UNDERSTANDING CIVIL RIGHTS LITIGATION

UNDERSTANDING CIVIL RIGHTS LITIGATION

Howard M. Wasserman
Professor of Law
FIU College of Law

ISBN: 978-0-7698-4583-8
eBook ISBN: 978-0-3271-8760-8

Library of Congress Cataloging-in-Publication Data

Wasserman, Howard M.
    Understanding civil rights litigation / Howard M. Wasserman, Professor of Law, FIU College of Law.
      pages cm
    Includes index.
    ISBN 978-0-7698-4583-8
  1. Civil rights--United States. 2. Civil procedure--United States. I. Title.
    KF4749.W39 2013
    342.7308'5--dc23
                                                                                    2013014377

NOTE TO USERS
To ensure that you are using the latest materials available in this area, please be sure to periodically check the LexisNexis Law School web site for downloadable updates and supplements at www.lexisnexis.com/lawschool.

Editorial Offices
121 Chanlon Rd., New Providence, NJ 07974 (908) 464 6800
201 Mission St., San Francisco, CA 94105-1831 (415) 908-3200
www.lexisnexis.com

MATTHEW◆BENDER

PREFACE

Several years ago, I argued that law schools should free the subject of Civil Rights Litigation (also called Constitutional Torts or Constitutional Litigation or Civil Rights) from its parent course of Federal Courts and offer both classes as a two-course sequence.[1] The increasing number of schools offering this separate class creates a need for a concise, accessible, organized, and comprehensive student-centered treatment of the subject. This book seeks to provide that compact-yet-complete treatment.

The book traces the entire process of civil rights litigation under 42 U.S.C. § 1983 and its federal analogs. It begins with the basic elements of a plaintiff's claim; considers the identities of possible defendants and the immunity defenses available to them; examines jurisdiction, procedural, and abstention barriers to recovery, and concludes with the remedies available to any plaintiff who successfully navigates the terrain. The book also discusses alternative, government-initiated mechanisms for enforcing civil rights through criminal and civil proceedings. Woven throughout are discussions of the history of federal civil rights legislation and litigation, as well as the dominant themes and principles that guide the jurisprudence in this area. Finally, the book offers "Puzzles" on various topics, presenting facts and details from recent lawsuits and decisions to illustrate the material.

I envision several uses for this book. It can function as a usable reference and supplemental guide for students taking Civil Rights or a Federal Courts course covering or focusing on § 1983 litigation. It can function as assigned course material in support of any casebook, as well as in support of a raw-case approach to Civil Rights (my preferred way of teaching the course). Students in such a class benefit from a supporting text that helps them synthesize cases and materials while providing background, nuance, policy, and detail beyond the canonical cases, which is what I hope this book does. The "Puzzles" become useful for class discussions and reviews and for a problem-oriented approach to the material. The book also includes appendices containing the United States Constitution and relevant provisions of the United States Code and Federal Rules of Civil Procedure, allowing it to serve as a statutory supplement for all course materials. Finally, I hope these multiple and varied uses allow the book to continue to function as a basic reference for those students who venture out as civil rights attorneys.

I want to thank FIU, FIU College of Law, and Dean R. Alexander Acosta for supporting this project and making this book possible. Brittany Dancel (Class of '14) and Altanese Phenelus (Class of '14) provided exemplary research assistance. All my love to my wife, Jennifer, and my daughter, Lily, who support me every day and in every way. Finally, thanks in advance to the professors, students, and attorneys who select and use this book; I hope you find it beneficial and workable and I welcome your comments and suggestions on how to make it even better.

Miami, Florida

May, 2013

---

[1] Howard M. Wasserman, *Civil Rights and Federal Courts: Creating a Two-Course Sequence,* 54 ST. LOUIS U. L.J. 821 (2010).

TABLE OF CONTENTS

TABLE OF CONTENTS

TABLE OF CONTENTS

TABLE OF CONTENTS

TABLE OF CONTENTS

TABLE OF CONTENTS

TABLE OF CONTENTS

Chapter 1

FEDERAL CIVIL RIGHTS LEGISLATION: HISTORY, THEMES, AND PRINCIPLES

Synopsis

§ 1.01   HISTORICAL BACKGROUND

The subject of civil rights legislation and litigation is a complex mixture of the modern and the historical and of action by the legislative, executive, and judicial branches. At times those actions complement one another, at times they conflict with one another. This area of law has its origins and foundation in statutes enacted during Reconstruction, but that lay largely dormant for almost a century; most of the canonical case law is less than 55 years old. The result is a paradoxically modern jurisprudential structure surrounding postbellum legislation. That combination creates some historically mixed analysis, with courts combining a focus on 19th-century legislative language, understandings, and intentions with modern judicial glosses for present-day applications and needs.

Most of the discussions and disputes in this area focus on precisely what that history was, what it shows, and how it should affect modern understandings and usage. A brief exploration of that history is thus necessary before we can explore modern civil rights jurisprudence.

[1]   Reconstruction Legislation

The Civil War ended in April 1865. With the war having explicitly become, through the Emancipation Proclamation, a conflict over the institution of slavery, and with the conflict in its waning months, Congress and President Lincoln sought to eliminate forever the institution of slavery and involuntary servitude in the United States. The resulting Thirteenth Amendment passed through Congress in

January 1865 and was ratified in December 1865.[1]

Southern states responded by enacting the so-called "Black Codes," a broad series of legislative restrictions designed to keep newly freedmen in a condition functionally approaching slavery by denying them most of the rights associated with citizenship and full membership in the socio-political community. With some variation from state to state, Blacks were prohibited from renting, owning, buying, and selling property; from engaging in certain businesses; from entering into and enforcing contracts; and from testifying or giving evidence against white citizens in court. Blacks (and their white Republican supporters) also faced disproportionately greater punishments than whites for the same crimes. Many states developed a system of peonage, under which freedmen found themselves working on the same land they had worked as slaves, this time to pay off debts owed to landowners (the former slave owners) and which the workers had little hope of ever paying off. Blacks who had been convicted of crimes often were made to work their sentences off in the unpaid employ of private landowners, again often the same landowners to whom they had been chattel just a few years prior.

Equally problematic was the rise in influence throughout the South of the Ku Klux Klan. The Klan and its members occupied and controlled many channels and institutions of state and local government. It also wielded such influence in southern society that government officials were unwilling or unable (usually both) to enforce the law and to protect minority rights in the face of Klan power. Either way, freedmen, Blacks, and their white supporters could not enjoy the benefits and protections of even neutral, non-discriminatory state laws or the equal enjoyment and enforcement of rights in southern states.

The Reconstruction Congress attempted to step into the breach. More significant than the Thirteenth Amendment's prohibition on the institution of slavery was its express delegation to Congress of power to "enforce" the amendment's substantive provisions through "appropriate legislation."[2] This represented the first new grant of federal legislative authority beyond the original enumerated powers of Article I. Congress understood this as an expansive grant of constitutional authority to legislate not only against the formal institution of slavery, but also against the "badges and incidents" of slavery — restrictions and disabilities on Blacks that remained or flowed from their prior condition of servitude and from the racial attitudes that supported that condition. "Radical Republicans" dominated Congress in these early years of Reconstruction and achieved much of their legislative success by overriding vetoes of Democratic President Andrew Johnson (who became president following the assassination of President Lincoln in April 1865).

The first exercise of this new legislative authority produced the Civil Rights Act of 1866. Section One sought to override the Black Codes by enumerating rights that all persons possess on equal terms regardless of race — including the rights to make and enforce contracts;[3] own, rent, buy, and sell property;[4] sue, be parties to

---

[1] U.S. CONST. amend. XIII, § 1 (1865).

[2] *Id.* § 2.

[3] 42 U.S.C. § 1981; Jett v. Dallas Indep. Sch. Dist., 491 U.S. 701 (1989). The statute prohibits race

lawsuits, and give evidence in court; serve on juries; and enjoy the full and equal benefit of the laws. Section Two imposed criminal penalties against officials acting under color of state or local law who willfully violated a person's federal rights, such as those rights enumerated in § 1,[5] and the Department of Justice initiated thousands of prosecutions against southern officials in the late 1860s and early 1870s. Section Three attempted to weaken the effect of Black Codes, establishing federal judicial jurisdiction over civil and criminal cases "affecting persons who are denied or cannot enforce" their § 1 rights in the state or local courts, thereby allowing more cases into federal court and away from state-law restrictions.

The nagging question over the 1866 Act was whether it constituted "appropriate legislation" to "enforce" the Thirteenth Amendment. The Supreme Court suggested that some provisions of the 1866 Act were not, at least in some applications,[6] although it never conclusively resolved the issue at the time. The Court ultimately upheld the substantive provisions of § 1 as valid enforcement legislation targeting the badges and incidents of slavery, but not until more than a century later.[7]

Nevertheless, to cure the constitutional uncertainty, Congress passed the Fourteenth Amendment, which was ratified in 1868. Section One prohibits States from depriving any person of the privileges or immunities of citizenship, depriving any person of life liberty, or property without due process of law, or denying any person the equal protection of the laws.[8] This general constitutional language was understood, at a minimum, to encompass the rights enumerated in the 1866 Act. Like the Thirteenth Amendment, the Fourteenth Amendment contained an enforcement provision, empowering Congress to enforce the Amendment's substantive provisions (primarily those in § 1) via appropriate legislation.[9]

Pursuant to the new (and broader) power of § 5, Congress passed the Civil Rights Act of 1870, which reenacted Sections 1 and 2 of the 1866 Act, this time on firmer constitutional authority. The 1870 Act also added a criminal conspiracy provision, prohibiting two or more persons from conspiring to intimidate or prevent freedmen or others from exercising the privileges or immunities secured by the Constitution or federal laws.[10] And in clear recognition of the Klan's power, that same section prohibited (and imposed criminal penalties on) two or more

---

discrimination in employment contracts. Johnson v. Railway Express Agency, Inc., 421 U.S. 454 (1975). In 1991, Congress amended § 1981 to define "make and enforce" to include "the making, performance, modification, and termination of contracts, and the enjoyment of all benefits, privileges, terms, and conditions of the contractual relationship." 42 U.S.C. § 1981(b); Civil Rights Act of 1991, Pub. L. No. 102-166, § 101, 105 Stat. 1077 (1991). Section 1981 often acts as a complement to Title VII of the Civil Rights Act of 1964 in employment discrimination litigation. See 42 U.S.C. § 2000e, et seq.

[4] 42 U.S.C. § 1982.

[5] 18 U.S.C. § 242. Congress added a scienter requirement in 1909. Act of March 4, 1909, 35 Stat. 1092 (1909).

[6] Blyew v. United States, 80 U.S. (13 Wall.) 581 (1872).

[7] Jones v. Alfred H. Mayer Co., 392 U.S. 409 (1968).

[8] U.S. Const. amend. XIV (1868).

[9] Id. § 5.

[10] 18 U.S.C. § 241; United States v. Kozminski, 487 U.S. 931 (1988).

persons "go[ing] in disguise on the highway, or on the premises of another, with intent to prevent or hinder his free exercise or enjoyment of any right or privilege" secured by federal law[11] — language explicitly referencing Klan rituals, dress, and activities and leaving little doubt as to the target of the provision. That same year, the states ratified the Fifteenth Amendment, prohibiting the denial or abridgement of the right to vote on account of race, color, or previous condition of servitude; the Amendment also allowed for "enforcement" via "appropriate legislation."[12]

The following year, Congress enacted the Ku Klux Klan Act of 1871, which was notable in several respects. It was, in title and content, an even-more explicit federal recognition of, and response to, the Klan's influence on southern government, society, laws, and institutions. It adopted private civil litigation (as opposed to government-initiated criminal prosecution) as the vehicle for enforcing newly created constitutional rights against state and local officials, swinging open the doors of the federal courthouse to private claims against members of the Klan and against governments and government officials influenced by the Klan's power.

Section One established a civil counterpart to § 2 of the 1866 and 1870 Acts, using similar language; codified at 42 U.S.C. § 1983 (and referred to by that shorthand); it provides:

> Every person who, under color of any statute, ordinance, regulation, custom, or usage, of any State or Territory or the District of Columbia, subjects, or causes to be subjected, any citizen of the United States or other person within the jurisdiction thereof to the deprivation of any rights, privileges, or immunities secured by the Constitution and laws, shall be liable to the party injured in an action at law, suit in equity, or other proper proceeding for redress.[13]

Although it took almost 100 years and some expansive judicial interpretation,[14] §1983 has become the cornerstone of modern constitutional and civil rights litigation, and it will be the primary focus of this book. Similarly, § 2 of the 1871 Act established a civil counterpart to the criminal conspiracy provision of the 1870 Act, creating a private cause of action against those who go in disguise on the highways or on another's property for purpose of depriving a person of the equal protection of laws or equal privileges and immunities.[15]

The last gasp of Reconstruction legislative activism was the Civil Rights Act of 1875. It included the first federal provision prohibiting, through threat of both civil and criminal penalties, discrimination because of race in all places of public accommodation, even if privately owned and operated. This marked the strongest effort to establish societal equality as a matter of federal law. The statute also prohibited states from discriminating because of race in jury selection.[16] That same

---

[11] *Id.*

[12] U.S. CONST. amend. XV (1870).

[13] 42 U.S.C. § 1983.

[14] Monroe v. Pape, 365 U.S. 167 (1961).

[15] 42 U.S.C. § 1985(3).

[16] Strauder v. West Virginia, 100 U.S. 303 (1880).

year, Congress granted federal district courts general "arising under" federal question jurisdiction,[17] making them the primary and powerful forum for vindicating every right under the federal Constitution, laws, and treaties.[18]

But the Supreme Court invalidated the public accommodations provisions in *The Civil Rights Cases* in 1883. A federal prohibition on private discrimination or segregation was not appropriate enforcement legislation under the Thirteenth Amendment, because the denial of access to places of public accommodation on the basis of race does not constitute a badge or incident or slavery. And it was not appropriate enforcement legislation under the Fourteenth Amendment, which empowered Congress to enact only "remedial" legislation regulating states and correcting constitutional violations by state and local governments, rather than direct legislation regulating the conduct of private (non-governmental) actors.[19]

[2]   From Non-Enforcement to Enforcement and Back

The removal of federal troops from the South in 1877 (as part of the compromise that resolved the disputed 1876 presidential election between Rutherford B. Hayes and Samuel J. Tilden and made Hayes President[20]) marked the official historical end of Reconstruction. The Court's decision in *The Civil Rights Cases* six years later, invalidating the final and most sweeping congressional attempt to establish legal and social equality, marked its legal end. Thus began a 60-year period with no meaningful federal creation, enforcement, or vindication of civil and constitutional rights by any of the three branches of the federal government.

Beginning around 1890, Jim Crow took root throughout the South,[21] receiving judicial imprimatur in *Plessy v. Ferguson* in 1896.[22] Following the doomed 1875 Act, Congress enacted no new civil rights legislation for more than 80 years. Nor was there much judicial activity. An often-cited statistic shows that from 1871–1920, there were only 21 reported civil actions brought under § 1983, most of them unsuccessful.[23] Similarly, the Department of Justice and the executive branch showed little interest in prosecuting constitutional violations by state and local officials or otherwise protecting civil rights. This inactivity had several causes. Part of the problem was political will — the lack of interest by any powerful parties or national political groups in taking on Southern-Democratic control of the South. Part of the problem was the state of substantive constitutional law: *Plessy* and separate-but-equal remained the prevailing interpretation of the Equal Protection Clause and there had been little or no incorporation of the Bill of Rights against

---

[17] Judiciary Act of Mar. 3, 1875, § 1, 18 Stat. 470 (1875) (codified at 28 U.S.C. § 1331).

[18] Steffel v. Thompson, 415 U.S. 452, 464 (1974).

[19] The Civil Rights Cases, 109 U.S. 3 (1883).

[20] MICHAEL J. KLARMAN, FROM JIM CROW TO CIVIL RIGHTS: THE SUPREME COURT AND THE STRUGGLE FOR RACIAL EQUALITY 14 (2004); C. VANN WOODWARD, THE STRANGE CAREER OF JIM CROW 52–53 (3d ed. 2002).

[21] *See generally* MICHAEL J. KLARMAN, FROM JIM CROW TO CIVIL RIGHTS: THE SUPREME COURT AND THE STRUGGLE FOR RACIAL EQUALITY (2004); C. VANN WOODWARD, THE STRANGE CAREER OF JIM CROW (3d ed. 2002).

[22] Plessy v. Ferguson, 163 U.S. 537 (1896).

[23] Comment, *The Civil Rights Act: Emergence of an Adequate Federal Civil Remedy?*, 26 IND. L.J. 361, 363 (1951).

the states.[24] It thus was unlikely that a state or local official or government could have violated a right, privilege, or immunity secured by the Constitution, so as to be liable in a § 1983 action or § 242 prosecution, because state officials and governments were not bound by most of the Bill of Rights.

This stance of non-enforcement began changing in the 1940s. The Supreme Court slowly, provision-by-provision, incorporated Bill of Rights liberties — most significantly the First,[25] Fourth,[26] Fifth,[27] and Eighth[28] Amendments — against state and local officials and governments through the Due Process Clause of the Fourteenth Amendment. Civil rights activists rediscovered § 1983 as the vehicle for federal litigation to challenge Jim Crow and *de jure* segregation, particularly in public service,[29] voting,[30] and education,[31] culminating most famously in *Brown v. Board of Education*.[32] At the same time, the Justice Department under President Franklin Delano Roosevelt and attorneys general Robert H. Jackson and Francis Biddle began prosecuting blatant, and often violent, violations of rights by Southern officials.[33] Finally, Congress enacted the first piece of federal civil rights legislation in almost 100 years when it enacted the Civil Rights Act of 1957, although the bill was watered-down in the legislative process and rendered largely toothless.[34]

By the 1960s, Congress, the executive, and the courts were, for arguably the first and only time, on the same page in seeking vigorous and proactive enforcement of civil and constitutional rights. The courts rediscovered the Reconstruction statutes, particularly § 1983 (§ 1 of the Ku Klux Klan Act of 1871), interpreting it broadly and making it the central vehicle for challenging constitutional violations in court and for vindicating constitutional rights.[35] The Court also created a federal analog to § 1983 for damages claims against federal officers for constitutional violations.[36] Courts also took bold steps to enforce school desegregation mandated in *Brown* through so-called "structural-reform injunctions"; these injunctions compelled schools to take broad, affirmative steps to achieve integration by fundamentally reforming the structure and administration

---

[24] Slaughter-House Cases, 83 U.S. 36 (1873).

[25] Everson v. Board of Education, 330 U.S. 1 (1947); Cantwell v. Connecticut, 310 U.S. 296 (1940); Near v. Minnesota, 283 U.S. 697 (1931); Gitlow v. New York, 268 U.S. 652 (1925).

[26] Mapp v. Ohio, 367 U.S. 643 (1961).

[27] Malloy v. Hogan, 378 U.S. 1 (1964).

[28] Robinson v. California, 370 U.S. 660 (1962).

[29] Hollins v. Oklahoma, 295 U.S. 394 (1935); Norris v. Alabama, 294 U.S. 587 (1935).

[30] Terry v. Adams, 345 U.S. 461 (1953); Smith v. Allwright, 321 U.S. 649 (1944).

[31] Sweatt v. Painter, 339 U.S. 629 (1950); Fisher v. Hurst, 333 U.S. 147 (1948).

[32] Brown v. Board of Educ., 347 U.S. 483 (1954).

[33] Screws v. United States, 325 U.S. 91 (1945); United States v. Classic, 313 U.S. 299 (1941).

[34] Civil Rights Act of 1957, Pub. L. No. 85-315, 71 Stat. 634 (1957).

[35] Monroe v. Pape, 365 U.S. 167 (1961).

[36] Bivens v. Six Unknown Named Agents of Federal Bureau of Narcotics, 403 U.S. 388 (1971).

of their public institutions.[37] Courts then expanded this model of judicially mandated and supervised reform to other state institutions, notably police departments, courts, hospitals, and prisons.[38]

Meanwhile, Congress engaged in its most significant civil rights lawmaking since Reconstruction, enacting strong laws to prohibit race, sex, and other discrimination in public accommodations, employment, education, voting, and housing.[39] Importantly, many of these laws were enacted and upheld not as exercises of the enforcement powers of the Reconstruction Amendments, but under a more-broadly understood congressional power to regulate interstate commerce.[40] Finally, the Department of Justice continued to bring federal criminal charges against the most extreme civil rights abuses by state and local officials, particularly officials connected with the Klan and trying to stop Blacks from voting and otherwise exercising their federal rights.[41]

This period of joint legislative, executive, and judicial enforcement did not last long, perhaps into the late 1970s. It soon gave way to the current period of judicial ascendance and under-enforcement (if not non-enforcement) of civil rights. The Supreme Court has narrowed its understanding of many substantive constitutional rights in § 1983 actions, narrowed the scope of damages claims against federal officials,[42] narrowed its interpretation of the Reconstruction statutes,[43] broadened the scope of many doctrines that limit official liability for constitutional violations,[44] and taken a skeptical view of broad federal injunctions[45] and limited the availability of attorney's fees to prevailing plaintiffs.[46] At the same time, the Supreme Court has narrowed the reach of congressional power under both the Commerce Clause and § 5 of the Fourteenth Amendment, thus narrowing Congress' power to enact new legislation protecting civil rights.[47]

This historical ebb-and-flow, judicial and legislative, will be apparent throughout this book. It affects and dictates the evolution of a number of different issues and

---

[37] Swann v. Charlotte-Mecklenburg Bd. of Educ., 402 U.S. 1 (1971); Green v. County School Board, 391 U.S. 430 (1968).

[38] MALCOLM M. FEELEY & EDWARD L. RUBIN, JUDICIAL POLICY MAKING AND THE MODERN STATE: HOW THE COURTS REFORMED AMERICA'S PRISONS (1998); Edward L. Rubin & Malcolm M. Feeley, *Judicial Policymaking and Litigation Against the Government*, 5 U. PA. J. CONST. L. 617 (2003).

[39] Fair Housing Act of 1968, Title VIII, Pub. L. No. 90-284, 82 Stat. 73 (1968); Voting Rights Act of 1965, Pub. L. No. 89-910, 79 Stat. 437 (1965); Civil Rights Act of 1964, Pub. L. No. 89-352, 78 Stat. 241 (1964).

[40] Katzenbach v. McClung, 379 U.S. 294 (1964); Heart of Atlanta Motel, Inc. v. United States, 379 U.S. 241 (1964).

[41] United States v. Price, 383 U.S. 787 (1966); United States v. Guest, 383 U.S. 745 (1966).

[42] Minneci v. Pollard, 132 S. Ct. 617 (2012); Ashcroft v. Iqbal, 556 U.S. 662 (2009).

[43] Connick v. Thompson, 131 S. Ct. 1350 (2011).

[44] Coleman v. Court of Appeals, 132 S. Ct. 1327 (2012); Pearson v. Callahan, 555 U.S. 223 (2009).

[45] Horne v. Flores, 559 U.S. 433 (2009); Milliken v. Bradley, 418 U.S. 717 (1974).

[46] Perdue v. Kenny A., 130 S. Ct. 1662 (2010); Sole v. Wyner, 551 U.S. 74 (2007); Buckhannon Bd. & Care Home, Inc. v. W. Va. Dep't of Health & Hum. Res., 532 U.S. 598 (2001).

[47] *Coleman*, 132 S. Ct. at 1333–34; United States v. Morrison, 529 U.S. 598 (2000); City of Boerne v. Flores, 521 U.S. 507 (1997).

areas of civil rights jurisprudence.

§ 1.02 PRINCIPLES AND THEMES

Constitutional and civil rights litigation, historically and in the present, reflects the influence of several recurring themes and principles. Some or all appear, explicitly or implicitly, as policy considerations guiding the enactment of federal legislation and the judicial interpretation and application of that legislation. Courts, attorneys, and students can organize and understand the material that follows around these principles and themes, using them to understand how the jurisprudence has formed and evolved, to predict how the doctrine may move over time, and to normatively evaluate the wisdom and effectiveness of the doctrine.

[1] Federalism

The precise shape of the law of civil rights and civil rights litigation depends on the accommodation of differing, often conflicting, visions of federalism and the balance of power between state (and local) government on one hand and the federal government on the other. The Reconstruction Amendments (Thirteenth, Fourteenth, and Fifteenth), particularly by establishing congressional enforcement authority, fundamentally shifted the balance away from the states and toward the federal government.[48] Having seen what states could do when left unchecked — slavery, a bloody war, the Black Codes, Jim Crow — the Fourteenth Amendment was designed to "make rights truly nationalized."[49]

The recurring question is how far and how dramatic this shift was, a question that often marks the point of departure among the Justices and among lower courts. Federalism affects how courts interpret existing civil rights legislation, particularly in deciding how much Congress shifted the federal/state balance toward greater federal power in a given piece of legislation. This can be a particularly difficult historical inquiry, since the relevant Congress did its work 150 years ago. Courts frequently accommodate federalism through clear-statement rules, demanding that Congress have made explicit when a statute fundamentally alters or undoes the federal-state balance; absent such a clear statement, the prevailing interpretation is the one most solicitous of state authority. Thus, for example, the Court has twice declared that a state is not a "person" subject to suit under § 1983 because Congress in 1871 did not provide an explicit textual statement defining person that broadly; absent such an express pronouncement, courts will not presume Congress burdened states and their sovereignty.[50] Courts also have done the same in reverse, holding that common law immunity defenses that existed in the 19th century survived passage of the 1871 Act and protect modern officer defendants from suit, although such defenses are nowhere mentioned in the statute.[51]

---

[48] Fitzpatrick v. Bitzer, 427 U.S. 445, 453–56 (1976).

[49] Eugene Gressman, *The Unhappy History of Civil Rights Legislation*, 50 MICH. L. REV. 1323 (1952).

[50] Will v. Mich. Dep't of State Police, 491 U.S. 58 (1989); Quern v. Jordan, 440 U.S. 332 (1979).

[51] Filarsky v. Delia, 132 S. Ct. 1657 (2012).

Federalism also informs judicial evaluation of the constitutionality of civil rights legislation. The scope of congressional power under the enforcement provisions of the Thirteenth, Fourteenth, and Fifteenth Amendments — and thus the constitutionality of congressional enactments pursuant to those powers — is defined with deference to federalism and state power. The result is that courts have invalidated multiple pieces of civil rights legislation throughout the past 150 years, particularly during and immediately after Reconstruction and again in the past two decades.[52]

Unfortunately, federalism often prevails without much analysis or explanation. Instead, the Court halts the conversation with the simple declaration that "it will not be thought"[53] that Congress (particularly the Reconstruction Congress) intended to extend its power so far, whether in enacting legislation or in framing the Fourteenth Amendment and arranging the new power structures.

[2] Majoritarianism

Counter-majoritarianism is the recurring ideal in all of constitutional law, notably in debates over the institution of judicial review.[54] But majoritarian concerns affect constitutional litigation more broadly than in just the question of whether a particular legislative enactment is constitutionally valid and whether a court should have the power to make that determination.

One question is how much deference courts should grant to the majoritarian branches to order and carry out their business. It informs how willing courts should be to second-guess executive conduct *ex post*, particularly discretionary law-enforcement decisions made in the heat of the moment. Courts struggle with how much "breathing room" to give officials to act vigorously without fear of suit and personal liability for any constitutional violations.

At the opposite end is the question of how willing or reluctant courts should be to enjoin executive officials from engaging in unconstitutional conduct or enforcing unconstitutional laws and policies. This is particularly important as to so-called structural-reform injunctions, courts command that executive officials take affirmative steps, under ongoing judicial supervision, to remedy existing and ongoing constitutional defects in government programs and institutions, often by limiting or controlling majoritarian discretion in funding, managing, and administering those institutions. Courts and commentators continue to debate whether such structural-reform orders are legitimate and appropriate, the extent to which the federal judiciary should oversee state institutions in the wake of a finding of unconstitutional behavior, and the extent to which courts should instead

---

[52] Coleman v. Court of Appeals, 132 S. Ct. 1327 (2012); United States v. Morrison, 529 U.S. 598 (2000); Kimel v. Florida Bd. of Regents, 528 U.S. 62 (2000); City of Boerne v. Flores, 521 U.S. 507 (1997); Civil Rights Cases, 109 U.S. 3 (1883).

[53] *Blyew v. United States*, 80 U.S. (13 Wall.) 581, 592 (1872).

[54] JOHN HART ELY, DEMOCRACY AND DISTRUST: A THEORY OF JUDICIAL REVIEW (1980); ALEXANDER M. BICKEL, THE LEAST DANGEROUS BRANCH: THE SUPREME COURT AT THE BAR OF POLITICS (1962); Barry Friedman, *The Birth of an Academic Obsession: The History of the Countermajoritarian Difficulty, Part 5*, 112 YALE L.J. 153 (2002).

trust the majoritarian institutions to correct their own constitutional defects and leave it to those institutions to decide how best to do so.[55]

A third issue is the extent to which the majoritarian branches should take the lead in enforcing constitutional rights and the extent to which courts should defer to that lead. The history of civil rights legislation demonstrates the salience of this theme. The key to the Fourteenth Amendment arguably was the enforcement power in § 5, allowing Congress and the executive to protect the new constitutional rights by enacting and vigorously enforcing new legislation. And, as discussed above, that is how things went in the early post-bellum period; the 1866 and 1870 Acts primarily relied on criminal penalties against states and state officials, with federal-government enforcement. In other words, enforcement strategies and choices remained largely in the hands of the majoritarian branches.

It was not until the Ku Klux Klan Act of 1871 that Congress shifted to private civil litigation in federal court as a way to enforce and vindicate civil and constitutional rights. With the revitalization of § 1983 in the past half-century, private litigation has become the dominant enforcement model. Private enforcement, in turn, rests on the notion of the "private attorney general;" plaintiffs, and the lawyers who represent them, vindicate public rights and the public interest by using private litigation to remedy individual violations of their own rights.[56] Judicial remedies for private constitutional injury compensate injured persons for past violations of their rights and deter and prevent future violations by forcing, directly or indirectly, changes to government policies and conduct.[57] Those changes inure not only to the benefit of the individual plaintiff, but to the general public. Private attorneys general offer an important supplement to government enforcement of federal rights and Congress has made private enforcement a central component of its enforcement schemes. Because government lacks the resources and ability to pursue every case or every isolated violation, it must focus on larger, structural, and systemic violations — cases that provide "more bang for the buck." The federal government also may lack the political will or interest to pursue constitutional litigation; recall that there was little enforcement by the federal executive from the end of Reconstruction until the 1940s.

Allowing private plaintiffs to bring more cases — even cases involving smaller, individual, and less systematic violations — and to succeed in those cases increases the overall level of federal constitutional enforcement, thereby benefitting the public as a whole. Congress acts on this theory by empowering private individuals to pursue civil litigation through the creation of private rights of action (such as § 1983 or the rights of action in new legislation)[58] and by providing incentives and

---

[55] MALCOLM M. FEELEY & EDWARD L. RUBIN, JUDICIAL POLICY MAKING AND THE MODERN STATE: HOW THE COURTS REFORMED AMERICA'S PRISONS (1998); ROSS SANDLER & DAVID SCHOENBROD, DEMOCRACY BY DECREE: WHAT HAPPENS WHEN COURTS RUN GOVERNMENT (2003).

[56] William B. Rubenstein, On What a "Private Attorney General" Is — And Why It Matters, 57 VAND. L. REV. 2129 (2004); Pamela S. Karlan, Disarming the Private Attorney General, 2003 U. ILL. L. REV. 183.

[57] Owen v. Independence, 445 U.S. 622 (1980); Carey v. Piphus, 435 U.S. 247 (1978).

[58] Newman v. Piggie Park Enterprises, Inc., 390 U.S. 400 (1968) (per curiam).

weapons to enable plaintiffs to sue successfully, notably by making attorney's fees available for prevailing plaintiffs.[59]

At the same time, the executive branch still retains and wields significant enforcement weapons — those established in the Reconstruction statutes,[60] as well as more recent enactments.[61] Thus, a recurring doctrinal issue is whether governmental or private enforcement should be preferred and how limits on the latter may be justified by the availability and expectation of the former.

[3] Procedural and Jurisdictional Burdens and Hurdles

The language of § 1 of the 1871 Act (§ 1983) is deceptively simple — any state actor who deprives a person of a federally protected right may be sued and held liable for legal (damages) or equitable (injunctive or declaratory) relief.[62]

But an elaborate body of procedural and jurisdictional limitations has been superimposed on this seemingly straightforward right of action — most judicially created and historically justified but nowhere mentioned in statutory text or legislative history. In fact, these procedural and jurisdictional issues form much of the core jurisprudence; they are at the heart of the debates on this subject and learning how to navigate them is at the heart of civil rights practice. These hurdles include official and governmental immunities, which absolve officials of liability even if they did violate a person's constitutional rights;[63] strict limits on respondeat superior, supervisory, and entity liability;[64] limits on the circumstances in which federal officers can be sued for damages;[65] limits on the types of constitutional rights that can be litigated;[66] and limits on the federal courts' adjudicative jurisdiction over many constitutional claims.[67] Some of these limits existed at common law in the 19th century and have been deemed incorporated into the 1871 Act. Others are judge-made limits driven by concerns for docket management and decisional authority. And still others reflect explicit judicial policy preferences for protecting the authority and discretion of officials in other governments and other branches of the federal government.

At the same time, courts have limited Congress's legislative authority, often by erecting hurdles in the process of enacting civil rights legislation, hurdles similarly not apparent from constitutional text. For example, the Court has restricted Congress' power to enact new civil rights legislation.[68] Courts demand unusual

---

[59] 42 U.S.C. § 1988(b); Perdue v. Kenny A., 559 U.S. 542 (2010); Evans v. Jeff D., 475 U.S. 717 (1986).

[60] United States v. Lanier, 520 U.S. 259 (1997).

[61] 42 U.S.C. § 14141.

[62] 42 U.S.C. § 1983.

[63] Van de Kamp v. Goldstein, 555 U.S. 335 (2009); Pearson v. Callahan, 555 U.S. 223 (2009).

[64] Connick v. Thompson, 131 S. Ct. 1350 (2011); McMillian v. Monroe County, 520 U.S. 781 (1997); Monell v. Dep't of Social Servs., 436 U.S. 658 (1978).

[65] Ashcroft v. Iqbal, 556 U.S. 662 (2009); Wilkie v. Robbins, 551 U.S. 537 (2007).

[66] Heck v. Humphrey, 512 U.S. 477 (1994).

[67] Younger v. Harris, 401 U.S. 37 (1971); Railroad Com. of Texas v. Pullman Co., 312 U.S. 496 (1941).

[68] United States v. Morrison, 529 U.S. 598 (2000).

clarity from Congress before finding that a particular statutory right is privately enforceable.[69] And state sovereign immunity prohibits Congress from imposing statutory obligations on states that go too far beyond the obligations already imposed by the Constitution, unless Congress makes explicit and detailed legislative findings as to past constitutional misconduct by states themselves.[70]

[4] Federal Rights, Federal Remedies, Federal Forums

A final theme goes to the unique importance and need for federal rights and remedies, as opposed to state rights and remedies, and of a federal forum in which to enforce those rights and remedies. This affects whether state legislatures can be trusted to not enact invidiously discriminatory laws and whether state courts can be trusted to vigorously protect rights and provide remedies for violations of rights. Of course, Reconstruction legislation was explicitly grounded on distrust of state institutions, given the recent experience of the Civil War, the Black Codes, and the socio-political influence of the KKK. The prevailing belief in Congress in 1871 was that federal legislation was necessary to override and undo the explicitly discriminatory Black Codes, as well as to provide a meaningful federal remedy where state law, though neutral and adequate in theory, was inadequate in practice, given discriminatory forces in society and in its legal institutions. Federal rights and federal remedies were the necessary and appropriate response to the state of law and society in the South.

The question becomes the importance of federal forums and institutions for vindicating and remedying violations of those federal rights. State courts are, of course, generally empowered to hear and resolve federal issues and they are expected, under the Supremacy Clause, to give the full scope to federal rights when they arise in state court litigation.[71] Again, however, the question is whether state courts can or will do so as a practical matter.

This forms the heart of the debate over "parity," the belief that state courts are equivalent to federal courts in their ability and willingness to protect individual federal rights.[72] By presuming parity, the availability of a federal forum becomes less important than the existence of the federal right; so long as the federal right exists, an individual is as well off litigating that right in state court as in federal court.

Whether one accepts parity depends on whether the theory and practice of constitutional litigation can escape its history. There long was good reason to question state courts' willingness or ability to enforce federal rights. U.S. history is very much about Southern resistance — through the Black Codes, Jim Crow, and massive resistance to *Brown* and integration.[73] That history and experience

---

[69] Gonzaga Univ. v. Doe, 536 U.S. 273 (2002); Alexander v. Sandoval, 532 U.S. 275 (2001).

[70] Coleman v. Court of Appeals, 132 S. Ct. 1327 (2012); Kimel v. Florida Bd. of Regents, 528 U.S. 62 (2000).

[71] U.S. CONST. art. VI.

[72] Burt Neuborne, *The Myth of Parity*, 90 HARV. L. REV. 1109 (1977).

[73] *See generally* MICHAEL J. KLARMAN, FROM JIM CROW TO CIVIL RIGHTS: THE SUPREME COURT AND THE STRUGGLE FOR RACIAL EQUALITY (2004).

motivated the activist Congresses during Reconstruction and the 1960s, as well as the federal courts in rediscovering and revitalizing Reconstruction legislation as the driver of constitutional enforcement. But much arguably has changed and the question of parity must be answered without regard to that history or our memories of the pre-Civil Rights, Jim Crow South.

Nevertheless, Burt Neuborne famously argued that parity remains a myth; even assuming the good faith of state courts and state judges and the proper functioning of state judiciaries, federal courts, and federal judges simply are better at protecting constitutional rights. Neuborne cites several factors for this, including federal judges' insulation from political and social pressures by virtue of Article III's structural protections of life tenure and guaranteed salary for federal judges;[74] federal judges' familiarity and technical competence with federal law; and the mindset that comes with being part of an elite institution such as the federal judiciary and tends toward greater protection of federal rights and interests.[75] Neuborne's arguments about parity have been questioned, particularly in recent years, as state courts have actually shown a greater willingness than federal courts to protect minority rights, especially on questions of equal protection.[76] More importantly, courts have roundly rejected the Neuborne view; numerous areas of civil rights litigation jurisprudence are grounded in an explicit assumption of parity, rejecting that there is anything special or necessary about a federal forum. Several doctrines flatly deny litigants a federal forum on federal issues, instead pushing them to litigate and (attempt to) enforce their federal rights in state court proceedings, at least in the first instance.[77]

§ 1.03   CONCLUSION

The remaining chapters of this book explore the jurisprudence of civil rights and constitutional litigation under § 1983 (and its federal counterparts). The history, principles, and themes introduced here run throughout this material. Readers should keep them in mind; they will enable readers to understand the origins and evolution of this jurisprudence, how the various rules and principles link together, whether the doctrine is normatively correct, and where it is likely to go in the future.

---

[74] U.S. Const. art. III § 1.

[75] Burt Neuborne, *The Myth of Parity*, 90 Harv. L. Rev. 1107 (1977).

[76] William B. Rubenstein, *The Myth of Superiority*, 16 Const. Comment. 599 (1999).

[77] *See, e.g.*, 28 U.S.C. § 2254(b); Granberry v. Greer, 481 U.S. 129 (1987); Allen v. McCurry, 449 U.S. 90 (1980); Younger v. Harris, 401 U.S. 37 (1971).

Chapter 2

ENFORCING FEDERAL RIGHTS

§ 2.01 OVERVIEW

18 U.S.C. § 242

Whoever, under color of any law, statute, ordinance, regulation, or custom, willfully subjects any person in any State, Territory, Commonwealth, Possession, or District to the deprivation of any rights, privileges, or immunities secured or protected by the Constitution or laws of the United States, or to different punishments, pains, or penalties, on account of such person being an alien, or by reason of his color, or race, than are prescribed for the punishment of citizens, shall be fined under this title or imprisoned not more than one year, or both * * *

42 U.S.C. § 1983

Every person who, under color of any statute, ordinance, regulation, custom, or usage, of any State or Territory or the District of Columbia, subjects, or causes to be subjected, any citizen of the United States or other person within the jurisdiction thereof to the deprivation of any rights, privileges, or immunities secured by the Constitution and laws, shall be liable to the party injured in an action at law, suit in equity, or other proper proceeding for redress, except that in any action brought against a judicial officer for an act or omission taken in such officer's judicial capacity, injunctive relief shall not be granted unless a declaratory decree was violated or declaratory relief was unavailable. For the purposes of this section, any Act of Congress applicable exclusively to the District of Columbia shall be considered to be a statute of the District of Columbia.

The Reconstruction Congress created two statutory vehicles for enforcing the Fourteenth Amendment's newly established rights — § 242 (§ 2 of the Civil Rights Act of 1866 enacted under the Thirteenth Amendment and re-enacted as § 2 of the Civil Rights Act of 1870 under the Fourteenth Amendment) and § 1983 (§ 1 of the Ku Klux Klan Act of 1871).[1] The provisions share several features, albeit with slightly different language.

First, the defendant must be a person — this is explicit in § 1983 and implicit in the word "whoever" in § 242. Both provisions were enacted (or re-enacted) pursuant to § 5 of the Fourteenth Amendment, to enforce the provisions of § 1 of that Amendment, which by its terms imposes limitations only on a "State." A "state" for Fourteenth Amendment purposes includes the state as an entity; local governments as entities; and state and local boards, agencies, departments, and other public entities. It also may include individuals employed by and acting on behalf of the state or local government or governmental agency, individuals whose conduct is fairly attributable to the state;[2] and individuals who contract to work for and on behalf of the state on any basis.[3] Meanwhile, § 1983's reference to "persons" suggests that individual government officers and employees are the primary targets of civil litigation, although the term could and does include legal persons. Thus, a proper defendant in a § 1983 action (or § 242 prosecution) must be the State for Fourteenth Amendment purposes and a person for § 1983 purposes.

Second, both statutes require that the person act "under color" of some law, statute, ordinance, regulation, custom, or usage of a state, territory, commonwealth, or the District of Columbia.

Third, the defendant must "subject[]" or "cause[] to be subjected" the victim or plaintiff to a "deprivation" of "rights, privileges, or immunities" secured or protected by the Constitution and laws. Section 242 is explicit that this means the Constitution and laws of the United States, while courts have read that requirement

---

[1] *See* Ch. 1.

[2] Lugar v. Edmondson Oil Co., 457 U.S. 922 (1982).

[3] Filarsky v. Delia, 132 S. Ct. 1657 (2012); West v. Atkins, 487 U.S. 42 (1988).

into § 1983.[4] In other words, the plaintiff (in a § 1983 claim) or the United States (in a § 242 prosecution) must prove that the defendant violated someone's federal constitutional or statutory rights. Importantly, however, neither § 1983 nor § 242 prohibits or regulates any conduct, establishes any rights, or imposes any duties of its own force. Rather, both are vehicles for enforcing federal rights and liberties emanating from some other source — the Constitution (specifically the Fourteenth Amendment, broadly understood) or some federal statutes.

The obvious difference between the two provisions goes to the nature of the remedies and penalties. Section 242 is a criminal provision, imposing imprisonment and fines for violations, through actions instituted by the federal government. Given its criminal nature, § 242 contains an express scienter element, requiring that the defendant "willfully" subject the victim to a deprivation, which the Court has interpreted to require specific intent to deprive a citizen of a specific constitutional right.[5] Section 1983 establishes a civil cause of action, granting the injured person the right to bring an action in law (seeking compensatory damages, punitive damages, and other monetary relief), a suit in equity (seeking an injunction or other equitable relief), or other "proper proceeding for redress" (seeking other available judicial remedies). The statute itself contains no state-of-mind requirement.

PART A
"UNDER COLOR" OF STATE LAW

§ 2.02 A PRELIMINARY WORD ON STATE ACTION AND UNDER COLOR OF LAW

The constitutional requirement of action by a state and the statutory requirement of a person acting "under color" of state law together reflect federalism considerations that seek to limit the reach of federal law and federal courts, protect the power of state institutions, and maintain an appropriate federal-state balance. This requirement "preserves an area of individual freedom by limiting the reach of federal law," allowing private persons to act free from constitutional liability or from constitutional limitations that are not intended to control individual conduct. It also avoids imposing liability on state or local governments for conduct they could not control, ensuring that government is only liable for constitutional violations " 'when it can be said that the State is responsible for the specific conduct of which the plaintiff complains' " because the conduct is somehow "fairly attributable" to the state.[6] Finally, the statutory "under color" requirement confines § 1983 to the

---

[4] *Lugar*, 457 U.S. at 930 (quoting Adickes v. S. H. Kress & Co., 398 U.S. 144, 150 (1970)).

[5] United States v. Lanier, 520 U.S. 259 (1997); Screws v. United States, 325 U.S. 91 (1945); John V. Jacobi, *Prosecuting Police Misconduct*, 2000 Wis. L. Rev. 789, 808–09. Congress added the "willfully" requirement in 1909, precisely to ease the severity of the criminal sanction. *Screws*, 325 U.S. at 100; Act of Mar. 4, 1909, 35 Stat. 1092 (1909).

[6] Brentwood Acad. v. Tennessee Secondary Sch. Athletic Ass'n, 531 U.S. 288, 295 (2001); *Lugar*, 457 U.S. at 936–37.

constitutional limits of the Fourteenth Amendment.[7] It ensures that the § 1983 claim is based on an actual violation of a constitutional right, since the Fourteenth Amendment is only violable by government, not private, actors.

The Supreme Court has described a two-step inquiry for establishing that a defendant is a person subject to suit under § 1983 on a constitutional claim. "First, the deprivation [of a federal right] must be caused by the exercise of some right or privilege created by the State or by a rule of conduct imposed by the State or by a person for whom the State is responsible . . . . Second, the party charged with the deprivation must be a person who may fairly be said to be a state actor."[8]

The two steps converge when the claim is directed against an officer who brings the weight of the state and his public office into his conduct; they diverge when the claim is against a private party over whom government or government officers exercise some control. Moreover, there is an often-confused relationship between the constitutional requirement of state action by a state actor and the statutory requirement of a person acting under color of state law. Courts often treat them as identical inquiries.[9] And as a default rule, the former establishes the latter. That is, if a person is a state actor under the Fourteenth Amendment, he also acts under color of state law. If there is state action there is action under color of law and if there is action under color of law there is state action.[10]

§ 2.03   STATE ACTION, ACTION UNDER COLOR, AND PUBLIC OFFICIALS

[1]   Expanding "Under Color"

The core of "under color" of law — the situation where conduct is obviously fairly attributable to the state — occurs when a public official, officer, or employee (whether someone with full-time status or those who contract to work for the government for a particular, limited time or purpose[11]) adheres to his formal obligations under state law and violates a person's constitutional rights because of a constitutional defect in the law or policy being followed or enforced.[12] Thus, there was no question of action under color of law in Civil Rights Era litigation directly challenging *de jure* state discrimination in public education[13] or electoral processes.[14] Nor is there a question when the defendant public officer acts within

---

[7] *Brentwood*, 531 U.S. at 295; *Lugar*, 457 U.S. at 950.

[8] *Lugar*, 457 U.S. at 937.

[9] *Brentwood*, 531 U.S. at 295 n.2; Chudacoff v. Univ. Med. Ctr., 649 F.3d 1143 (9th Cir. 2011); Almand v. DeKalb County, 103 F.3d 1510, 1513–14 n.7 (11th Cir. 1997).

[10] *Lugar*, 457 U.S. at 935 & n.18; Butler v. Sheriff of Palm Beach County, 685 F.3d 1261, 1265 n.5 (11th Cir. 2012); Abbott v. Latshaw, 164 F.3d 141, 145 (3d Cir. 1998).

[11] Filarsky v. Delia, 132 S. Ct. 1657 (2012); West v. Atkins, 487 U.S. 42 (1988).

[12] Lane v. Wilson, 307 U.S. 268 (1939); Nixon v. Herndon, 273 U.S. 536 (1927).

[13] Brown v. Board of Educ., 347 U.S. 483 (1954); Sweatt v. Painter, 339 U.S. 629 (1950).

[14] *Lane*, 307 U.S. at 274.

the range of executive discretion authorized by state law in the enforcement of state and local law.[15]

The question is whether "under color" extends further to also reach public officials who, acting within the scope of employment and in the course of performing official duties, engage in conduct contrary to, inconsistent with, or in direct violation of state law and their state obligations, where that conduct also deprives someone of his federal constitutional rights. The Supreme Court initially addressed this situation in two § 242 prosecutions.

In *United States v. Classic*, several county election officials were prosecuted for depriving Blacks of the right to vote when the officials failed to count votes, altered ballots to show votes for different candidates, and falsely certified the election results — all directly contrary to their state law obligations to count votes and properly certify the election results. Although violative of state law, the officials' conduct also deprived African American voters of their federal constitutional right to vote.[16] A four-justice majority held that the federal prosecution could proceed; the election officials acted under color of state law because "[m]isuse of power, possessed by virtue of state law and made possible only because the wrongdoer is clothed with the authority of state law, is action taken 'under color' of state law."[17] Public officials act under color of law when they disregard their express legal obligations in the course of performing their official public duties, where doing so deprives an individual of her constitutional rights.

The same issue arose four years later in *Screws v. United States*, this time in the prosecution of a Southern sheriff and a posse of his deputies for the prolonged and fatal assault and beating of a handcuffed African American arrestee outside the jailhouse.[18] A four-justice plurality rejected the argument that the officers did not act under color of law because their actions constituted crimes and/or torts under state law, insisting instead that conduct could violate state law and still violate the federal Constitution. The case was indistinguishable from *Classic*.[19] In both, government officers misused state-granted power. The law-enforcement officers here acted within the scope of their state authority because they were empowered to make arrests, to take someone into custody, and to take necessary steps to make an arrest effective; they acted without their authority only because they then used excessive force in the course of effecting that arrest.[20] The Court reaffirmed *Classic*'s formulation of under color, then went further to insist that "it is clear that under 'color' of law means under 'pretense' of law." All acts taken in performance of official duties are included within "under color," both where officers "hew to the line of their authority" (in following and enforcing unconstitutional laws) and where officers "overstep" that authority.[21]

---

[15] Hague v. CIO, 307 U.S. 496 (1939).

[16] United States v. Classic, 313 U.S. 299, 307–09 (1941).

[17] *Id.* at 326.

[18] Screws v. United States, 325 U.S. 91, 92–93 (1945).

[19] *Id.* at 110.

[20] *Id.* at 111.

[21] *Id.*

[2]   *Monroe v. Pape* and "Under Color" in § 1983

Classic and *Screws* did not necessarily resolve the meaning of "under color" for purposes of § 1983. That happened 16 years later in *Monroe v. Pape*,[22] the case that commentators rightly regard as launching modern civil rights litigation.[23]

Thirteen Chicago police officers investigating a murder entered the home of James Monroe, an African American man, and his family in the middle of the night, without a warrant. They dragged James out of bed (naked) and made him stand in the living room; they also made James' wife (also naked) and his children stand in the living room. Officers then ransacked the entire house, emptying drawers and ripping mattresses. They also allegedly pushed, hit, or kicked James and several other family members and used racial epithets in talking to the family. James was arrested and detained for 10 hours, without being taken before a magistrate or allowed to call his attorney or family. He was released the following day when the witness (the wife of the murder victim) was unable to identify Monroe in a line-up.[24] Monroe then sued the City of Chicago, Chief of Detectives Pape (who lead the officers into the house), and the other officers.

As in *Screws*, police abused authority they possessed as law enforcement officers, engaging in conduct that not only was not authorized by state law, but was in fact directly contrary to it and actionable under it. The officers' conduct violated the Illinois Constitution and Illinois statutory and common law, Illinois law provided civil remedies for those violations, and the Illinois courts were open and available to provide full redress.[25]

For the first time, a full majority (eight justices) agreed to the broad construction of under color offered in *Screws* and *Classic*. And for the second time, the Court rejected a request to reconsider *Classic* and the misuse-of-authority standard.[26] Writing for the Court, Justice Douglas concluded that the phrase should have the same construction in both civil and criminal contexts, given that § 1983 was explicitly modeled on § 242. The group of defendants subject to civil suit should be at least as broad as the group of defendants subject to criminal prosecution.

Justice Douglas adopted a purposivist approach to § 1983, looking at the debates over the Ku Klux Klan Act of 1871 to identify three main aims of § 1. The first was to "override certain kinds of state laws," most notably the Black Codes, that explicitly burdened or disabled freedmen from most incidents and rights of political and civil society. Section 1983 thus provided for federal civil lawsuits to invalidate

---

[22]   Monroe v. Pape, 365 U.S. 167 (1961).

[23]   Gene R. Nichol, Jr., *Federalism, State Courts, and Section 1983*, 73 Va. L. Rev. 959, 968–69 (1987).

[24]   *Monroe*, 365 U.S. at 169–70; Myriam E. Gilles, *Police, Race and Crime in 1950s Chicago:* Monroe v. Pape *as Legal Noir, in* Civil Rights Stories 41, 48–52 (Myriam E. Gilles and Risa L. Goluboff eds., 2008). Ultimately, the victim's wife confessed that she and her lover had conspired to commit the murder. *Id.* at 52.

[25]   *Monroe*, 365 U.S. at 172.

[26]   *Id.* at 187.

invidious state statutes that abridged the rights or privileges of citizens.[27]

The second aim was to provide a federal remedy where state law on the books and as written was inadequate to protect the person's rights.[28]

The third aim, on which the *Monroe* Court focused, gave the statute its true breadth: To "provide a federal remedy where the state remedy, though adequate in theory, was not available in practice."[29] Congress in 1871 legislated against the pervasive legal, political, and social influence of the Klan throughout the South. Congress' concern was not limited to situations in which the Klan controlled the engines of state government and directly enacted or enforced unconstitutional laws. Rather, Congress wanted to provide a remedy "against those representing a State in some capacity [who] were unable or unwilling to enforce a state law" because of the Klan's societal influence and control. In such cases, there was "no quarrel with the state law on the books. It was their lack of enforcement that was the nub of the difficulty." The federal remedy must be available where any state law might not be enforced or where state rights might be denied, where there is a risk of discriminatory enforcement or non-enforcement because of "prejudice, passion, neglect, intolerance, or otherwise."[30]

Importantly, history quickly falls away from the analysis. While enacted in a particular historical context and in response to a particular historical problem, § 1983 is written in general terms. Its policies were as applicable to Illinois in 1961 as to the Klan-influence South in 1871[31], even if the same socio-legal pathologies no longer were in play.

Moreover, Congress designed the federal remedy to supplement the state remedy, given the possibility that the latter might be inadequate.[32] Plaintiffs need not seek and have refused state rights and remedies as a condition precedent to resorting to federal court and federal remedies. Nor is it significant that the same conduct by the same defendants could constitute both a state tort and the deprivation of a constitutional right; the latter is a significantly different and unique legal right, deserving of a different and unique remedy.[33]

Congress decided in 1871 that federal civil remedies should be available in federal court simply because state law remedies might be practically unavailable or inadequate because, historically, they were.[34]Section 1983 thus establishes a wholesale approach to the relationship between federal and state remedies, in light of historical suspicions about state law and state processes that motivated the Reconstruction Congress. A plaintiff need not make a retail showing of inadequacy in each case to proceed on a § 1983 claim in federal court. She simply may proceed

---

[27] *Id.* at 173.

[28] *Id.* at 173–74.

[29] *Id.* at 174.

[30] *Id.* at 174–80.

[31] *Id.* at 183.

[32] *Id.* at 196.

[33] *Id.* at 196 (Harlan, J., concurring).

[34] *See* Mitchum v. Foster, 407 U.S. 225, 241–42 (1972).

to show that an individual, acting under the pretense of state authority, acted in a way that deprived her of her constitutional rights.

[3] Public-official defendants after *Monroe*

Monroe, adapting *Screws* and *Classic* to § 1983, establishes that a defendant acts under color of law when he misuses state-granted power and when his misconduct is possible only because he is "clothed" with the authority, or pretense of authority, of state law. A public officer may be sued for all acts performed within the scope of his employment, whether state law formally authorizes the conduct, formally prohibits the conduct, or is silent about the conduct.

"Under color" analysis focuses on whether the defendant officer wields actual or apparent authority given by the State and whether that authority enables him to engage in the conduct at issue. As one court of appeals explains it, a government officer acts under color of law when his conduct "occurs in the course of performing an actual or apparent duty of his office, or [when] the conduct is such that the actor could not have behaved in that way but for the authority of his office."[35] This includes conduct done only under the "pretense" of authority or law, even in the total absence of any actual authority.[36] In fact, so long as there is pretense of authority, conduct can be under color of law even if based, in whole or in part, on personal animus between the officer and the plaintiff.[37] But the challenged conduct must relate in some "meaningful way" to the defendant's governmental status or to the performance of his official functions.[38] It must be an act that is part of the officer's public duties (even if done in a way exceeding the scope of those duties) or purportedly taken in the course of his actual duties and under pretense of authority connected to his official position.[39] That an actor is a government official does not alone mean he acts under color for all his conduct, however, even where the conduct bears a loose connection to his job functions.[40]

A government officer also may be "clothed" with state authority where he acts entirely outside the scope of employment and is in no way performing public or governmental duties, but carries and wields the badges of state authority to enable the conduct. This can be thought of in terms of but-for causation — whether the defendant could have committed these acts without his state authority or, stated differently, whether a purely private person could have engaged in precisely the same conduct in precisely the same circumstances.[41]

---

[35] Martinez v. Colon, 54 F.3d 980, 986 (1st Cir. 1995).

[36] Butler v. Sheriff of Palm Beach County, 685 F.3d 1261, 1268 (11th Cir. 2012).

[37] There was some evidence that Sheriff Screws held a personal grudge against the victim of that beating. *Screws*, 325 U.S. at 93.

[38] Waters v. City of Morristown, 242 F.3d 353, 359 (6th Cir. 2001) (citing Zambrana-Marrero v. Suarez-Cruz, 172 F.3d 122, 126 (1st Cir. 1999)).

[39] Wilson v. Price, 624 F.3d 389, 393 (7th Cir. 2010); Dossett v. First State Bank, 399 F.3d 940, 949–50 (8th Cir. 2005).

[40] *Butler*, 685 F.3d at 1268–69; Johnson v. Knowles, 113 F.3d 1114, 1117 (9th Cir. 1997).

[41] *Butler*, 685 F.3d at 1267–69.

The latter situation most commonly arises with respect to off-duty law enforcement officers. These officers are unique even among public officials — they possess legal authority to use physical, and even deadly, force; to seize and detain people or threaten to do so; and to disobey traffic and other public regulations. The question is what happens when an officer wields the ordinary authority attached to his job entirely outside the scope of that job. These cases often turn on the extent to which the defendant implicitly or explicitly suggests to observers that he is acting as a law-enforcement officer and within the scope of his employment, as by flashing the trappings or indicia of state authority. Relevant facts may include whether the officer is in uniform, whether he displays his badge, whether he carries or flashes his service weapons, whether he is driving an official vehicle, and whether he identifies himself as a police officer.[42] Courts also may look to the underlying circumstances that put the off-duty officer in that situation and whether they connect him to the police department or to his position and power as a member of the department.[43]

[4]   Under Color of Law Puzzles: Public-Official Defendants

The following situations result in a § 1983 action against the officers. Consider whether the defendants acted under color of law under the Monroe standard; think about what facts are significant and what additional facts may be necessary for a court to resolve the question.

1. *Two New York City police officers remove a fan from Yankee Stadium during a baseball game because he left his seat during the playing of "God Bless America," in violation of team policy; the fan alleges his removal violates his First Amendment rights. The off-duty officers are working at the stadium pursuant to the Police Department's "Paid Detail Program," through which private companies and events hire uniformed police officers to provide security at various venues, including ballgames. The primary purpose of the program is to "provide a highly visible police presence" at events and venues; it incidentally provides off-duty officers an opportunity to earn additional income. Participating officers are required to wear full uniform, carry handcuffs and service firearms, carry a department radio, and conform to all department grooming and appearance standards. They are subject at all times to department rules and regulations, including regulations regarding courtesy and contact with the public. At larger venues (such as a baseball stadium), the officers report to a superior NYPD officer working in the detail program in a supervisory capacity. Officers are responsible for taking all "proper police action in accordance with the circumstances" in working these private events. The officers also are subject to control by the hiring business or venue.*[44]

2. *During a preliminary hearing in a state criminal prosecution, the assistant district attorney becomes enraged with defense counsel. After a brief shouting match, the ADA shoves, punches,, and tackles the defense attorney onto a tabletop.*

[42] Pickrel v. City of Springfield, 45 F.3d 1115 (7th Cir. 1995).

[43] *Butler,* 685 F.3d at 1267–68; Almand v. DeKalb County, 103 F.3d 1510, 1514–15 (11th Cir. 1997).

[44] Complaint in *Campeau-Laurion v. Kelly,* No. 09-CV-3790 (S.D.N.Y. 2009).

The defense attorney alleges excessive force in violation of the Fourth Amendment and a violation of due process under the Fourteenth Amendment.

3. *Plaintiffs are three women who sue Judge David Lanier, an elected state chancery judge. Judge Lanier has jurisdiction over divorce, child custody, and child support matters, as well as supervisory responsibilities for the court's clerical and secretarial employees. All three women go to Lanier's chambers on various occasions, whether as part of a job interview, pursuant to their job responsibilities, or to discuss custody matters pending in Lanier's court to which they are parties. At various points, Lanier threatens each with loss of a job, court case, or custody of her child if she does not come to chambers and submit to his sexual advances. Once in chambers, Lanier assaults, sexually assaults, and rapes the women. He also stalks them and makes harassing phone calls, continuing to threaten them with adverse employment or legal consequences.*[45]

4. *Martinez is a member of the Puerto Rico police force. One morning at work, he is accosted on four different occasions by Valentin, a fellow officer. Three times, Valentin aims his cocked service revolver at Martinez and asks Martinez if he is scared. The third time, the gun discharges, severely injuring Martinez.*[46]

[5] State Actors and State Action

There is a somewhat convoluted relationship between the Fourteenth Amendment requirement of state action and the § 1983 requirement of a person acting under color of state law. As stated previously, courts often treat them as identical inquiries. And as a default rule, if a person is a state actor, he acts under color of state law, and if there is state action there is action under color of state law.[47]

One notable exception is *Polk County v. Dodson.* A convicted prisoner sued his former defense attorney, a public defender who had been assigned to handle his appeal but had requested to withdraw when she concluded that the appeal was wholly frivolous; the plaintiff alleged that the withdrawal violated his constitutional right to counsel.[48] There obviously is both a state actor and state action here — the attorney is a full-time employee of a county agency, performing her official job duties for a county-created and -funded agency, and exercising the professional discretion and responsibility her government job requires.

But the Supreme Court held that the lawyer did not act under color of state law for § 1983 purposes, given the nature of the attorney-client relationship. An attorney, even a publicly funded or employed one, acts as the adversary of the state when performing her traditional function as counsel for a defendant in a criminal proceeding. A public defender works on behalf of her client within an adversary system, advancing " 'the undivided interest of his client,' " rather than on behalf of

---

[45] Archie v. Lanier, 95 F.3d 438 (6th Cir. 1996); *see also* United States v. Lanier, 520 U.S. 259 (1997).

[46] Martinez v. Colon, 54 F.3d 980 (1st Cir. 1995).

[47] Lugar v. Edmondson Oil Co., 457 U.S. 922, 935 & n.18 (1982); *Butler,* 685 F.3d at 1265 n.5.

[48] Polk County v. Dodson, 454 U.S. 312, 314–15 (1981).

or in concert with the state.[49] The public defender's job is to oppose the representatives and interests of the state. Her traditional representation functions are in no way dependent on state authority; in fact, the assumption underlying the very concept of a public defender is that she will zealously represent the interests of the defendant against the state, exercising her own professional judgment, free of all state control or influence.[50] The attorney-client relationship and the attorney's ethical obligations render representation a private function, no different than representation by a paid or court-appointed private attorney.

Polk County can be understood as a judicial effort to protect the unique institution of the public defender, in light of its function in ensuring constitutionally required representation to indigent criminal defendants.[51] A different conclusion could have opened the door for every person convicted of a crime to use § 1983 litigation to challenge the representation afforded by his public defender, functionally seeking federal judicial review of his conviction. This obviously would affect the federal judicial docket, forcing district courts to review state criminal proceedings in a manner not within the ambit of § 1983.[52] It also would have provided criminal defendants represented by a public defender a unique opportunity for federal review not available to those represented by private counsel, even court-appointed private counsel, who do not act under color of state law in their roles as officers of the court.[53]

Given the focus on the traditional lawyering function, *Polk County* does not mean that a public defender, or the state office of public defender, never acts under color of state law. Instead, the Court recognized that a public defender could act under color of law in performing functions other than client representation — functions that do not place the official or agency in an adverse position to the state, such as hiring, firing, and performing other administrative or investigative functions.[54] This shows that the controlling feature in *Polk County*'s "under color" analysis remains the uniqueness of the attorney-client relationship, entailing exercise of professional judgment within an adversarial process immune from state control.[55] It also highlights the precision needed in defining the relationship between constitutional state action and statutory action under color of state law.

This understanding of *Polk County* became clear several years later in *West v. Atkins*, an action by a prisoner against the private physician contracted by the

---

[49] *Id.* at 318–19.

[50] *Id.* at 321–22.

[51] *Id.* at 320, 324; *but see id.* at 331 (Blackmun, J., dissenting).

[52] Although other doctrines might handle most of these cases. Heck v. Humphrey, 512 U.S. 477 (1994); *infra* § 5.07.

[53] *Polk County*, 454 U.S. at 318 & n.7; Rodriguez v. Weprin, 116 F.3d 62 (2d Cir. 1997); Mills v. Criminal Dist. Court # 3, 837 F.2d 677 (5th Cir. 1988).

[54] *Polk County*, 454 U.S. at 324–25; Miranda v. Clark County, Nev., 319 F.3d 465, 469 (9th Cir. 2003) (holding that administrator acts under color in enforcing office policy requiring potential clients to take polygraph).

[55] *Polk County*, 454 U.S. at 321, 324–25; The Court subsequently applied *Polk County*'s "acting-on-behalf-of-the-state" concept to the constitutional state action requirement. *See* Georgia v. McCollum, 505 U.S. 42, 53 n.9 (1992) (citing Blum v. Yaretsky, 457 U.S. 991, 1009 n.20 (1982)).

state to provide prison medical services. The court of appeals had interpreted *Polk County* to mean that all professionals do not act under color of state law when acting in their professional capacities, but the Supreme Court rejected that approach. Doctors are different than attorneys because their relationship with the state is cooperative rather than adversarial; their professional and ethical obligations are consistent with the state's mission and obligation to provide constitutionally adequate medical care to prisoners. In fact, the state established specific patient-care guidelines and protocols that doctors were obligated to follow.[56]

[6]   A Dissenting View on Under Color

The expansive view of under color of state law established in *Classic*, *Screws*, and *Monroe* did not receive unanimous approval of the Supreme Court. Justice Roberts dissented in *Screws*, joined by Justices Frankfurter and Jackson; Justice Frankfurter, the only of the three remaining on the Court in 1961, dissented alone in *Monroe*. Both dissents closely examined the legislative history of the 1866 Act (which produced § 242, the model for § 1983), concluding that Congress only intended federal authority to punish those who claimed state authority, not those who offended state authority in their actions. The broader interpretation impermissibly interposed federal courts into the prosecution of purely local crimes and common law torts.

The divide between the majorities and dissents in both cases reflects many of the overarching themes of federal civil rights law and a divide over what those themes mean. While everyone recognized the changes to federalism wrought by the Fourteenth Amendment and legislation enforcing that Amendment, the dissents insisted that Congress did not intend the sort of "distortion of federal power" or "revolutionary break with the past overnight"[57] or departure from the "presuppositions of our federal system"[58] that comes from federalizing localized misconduct by one co-citizen (who happens to work for the government) against another. State courts were to remain the "primary guardians of that fundamental security of persons and property" in individual disputes.[59] Importantly, the dissenters agreed that Congress could have adopted a broader approach, but insisted that it did not do so; it failed to provide any sufficiently clear statutory declaration of such a fundamental shift of power and responsibility. Absent that statement, it is not for the Court to make the legislative policy judgments necessary to effect that transfer.

Both dissents did recognize that an officer might act under color of law even where his conduct is not formally authorized by state law, pointing to the "custom" or "usage" language in both statutes. Federal law should "reach, as well, official conduct which, because engaged in 'permanently and as a rule,' or 'systematically,' came through acceptance by law-administering officers to constitute 'custom, or

---

[56] West v. Atkins, 487 U.S. 42, 50–51, 55–57 (1988).

[57] Screws v. United States, 325 U.S. 91, 142–44 (1945) (Roberts, J., dissenting).

[58] Monroe v. Pape, 365 U.S. 167, 237 (1961) (Frankfurter, J., dissenting).

[59] *Id.* at 237 (Frankfurter, J., dissenting).

usage' having the cast of law."[60] But this requires a "settled state practice" or a "systematic pattern of official action or inaction," such that it prevents "effective and adequate reparation by the State's authorities."[61] Only if the state remedy is formally or functionally unavailable should federal law (and federal courts) interpose itself.

As discussed, the *Screws/Monroe* standard takes a wholesale approach to under color, making § 1983 actions broadly available. By contrast, the dissenting approach would require a detailed, case-by-case inquiry into whether this particular state has a custom or usage of non-enforcement or discriminatory enforcement as to this law or this class of defendants or plaintiffs.

Justice Frankfurter's *Monroe* dissent acknowledged that this creates difficult questions of proof. He rejected, however, the notion that this imposes an exhaustion requirement, which would "effectively nullify" § 1983 as a vehicle for recovering damages and would be inconsistent with efficient judicial administration.[62] After all, that a plaintiff seeks a state remedy and loses does not mean the state remedy is so fundamentally inadequate that there is a custom or usage of non-enforcement. But Frankfurter did not indicate how a plaintiff can otherwise show this policy or custom of state non-enforcement — perhaps by showing a complete absence of any history of successful lawsuits or prosecutions or a history of unequal enforcement. He only made the obvious point that federal district courts must resolve intricate and uncertain questions of state law all the time, so there is nothing fundamentally different about this one.[63]

§ 2.04 STATE ACTION, UNDER COLOR, AND PRIVATE ACTORS

While *Classic*, *Screws*, and *Monroe* expand the circumstances under which a public officer, official, or employee acts under color of law, there also are situations in which an ostensibly private actor acts under color of law. The Fourteenth Amendment's "ambit cannot be a simple line between States and people operating outside formally governmental organizations."[64] Under certain facts and circumstances, the conduct of a putatively private individual, entity, or organization should be treated as if the State caused the conduct to be performed, such that courts will find that the private actor is a state actor, acts under color of law, and can be subject to constitutional liability. Courts describe this as "joint participation" between the government and the private actor, such that putatively private conduct "may be fairly treated as that of the State itself."[65]

The Supreme Court has suggested a range of tests or factors that establish joint participation, all of which reflect "different ways of characterizing the necessarily

---

[60] *Id.* at 236 (Frankfurter, J., dissenting).

[61] *Id.* (Frankfurter, J., dissenting).

[62] *Id.* at 245 (Frankfurter, J., dissenting).

[63] *Id.* at 246 (Frankfurter, J., dissenting).

[64] *Brentwood*, 531 U.S. at 295.

[65] *Brentwood*, 531 U.S. at 295; Lugar v. Edmondson Oil Co., 457 U.S. 922, 937 (1982).

fact-bound inquiry that confronts the Court in such a situation."[66] It also has suggested these are not necessarily competing tests, but more "a host of facts that can bear on the fairness" of attributing state authority to private conduct on a given set of facts.[67] Whether viewed as tests or criteria, they often are best understood as much for what they do not reach as for what they do reach. Most are difficult to establish, which is consistent with the policy concerns underlying the state action/under color requirement and the Court's stated desire to limit the reach of federal law, the burden on individual conduct, and the liability of states.[68]

[1] Traditional, Exclusive Public Function

This test looks to whether a private actor has undertaken a function that is "traditionally the exclusive prerogative of the state."[69] It ensures that government cannot skirt its constitutional obligations by delegating tasks to private actors. But the test is intentionally narrow and rarely satisfied. The function at issue must not only be one government traditionally performs, but one that only government, and no other actor, traditionally performs. And very few state functions are historically reserved exclusively to the government.[70]

This is largely limited to functions that are essential to sovereignty,[71] particularly where the state has a constitutional obligation to provide the service and has instead fully delegated it to the private entity. These may include administering general and primary elections,[72] operating and administrating a municipality,[73] operating and maintaining a municipal park,[74] operating a volunteer fire department,[75] exercising plenary police authority to arrest and detain people,[76] and controlling domestic animals in the community.[77] They also include selecting a jury as part of judicial proceedings, including the use of peremptory challenges by private parties in civil litigation[78] and private defendants in a criminal prosecution.[79] The prevailing view in the lower courts is that operating prisons and jails qualifies as traditional and exclusive, thus private prison companies and their employees act under color of state law for § 1983 purposes.[80] On the other hand, it

---

[66] *Lugar*, 457 U.S. at 939.

[67] *Brentwood*, 531 U.S. at 296.

[68] *Lugar*, 457 U.S. at 936–37; *supra* § 2.02.

[69] Rendell-Baker v. Kohn, 457 U.S. 830, 842 (1982); Craig v. Floyd County, 643 F.3d 1306, 1310 (11th Cir. 2011).

[70] Flagg Bros., Inc. v. Brooks, 436 U.S. 149, 158 (1978).

[71] *Id.* at 163.

[72] Terry v. Adams, 345 U.S. 461 (1953).

[73] Marsh v. Alabama, 326 U.S. 501 (1946).

[74] Evans v. Newton, 382 U.S. 296 (1966).

[75] Goldstein v. Chestnut Ridge Volunteer Fire Co., 218 F.3d 337 (4th Cir. 2000).

[76] Romanski v. Detroit Entm't, L.L.C., 428 F.3d 629 (6th Cir. 2005).

[77] Fabrikant v. French, 691 F.3d 193 (2d Cir. 2012).

[78] Edmonson v. Leesville Concrete Co., 500 U.S. 614 (1991).

[79] Georgia v. McCollum, 505 U.S. 42 (1992).

[80] Craig v. Floyd County, Ga., 643 F.3d 1306 (11th Cir. 2011); Rosborough v. Management & Training

does not include operating schools[81] or hospitals and health-care facilities;[82] accrediting training and educational programs;[83] providing counseling to minors, even when done pursuant to a court order;[84] or regulating interscholastic athletics[85] — none of these functions ever has been the exclusive province of government or an aspect of sovereignty.

The idea of constitutional obligation to perform a function further explains the Court's decision in *West v. Adkins* that a private physician contracting with the state to provide prison medical services acts under color of law; because the state has a constitutional obligation to provide adequate medical care to prisoners, it cannot avoid the constitutional limits by delegating its responsibility to a private person.[86] Lower courts have followed suit.[87] More recently, the Supreme Court considered a claim against a private attorney who contracted with a municipality to investigate and report on alleged misconduct by a municipal firefighter.[88] No one disputed that the attorney acted under color of law,[89] a conclusion that must be understood in similar terms — government only can function as an institution and only can carry out its traditional (sovereign) governing obligations by acting through its officers, whether it hires them as full-time employees or as contract workers.

[2] Conspiracy

United States v. Price involved a § 242 prosecution of three Southern local law-enforcement officials and 15 non-official community members (some of whom were Klan members) in the notorious deaths of three civil rights workers in Philadelphia, Mississippi, in 1964.[90] According to the indictment, a deputy sheriff arrested and jailed the three men, then released them from custody. The deputy then followed them from the jail in his car, stopped and seized them a second time, and drove them to a place on an unpaved road; they were again set loose and intercepted by the other men, according to plan. Some or all of the group then shot and killed the three men, while others transported and buried the bodies in an

---

Corp., 350 F.3d 459 (5th Cir. 2003) (per curiam); Street v. Corrections Corp. of Am., 102 F.3d 810 (6th Cir. 1996); *but cf.* Minneci v. Pollard, 132 S. Ct. 617 (2012).

[81] Rendell-Baker v. Kohn, 457 U.S. 830 (1982).

[82] Blum v. Yaretsky, 457 U.S. 991 (1982).

[83] McKeesport Hosp. v. Accreditation Council for Graduate Medical Educ., 24 F.3d 519 (3d Cir. 1994).

[84] Reguli v. Guffee, 2010 U.S. App. LEXIS 6767 (6th Cir. Mar. 31, 2010).

[85] *Brentwood*, 531 U.S. at 288; National Collegiate Athletic Ass'n v. Tarkanian, 488 U.S. 179, 197 n.18 (1988).

[86] West v. Atkins, 487 U.S. 42, 55–56 (1988).

[87] Americans United for Church & State v. Prison Fellowship Ministries, Inc., 509 F.3d 406 (8th Cir. 2007).

[88] Filarsky v. Delia, 132 S. Ct. 1657 (2012).

[89] The issue before the Court was whether the contract attorney could avail himself of a qualified immunity defense, as would a regular municipal employee. *Filarsky*, 132 S. Ct. at 1660; *infra* § 3.16.

[90] United States v. Price, 383 U.S. 787 (1966). The events underlying *Price* were loosely depicted in the film *Mississippi Burning*. MISSISSIPPI BURNING (Orion Pictures 1988).

earthen dam outside of town.[91]

The Court reversed dismissal of the § 242 charges against the 15 private individuals, holding that the joint conspiracy between private actors and government officials (themselves unquestionably acting under color of law as construed in *Screws*) made the private individuals "willful participant[s]" in joint activity. The "brutal joint adventure was made possible by state detention and calculated release of the prisoners by an officer of the State." It was part of the "monstrous design," a "joint activity from start to finish." And the private persons who "took advantage of the participation by state officers in accomplishment of the foul purpose alleged must suffer the consequences of that participation."[92]

The language in *Price* suggests an important limitation on the conspiracy test — the conduct engaged in must be blatantly, obviously, even monstrously unlawful and the private and public actors must intentionally agree to engage in that obviously unlawful conduct. Mere invocation of governmental authority or legal processes by a private actor is not sufficient to establish a public-private conspiracy. Much turns on the intent of the private individual and the nature of the joint action between the private person and the state actor.

In *Dennis v. Sparks*, a private company bribed a state-court judge to issue an injunction preventing the production of minerals from oil leases owned by Sparks; a unanimous Supreme Court held that Sparks could sue the company under § 1983. While requesting and obtaining the injunction is not sufficient to place the company under color, the allegations that the company bribed and corruptly conspired with the judge to get the injunction changes the analysis.[93] Similarly, when a private person complains and asks police to enforce the laws on his behalf, it does not establish action under color by that person as to any subsequent unconstitutional conduct by the officers themselves in responding to that request.[94] But a private storeowner who agrees in advance with police to unlawfully deny a customer service because of her race and to cause her subsequent arrest may act under color.[95]

[3] Symbiotic Relationship

Established in *Burton v. Wilmington Parking Authority*,[96] this is one of the broadest and most controversial approaches to under color.

The Eagle Coffee Shoppe was a private restaurant operating in a parking garage owned by the Wilmington Parking Authority, a Delaware agency, which

---

[91] *Price*, 383 U.S. at 789–91.

[92] *Id.* at 794–95.

[93] Dennis v. Sparks, 449 U.S. 24, 29 (1980).

[94] Dunn v. Carrier 2005 U.S. App. LEXIS 10511 (2d Cir. June 7, 2005) (complaint by private resident at his home); Peng v. Hu, 335 F.3d 970 (9th Cir. 2003) (complaint to police about theft); Moore v. Marketplace Restaurant, Inc., 754 F.2d 1336 (7th Cir. 1985) (restaurant manager complained to police about customers' failure to pay for meals).

[95] Adickes v. S. H. Kress & Co., 398 U.S. 144, 152 (1970).

[96] Burton v. Wilmington Parking Auth., 365 U.S. 715 (1961).

leased the restaurant space to Eagle under a 20-year renewable lease. The restaurant was sued for violating Equal Protection by refusing to serve an African American man. In finding that Eagle acted under color, the Court's analysis focused on the "peculiar relationship" of the restaurant to the publicly owned parking facility, which conferred on each "an incidental variety of mutual benefits."[97] The exchange of those mutual benefits established joint participation and thus action under color.

The government benefitted from having the restaurant there, since it needed money from long-term commercial leases to even build the garage. Guests of the restaurant had a convenient place to park and the restaurant traffic created additional demand for parking. By renting in a building owned by a government agency, Eagle knew that improvements to the space would not result in higher property taxes on the owner or on the passage of those taxes to it (as the lessee) as higher rent. Finally, Eagle acknowledged that its business would be hurt if it served African Americans; because better business for Eagle meant continued payment of rents, the government was functionally profiting from private discrimination. This last point is critical, because it ties the under color inquiry to the challenged race discrimination: It is not that government is profiting from the restaurant's operations, but that government is profiting directly from the challenged unconstitutional conduct.[98]

The Court then concluded:

> Addition of all these activities, obligations and responsibilities of the Authority, the benefits mutually conferred, together with the obvious fact that the restaurant is operated as an integral part of a public building devoted to a public parking service, indicates that degree of state participation and involvement in discriminatory action which it was the design of the Fourteenth Amendment to condemn.[99]

There is some debate as to the continued vitality of *Burton*. The Court did not mention *Burton* or symbiotic relationship in its most recent "under color" case.[100] And *Burton* is in many ways a *sui generis* case, a product of an unusual business relationship and the extremes that faced the Court at the height of the Civil Rights Movement. This history makes *Burton* "seminal, albeit somewhat idiosyncratic."[101] One scholar argues that the *Burton* test "really represented an open-ended inquiry into the relationship between the state and the private entity in order to ascertain whether it would be fundamentally fair to hold the private entity accountable for constitutional violations."[102]

---

[97] *Id.* at 724.

[98] *Id.* at 723–24.

[99] *Id.*

[100] *Brentwood*, 531 U.S. at 288.

[101] Crissman v. Dover Downs Entm't, 289 F.3d 231, 246 (3d Cir. 2002) (en banc) (citing Brown v. Philip Morris, Inc., 250 F.3d 789, 803 (3d Cir. 2001)).

[102] Ronald J. Krotoszynski, *A Remembrance of Things Past?: Reflections on the Warren Court and the Struggle for Civil Rights*, 59 WASH. & LEE. L. REV. 1055, 1063 (2002).

Some lower courts thus have suggested that *Burton* should be limited to its unique fact pattern.[103] Of course, *Burton* no longer is necessary in the particular context of private race discrimination in spaces such as restaurants. A plaintiff instead can proceed under Title II of the Civil Rights Act of 1964, a statute enacted under the Commerce Clause, which prohibits discrimination because of race in privately owned places of public accommodation, such as restaurants, operating in interstate commerce.[104] He no longer needs to establish state action or action under color of law because he no longer needs to frame the case under the Fourteenth Amendment or § 1983.

[4] Close Nexus

This test asks whether there is a close connection between the government and the private actor's challenged conduct. The government must be responsible — through compulsion, coercion, control, facilitation, overwhelming government encouragement, enforcement, or otherwise — for the specific private conduct of which the plaintiff complains. Mere government approval, authorization, or acquiescence is not sufficient; the government must affirmatively aid the private conduct.[105] The nexus must be to the precise action, conduct, or decision being challenged; a relationship between government and the private actor, even a close one, is not sufficiently connected to the specific conduct or decision itself.[106]

Like the public function test, close nexus can be understood as much for what does not satisfy it as what does. Extensive state regulation,[107] state provision of funding or other benefits,[108] and state licensing of the entity,[109] even to the point of granting a monopoly, do not establish the necessary nexus. Neither does delegation of state power, at least where the state formally retains regulatory authority and ultimate responsibility for implementing the decision of the private organization as its own.[110] The narrowness of this test is again grounded in the need to limit the scope of constitutional duty and liability. So many people, entities, and businesses receive public funds or are subject to regulation or licensing that too broad an

---

[103] *Crissman*, 289 F.3d at 244.

[104] Civil Rights Act of 1964, Title II, Pub. L. No. 88-352, 78 Stat. 241 (1964) (codified at 42 U.S.C. § 2000a); Katzenbach v. McClung, 379 U.S. 294 (1964).

[105] *Compare* Harvey v. Plains Twp. Police Dep't, 635 F.3d 606, 610–11 (3d Cir. 2011) (reasonable jury could have found that officer intervened and aided one private party, so as to cause the constitutional violation), *and* Abbott v. Latshaw, 164 F.3d 141, 147 (3d Cir. 1998) (finding action under color where defendant did not remain neutral in overseeing dispute between private persons), *with* Barrett v. Harwood, 189 F.3d 297, 302–03 (2d Cir. 1999) (no action under color where officer did nothing to facilitate private action).

[106] McKeesport Hosp. v. Accreditation Council for Graduate Med. Educ., 24 F.3d 519, 525 (3d Cir. 1994).

[107] American Mfrs. Mut. Ins. Co. v. Sullivan, 526 U.S. 40 (1999) (private workers' compensation insurer); Blum v. Yaretsky, 457 U.S. 991 (1982) (nursing home); Jackson v. Metropolitan Edison Co., 419 U.S. 345 (1974) (electric utility).

[108] Rendell-Baker v. Kohn, 457 U.S. 830 (1982) (private school).

[109] *Blum*, 457 U.S. at 1011–12; Moose Lodge No. 107 v. Irvis, 407 U.S. 163 (1972); Den Hollander v. Copacabana Nightclub, 624 F.3d 30 (2d Cir. 2010).

[110] *McKeesport Hosp.*, 24 F.3d at 525.

understanding would dramatically expand who acts under color and thus who is subject to constitutional obligations and liability.

In *Moose Lodge No. 107 v. Irvis*, the plaintiff challenged the racially discriminatory guest policies of a private club that owned a state liquor license. The Court held that receipt of the license, and the regulations that went with it, did not place the lodge under color. But state liquor control board regulations also required that all licensees comply with all provisions of their constitutions and by-laws; one of Moose Lodge's by-laws limited membership and guest services only to "white male Caucasians." Thus, by requiring the club to comply with this discriminatory provision of its own by-laws, state regulations coerced or compelled the specific unconstitutional conduct of which the plaintiff complained (denial of service on account of race), changing the nature of the regulation and thus the nature of the lodge.[111] By contrast, a bar does not act under color of law in holding "Ladies Night," where the state merely grants the bar a liquor license and does nothing to establish or enforce the allegedly discriminatory policy or practice.[112]

The narrowness of the close nexus test shifts litigation efforts back onto the government that licenses, regulates, or delegates — arguably where constitutional litigation should focus. If government delegates authority to a private entity, government enforcement of the entity's private regulations or decisions converts those private decisions into public regulations. The government itself becomes liable for carrying out or acquiescing in the private decisions that cause a constitutional violation when publicly enforced.[113]

[5] Entwinement

The Court's most recent statement on state action/action under color of law came in 2001 in *Brentwood Academy v. Tennessee Secondary School Athletic Association*, a unique case in several respects.

First, it was a First Amendment free speech case rather than an equal protection or due process case. A private parochial high school challenged enactment and enforcement of anti-recruiting rules by the state high school athletic association, after the school was placed on probation for writing recruiting letters to incoming students; it alleged that the rules violated the school's freedom of speech. The defendant was a not-for-profit association created by Tennessee law for the purpose of regulating interscholastic athletic competition in the state.[114]

Second, the case had been anticipated in dicta several years prior. In *NCAA v. Tarkanian*, the Court held that the NCAA, the body that regulates intercollegiate athletics, does not act under color of state law in establishing rules to be enforced by member schools, including by a public university such as the University of Nevada-Las Vegas. The NCAA could not be said to act under color of law of any state because it was composed of hundreds of member schools, including public

---

[111] Moose Lodge No. 107 v. Irvis, 407 U.S. 163 (1972).

[112] Comiskey v. JFTJ Corp., 989 F.2d 1007 (8th Cir. 1993).

[113] National Collegiate Athletic Ass'n. v. Tarkanian, 488 U.S. 179, 194 (1988).

[114] *Brentwood*, 531 U.S. at 291–93.

schools from all fifty states.[115] The Court suggested that the analysis might be different if the regulating body were created or empowered by the laws of a single state.[116] *Brentwood* presented that very situation.

Third, the Court spoke, arguably for the first time, about "entwinement" of government and government policies in management and control of the purportedly private entity.[117] It is not clear, however, whether entwinement constitutes a new, independent test, or whether it is an offshoot of the close nexus test. The *Brentwood* Court quoted close nexus cases and the close nexus standard, then seemed to broaden it by insisting that it is a matter of "normative judgment," with criteria that "lack rigid simplicity," in which no one fact is necessary or sufficient.[118] On the other hand, entwinement uniquely focuses on actors — on the private entity and its connection to the government — rather than on precise challenged conduct.[119] One commentator explains entwinement as a return to the flexible methodology of the *Warren* Court, eschewing rigid tests in favor of taking bits and pieces of several tests where the facts do not support any one standing alone.[120] Entwinement is less a singular test than a gestalt analysis of whether the Constitution should apply to the actors and facts at hand.

It seems clear that close nexus was not satisfied in *Brentwood*. The TSSAA, a private body, created the anti-recruiting rules and formal state policy did not require, coerce, or compel their creation or enforcement. At one time the association had been designated by the State Board of Education as the official organization for supervising and regulating interscholastic athletics and the Board specifically approved the association's rules and regulations. While such a combination of delegation and state review authority might have been sufficient to establish close nexus (as a district court held in 1995), the Board dropped that express designation and delegation in 1996, replacing it with a statement recognizing the association's regulatory role and authorizing public schools to voluntarily maintain membership.[121]

Instead, *Brentwood* focused on the connection among the state and private entities, insisting that the "nominally private character of the Association is overborne by the pervasive entwinement of public institutions and public officials in its composition and workings."[122] The Court focused on the reality of the organization's operations and relationships and found entwinement — both from the bottom up and from the top down.

From the bottom up, public schools comprised 84% of the association's membership, each school represented by an official who worked with the

---

[115] *Tarkanian*, 488 U.S. at 193.

[116] *Id.* at 193 n.13.

[117] *Brentwood*, 531 U.S. at 298.

[118] *Id.* at 295.

[119] *Id.* at 298.

[120] Ronald J. Krotoszynski, *A Remembrance of Things Past?: Reflections on the Warren Court and the Struggle for Civil Rights*, 59 Wash. & Lee. L. Rev. 1055, 1065–67 (2002).

[121] *Brentwood*, 531 U.S. at 300–01.

[122] *Id.* at 298.

association in her official capacity as part of her job responsibilities. Each official had a vote in selecting the association's governing legislative and executive bodies, which were staffed by people chosen from among eligible school officials. Public schools and public school officials essentially exercised their own authority, working through the association, to meet their responsibilities in regulating interscholastic athletics, an integral element of secondary public schooling. Association revenues came from member fees and gate receipts from tournaments held among member schools (again, the overwhelming majority of which were public). In short, there would be no recognizable or functioning association without the public school officials who control its functions and work on its behalf.[123]

From the top down, members of the State Board of Education served as *ex officio* non-voting members of the TSSAA's executive and legislative bodies. Moreover, the Court placed little significance on the state's withdrawal of the express designation of the association as regulator, because that did not affect the "momentum" of its continued involvement with the state. The removal of the formal delegation "affected nothing but words," simply "winks and nods," a formality that ignores the "practical certainty in this case that public officials will control operation of the Association."[124]

[6]   Under Color of Law Puzzle

Return to the lawsuit by the fan removed from a baseball stadium for refusing to stand during "God Bless America," arguably in violation of his First Amendment rights. In addition to suing the police officers who removed him from the park, the fan also sues the baseball team that uses the stadium. The team is a private entity. According to the complaint, the stadium is owned by the city and leased to the team on "extremely favorable terms." The city receives either rent or a percentage of revenue from admissions and concessions at games, as well as a portion of revenue from parking fees. The team began singing "God Bless America" to honor the United States and the military. It established the policy of prohibiting movement during the song in response to spectator complaints that having people moving during the song shows a lack of respect to the United States and makes it impossible for them to enjoy their experience at the stadium. The team relies on uniformed off-duty police officers, hired pursuant to a detailed formal city program, to enforce the policy regarding moving during the song.[125]

Consider whether the team, although a private entity, acts under color of law under any of the tests discussed.

---

[123] *Id.* at 299–300.

[124] *Id.* at 301.

[125] *Supra* § 2.03[4], Puzzle 1. *See* Complaint in *Campeau-Laurion v. Kelly*, No. 09-CV-3790 (S.D.N.Y. 2009); *cf.* Ludtke v. Kuhn, 461 F. Supp. 86 (S.D.N.Y. 1978).

§ 2.05   STATE ACTION WITHOUT A STATE ACTOR

In *Polk County*, the Court held that a public defender, a state employee who obviously is a state actor, is not engaged in state action (or action under color of state law) because the attorney does not act on behalf of the state in defending a client in a criminal prosecution.[126] *Polk County* marks the exception to the default rule that a state actor acts under color of state law.[127] We now consider the converse — when a person or entity who is not obviously a state actor nevertheless acts under color of state law (or engages in state action).

Private parties to civil litigation necessarily utilize or attempt to avail themselves of legal rules and processes, some of which may be constitutionally suspect. State action is present in such cases because the state establishes the legal rules and procedures sought to be utilized or enforced in state-created and controlled judicial processes; as a result, private parties can assert constitutional defenses or objections to those rules. For example, in *New York Times v. Sullivan*, the Supreme Court held that a private defendant sued by a private plaintiff for defamation could defend against liability by challenging state defamation law under the First Amendment; the Court recognized that state action was present where the courts were asked to apply a state-enacted legal rule that allegedly violated the First Amendment.[128] It did not matter that they were asked to do so only in the context of a purely private dispute initiated by a non-state actor.[129]

Similarly, the Court held in a series of cases that state garnishment and pre-judgment attachment procedures were subject to procedural due process challenges by debtors-defendants. Again, state action was present because the state created these procedures and they were utilized in state-created courts, even when initiated or wielded by one private party in a dispute with another private party.[130] Although one of these cases was a § 1983 action, the constitutional claim in that case sought to enjoin enforcement of the attachment procedure and primarily targeted the state attorney general as defendant.[131] Finally, the two cases in which the Supreme Court established that equal protection controls the conduct of private litigants in jury selection arose on appeal of the judgments in the underlying cases, not in § 1983 actions.[132]

A distinct question is whether a private civil litigant, such as the creditor-plaintiff who avails itself of those constitutionally defective procedures, can be sued for damages under § 1983 by the debtor-defendant, on the ground that the creditor, in availing itself of those procedures, has become a state actor who acts under color of state law. The Court twice considered this question, reaching divergent conclusions.

---

[126] Polk County v. Dodson, 454 U.S. 312 (1981); *supra* § 2.03[5].

[127] Chudacoff v. Univ. Med. Ctr., 649 F.3d 1143 (9th Cir. 2011).

[128] New York Times Co. v. Sullivan, 376 U.S. 254, 265 (1964).

[129] *Id.*

[130] North Georgia Finishing, Inc. v. Di-Chem, Inc., 419 U.S. 601 (1975); Mitchell v. W. T. Grant Co., 416 U.S. 600 (1974).

[131] Fuentes v. Shevin, 407 U.S. 67 (1972).

[132] Georgia v. McCollum, 505 U.S. 42 (1992); Edmonson v. Leesville Concrete Co., 500 U.S. 614 (1991).

In *Flagg Bros., Inc. v. Brooks*, Flagg Bros. stored the plaintiff's furniture after the plaintiff and her family were evicted from their apartment; when the plaintiff disputed certain charges associated with moving and storage and the parties could not resolve the dispute, Flagg Bros. threatened to sell the furniture pursuant to a state-law warehouseman's lien. Instead, Brooks brought a § 1983 action against Flagg Bros., seeking damages and an injunction against the threatened sale. The Supreme Court held that Flagg Bros. did not become a state actor in availing itself of state-created procedures. It was not exercising a traditional and exclusive public function, because the resolution of private commercial disputes between debtor and creditor (which the lien statute was designed to accomplish) was not a sovereign function.[133] There also was no close nexus, because state law authorizing the sale of property by the warehouseman was not the same as state law ordering or coercing the sale.[134]

Just four years later, however, the Court held in *Lugar v. Edmondson Oil Co.* that a private litigant was subject to a § 1983 damages claim for utilizing pre-judgment attachment procedures. Edmondson Oil sued Lugar on a commercial debt in Virginia state court. As part of that litigation, Edmondson sought to secure a potential judgment by seizing some of Lugar's property; in accordance with state law, Edmondson filed an *ex parte* petition stating its belief that Lugar might dispose of his property as a way to defeat creditors and the clerk of court issued a writ of attachment, which was executed by the county sheriff. Thirty-four days later, the state trial court held a hearing and dismissed the attachment. Lugar then filed a § 1983 action in federal court against Edmondson and its president, seeking damages resulting from the erroneous attachment.[135]

The key to the Court's decision that Edmondson could be sued under § 1983 was the essential overlap between state action and action under color. A debtor-defendant in a state-court debt collection proceeding (such as Lugar) could challenge the constitutionality of the creditor-plaintiff's resort to attachment procedures. Thus, the *Lugar* Court said for the first time, it is "difficult to understand why that same behavior by the state-court plaintiff should not provide a cause of action under § 1983."[136] There was "little or no reason" to deny the federal action, since § 1983 was designed to provide judicial redress for just such constitutional violations; reading "under color" to disallow suits challenging some Fourteenth Amendment violations would be "wholly inconsistent" with § 1983's purpose of providing a vehicle to challenge unconstitutional state laws.[137] The Court then adopted and applied a broad understanding of "joint participation," finding action under color in light of the willful joint engagement of Edmondson with state officials — the clerk who granted the writ of attachment and the sheriff who executed it — in seizing Lugar's property, even if the attachment ultimately was dismissed.[138]

---

[133] Flagg Bros., Inc. v. Brooks, 436 U.S. 149, 153–54, 160, 163 (1978).

[134] *Id.* at 164.

[135] Lugar v. Edmondson Oil Co., 457 U.S. 922, 924–25 (1982).

[136] *Id.* at 934.

[137] *Id.*

[138] *Id.* at 940–42.

Lugar is unique in several respects and has largely remained an outlier decision.[139] First, it is part of a trilogy of state-action cases from 1982, but the only one in which the Court found state action.[140]

Second, as the dissents argued, *Lugar* is inconsistent with the prevailing understanding that private parties should be free to resort to presumptively valid state legal processes and legal rules, which typically does not place them under color of law.[141] Although the majority insisted that its holding was limited to the "particular context" of prejudgment attachment procedures, the dissent correctly argued that such a limitation lacked any principled basis; there simply is no meaningful difference between prejudgment attachment and other litigation strategies and procedures, such as requesting injunctive relief (which often is done *ex parte*) or summoning police to investigate a suspected crime.[142] If resort to prejudgment attachment places the creditor under color of state law, so should resort to other legal and judicial processes.

Third, it is inconsistent with the accepted notion that private parties, attorneys, and other litigation actors are not subject to suit under § 1983 for their ordinary litigation conduct.[143] Unless the joint public/private conduct is manifestly unlawful (such as bribing a judge to issue an injunction[144]), a private participant in judicial processes should be able to pursue efforts to obtain legal relief without becoming a state actor (or an actor under color of state law) subject to § 1983 and constitutional suit and liability.

PART B
RIGHTS, PRIVILEGES, OR IMMUNITIES SECURED BY THE CONSTITUTION

U.S. Constitution amend. XIV (1868)

No State shall make or enforce any law which shall abridge the privileges or immunities of citizens of the United States; nor shall any State deprive any person of life, liberty, or property, without due process of law; nor deny to any person within its jurisdiction the equal protection of the laws.

---

[139] *But cf.* Wyatt v. Cole, 504 U.S. 158 (1992) (considering availability of qualified or good-faith immunity to private defendant, while implicitly accepting underlying § 1983 claim).

[140] Blum v. Yaretsky, 457 U.S. 991 (1982); Rendell-Baker v. Kohn, 457 U.S. 830 (1982).

[141] *Lugar*, 457 U.S. at 943 (Burger, C.J., dissenting); *id.* at 944 (Powell, J., dissenting).

[142] *Compare id.* at 951 & n.8 (Powell, J., dissenting) *with id.* at 939 n.21 (majority opinion).

[143] Edmonson v. Leesville Concrete Co., 500 U.S. 614, 622 (1991); Tahfs v. Proctor, 316 F.3d 584 (6th Cir. 2003); Jordan v. Fox, Rothschild, O'Brien & Frankel, 20 F.3d 1250 (3d Cir. 1994).

[144] Dennis v. Sparks, 449 U.S. 24 (1980).

§ 2.06 CONSTITUTIONAL RIGHTS ENFORCEABLE

Both the Civil Rights Act of 1870 (in which § 242 was reenacted) and the Ku Klux Klan Act of 1871 (of which § 1983 was a part) were passed pursuant to Congress' power under § 5 of the Fourteenth Amendment to "enforce the provisions" of the Amendment by "appropriate legislation."[145] The primary rights, privileges, or immunities secured by the Constitution are those in § 1 of the Amendment. A plaintiff (or the government in a § 242 prosecution) must plead and prove that the victim was "deprived" of some of the wide range of rights recognized and protected by § 1.

First, § 1 prohibits states from depriving persons of the equal protection of the laws, which also reaches employment discrimination and harassment claims by public employees.[146] Second, § 1 prohibits states from abridging the "privileges or immunities of citizens of the United States," although that provision has been largely stripped of any meaning or use.[147]

Third, § 1 prohibits states from depriving any persons of life, liberty, or property without due process of law.[148] This due process rubric has been broken into several categories of distinct rights. "Procedural due process" guarantees that fundamentally fair procedures are followed before a person can be executed, imprisoned, fined, or deprived of any other property or liberty interest.[149]

"Substantive due process" prohibits certain government conduct, regardless of procedures used.[150] This, in turn, encompasses three distinct classes of rights.

First, substantive due process incorporates most of the specific protections, rights, and liberties of the Bill of Rights and subjects states to their control and regulation:[151] these include First Amendment liberties of press,[152] religious freedom,[153] and speech,[154] including claims by public employees challenging speech-related employment sanctions;[155] Second Amendment liberty to keep and bear arms;[156] Fourth Amendment protections against unreasonable searches and seizures,[157] which include claims for excessive force;[158] much of the Fifth Amendment,

---

[145] U.S. Const. amend. XIV, § 5 (1868).

[146] Id. (1968); see, e.g., Valentine v. City of Chicago, 452 F.3d 670 (7th Cir. 2006).

[147] McDonald v. City of Chicago, 130 S. Ct. 3020, 2060-63 (2010) (Thomas, J., concurring in part and concurring in the judgment).

[148] U.S. Const. XIV, § 1 (1868).

[149] Zinermon v. Burch, 494 U.S. 113, 125–26 (1990).

[150] Id. at 125.

[151] Id.; Cf. McDonald, 130 S. Ct. at 3059 (Thomas, J., concurring in part and concurring in the judgment) (arguing that the Privileges or Immunities Clause is the proper source of incorporation of the Bill of Rights).

[152] Near v. Minnesota, 283 U.S. 697 (1931).

[153] Everson v. Board of Education, 330 U.S. 1 (1947); Cantwell v. Connecticut, 310 U.S. 296 (1940).

[154] Gitlow v. New York, 268 U.S. 652 (1925).

[155] Garcetti v. Ceballos, 547 U.S. 410 (2006); Branti v. Finkel, 445 U.S. 507 (1980).

[156] McDonald v. City of Chicago, 130 S. Ct. 3020 (2010).

[157] Mapp v. Ohio, 367 U.S. 643 (1961).

including protections against self-incrimination[159] and taking of property without just compensation;[160] and Eighth Amendment protections against cruel and unusual punishment.[161] The last encompasses all claims by prisoners challenging conditions of confinement;[162] this includes cases relating to use of force by corrections officers,[163] prison safety,[164] provision of medical care, medical malpractice, and denial of medical care,[165] and all other aspects of life and conditions in prison.[166]

Second, substantive due process includes unenumerated rights, notably the right to privacy[167] and the right to reproductive freedom.[168] Infringements on recognized unenumerated fundamental rights generally are subject to strict scrutiny, while new rights will be recognized only if they are "deeply rooted in this nation's history and tradition" and "implicit in the concept of ordered liberty."[169]

Third, substantive due process includes a fallback, tort-like catch-all prohibition on "outrageous" or constitutionally "arbitrary" government misconduct, particularly executive misconduct that is so outrageous and egregious as to "shock the conscience."[170]

In addition, the Fifteenth Amendment protections against racial discrimination in voting are enforceable through § 1983.[171]

On the other hand, the Supremacy Clause does not establish substantive rights enforceable through § 1983. The Supremacy Clause does not, by its own force, create any enforceable rights; it instead is purely structural, declaring that federal rights get priority whenever they come in conflict with state law.[172] In other words, the Supremacy Clause is the reason a plaintiff can recover under § 1983 for violations of other constitutional provisions by state officials acting under color of state law; the Supremacy Clauses establishes that federal constitutional rights

---

[158] Graham v. Connor, 490 U.S. 386 (1989).

[159] Malloy v. Hogan, 378 U.S. 1 (1964); *but see* Chavez v. Martinez, 538 U.S. 760, 772 (2003) (plurality opinion of Thomas, J.) (rejecting plaintiff's argument that failure to read *Miranda* warnings could be basis for § 1983 action).

[160] San Remo Hotel, L.P. v. City & County of San Francisco, 545 U.S. 323 (2005); Dolan v. City of Tigard, 512 U.S. 374 (1994).

[161] Robinson v. California, 370 U.S. 660 (1962).

[162] Farmer v. Brennan, 511 U.S. 825 (1994); Estelle v. Gamble, 429 U.S. 97 (1976).

[163] Whitley v. Albers, 475 U.S. 312 (1986).

[164] *Farmer*, 511 U.S. at 833.

[165] West v. Atkins, 487 U.S. 42 (1988); *Estelle*, 429 U.S. at 103–05.

[166] Turner v. Safley, 482 U.S. 78 (1987) (regulations relating to inmate marriages and correspondence).

[167] Griswold v. Connecticut, 381 U.S. 479 (1965).

[168] Planned Parenthood v. Casey, 505 U.S. 833 (1992).

[169] Washington v. Glucksberg, 521 U.S. 702, 721–22 (1997); County of Sacramento v. Lewis, 523 U.S. 833, 860 (1998) (Scalia, J., concurring in the judgment).

[170] *Lewis*, 523 U.S. at 847–48.

[171] Osburn v. Cox, 369 F.3d 1283 (11th Cir. 2004); LaRouche v. Fowler, 152 F.3d 974 (D.C. Cir. 1998).

[172] Golden State Transit Corp. v. Los Angeles, 493 U.S. 103, 107–08 (1989).

prevail over contrary state laws, policies, and actions.

§ 2.07 SUBSTANTIVE DUE PROCESS

[1] State of Mind

Section 1983 contains no statutory state-of-mind requirement, a critical difference with its criminal counterpart, which requires that the defendant "willfully" subject the victim to the deprivation of rights.[173] This does not mean that § 1983 imposes strict liability, however. Rather, § 1983 incorporates the state-of-mind requirement attached to the underlying federal constitutional right being enforced. We can think of § 1983 as an empty vessel or clear glass, taking the size, shape, and color of the substantive right being enforced.

Different constitutional rights have different state of mind requirements. Fourth Amendment claims are subject to a reasonableness standard — the defendant officer is liable if the search or seizure is unreasonable.[174] Equal Protection requires intentional discrimination.[175] First Amendment claims require a showing that the defendant officer did something because of, and in retaliation for, the plaintiff's exercise of First Amendment liberty or with the purpose of halting that exercise.[176]

For some rights, the state of mind depends on the factual circumstances at issue. Consider the Eighth Amendment. If the officer has an opportunity to deliberate or to consider his conduct prior to acting — as in providing medical care or taking steps to protect inmates from a risk of violence at the hands of other inmates — the plaintiff must show that the defendant acted with deliberate indifference.[177] That means subjective recklessness, meaning the defendant has actual knowledge of facts indicating a substantial or excessive risk of serious harm and unreasonably acts or fails to act despite that knowledge.[178] On the other hand, if the officer has no opportunity to deliberate because the situation is fast-moving, immediate, or emergent — for example, responding to a prison riot — the plaintiff must show that the defendant inflicted unnecessary and wanton pain and suffering, as by force not "in a good faith effort to maintain or restore discipline," but "maliciously and sadistically for the very purpose of causing harm."[179]

Courts apply a similar split for outrageous executive misconduct substantive due process claims — deliberate indifference (defined the same way) if the officer has

---

[173] *Compare* 18 U.S.C. § 242 ("Whoever . . . willfully subjects") *with* 42 U.S.C. § 1983 ("Every person who . . . subjects"); Parratt v. Taylor, 451 U.S. 527, 534 (1981); *infra* § 2.10.

[174] Saucier v. Katz, 533 U.S. 194 (2001).

[175] Washington v. Davis, 426 U.S. 229 (1976); McCauley v. City of Chicago, 671 F.3d 611 (7th Cir. 2011).

[176] Ashcroft v. Iqbal, 556 U.S. 662 (2009); Gronowski v. Spencer, 424 F.3d 285 (2d Cir. 2005); Tatro v. Kervin, 41 F.3d 9 (1st Cir. 1994).

[177] Farmer v. Brennan, 511 U.S. 825, 828–29 (1994); Estelle v. Gamble, 429 U.S. 97, 104–05 (1976).

[178] *Farmer*, 511 U.S. at 837.

[179] Whitley v. Albers, 475 U.S. 312, 320–21 (1986).

time and opportunity for deliberation, intent to harm if he does not.[180]

[2] Identifying the Appropriate Constitutional Right

It may not always be clear what constitutional right the plaintiff can or should assert and multiple rights arguably could be triggered on one set of facts or circumstances. At times courts allow this. For example, discrimination may be because of both religion and national origin, subject to challenge on both Free Exercise and equal protection grounds.[181]

At other times, courts demand a higher degree of precision, under the principle *lex specialis derogate general* — the specific law prevails over the general law. This is particularly salient at the intersection of outrageous-misconduct substantive due process and other rights, where the Court has made clear that the former is a fallback to be used only when some explicit textual source is inapplicable.[182] Whether a claim should be analyzed under a specific provision or general due process depends on the precise facts, which in turn determines the applicable state of mind and the ease with which a plaintiff may be able to prove her case.

This was the issue facing the Supreme Court in *County of Sacramento v. Lewis*. Lewis was a passenger on a motorcycle involved in a high-speed police chase. After a little over a mile of weaving in and out of traffic at more than 100 mph, the motorcycle tipped over while trying to execute a turn. Given the speed at which they were traveling in pursuit, the police were unable to stop their car in time; it skidded into Lewis at 40 mph, throwing his body about 70 feet down the road and causing massive and ultimately fatal injuries.[183] In the subsequent § 1983 action by Lewis' estate, the Court held that the plaintiff had to proceed under substantive due process; the Fourth Amendment was not implicated in the case because there had been no search or seizure. A seizure occurs "only when there is a governmental termination of freedom of movement *through means intentionally applied.*"[184] The officers did not stop Lewis; Lewis was stopped by the motorcycle crash and by the car striking him, neither of which was caused by any officer's intentional act. This contrasts with an officer shooting a fleeing felon, which does constitute a seizure because the officer's intentional act of firing a shot terminated the victim's freedom of movement.[185] It also contrasts with an officer who terminates a high-speed chase by deliberately ramming the fleeing suspect's car pursuant to departmental procedures and with permission from his supervisory officers.[186]

Once a case moves from the Fourth Amendment into substantive due process, of course, the plaintiff must show a significantly higher state of mind. In *Lewis*, the

---

[180] County of Sacramento v. Lewis, 523 U.S. 833, 851, 854 (1998); Sitzes v. City of W. Memphis Ark., 606 F.3d 461, 476 (8th Cir. 2010).

[181] Ashcroft v. Iqbal, 556 U.S. 662 (2009).

[182] *Lewis*, 523 U.S. at 842; Evans v. Chalmers, 703 F.3d 636, 646 n.2 (4th Cir. 2012).

[183] *Lewis*, 523 U.S. at 836–38.

[184] *Id.* at 843–44 (emphasis in original) (citing Brower v. County of Inyo, 489 U.S. 593, 596–97 (1989)).

[185] *Id.* at 842–44 (discussing and applying Graham v. Connor, 490 U.S. 386 (1989)).

[186] Scott v. Harris, 550 U.S. 372 (2007).

Court held that the claim failed because the officer's conduct, while perhaps inconsistent with police protocol and arguably unreasonable, was not conscience-shocking, a stringent standard that reaches only the "most egregious official conduct"[187] undertaken with intent to harm.[188]

We see similar analysis in *Chavez v. Martinez*. The plaintiff was shot several times during an encounter with police. During a 45-minute period in which the plaintiff was receiving off-and-on medical treatment at the hospital, a police officer questioned him, repeatedly asking what happened. His responses included statements that he was choking, that he was dying, and that he did not want to die; pleading for air; begging for medical treatment; and finally agreeing to tell what happened if he could get treated.[189] In a separate opinion, Justice Stevens described this as the "functional equivalent of an attempt to obtain an involuntary confession from a prisoner by torturous methods."[190] Although the officer never gave the plaintiff his *Miranda* warnings as required by the Fifth Amendment's Self-Incrimination Clause,[191] he was not charged with anything, so his statements never were used in court.[192] A majority of the justices held that the plaintiff could not assert a violation of the right against self-incrimination (as incorporated through the Fourteenth Amendment). Because the unwarned statements never were used against him, he never was compelled to be a witness against himself; mere coercion in questioning, even to the point of imposing physical pain, does not produce compelled testimony absent actual use of the statements as testimony in a prosecution.[193] Instead, the claims arising from the infliction of physical pain must be evaluated under the catchall substantive due process rubric, with the accompanying heightened standard of egregious conduct and intent to harm; a majority of the Court remanded for the lower court to perform that analysis.[194]

[3] "Not a Font of Tort Law"

Courts are careful to maintain a sharp line between due process and ordinary tort law, repeatedly insisting that § 1983 and the Constitution are "not a font of tort law to be superimposed upon whatever systems may already be administered by the States."[195] Ordinary torts do not become constitutional violations merely

---

[187] *Lewis*, 523 U.S. at 848.

[188] *Id.* at 853–54.

[189] Chavez v. Martinez, 538 U.S. 760, 763–65 (2003); *id.* at 784–86 (Stevens, J., concurring in part and dissenting in part).

[190] *Id.* at 783–84 (Stevens, J., concurring in part and dissenting in part).

[191] U.S. Const. amend. V (1791); Miranda v. Arizona, 384 U.S. 436 (1966).

[192] *Chavez*, 538 U.S. at 764.

[193] *Id.* at 772 (plurality opinion of Thomas, J.); *id.* at 777 (Souter, J., joined by Breyer, J., concurring in the judgment).

[194] *Id.* at 779–80 (majority opinion of Souter, J.); *but see id.* at 773–74 (opinion of Thomas, J.) (insisting that no remand was necessary and concluding that the plaintiff's due process rights were not violated).

[195] Paul v. Davis, 424 U.S. 693, 701 (1976); San Gerónimo Caribe Project, Inc. v. Acevedo-Vilá, 687 F.3d 465, 480-81 (1st Cir. 2012).

because committed by government officials.[196] In *Paul v. Davis*, for example, police officers posted public notices falsely stating that the plaintiff had written bad checks; the Court rejected the plaintiff's substantive due process claim, insisting that this was ordinary defamation and had not been constitutionalized simply because it happened to be committed by police officers.[197] And any stigma caused by the false statements does not create a sufficient constitutional injury.[198] On the other hand, courts may allow recovery in so-called "stigma-plus" cases, where a stigmatic injury associated with false statements by government officials is accompanied by some other independent constitutional violation, such as an unlawful arrest or seizure.[199]

This explains why courts so closely police whether conduct truly shocks the conscience and genuinely is done with the requisite high degree of intent; that heightened state of mind marks the line between a constitutional violation and an ordinary tort. The scope of substantive due process must remain narrow in order to not simply be a constitutional replacement for state tort law.[200] Thus, whether conduct truly shocks the conscience is a question of law for the court, not a question of fact for the jury.[201]

§ 2.08   PROCEDURAL DUE PROCESS

The procedural component of due process ensures that the state provides fundamentally fair process in connection with any deprivation of life, liberty, or property. It is subject to a two-step analysis. It first asks if the plaintiff has been deprived of a recognized interest in life, liberty, or property.[202] The plaintiff must have some interest which creates personal rights, and she must have suffered a deprivation or loss of that interest. If the plaintiff does not have a liberty or property interest or if she does not suffer any deprivation of that interest, her due process rights have not been violated. Second, if (and only if) there is deprivation of a recognized interest, the court asks whether the plaintiff received sufficient process at some point with respect to that interest.[203] Sufficient process means a party receives notice and a meaningful opportunity to be heard in a meaningful manner, with the goal of ensuring an accurate determination of the propriety of any deprivation.[204]

A procedural due process violation occurs not with the deprivation of the liberty or property interest, but only if and when adequate process has not been provided

---

[196] DeShaney v. Winnebago County Dep't of Social Servs., 489 U.S. 189, 202 (1989).

[197] *Paul*, 424 U.S. at 709–10.

[198] *Id.*

[199] *Evans*, 703 F.3d at 654–55 & n.12.

[200] Sitzes v. City of W. Memphis Ark., 606 F.3d 461, 467 (8th Cir. 2010).

[201] *Id.*

[202] Kentucky Dep't of Corr. v. Thompson, 490 U.S. 454, 460 (1989).

[203] *Id.*

[204] Ludwig v. Astrue, 681 F.3d 1047 (9th Cir. 2012); Greenbriar Vill., L.L.C. v. Mt. Brook City, 345 F.3d 1258 (11th Cir. 2003); *see also* Mathews v. Eldridge, 424 U.S. 319, 333 (1976).

with respect to that deprivation.[205] The constitutional problem is not the deprivation but the absence or insufficiency of process surrounding that deprivation.[206] In other words, a person may properly be deprived of liberty or property, yet a constitutional violation still occurs because she does not receive adequate process. Conversely, even if the deprivation is wrongful and a person should not have had her liberty or property taken away, the constitutional claim fails if the process provided is fundamentally fair or if the party has received all the process that is due. Claims targeting the deprivation of liberty or property itself, as opposed to the failure of process, sound in substantive due process, not procedural due process.

[1] Deprivation of Liberty or Property Interest

Courts first must identify when and if a deprivation of liberty or property occurs, which turns in part on the defendant's state of mind.

In *Parratt v. Taylor*, prison officials negligently lost a hobby kit worth $23.50, which had been mailed to the prisoner and delivered to the prison, but never passed along to him in accordance with prison regulations. The Court held that a deprivation of property had occurred, because the plaintiff had lost his property as a result of government conduct, even if that conduct was merely negligent.[207]

Several justices questioned whether this sort of unintentional, negligent act was the kind of deprivation of property with which the Fourteenth Amendment should be concerned.[208] Five years later, the Court overturned this piece of *Parratt*. In *Daniels v. Williams*, an inmate in a county jail was injured when he tripped on a pillow that had been negligently left in a prison stairwell.[209] In the companion case of *Davidson v. Cannon*, a prisoner was injured when he was assaulted by a fellow inmate; the plaintiff had notified prison officials in writing that he had been threatened, but officials either did not regard the matter as urgent or forgot about the note. The plaintiff did not argue that the officers acted with deliberate or callous indifference, only that they had negligently failed to protect him from his fellow inmate.[210]

In both cases, the Court held that no deprivation of liberty in the "constitutional sense" had occurred because the defendants had only been careless, rather than intentional, in their conduct.[211] Adopting Justice Powell's concurring opinion from *Parratt*, the Court stated that "deprive" in the Fourteenth Amendment connotes more than a negligent act. Due process is concerned with affirmative abuse of governmental power, which entails some deliberate or intentional action by the

---

[205] Zinermon v. Burch, 494 U.S. 113, 126 (1990).

[206] Carey v. Piphus, 435 U.S. 247 (1978).

[207] Parratt v. Taylor, 451 U.S. 527 (1981).

[208] *Id.* at 544–45 (Stewart, J., concurring) (calling it "entirely doubtful"); *id.* at 546 (Powell, J., concurring in the result).

[209] Daniels v. Williams, 474 U.S. 327, 328 (1986).

[210] Davidson v. Cannon, 474 U.S. 344, 345–46 (1986).

[211] *Daniels*, 474 U.S. at 330–32; *Davidson*, 474 U.S. at 347–48.

state.[212] Treating an injury caused by a failure to provide due care as a constitutional deprivation would "trivialize the centuries-old principle of due process of law."[213] Because no intentional deprivation occurred in either case, it was not necessary to discuss the adequacy of processes or remedies provided; the Due Process Clause does not, as a constitutional matter, require remedial or compensatory procedures for non-intentional deprivations by government officers.

This again reflects the distinction between the Constitution and ordinary state tort law. The Constitution only requires a remedy against intentional acts by government officials, not for ordinary torts. While the state may (and typically does) provide remedies for non-intentional acts, the Constitution does not require such remedies or in any way dictate their procedural sufficiency. And a § 1983 claim cannot be the vehicle for questioning those processes.

[2] What Process Is Due

If, and only if, the state has deprived the plaintiff of a liberty or property interest through intentional (not merely negligent) misconduct, the court then considers what process is due and whether the process that has been provided is sufficient. Due process requires that, at some point, the state provide a meaningful hearing with respect to the deprivation, either to prevent a wrongful deprivation from occurring or to remedy a wrongful deprivation that already has occurred. The general rule is that a person is entitled to process prior to the deprivation.[214] But post-deprivation process may be constitutionally sufficient where that is all that the state can feasibly provide; given the nature of some deprivations, it may be impossible for government to provide a pre-deprivation hearing under formal state-authorized procedures.[215]

This situation first arose in *Parratt*. Although (at least according to the majority) there had been a deprivation of the plaintiff's property interest, there was no due process violation because that deprivation did not occur pursuant to established state procedures. Instead, the deprivation resulted from the unauthorized failure of state agents to follow established state procedures for delivering mail to prisoners. The state could not predict, control, or prevent such a "random and unauthorized act," and thus could not provide process in advance of the deprivation. Although it perhaps is predictable that random and unauthorized acts may occur, it is impossible to know who would commit such acts, what the acts would be, or when they might occur, making a pre-deprivation hearing impossible.[216]

Where a pre-deprivation hearing is not feasible, due process is satisfied by the availability of fair tort procedures through which persons can bring claims against

---

[212] *Daniels*, 474 U.S. at 330 (citing *Parratt*, 451 U.S. at 548–49 (Powell, J., concurring in the result)).

[213] *Daniels*, 474 U.S. at 332.

[214] *Zinermon*, 494 U.S. at 127; *Parratt*, 451 U.S. at 537.

[215] *Zinermon*, 494 U.S. at 128–29.

[216] *Parratt*, 451 U.S. at 541, 543–44.

the state or state officers to recover for their losses after the fact.[217] That state procedures are different, limited, or do not provide the same remedies or procedures as a federal § 1983 claim does not mean those procedures are not meaningful or adequate. State tort claims satisfy the Fourteenth Amendment even if, as in *Parratt*, the process would run against the state rather than the individual officer, no punitive damages are available, and the plaintiff does not enjoy a jury right in those proceedings.[218] State process is constitutionally adequate even when state processes may be lengthy, uncertain or speculative, when defenses such as government immunity may be available, or when they may require plaintiffs to assert a number of different types of claims against different parties.[219] So long as the state process is fundamentally fair, it cannot "readily be characterized as inadequate to the point that it is meaningless or nonexistent."[220] On the other hand, post-deprivation remedies do not satisfy due process where the deprivation occurs pursuant to or in accordance with established state procedures; in cases not involving a random-and-unauthorized act, due process demands pre-deprivation process.[221]

The Court confirmed this approach in *Hudson v. Palmer.* The random-and-unauthorized deprivation of property there was intentional — an unauthorized search and "shakedown" of a prisoner's cell, during which some of the prisoner's non-contraband property was destroyed.[222] The Court held that, in terms of the practicality of pre-deprivation process, there is no logical distinction between negligent and intentional deprivations of property. "The state can no more anticipate and control in advance the random and unauthorized intentional conduct of its employees than it can anticipate similar negligent conduct."[223] Thus, a random-and-unauthorized intentional deprivation of property is subject to the same analysis as a random negligent deprivation of property — pre-deprivation process is not required because it is not feasible and due process is not violated so long as meaningful post-deprivation remedies are available.

Finally, in *Zinermon v. Burch*, the Court made clear that the random-and-unauthorized distinction controls with respect to deprivations of liberty as well as property.[224] As to both, government is unable to provide pre-deprivation process where the deprivation is random and unauthorized, while it is able to provide pre-deprivation process where the deprivation is not random and unauthorized.

---

[217] *Id.* at 543–44.

[218] *Id.*

[219] Easter House v. Felder, 910 F.2d 1387, 1405–06 (7th Cir. 1990).

[220] *Id.* at 1406.

[221] Hudson v. Palmer, 468 U.S. 517, 568 (1984) (citing Logan v. Zimmerman Brush Co., 455 U.S. 422(1982)).

[222] *Hudson*, 468 U.S. at 519–20.

[223] *Id.* at 533.

[224] *Zinermon*, 494 U.S. at 132.

[3] Post-deprivation or Pre-deprivation Process

If a deprivation is random and unauthorized, the constitutional claim fails so long as reasonably meaningful and fair post-deprivation process is available. Due process does not replace or displace state tort law, nor does it move basic tort claims into federal court and federal constitutional analysis; it only demands that state law be fundamentally fair and not practically nonexistent.[225]

A constitutional due process claim thus will lie only where a plaintiff suffers deprivation that is not random and unauthorized and does not receive process prior to that deprivation. That line forms the analytical heart of *Zinermon v. Burch.*

The plaintiff was "voluntarily" admitted to a mental health facility when he signed forms consenting to admission and treatment, although at the time staff evaluation forms stated that he was "hallucinating, confused, and psychotic" and believed he was in heaven. Three days later, he was transferred to a state mental health facility, which also voluntarily admitted him when he signed forms requesting admission and treatment, although further evaluations described him as appearing distressed and confused, "extremely psychotic," disoriented, "apparently paranoid," and hallucinating. The plaintiff remained in the state facility for five months, never receiving a hearing regarding his hospitalization and treatment.[226]

The state had established a comprehensive statutory scheme governing admission to state mental health facilities, built on a divide between voluntary and involuntary admissions. Any person could be voluntarily admitted for treatment by providing express and informed written consent, based on sufficient explanation and disclosure as to ensure a "knowing and willful decision without any element of force, fraud, deceit, duress, or other form of constraint or coercion." A voluntarily admitted patient could request discharge at any time and the facility was obligated to notify the patient of his right to seek discharge. A person also could be involuntarily admitted for treatment. Involuntary admission occurred on the recommendation of a facility administrator and two mental-health professionals that the person was likely "to injure himself or others" or was in "need of care or treatment which, if not provided, may result in neglect or refusal to care for himself and . . . such neglect or refusal poses a real and present threat of substantial harm to his well-being." Certain procedural protections accompany involuntary placement, including a right to notice, a judicial hearing with appointed counsel, access to medical records and personnel, and an independent expert examination. Involuntary admission would last six months, after which the patient must be discharged or a court order sought for further treatment. State law also provided for short-term emergency commitments, after which the patient must be discharged, voluntarily admitted, or involuntarily admitted pursuant to required procedures.[227]

The plaintiff in *Zinermon* argued that he had not been mentally competent to provide knowing and voluntary consent for admission, as indicated by the medical

---

[225] *Parratt*, 451 U.S. at 543–44; *Easter House*, 910 F.2d at 1405–06.

[226] *Zinermon*, 494 U.S. at 118–20.

[227] *Id.* at 122–23.

evaluations and treatment notes. The state therefore was obligated to provide pre-deprivation procedural protections to determine whether a potential voluntary admission was actually competent to place himself in the hospital, or if not, whether he should have been involuntarily placed.

The Court began its analysis with *Parratt* and *Hudson*, asking whether this was a case in which the deprivation was random and unauthorized, rendering pre-deprivation process impracticable or impossible and thus unnecessary. The majority concluded that *Parratt/Hudson* did not apply because the state had delegated to hospital officials broad, uncircumscribed power to deprive patients of their liberty; officers who wield that power as a matter of state law and fail to provide or adhere to necessary procedural safeguards cannot rely on *Parratt* and *Hudson* to escape liability.[228]

The Court identified three reasons *Parratt* and *Hudson* did not control.

First, the violation was not unpredictable, because it was foreseeable that a person requesting treatment might be incapable of informed consent and that officials with the power to initiate process might fail to do so. Moreover, officials could predict precisely when in the process the deprivation would take place — at the time of admission when the patient is completing forms, at which point there was an obvious risk of officials taking the patient's consent (and ability to knowingly consent) at face value and not truly delving into his ability to give knowing and informed voluntary consent.[229]

Second, pre-deprivation process was feasible. The state already had established procedures for involuntary placements and those procedures could be used to determine whether potential voluntary patients were able to give informed consent.[230] Functionally, the claim became that defendants failed to adhere to their own placement procedures already in place. This contrasted with *Hudson*, where the defendant prison guard was bent on effecting the substantive deprivation (destroying the inmate's property) and would have done so regardless of any procedural protections in place.

Third, the deprivation was not unauthorized. The state had delegated to hospital officials the power and authority to effect the deprivation at issue by admitting patients, along with the concomitant duty to initiate procedures so as to prevent unlawful confinement.[231] When public officers are empowered to provide process in the course of effecting a deprivation, they should be subject to constitutional liability when they fail to do so. By contrast, the defendants in *Parratt* and *Hudson* had no similar authority to effect the deprivations at issue and no duty or authority to initiate pre-deprivation procedures.

The outcome-determinative question is whether a deprivation is random, unauthorized, and unforeseeable, which determines whether the case falls on the *Parratt/Hudson* or the *Zinermon* side of the analysis. An illustrative case is the

---

[228] *Id.* at 135–36.

[229] *Id.* at 136.

[230] *Id.* at 136–38.

[231] *Id.* at 138–39.

Fourth Circuit's decision in *Bogart v. Chappell*. After hearing concerns about the number of animals a woman was keeping at her home, the local Humane Society, animal-control officials, and the county sheriff executed a search warrant on her property; she was arrested and charged with mistreating animals in violation of state law. More than 200 dogs and cats were seized from the property and all but two dogs and few cats were euthanized by the next morning. The woman alleged that the mass killing of her animals, which was ordered by the head of the Humane Society and overseen by the supervisor of animal control, violated procedural due process.[232]

A majority of the panel held that *Parratt/Hudson* rather than the *Zinermon* controlled; although the plaintiff was deprived of property — her animals were killed — the deprivation was random, unauthorized, and unforeseeable.[233] The defendants were not authorized under any circumstances to euthanize the animals, but instead were obligated to care for them until a state court adjudicated the plaintiff's rights to the animals; by euthanizing the animals, the defendant officials engaged in unauthorized and thus unforeseeable conduct. Second, the defendants did not wield discretion to provide (or not provide) process. Third, the state had not delegated to the defendants the authority to initiate procedural safeguards; they only had a nondiscretionary duty to care for the animals pending the outcome of state court proceedings.[234] Having found that *Parratt* and *Hudson* controlled, the court could dispose of the constitutional claim in one sentence, given the unquestioned availability of post-deprivation state tort remedies which the court declared (albeit without analysis) to be "reasonable."[235]

Bogart reflects a fairly narrow reading of *Zinermon*, a point the dissent pursued. The defendant officers were, in fact, obligated to initiate process. State law required them to petition a state court for a hearing about the animals immediately following the seizure — in other words, to initiate pre-deprivation process — and to carry out the "humane disposition" of the animals if Bogart was adjudicated unable to care for them. The defendants' misconduct was their failure to initiate that process, in accordance with their state-law duty, before effecting the deprivation by euthanizing the animals.[236] These defendants thus were situated identically to the defendants in *Zinermon* — charged by state law with initiating pre-deprivation process before effecting the deprivation (admitting patients or euthanizing animals) but failing to do so.

[4] Legalist Model vs. Governmental Model

Confusion in the procedural due process cases stems from seemingly contradictory approaches to § 1983. The dissenting opinion in *Bogart* adopted Larry Alexander's taxonomy, which distinguishes between "legalist" and

---

[232] Bogart v. Chappell, 396 F.3d 548, 551–53 (4th Cir. 2005).

[233] *Id.* at 561.

[234] *Id.* at 561–63.

[235] *Id.* at 563.

[236] *Id.* at 567 n.1 (Williams, J., dissenting).

"governmental" models of § 1983 liability.[237] Under the governmental model, liability attaches when a government actor engages in conduct in the scope of his employment and with the apparent force of his government authority that violates a constitutional right; this model is reflected in *Monroe v. Pape*, which expressly rejected the argument that, because the officers' conduct was prohibited by state law, they could not act under color of law.[238] Under the legalist model, § 1983 liability attaches only where state lawmakers, through formal state law and policy, endorse the violation; this is the model urged by Justice Frankfurter in his *Monroe* dissent and it is reflected in *Parratt* and *Hudson*, where the court found no constitutional violation when state law itself did not cause the deprivation of liberty or property.[239]

The simplest explanation for the divide is that the legalist model applies to procedural due process claims, while the governmental model applies to all other constitutional rights.[240] Whether this divide makes normative sense, it at least is straightforward. But *Zinermon* contradicts the simple divide by applying what looks like the governmental model to a procedural due process clam, albeit without overruling *Hudson*.[241] The result is jurisprudence "resembling the path of a drunken sailor,"[242] a violation of the essential judicial "law of noncontradiction" that leaves litigants and lower courts "completely at sea,"[243] and the occasional plea from lower courts for Supreme Court clarification and guidance.[244]

A better way to reconcile the jurisprudence is that it reflects not competing or conflicting models of § 1983 liability, but rather differences in when the underlying constitutional right has been violated. Obviously, if the underlying constitutional right has not been violated, the plaintiff has not been subjected to a "deprivation" of a right, privilege, or immunity secured by the Constitution and thus cannot prevail on a § 1983 claim. Most constitutional violations occur at the time the defendant acts[245] — the Fourth Amendment is violated when officers search a home without a warrant or when they arrest a person and bring him into custody; the First Amendment is violated when the individual is denied the opportunity to speak; a substantive due process violation occurs when the outrageous, conscience-

---

[237] *Id.* at 564 (Williams, J., dissenting) (citing Larry Alexander, *Constitutional Torts, the Supreme Court, and the Law of Noncontradiction: An Essay on* Zinermon v. Burch, 87 Nw. U. L. Rev. 576 (1993)).

[238] *Bogart*, 396 F.3d at 564 (Williams, J., dissenting); Larry Alexander, *Constitutional Torts, the Supreme Court, and the Law of Noncontradiction: An Essay on* Zinermon v. Burch, 87 Nw. U. L. Rev. 576, 577 (1993).

[239] *Bogart*, 396 F.3d at 564 (Williams, J., dissenting); Larry Alexander, *Constitutional Torts, the Supreme Court, and the Law of Noncontradiction: An Essay on* Zinermon v. Burch, 87 Nw. U. L. Rev. 576, 576–77 (1993); *supra* § 2.03[2].

[240] *Bogart*, 396 F.3d at 564 (Williams, J., dissenting).

[241] *Id.* at 564–65 (Williams, J., dissenting).

[242] Easter House v. Felder, 910 F.2d 1387, 1409 (7th Cir. 1990) (Easterbrook, J., concurring).

[243] Larry Alexander, *Constitutional Torts, the Supreme Court, and the Law of Noncontradiction: An Essay on* Zinermon v. Burch, 87 Nw. U. L. Rev. 576, 596 (1993); *see also Bogart*, 396 F.3d at 565 (Williams, J., dissenting) ("Lower courts were, it seemed, free to choose whichever model they preferred.").

[244] San Gerónimo Caribe Project, Inc. v. Acevedo-Vilá, 687 F.3d 465, 498 (1st Cir. 2012) (Lipez, J., concurring).

[245] *Zinermon*, 494 U.S. at 125.

shocking behavior takes place. On the other hand, a procedural due process violation is complete only when the state has not accorded all the process that is due for a willful deprivation of property or liberty.[246]

The divide between *Parratt/Hudson* and *Zinermon* is about when procedural due process has been violated, which depends on what process is due. In *Parratt* and *Hudson*, because the loss of property was random and unauthorized, only state post-deprivation remedy was possible; that therefore constituted all the process due, so there was no completed procedural due process violation given adequate and available post-deprivation process. Because there was no completed violation, there could be no § 1983 liability. On the other hand, because the loss of liberty in *Zinermon* was not random, unauthorized, or unforeseeable, pre-deprivation process was possible; once the plaintiff was admitted without required pre-deprivation process, there was a completed procedural due process violation and therefore § 1983 liability.

Zinermon looks like *Monroe*, and not like *Parratt/Hudson*, not because of different models of § 1983 liability, but because of differences in if and when the respective underlying constitutional violations became complete.In both *Monroe* and *Zinermon*, plaintiffs could succeed on their § 1983 claims because both arguably had been subjected to an actual, completed "deprivation" of a constitutional right. The plaintiffs in *Parratt* and in *Hudson*, on the other hand, were not deprived of any constitutional right because the possibility of state post-deprivation remedies undermined an element of the constitutional claim.

[5] Procedural Due Process Puzzle

In 2000, San Geronimo Caribe Project ("SGCP"), a private company, obtained approval for a multi-million dollar development project involving mixed residential, commercial, and tourism uses in Puerto Rico. In furtherance of the project, SGCP purchases a number of parcels of land, initially obtains all necessary permits from the Regulations and Permits Administration ("ARPE"), and in 2002 begins the first phase of construction. Over time, the development project becomes highly controversial, triggering public demonstrations around the development site and government investigations over concerns for public access to the development and contested ownership of some lands on which construction is taking place. The Secretary of the Puerto Rico Department of Justice identifies concerns about land ownership and recommends that all executive agencies reevaluate all previous permitting decisions.

Puerto Rico's governor orders all administrative agencies to suspend all permits and halt construction for an initial period of 60 days. ARPE does so, relying on state-created "emergency adjudicatory procedures," which allow for temporary suspension of licenses without notice, formal hearing, or opportunity to present evidence, as required by ordinary administrative procedures. Emergency procedures are appropriate "in any situation in which there is imminent danger to the public health, safety and welfare or which requires immediate action." ARPE cites the DOJ Secretary's investigation and

---

[246] *Id.* at 126.

recommendation, as well as public safety threats from the public demonstrations.

SGCP initiates state-court litigation challenging the suspension of the permits; the Puerto Rico Supreme Court agrees, holding that the governor and ARPE improperly invoked emergency procedures in immediately suspending the permits and halting construction. Ultimately, construction is halted for 63 days. Following reinstatement of the permits, SGCP brings a § 1983 action in federal court, alleging a violation of procedural due process in the suspension of construction and the improper exercise of emergency procedures; named defendants are ARPE, the governor, and the Secretary of DOJ.[247]

Consider whether the procedural due process claim can succeed, particularly where the claim falls on the line between Parratt/Hudson *and* Zinermon.

§ 2.09 SUBSTANTIVE DUE PROCESS AND GOVERNMENT FAILURE TO ACT

[1] *DeShaney v. Winnebago County Dep't of Social Services*

In 1983, four-year-old Joshua DeShaney was severely beaten by his father and suffered severe and permanent brain damage. State child-welfare officials had been monitoring the family for some time over multiple complaints and reports of suspected abuse, including multiple reports from hospital emergency room personnel who treated Joshua for suspicious injuries. At one point, Joshua was temporarily removed from his father's custody on suspicion of abuse, but he was returned a few days later. A state caseworker made monthly visits to the home, observing suspicious injuries and a problematic living situation; she "dutifully recorded" her observations and suspicions, but neither she nor state child-welfare agencies did anything further, even after the caseworker did not see Joshua on consecutive visits when told he was too sick.[248]

The Supreme Court rejected a substantive due process claim brought by Joshua's mother on his behalf. The Fourteenth Amendment creates no affirmative constitutional right to government aid against or protection from private third-party violence and imposes no affirmative duty on a state to provide that aid; thus a state's failure to protect does not violate substantive due process.[249] States have no obligation to provide citizens with particular protective services, thus government and government officers cannot be liable for injuries caused by third-party actors, even when the injuries might have been averted had such services been provided. The Fourteenth Amendment protects only against a state's affirmative act of restraining the individual, "not its failure to act to protect his liberty interests against harms inflicted by other means."[250] While state law could impose affirmative duties of care and protection on public officials, the Fourteenth

---

[247] San Gerónimo Caribe Project, Inc. v. Acevedo-Vilá, 687 F.3d 465 (1st Cir. 2012).

[248] DeShaney v. Winnebago County Dep't Social Servs., 489 U.S. 189, 191–93 (1989).

[249] *Id.* at 197.

[250] *Id.* at 200.

Amendment does not constitutionalize those duties.[251]

DeShaney remains one of the Court's most controversial decisions.[252] This is partly due to the tragic facts that both the majority and dissent recognized,[253] best captured by Justice Blackmun, who wound up his dissent with "Poor Joshua!"[254] This is partly due to the possibility that, apart from whether substantive due process imposes any affirmative duties, the majority wrongly applied even its negative conception of due process. As Justice Brennan argued in the primary dissent, the state may have been more than a passive bystander to third-party misconduct, having taken affirmative steps that caused or contributed to Joshua's injuries, notably by actively monitoring the family but failing to follow through on that monitoring or on the obvious indications of continued abuse.[255]

Nevertheless, *DeShaney* remains a hurdle to substantive due process claims where a private third party's conduct is the primary cause of injury but the conduct and injury occur against a background of some action by the state and state actors. Efforts to work around that limitation have focused on language from *DeShaney* itself.

[2]   Working Around *DeShaney*: Special Relationship

In rejecting the due process claim, *DeShaney* emphasized the absence of a "special relationship" between the state and Joshua that would impose on the state an affirmative duty to provide care, protection, and aide. When "the State takes a person into its custody and holds him there against his will, the Constitution imposes upon it a corresponding duty to assume some responsibility for his safety and general well-being." By taking a person into custody or other restraint, the state limits his ability to act on his own behalf, forces him to remain in a particular place and under particular conditions, and renders him unable to care for himself; the state thus assumes an affirmative duty to provide for all the basic needs he no longer can, including "reasonable safety," food, shelter, clothing, and medical care.[256] Failure to adhere to that duty thus conform the basis for constitutional liability.

Government-imposed restraint on the individual's ability to protect herself must be ongoing at the time of the third-party misconduct. In *DeShaney*, the Court declined to recognize a special relationship with Joshua based on the state having once temporarily removed him from the home; once Joshua returned to his father's home and custody, he was in the same position as if the state had not acted at all.[257]

---

[251] *Id.* at 201–02.

[252] Akhil Reed Amar & Daniel Widawsky, *Child Abuse as Slavery: A Thirteenth Amendment Response to* DeShaney, 105 HARV. L. REV. 1359 (1992); David Strauss, *Due Process, Government Inaction, and Private Wrongs*, 1989 SUP. CT. REV. 53.

[253] *DeShaney*, 489 U.S. at 191, 202–03; *id.* at 211–12 (Brennan, J., dissenting); *id.* at 213 (Blackmun, J., dissenting).

[254] *Id.* at 213 (Blackmun, J., dissenting).

[255] *Id.* at 210 (Brennan, J., dissenting).

[256] *Id.* at 200.

[257] *Id.* at 201.

The custodial relationship also must be complete and involuntary; that the state was monitoring Joshua and the household for suspected abuse was not sufficient.

Lower courts label this the "special relationship" exception to *DeShaney*.[258] *DeShaney* recognized incarceration and involuntary institutionalization as two obvious special relationships;[259] several circuits have extended the exception to children in foster care, who are involuntary wards of the state.[260] On the other hand, lower courts have uniformly rejected the exception as to public schools, which do not involve a comparably coercive or involuntary custodial relationship.[261] Parents are not stripped of their ability to protect their children in sending them to public school, since the children return home every night and parents remain the primary source for their children's basic needs. And neither state compulsory education rules nor the school's *in loco parentis* role make the relationship with the student involuntary, since parents can comply with compulsory education laws by sending their children to private school, home-schooling them, or making other arrangements for their education.[262]

[3] Working Around *DeShaney*: State-Created Danger

The *DeShaney* Court also explained that while "the State may have been aware of the dangers that Joshua faced in the free world, it played no part in their creation, nor did it do anything to render him any more vulnerable to them."[263] From that, most,[264] but not all,[265] federal courts of appeals have recognized the "state-created danger" exception, under which states and state officials can be liable for substantive due process violations where they affirmatively create or enhance the danger or risk of harm to a particular individual at the hands of some third party or outside circumstances, creating or exacerbating harm the victim would not have faced but for the state's action.

---

[258] Doe v. Covington County Sch. Dist., 675 F.3d 849 (5th Cir. 2012) (en banc); Patel v. Kent Sch. Dist., 648 F.3d 965 (9th Cir. 2011); D.R. v. Middle Bucks Area Vocational Technical School, 972 F.2d 1364 (3d Cir. 1992).

[259] *DeShaney*, 489 U.S. at 200.

[260] *Doe*, 675 F.3d at 856; Nicini v. Morra, 212 F.3d 798, 808–09 (3d Cir. 2000) (en banc).

[261] *Doe*, 675 F.3d at 857–58; *Patel*, 648 F.3d at 968–69; Hasenfus v. LaJeunesse, 175 F.3d 68 (1st Cir. 1999); Doe v. Claiborne County, 103 F.3d 495, 510 (6th Cir. 1996); *D.R.*, 972 F.2d at 1370–73.

[262] *Doe*, 675 F.3d at 856–58; *but see id.* at 878–79 (Wiener, J., dissenting) (citing *D.R.*, 972 F.2d at 1380 (Sloviter, C.J., dissenting)).

[263] *DeShaney*, 489 U.S. at 201.

[264] *See* Gray v. Univ. of Colo. Hosp. Auth., 672 F.3d 909 (10th Cir. 2012); *Patel*, 648 F.3d at 974; Okin v. Vill. of Cornwall-on-Hudson Police Dep't, 577 F.3d 415 (2d Cir. 2009); Waybright v. Frederick County, 528 F.3d 199 (4th Cir. 2008); Butera v. District of Columbia, 235 F.3d 637 (D.C. Cir. 2001); Kallstrom v. City of Columbus, 136 F.3d 1055 (6th Cir. 1998); Kneipp by Cusack v. Tedder, 95 F.3d 1199 (3d Cir. 1996); Reed v. Gardner, 986 F.2d 1122 (7th Cir. 1993).

[265] *Doe*, 675 F.3d at 864–65 (declining to recognize exception, although identifying elements of test); Velez-Diaz v. Vega-Irizarry, 421 F.3d 71, 80 & n.3 (1st Cir. 2005) (circuit has discussed theory but never found it applicable); Vaughn v. City of Athens, 176 F. App'x 974; 2006 U.S. App. LEXIS 9993 (11th Cir. 2006) (court no longer considers theory valid).

Mere knowledge of a risk of private danger is not sufficient. And the officers must take action; the critical distinction, from *DeShaney* itself, is between passive failure to stop private misconduct or injury and active facilitation of that harm. These cases became very fact-dependent, as much turns on whether that affirmative government act is the driving force of the plaintiff's injury. For example, a due process claim could go forward where police arrested the sober driver, left a drunk passenger in the car with the keys, and the drunk passenger then drove while intoxicated and injured other drivers.[266] But it could not go forward where the designated driver himself left the keys in the ignition while he voluntarily went to speak with police officers inside the station.[267]

A plaintiff must show that government officials somehow affirmatively used their authority to create or worsen a specific person's circumstances or conditions and to make that person more vulnerable to outside harms, causing a foreseeable injury at the hands of a third party that would not have occurred absent the officers' affirmative acts.[268] The underlying theory is that the victim was safer before the officers acted than she was after they acted. Some courts also demand that the increased risk be specific to an identifiable person, not merely to the public at large; courts get at this by requiring some relationship, connection, or interaction between the government officials and the victim.[269] Finally, because these claims sound in substantive due process, the plaintiff must show that the officers acted in willful disregard of, or deliberate indifference to, her safety and the risk created by their conduct; this means the officers know of and disregard foreseeable dangers likely to result from their conduct.[270]

While recognizing the state-created danger theory, courts have been generally reluctant to accept such claims. Because a third party causes the ultimate harm, the state actor must play a significant role in the situation in which the harm occurs. Indeed, a plaintiff may be more likely to succeed where the harm is caused not by some independent third person, but by circumstances or conditions to which the officer contributes or worsens.

In the Third Circuit case of *Kneipp v. Tedder*, the defendant police officers stopped Joseph and Samantha Kneipp on a winter evening, while the couple was walking home from a night of drinking at a tavern. Both were visibly intoxicated; Samantha had a blood alcohol level of 0.25, was having trouble walking or standing up, and smelled of alcohol and urine. Officers allowed Joseph to leave the scene and return home to check on the couple's son, while Samantha remained behind. Rather than arresting her, taking her to the hospital, or escorting her home, the officers told Samantha to go home, then left the scene. In her drunken state, Samantha fell down an embankment across the street from their apartment;

---

[266] Reed v. Gardner, 986 F.2d 1122 (7th Cir. 1993).

[267] Gregory v. Rogers, 974 F.2d 1006 (8th Cir. 1992).

[268] *Patel*, 648 F.3d at 974; *Okin*, 577 F.3d at 428–29; *Kneipp*, 95 F.3d at 1208–09.

[269] *Kneipp*, 95 F.3d at 1209 & n.22.

[270] *Patel*, 648 F.3d at 974; Phillips v. County of Allegheny, 515 F.3d 224, 240–41 (3d Cir. 2008); King v. E. St. Louis Sch. Dist. 189, 496 F.3d 812, 818–19 (7th Cir. 2007).

exposure to the cold, caused hypothermia and loss of blood to her brain, resulting in permanent brain damage.[271]

The court held that the plaintiff presented sufficient evidence to support a state-created danger claim. Given her obvious level of intoxication, it was foreseeable that Samantha would have been unable to walk and thus more likely to not make it home if left unescorted. The officers acted in willful disregard of Samantha's safety, given that they admitted knowing she was drunk. They used their power as police officers to initially stop and detain her, separate her from Joseph by sending him home, and force her to find her way home alone in her drunken state.[272] They put Samantha in a worse position and made her more vulnerable to the elements than she otherwise would have been had they allowed her to remain with her husband. But for police intervention, Joseph would have continued escorting her home, where she would have been safe (or at least safer).[273]

The Ninth Circuit confronted a similar situation in *Penilla v. City of Huntington Park*. Police officers responded to a 911 call about a medical emergency, then found a man on his front porch in "grave need of medical care." The officers canceled the request for paramedics, broke the lock and door jamb on the front door of his residence, moved him inside the house and away from public view, locked the door, and left the premises. The man died of respiratory failure. Although his death was a product of his medical condition and not the affirmative actions of the officers, their conduct made him more vulnerable to the effects of that condition, placing him in a more precarious position than the one in which they found him.[274]

On the other hand, courts reject state-created danger claims where the injury is caused by a private third-party actor with whom the officers have minimal or no involvement or control or where the officers do not deliberately create the situation in which the third party acts to harm the victim.[275] A claim arising from third-party violence demands something more, such as evidence that officers condoned or endorsed the private conduct, whether explicitly or implicitly.

A good illustration is the Second Circuit's decision in *Dwares v. City of New York*. The plaintiff was participating in a public demonstration at which an

---

[271]   *Kneipp*, 95 F.3d at 1201–03.

[272]   *Id.* at 1208–09.

[273]   *Id.* at 1209.

[274]   Penilla by & Through Penilla v. City of Huntington Park, 115 F.3d 707 (9th Cir. 1997).

[275]   *See, e.g.*, Gray v. Univ. of Colo. Hosp. Auth., 672 F.3d 909 (10th Cir. 2012) (public hospital's false guarantee of continuing supervision of patient's condition not affirmative act); Jackson v. Indian Prairie Sch. Dist. 204, 653 F.3d 647 (7th Cir. 2011) (school district not liable when student with autism attacked teacher in classroom); Patel v. Kent Sch. Dist., 648 F.3d 965 (9th Cir. 2011) (school district not liable where developmentally disabled student had sexual relations with classmate in school bathroom); Estate of Smithers v. City of Flint, 602 F.3d 758 (6th Cir. 2010) (city not liable when arrestee released from custody, returned to house, and shot several people); Waybright v. Frederick County, 528 F.3d 199 (4th Cir. 2008) (county not liable for death in firefighter training exercises); Soto v. Flores, 103 F.3d 1056 (1st Cir. 1997) (police officers notified subject of domestic violence complaint, subject killed children and self); Carlton by Carlton v. Cleburne County, 93 F.3d 505 (8th Cir. 1996) (no liability in collapse of publicly maintained bridge); Vaughn v. City of Athens, 176 F. App'x 974, 2006 U.S. App. LEXIS 9993 (11th Cir. 2006) (police officers sending informant to drug buy in face of warning that target might kill informant did not engage in conscience-shocking conduct).

American flag was burned. A group of skinheads standing nearby attacked the plaintiff, repeatedly hitting him over the head with a bottle and chasing him out of the park in a 10-minute attack. The attack occurred in the presence of several police officers who made no effort to intervene, protect the plaintiff, or arrest the attackers.[276] In his complaint, citing to a newspaper interview with one of the attackers, the plaintiff alleged that the officers had assured them in advance that police would not interfere to stop the attacks or arrest them so long as they did not get totally out of control. These allegations took the case beyond one in which officers stood still and did nothing in the face of private violence in suspicious circumstances and into the realm of state actors affirmatively enabling private conduct in a way that reasonably increased the likelihood that private actors would be willing to act, believing they could do so with impunity.[277]

The Second Circuit adhered to that distinction more recently in *Pena v. DePrisco.* Police officer Grey went on a 12-hour drinking binge between shifts; this included drinking with fellow officers and supervisors in the precinct parking lot and at a strip club, as well as driving his supervising officer to and from that club. Several on-duty officers and supervisors observed him in a visibly intoxicated state during this period, but did nothing to stop him from getting back in his car and driving off. While driving back to the precinct to begin his next shift, the officer ran several red lights and struck and killed three pedestrians.[278] A § 1983 action followed against multiple defendants, including several of the officers who drank with him or observed the drinking binge. The court held that, to the extent plaintiffs alleged that these officers stood by and failed to intercede, the due process claim failed under the state-created danger exception. But the plaintiffs could proceed on the strength of allegations that, through their own conduct (such as drinking with Grey and having him drive them around the city in his intoxicated state so they all could drink more), the on-duty officers and supervisors encouraged and condoned the drinking and driving, communicated encouragement of that behavior, and let him know he could continue to do so with impunity.[279]

More recently, that same court emphasized that police encouragement of private misconduct can be implicit rather than explicit. It found at least a triable issue where evidence showed that officers responding to a domestic-violence call chatted with the alleged abuser about football, did not arrest him even when he admitted that he sometimes had to slap his girlfriend around, and failed to file incident reports in the later of a series of escalating domestic-violence calls and complaints. Although none of this qualified as explicit assurances to an aggressor that he would not be arrested, they "plainly transmitted the message that what he did was permissible and would not cause him problems with authorities" and that his violence would go unpunished.[280]

---

[276] Dwares v. New York, 985 F.2d 94, 96–97 (2d Cir. 1993).

[277] *Id.* at 99.

[278] Pena v. Deprisco, 432 F.3d 98, 103–04 (2d Cir. 2005).

[279] *Id.* at 110–12.

[280] *Okin*, 577 F.3d at 429–31.

Finally, state-created danger arguments can be bolstered by explicit allegations of a conspiracy between officers and private actors, as in *Dwares*.[281] Such allegations serve two purposes. First, they allow the plaintiff to sue the private actors; by virtue of conspiratorial joint participation, he acts under color for § 1983 purposes.[282] Second, they establish necessary active, participation by the officers — affirmatively agreeing and conspiring with the individuals — that creates and enables the private danger, thereby causing the constitutional violation.[283]

[4] Working Around *DeShaney*: Procedural Due Process

A third approach has been to recast the constitutional violation as an infringement on some other right. One possibility is procedural due process. This again derives from *DeShaney* itself, where the Court explicitly declined to consider an argument that state child-protection laws gave the plaintiff an "entitlement" to receive protection, such that the state's failure to protect that entitlement amounted to a failure to provide required process.[284]

The Court rejected this argument in *Town of Castle Rock v. Gonzales*. That claim was brought by a woman on behalf of her three deceased daughters who had been murdered by her estranged husband before he was killed by police; the husband had taken the children for the day in violation of a domestic-violence restraining order and police had ignored the mother's repeated requests over a 10-hour period to comply with the order and find and arrest her husband.[285] A substantive due process claim obviously was barred by *DeShaney*; the children were killed by a private third-party and the police had nothing to do with his actions or with directly enabling or encouraging his actions; they did not act affirmatively to place the children in a worse situation and they did not enjoy a custodial relationship with the children.

The mother instead tried to argue that her and her children's procedural due process rights were violated by police failure to properly enforce the restraining order in response to repeated requests. The claim failed, however, because the restraining order did not grant her or the children an entitlement to police enforcement, which meant there was no property interest sufficient to trigger due process obligations.[286] Although the restraining order contained language requiring police to take some enforcement action ("A peace office shall use every reasonable means to enforce a restraining order"; "A peace officer shall arrest, or . . . seek a warrant for the arrest of a restrained person"; "A peace officer shall enforce a valid restraining order whether or not there is a record of the restraining order in the registry"[287]), that language must be understood in light of well-established traditions of police discretion, particularly in cases in which the

---

[281] *Dwares*, 985 F.2d at 97.

[282] *Supra* § 2.04[2].

[283] *Dwares*, 985 F.2d at 97, 99–100.

[284] *DeShaney*, 489 U.S. at 195 n.2.

[285] Town of Castle Rock v. Gonzales, 545 U.S. 748, 751–54 (2005).

[286] *Id.* at 759–60, 766; *supra* § 2.08[1].

[287] *Id.* at 761–62.

restrained person is not at the scene and the police would have to search for him.[288] Further, it was unclear what means of enforcement the plaintiff should be entitled to — having the officer arrest her husband, having them seek a warrant, or having them simply use "every reasonable means" to effect an arrest.[289]

Even if the restraining order and state law did create an entitlement, it still did not follow that entitlement to enforcement constituted a property interest for the first prong of procedural due process analysis, as that entitlement "would not . . . resemble any traditional conception of property."[290] Justice Souter elaborated on this point in a concurring opinion. The plaintiff essentially was arguing for a property interest in process in and of itself. But due process distinguishes the underlying property interests to be protected from the procedural obligations that the Constitution imposes on states to protect those interests. There first must be an identifiable, protectable substantive property interest before the state is constitutionally obligated to afford any process at all. Although state law created a body of beneficial procedures, that alone did not establish a property interest in those procedures.[291]

[5] Working Around *DeShaney*: Equal Protection and Other Rights

Finally, *DeShaney* stated that, while the state has no obligation to provide its citizens with protective services, when it does provide protective services it may not selectively deny them to certain disfavored minorities or groups in a way that violates some other substantive constitutional provision.[292] Thus a plaintiff could assert failure to protect as equal protection claim by showing that officers protected some members of the public but not her and that the failure to protect her was because of her sex, race, or other protected classification.[293] Lower courts also have recognized claims where the inaction was in retaliation for the victim's exercise of some other constitutional liberty, such as the First Amendment.[294] Thus, in a case such as *Dwares*, a plaintiff might show that the officers stood by and did nothing because they disagreed with his expression or wanted to see him punished for that expression, and that such animus drove their failure to protect. Importantly, however, both equal protection and First Amendment claims require a showing that group animus or the plaintiff's message or viewpoint motivated the officers' inaction, at least in part.[295] This ensures that equal protection does not

---

[288] *Id.* at 763.

[289] *Id.* at 763–64.

[290] *Id.* at 766.

[291] *Id.* 771–72 (Souter, J., concurring).

[292] *DeShaney*, 489 U.S. at 197 n.3.

[293] McCauley v. City of Chicago, 671 F.3d 611 (7th Cir. 2011); Elliot-Park v. Manglona, 592 F.3d 1003 (9th Cir. 2010); Okin v. Vill. of Cornwall-on-Hudson Police Dep't, 577 F.3d 415 (2d Cir. 2009); Schroeder v. Hamilton Sch. Dist., 282 F.3d 946 (7th Cir. 2002)

[294] Estate of Smith v. Town of W. Hartford, 186 F. Supp. 2d 146 (D. Conn. 2002).

[295] *Schroeder*, 282 F.3d at 950–51; Soto v. Flores, 103 F.3d 1056, 1066 (1st Cir. 1997); Watson v. Kansas City, Kan., 857 F.2d 690, 694 (10th Cir. 1988).

become "an end-run around the *DeShaney* principle."[296] But it also renders these cases similarly difficult to prove.[297]

Equal protection arguments frequently have arisen in challenges to non-enforcement or under-enforcement of domestic violence laws and domestic-violence protective orders. Such cases must thread a thin needle. *DeShaney* forecloses a substantive due process claim because the source of the injury is the abusive partner and a restraining order does not (except on unusual facts) create a special relationship or state-created danger. *Castle Rock* forecloses a procedural due process claim in light of police enforcement discretion. The next move for plaintiffs is to argue that the failure to enforce restraining orders and pursue domestic violence cases — and the failure of police departments to create policies making domestic-violence enforcement a department priority — is motivated by animus against women or against domestic violence victims as a class.[298] Courts have been generally unreceptive to such claims, however. Plaintiffs must show both that police are enforcing domestic violence laws less vigorously than other crimes and that the reason is gender-based discriminatory animus, as opposed to policy choices about allocation of limited enforcement resources or prioritization of police activities.[299] Even evidence that the officers involved expressly disliked or disagreed with state laws requiring more rigorous enforcement of domestic violence laws, may not be sufficient to establish gender-based animus in their non-enforcement decisions.[300]

§ 2.10 DUE PROCESS, INTENT, AND CRIMINAL PROSECUTION

Section 242, enacted as § 2 of the Civil Rights Act of 1866 and reenacted as § 2 the Civil Rights Act of 1870, is the model for, and criminal counterpart to, § 1983.[301] Like its civil counterpart, § 242 utilizes the broad "misuse of authority" and "clothed with authority" standard for defining when a government officer acts under color of law.[302] And like the civil statute, it defines proscribed conduct by cross-referencing and incorporating law from other sources, namely all of the Constitution and laws of the United States.[303]

But as a criminal prohibition, § 242 potentially runs afoul of the due process prohibition against a vague law that "lacks an ascertainable standard of guilt" or

---

[296] Beltran v. City of El Paso, 367 F.3d 299, 304 (5th Cir. 2004).

[297] *McCauley*, 671 F.3d at 621.

[298] *McCauley*, 671 F.3d at 619; *Okin*, 577 F.3d at 438; Burella v. City of Philadelphia, 501 F.3d 134 (3d Cir. 2007); *Beltran*, 367 F.3d at 306; *Soto*, 103 F.3d at 1066.

[299] *McCauley*, 671 F.3d at 619; *Burella*, 501 F.3d at 149; *Beltran*, 367 F.3d at 305; *Soto*, 103 F.3d at 1066–67, 1072.

[300] *Soto*, 103 F.3d at 1072.

[301] Adickes v. S. H. Kress & Co., 398 U.S. 144, 214–15 n.23 (1970); United States v. Price, 383 U.S. 787, 794 n.7 (1966); United States v. Temple, 447 F.3d 130, 143 (2d Cir. 2006).

[302] Screws v. United States, 325 U.S. 91 (1945); *supra* § 2.03.

[303] United States v. Lanier, 520 U.S. 259, 264–65 (1997); Lynch v. Household Fin. Corp., 405 U.S. 538, 549 n.16 (1972).

that does not permit "men of common intelligence" to reasonably understand what is proscribed by the statute.[304] Federal prosecutors seeking to enforce § 242 thus confront an irony — a statute enacted to enforce the Fourteenth Amendment's Due Process Clause and protect the rights of private individuals is limited by the aspect of due process that prohibits laws that fail to provide sufficient notice to would-be violators, in this case government officers accused of constitutional violations.[305]

The solution is a saving construction of § 242, in which the phrase "willfully deprives" requires proof that the accused act with specific intent to "deprive a person of a federal right which has been made specific either by the express terms of the Constitution or laws of the United States or by decisions interpreting them."[306] The defendant need not be thinking in "constitutional terms" at the time of his actions; it is sufficient that his aim in engaging in some conduct is not to perform his duties but to deprive an individual of a right protected by the Constitution.[307] This limits § 242's reach only to rights "fairly warned of" at the time of the charged conduct.[308] This construction dramatically limits the scope of criminal civil rights prosecutions,[309] but that limitation is necessary to resolve constitutional doubt about the statute.

Of course, many of the constitutional rights enforced through § 242 are themselves written in vague terms that do not provide greater guidance or notice. A constitutional right can be made specific either by the plain constitutional text as to a narrow, clear right (such as the right to vote[310]) or by judicial decisions interpreting, construing, and applying broader constitutional language, such as due process of law.[311] The Court subsequently clarified that making a broader right specific does not require a decision by the Supreme Court and does not require prior case law with facts "fundamentally similar" to the case being prosecuted; fair warning simply requires that the unlawfulness of some conduct under the Constitution be "apparent" by virtue of the state of textual and decisional law.[312]

Thus, police officers are on notice that they violate due process in acting as prosecutor, judge, jury, and executioner in beating an arrestee to death and are properly punished if that was their intent.[313] Similarly, a judge potentially should be on notice, even absent precisely similar case law, that committing sexual assault

---

[304] *Lanier*, 520 U.S. at 265–66; *Screws*, 325 U.S. at 103.

[305] *Lanier*, 520 U.S. at 265.

[306] *Screws*, 325 U.S. at 103–04; *see also* United States v. Kozminski, 487 U.S. 931, 941 (1988) (applying same standard to 18 U.S.C. § 241, § 242's companion conspiracy statute, which originated as § 3 of the Civil Rights Act of 1870).

[307] *Screws*, 325 U.S. at 106.

[308] *Lanier*, 520 U.S. at 267 (citing *Kozminski*, 487 U.S. at 941).

[309] John V. Jacobi, *Prosecuting Police Misconduct*, 2000 Wis. L. Rev. 789, 808–09.

[310] *Screws*, 325 U.S. at 106 (discussing United States v. Classic, 313 U.S. 299 (1941)).

[311] *Screws*, 325 U.S. at 106.

[312] *Lanier*, 520 U.S. at 268, 271.

[313] *Screws*, 325 U.S. at 106. Prosecution of the police violence against suspects at issue is *Screws* now proceeds under the Fourth Amendment's prohibition on unreasonable seizures, which includes a prohibition on unreasonable or excessive force. Koon v. United States, 518 U.S. 81, 88 (1996).

under the authority of his office violates his victims' due process rights to bodily integrity and freedom from conscience-shocking behavior.[314]

PART C
"AND LAWS"

§ 2.11 OVERVIEW

The basic textual argument for enforcing federal statutes through § 1983 is that it creates a cause of action for deprivations of rights, privileges, or immunities secured by "the Constitution *and laws.*"[315] The statutory word "laws" must refer to something other than the Constitution, otherwise the language is surplussage. The only thing "and laws" could mean is federal statutes. Moreover, because the phrase is unmodified, it means § 1983 allows claims of violations of all federal statutes, not only civil rights or equal-protection statutes, even though equality concerns motivated the Fourteenth Amendment and the § 5 enforcement power through which Congress enacted § 1983.[316]

A § 1983 claim generally has two elements (1) the defendant must act under color of state law and (2) the plaintiff must have been deprived of a right, now including one created by a federal statute. An "and laws" claim imposes a third element: the federal statute must create rights in the plaintiff that are enforceable through § 1983. This new element becomes the analytical focus in "and laws" cases.

§ 2.12 PRELIMINARY JURISDICTIONAL CONCERN

"And laws" claims present an initial jurisdictional quirk. Section 1983 creates a cause of action, providing a vehicle that allows the plaintiffs into court. But to bring the claim in federal district court,[317] the court must possess jurisdiction over the action from some other source. There are two possible statutory bases for jurisdiction over a § 1983 claim. The first is 28 U.S.C. § 1331, which grants district courts original jurisdiction over "all civil actions arising under the Constitution, laws, or treaties of the United States"; at a minimum, this is satisfied where the cause of action and the rule of decision (that is, the right asserted) are created by federal law,[318] which obviously includes a § 1983 claim to enforce federal law. Prior to 1980, § 1331 also contained a $10,000 amount-in-controversy requirement.[319] The second source of jurisdiction is 28 U.S.C. § 1343(a)(3), which was a different provision of the Ku Klux Klan Act of 1871; it grants district courts original

---

[314] *Lanier*, 520 U.S. at 261–62.

[315] 42 U.S.C. § 1983 (emphasis added).

[316] Maine v. Thiboutot, 448 U.S. 1, 6–8 (1980).

[317] State courts, which are courts of general jurisdiction, exercise concurrent jurisdiction over § 1983 actions. *See* Haywood Drown, 556 U.S. 729, 735 (2009).

[318] 28 U.S.C. § 1331; Mims v. Arrow Fin. Servs., LLC, 132 S. Ct. 740, 748 (2012).

[319] Maine v. Thiboutot, 448 U.S. 1, 8 n.6 (1980). Congress eliminated it in 1980. Federal Question Jurisdictional Amendments Act of 1980, Pub. L. No. 96-486, 94 Stat. 2369 (1980).

jurisdiction "of any civil action authorized by law to be commenced by any person . . . [t]o redress the deprivation, under color of any State law, statute, ordinance, regulation, custom or usage, of any right, privilege or immunity secured by the Constitution of the United States or by any Act of Congress providing for equal rights of citizens."[320] Stated more succinctly, it grants district courts jurisdiction over civil actions commenced under § 1983 for violations of rights under the Constitution and some federal statutes.

But note the potential gap between cause of action and federal jurisdictional grant, at least prior to 1980. *Thiboutot* held that § 1983 allows claims for violations of all federal statutes, regardless of the subject matter of the statute. Section 1331 grants jurisdiction over all civil actions to enforce the Constitution and all statutes (including a § 1983 action to enforce another federal statute), but only for claims of more than $10,000. Section 1343(a)(3) grants jurisdiction only over § 1983 "and laws" actions asserting rights under statutes providing for equal rights. But this means that claims for violations of non-equality statutes worth $10,000 or less could not be brought in federal court, because while there was a cause of action, the district court lacked jurisdiction; § 1331 would not be satisfied because the amount-in-controversy is not met and § 1343(a)(3) would not be satisfied because the claim does not involve a right under a statute providing for equal rights. The *Thiboutot* majority insisted this gap was not inherently illogical, but simply reflected Congress' intent not to have certain low-value statutory claims litigated in federal court, and to leave those smaller claims in state court.[321]

Removing § 1331's amount-in-controversy requirement eliminates the gap between cause of action and jurisdictional grant; there no longer is a case in which a § 1983 claim is available but cannot be brought in federal court. What does remain are gaps and overlaps as to which jurisdictional statute a plaintiff should assert in bringing a claim. Both statutes provide jurisdiction over constitutional claims[322] and over claims to enforce equality-making statutes, while § 1331 alone provides jurisdiction over claims for violations of all other statutes, all regardless of amount in controversy.[323]

§ 2.13   PRELIMINARY CONSTITUTIONAL ISSUES

It is easy, but erroneous, to see "and laws" cases after *Thiboutot* as an attempt to impermissibly assert the Supremacy Clause as an enforceable constitutional right.[324] Instead, "and laws" claims function through Supremacy Clause-mandated preemption; the federal statute prevails over contrary state laws, regulations, policies, or practices because the federal statute is the supreme law of the land.[325] For example, the claim in *Thiboutot* was that state officials followed state law and

---

[320] 28 U.S.C. § 1343(a)(3).

[321] *Thiboutot*, 448 U.S. at 8 n.6.

[322] *See* Kulick v. Pocono Downs Racing Ass'n, 816 F.2d 895, 898 n.4 (3d Cir. 1987) (labeling § 1343(a)(3) an "anachronism" in light of statutory changes).

[323] *Infra* § 5.01.

[324] *Supra* § 2.06.

[325] Golden State Transit Corp. v. Los Angeles, 493 U.S. 103, 107–08 (1989); U.S. Const. art. VI.

policy in calculating and providing public benefits, but that those calculations contradicted requirements of the Social Security Act.[326] The Supremacy Clause still functions structurally and not as a source of right in these cases; supremacy merely dictates that when state law and practice in determining federal benefit entitlements conflict with federal law, the latter controls. Whether federal law preempts state law and whether an "and laws" claim is available entail distinct legal inquiries. Preemption does not necessarily mean a § 1983 "and laws" action will succeed, nor does preemption preclude such a claim under an appropriate statute.[327]

§ 2.14 ENFORCING FEDERAL STATUTES

Federal statutory rights can be enforced in private civil litigation in any of three ways. First, the statute creating the federal right may expressly establish a private right of action.[328] Second, courts may imply a private right of action from the right-creating statute.[329] Third, the statute can be enforced through § 1983 in an "and laws" action.[330] The latter two enforcement mechanisms often come into play with respect to Spending Clause[331] enactments; programs are created and funded by federal law but administered by states or other public and private entities, with Congress dictating rules that recipients or administrators of those funds must follow. Plaintiffs in these cases are claiming that the federal funds are being handled and distributed in violation of, or inconsistent with, the requirements of the federal statute and in a way that violates the plaintiffs' rights under that statute.[332]

As we now see, the latter two enforcement mechanisms often overlap.

[1] Section 1983 "and Laws" Actions

Whether a federal statute can be privately enforced through a § 1983 "and laws" action entails a two-step inquiry.

First, the statute to be enforced must "unambiguously confer[]" a right on the plaintiff.[333] Section 1983 allows an action to remedy a deprivation of "rights, privileges, or immunities," meaning a plaintiff only can enforce rights, not laws and not mere interests or benefits. The underlying statute must impose binding obligations on government that are not too vague or amorphous and that are sufficiently specific to be judicially enforceable; congressional preferences or even

---

[326] Maine v. Thiboutot, 448 U.S. 1, 3–4 (1980).

[327] *Golden State Trans.*, 493 U.S. at 108.

[328] 42 U.S.C. § 2000e-5(f) (employment provisions of Civil Rights Act of 1964); 42 U.S.C. § 12117 (employment provisions of Americans with Disability Act); 42 U.S.C. § 2000a-3(a) (public accommodations provisions of Civil Rights Act of 1964); 42 U.S.C. § 12188(a) (public accommodations provisions of ADA); 42 U.S.C. § 2000bb-1(c) (Religious Land Use and Institutionalized Persons Act).

[329] Alexander v. Sandoval, 532 U.S. 275 (2001); Cannon v. University of Chicago, 441 U.S. 677 (1979).

[330] Gonzaga Univ. v. Doe, 536 U.S. 273 (2002); Golden State Transit Corp. v. Los Angeles, 493 U.S. 103 (1989); Maine v. Thiboutot, 448 U.S. 1 (1980).

[331] U.S. Const. art. I, § 8, cl. 2

[332] *Gonzaga*, 536 U.S. at 280–82; *Cannon*, 441 U.S. at 680–82.

[333] *Gonzaga*, 536 U.S. at 281–82.

congressional "nudges" toward certain behavior are not sufficient.[334] In deciding whether a statute creates rights, courts examine the statute's text and structure, legislative history, and judicial interpretations, which are treated as if part of the text.[335] The statute must employ "rights-creating language," typically language speaking of the persons benefited by the statute rather than of the policies of the federal agency charged with providing funds.[336] The statute, by its terms or as interpreted, must create "obligations 'sufficiently specific and definite' to be within the 'competence of the judiciary to enforce.'"[337] And the plaintiff must be part of the class of intended beneficiaries of that right.[338]

If the plaintiff shows that a statute creates an individual right, the right is presumptively enforceable through § 1983. The government may rebut that presumption by showing that Congress specifically foreclosed § 1983 as a means of enforcing that particular statute; intent to foreclose could be expressed in the statute itself or implied when the statute includes a sufficiently comprehensive and carefully tailored enforcement scheme that is incompatible with individual enforcement under § 1983.[339] This is especially so when the statutory scheme is more restrictive than § 1983. Courts must defer to this alternative scheme, which may intentionally provide particular remedies,[340] impose unique procedural requirements such as exhaustion of administrative remedies,[341] or be uniquely streamlined and expedited to respond to special statutory needs.[342] To take an obvious example: Title VII of the Civil Rights Act of 1964 creates a right to be free from adverse employment action because of race or sex. No one ever attempts to enforce it through § 1983, however, because Title VII contains its own enforcement scheme requiring that plaintiffs exhaust administrative processes before the Equal Employment Opportunity Commission prior to filing suit in federal court. That enforcement scheme, and its exhaustion requirement, would be undermined if a plaintiff could use § 1983 (which does not contain an exhaustion requirement) as the vehicle into federal court to enforce those statutory rights.

On the other hand, absence of any remedial scheme in the underlying statute might suggest that Congress did not preclude a § 1983 claim.[343] In fact, the absence of a specific statutory scheme may leave § 1983 as the exclusive federal remedy for violations of the underlying statute. This is the case for claims against local governments under 42 U.S.C. § 1981 (§ 1 of the Civil Rights Act of 1866), which prohibits discrimination because of race in the making and enforcing of

---

[334] *Gonzaga*, 536 U.S. at 283–85; *Golden State*, 493 U.S. at 108–09; Wright v. Roanoke Redevelopment & Housing Authority, 479 U.S. 418, 423–24 (1987); Pennhurst State Sch. & Hosp. v. Halderman, 451 U.S. 1, 19 (1981).

[335] *Golden State*, 493 U.S. at 111–12.

[336] *Gonzaga*, 536 U.S. at 283–84.

[337] *Golden State*, 493 U.S. at 108; *Pennhurst*, 451 U.S. at 19.

[338] *Gonzaga*, 536 U.S. at 287.

[339] *Id.* at 284 & n.4.; *Golden State*, 493 U.S. at 106–07.

[340] City of Rancho Palos Verdes v. Abrams, 544 U.S. 113 (2005).

[341] 42 U.S.C. § 2000e-5(b), (f) (Title VII of Civil Rights Act of 1964).

[342] *City of Rancho Palos Verdes*, 544 U.S. at 122–23.

[343] Wilder v. Virginia Hosp. Ass'n, 496 U.S. 498, 520–21 (1990); *Wright*, 479 U.S. at 424–25, 427–28.

contracts; § 1981 itself provides no mechanism for enforcement against the government, so claims against municipalities and individual state actors must use § 1983 as the cause of action to enforce underlying § 1981 rights.[344]

[2]   Implied Rights of Actions

The second way to establish private enforcement, particularly for Spending Clause enactments, is for the courts to find a right of action implied from the statute itself. This has become a doctrinal flashpoint, with Justice Scalia rejecting entirely the validity of a federal judicial power to create causes of action and calling on the Court to abandon this line of cases and the exercise of this power.[345]

In *Cort v. Ash*,[346] the Court identified four factors that determine whether a federal statute contains an implied right of action; separation of powers concerns motivate all four factors and the touchstone for each is the intent of Congress in enacting the statute.

(1)   The statute creates a federal right or imposes a federal duty in favor of the plaintiff as "one of the class for whose especial benefit the statute was enacted."[347] The Court recently identified this as the necessary, if not always sufficient, factor.[348]

(2)   Indications in the statute, explicit or implicit, of congressional intent to either create or deny a private remedy.[349] This may mean that Congress created an express judicial right of action, obviating the need for an implied right. It may mean Congress explicitly prohibited private actions under the statute, although that is less common. Courts also may presume congressional intent to preclude a private right of action from the availability of other statutory remedies, particularly an elaborate administrative relief process.

(3)   A private right must be consistent with the primary (as opposed to secondary) purposes of the statutory scheme.[350]

(4)   Courts must consider federalism concerns and whether the federal right of action that would be implied is more appropriately an area of state concern that should be relegated to state law.[351]

---

[344] Jett v. Dallas Indep. Sch. Dist., 491 U.S. 701, 733 (1989) (plurality opinion); McCormick v. Miami Univ., 693 F.3d 654 (6th Cir. 2012); McGovern v. City of Philadelphia, 554 F.3d 114 (3d Cir. 2009); *but see* Federation of African Am. Contractors v. City of Oakland, 96 F.3d 1204 (9th Cir. 1996) (holding that Civil Rights Act of 1991 overruled *Jett* and created stand-alone right of action against municipalities under § 1981 itself).

[345] Corr. Servs. Corp. v. Malesko, 534 U.S. 61, 75 (2001) (Scalia, J., concurring).

[346] Cort v. Ash, 422 U.S. 66 (1975).

[347] *Id.* at 78.

[348] Alexander v. Sandoval, 532 U.S. 275, 288–89 (2001).

[349] *Cort*, 422 U.S. at 82–83.

[350] Cannon v. University of Chicago, 441 U.S. 677, 703–04 (1979).

[351] *Id.* at 708–09.

The two most significant private rights of action have been implied in two essential equality-promoting provisions. Using identical language, Title VI of the Civil Rights Act of 1964 prohibits discrimination because of race, color, and national origin[352] and Title IX of the Education Amendments Act of 1972 prohibits discrimination because of sex[353] in programs and other activities receiving federal funds. The Supreme Court has implied a private right of action from Title IX, emphasizing that the statute creates a federal right.[354] And because Title IX was modeled after Title VI, which by 1972 had been held by lower courts to include an implied right of action, the latter also is treated as privately enforceable.[355] But courts must perform a precise and targeted inquiry into whether there is an implied right of action under a specific provision of law as to a specific class of persons and for a specific remedy. That there is a private right of action under one part of Title VI does not mean there is an implied right of action under the rest of that title.

In *Alexander v. Sandoval*, plaintiffs challenged an Alabama policy requiring that drivers' license exams be administered only in English, which plaintiffs argued had the effect of discriminating against them on the basis of national origin, by preventing non-English speaking residents, who often hale from foreign countries, from obtaining drivers' licenses.[356] To resolve the issue, the Court had to consider two distinct provisions of Title VI. Section 601,[357] the direct restriction on national-origin discrimination by recipients of federal funds, prohibits only intentional discrimination.[358] Section 602 authorizes federal agencies to "effectuate" the anti-discrimination rule from § 601;[359] under that delegation, the Department of Justice promulgated regulations prohibiting all policies, criteria, or methods of administration having the effect of discriminating on the basis of race, color, or national origin. The claim in *Alexander* was that the state's English-only policy had a discriminatory impact, thus it only could have been brought under the DOJ regulations, enacted pursuant to § 602, not under § 601.

The claim therefore could proceed only if § 602 implied a private right of action, a separate question from the established conclusion that § 601 does so. The Court held that § 602 failed on the first *Cort* factor, because it lacked the necessary language creating an enforceable federal right. The majority distinguished between statutes that focus on the person regulated and statutes that focus on the individuals protected, with the latter more likely to reflect congressional intent to create an enforceable individual right.[360] Section 602 was even one step further removed, since its language was directed not at the rights-holder (the citizens) or

---

[352] *Alexander*, 532 U.S. at 279–80; 42 U.S.C. § 2000d.

[353] *Cannon*, 441 U.S. at 681–83; 20 U.S.C. § 1681.

[354] *Cannon*, 441 U.S. at 689–94.

[355] *Alexander*, 532 U.S. at 279–80.

[356] *Id.* at 278–79.

[357] 42 U.S.C. § 2000d.

[358] *Alexander*, 532 U.S. at 280.

[359] 42 U.S.C. § 2000d-1.

[360] *Alexander*, 532 U.S. at 288–89.

the recipient of the regulated federal funds (the State of Alabama), but at the federal agencies charged with distributing funds, regulating the recipients, and protecting rights-holders.[361] Moreover, the power of the federal agency to withhold funds from the particular program — albeit only after following specific, heightened, and deliberately slow administrative procedures — provided an alternative remedial mechanism, further undermining any suggestion that Congress intended to establish privately judicially enforceable rights under § 602.[362]

[3] Linking the Analyses

Dissenting in *Alexander*, Justice Stevens argued that these and future plaintiffs should refile the identical challenge to state English-only policies by filing a § 1983 "and laws" action to enforce § 602 and the regulations.[363] Up to this point, the Court had suggested that the legal standard for whether a statute could be enforced through § 1983 was different than the standard for whether a private right of action could be implied from the statute itself.[364] Moreover, "and laws" claims are not subject to the same separation-of-powers objections as implied rights. Courts are not wielding authority that arguably belongs solely to Congress in allowing § 1983 "and laws" actions.[365] In enacting § 1983, Congress itself created an express private cause of action to enforce rights, privileges, or immunities derived from a range of sources of federal law, including federal statutes.

Nevertheless, one year after *Alexander*, the Court in *Gonzaga University v. Doe* insisted that the first step of the § 1983 analysis is the same as the first step in the implied right-of-action analysis. Both require that Congress intended to create an enforceable individual federal right by establishing personal rights in the underlying statute, with a demand for the same specific language conferring rights on a class of specified beneficiaries.[366]

Gonzaga involved a claimed violation of the Federal Educational Records Privacy Act ("FERPA") by a private university. The university reported to the state agency responsible for teacher certification allegations that the plaintiff, a recent graduate, had sexually assaulted another student, causing the state to deny the plaintiff his teaching certification.[367] FERPA is a Spending Clause enactment requiring educational institutions receiving federal funds to regulate access and disclosure of educational records. The statute provides that "[n]o funds shall be made available under any applicable program to any educational agency or

---

[361] *Id.* at 289.

[362] *Id.* at 289–90.

[363] *Id.* at 302 (Stevens, J., dissenting).

[364] Wilder v. Virginia Hosp. Ass'n, 496 U.S. 498, 508 n.9 (1990).

[365] Cannon v. University of Chicago, 441 U.S. 677, 730 (1979) (Powell, J., dissenting).

[366] Gonzaga Univ. v. Doe, 536 U.S. 273, 283–85 (2001).

[367] The plaintiff filed his § 1983 action in state court, which found that the university acted under color of state law by disclosing this information to a state agency as part of the state-law teacher certification process. This is a questionable conclusion given prevailing understandings of "under color," but the Supreme Court declined to grant certiorari on that issue. *Gonzaga*, 536 U.S. at 277 n.1; *supra* § 2.04.

institution which has a policy or practice of permitting the release" of education records without consent,[368] while also authorizing the Secretary of Education to enforce the statute, specifically by withholding federal funds from any educational institution that fails to comply with federal law.[369]

Once the Court established that the implied right and § 1983 inquiries entailed the same first step, *Alexander* essentially controlled the outcome. Like § 602, FERPA does not contain rights-creating language directed to the rights-holder. The statute is addressed to the Secretary of Education and her control over the distribution of federal funds, a "focus . . . two steps removed from the interests of individual students and parents" that would show an individual entitlement enforceable through § 1983.[370] The statute also focused at the macro level on institutions and their policies and practices to ensure proper protections in the aggregate, rather than at the micro level on individual instances of disclosure or on the non-disclosure rights of any particular individual.

Both the § 1983 and implied right inquiries reach the second step only if the underlying statute creates an enforceable individual right. At that point the analyses, while still focusing on congressional intent, diverge. Under the implied rights analysis, courts must determine whether Congress affirmatively wanted this statutory right to be enforced through private civil litigation; under § 1983, the statutory right is presumptively enforceable absent a clear indication that Congress affirmatively did not want private enforcement of the underlying statute.[371] These different defaults make sense. Section 1983 is an existing litigation vehicle that Congress previously enacted specifically to enforce federal rights established elsewhere. We can presume that Congress wants an existing cause of action put to use enforcing new rights, unless it affirmatively provides to the contrary in subsequently enacted legislation.

Fitzgerald v. Barnstable School Committee further considered the link at the second step of the two inquiries. A grade-school-age girl was subject to sexually based bullying on the bus and at school and officials did nothing to stop or protect her from the harassment, all allegedly in violation of Title IX.[372] The plaintiff sought damages for the violation of her statutory rights under both the statute's implied right of action and § 1983.

The Court unanimously held that the implied right of action did not preclude a § 1983 "and laws" claim to enforce the same statute and a plaintiff can utilize both enforcement vehicles. While the inclusion of an express right of action in a statute is indicative of congressional intent to preclude a § 1983 action, the Court was unwilling to draw the same inference about legislative intent from an implied right of action, since, by definition, Congress said nothing in the statute about § 1983.[373] Moreover, Title IX lacks the sort of comprehensive, carefully tailored, or restrictive

---

[368] 20 U.S.C. § 1232g(b)(1).

[369] 20 U.S.C. § 1232g(f).

[370] *Gonzaga*, 536 U.S. at 287.

[371] *Id.* at 284 & n.4.

[372] Fitzgerald v. Barnstable Sch. Comm., 555 U.S. 246, 248–50 (2009).

[373] *Id.* at 255–57.

statutory enforcement scheme that generally precludes § 1983 actions. Title IX is enforceable by private civil litigation (as well as withdrawal of federal funds), but the remedies are identical to those available in the § 1983 action and do not require special notice, administrative exhaustion, or other special procedures. Thus, allowing the § 1983 claim "will neither circumvent required procedures, nor allow access to new remedies" not already available in the implied cause of action drawn from Title IX itself.[374]

[4] Alternative Enforcement Mechanisms

Because many of these cases involve Spending Clause enactments, the primary enforcement mechanism for noncompliance is withholding federal funds from the violating recipient or from the particular funded program in which the violation occurred. This point is central to both *Alexander* and *Gonzaga*, where the Court emphasized statutory language directed to the federal agency and the agency's special responsibility for ensuring compliance with federal law through the control of federal moneys.[375]

The problem with relying on withholding funds as the central means of enforcement is that it is a severe, and thus unlikely, sanction to impose for individual or isolated violations. This illustrates two related points — 1) the practical and political constraints on government, as opposed to private, enforcement of civil rights, and 2) the tension between catching and remedying individual, as opposed to systemic, civil rights violations. It would be an extreme, arguably unwarranted move for the Secretary of Education to withdraw all federal funds from Gonzaga University because of an apparent single instance of improper disclosure of student records. But absent some vehicle for private enforcement (whether § 1983 or implied rights of action), that single statutory violation goes unremedied (assuming no wave of similar incidents and no broader systemic problems at Gonzaga University). The federal government lacks the time, resources, and political will to root out every minor statutory violation, especially with such a blunderbuss weapon as withdrawal of funds. It must focus on larger, systemic violations which might justify stripping funds, while leaving smaller violations untouched. *Gonzaga* and *Alexander* thus have been criticized for undermining the centrality of private civil rights enforcement and of the private attorney general who (as plaintiff or plaintiff's attorney) takes on private litigation in service of the broader public interest.[376]

§ 2.15 PARALLEL CONSTITUTIONAL AND STATUTORY CLAIMS

Congress protects and enforces the Constitution in either of two ways. First, it creates new statutory rights, whether broader, narrower, or co-extensive with constitutional rights themselves, usually with some process for private enforcement

---

[374] *Id.*

[375] *Id.* at 254–55; *Gonzaga*, 536 U.S. at 278; *Alexander*, 532 U.S. at 289.

[376] Pamela S. Karlan, *Disarming the Private Attorney General*, 2003 U. ILL. L. REV. 183, 187.

of those rights. Second, it enacted § 1983 as a vehicle for direct judicial enforcement of the Constitution itself. The issue is what happens when the same conduct, transaction, or occurrence by the same or multiple connected defendants violates both a constitutional right and a statutory right. Can a plaintiff pursue both claims? Or does the statutory claim preclude the independent § 1983 constitutional claim?

This was the second issue in *Fitzgerald v. Barnstable School Committee*, where the plaintiff alleged that the public school's failure to stop sexual harassment and bullying violated the Equal Protection Clause as well as Title IX.[377] This again was a matter of congressional intent — whether Congress intended the rights in Title IX to be exclusive, precluding any assertion of constitutional rights. But here the comparison is not between remedial schemes, but between the nature and scope of distinct statutory and constitutional rights. Where the contours of the rights and protections — who can be sued, the conduct that can form the basis for a claim, and the applicable legal standard — diverge, it is unlikely that Congress intended to preclude § 1983 constitutional actions.[378] The question, moreover, is not whether Congress expected or anticipated statutory and constitutional claims to proceed side-by-side, but whether Congress intended to preclude that possibility.[379] And the Court "should 'not lightly conclude that Congress intended to preclude reliance on § 1983 as a remedy for a substantial equal protection claim.' "[380]

Applying these considerations, *Fitzgerald* held that Title IX does not preclude a parallel and concurrent equal protection claim. First, Title IX regulates educational entities that receive federal funds, but not school officials, teachers, or other individuals; the equal protection claim is necessary to reach these individual actors. Second, while Title IX reaches all educational institutions receiving funds, including private ones, § 1983 only reaches individual officials who act under color of state law. Third, certain conduct that may violate equal protection is exempt from Title IX's prohibitions, such as traditionally single-sex schools and discrimination in elementary and secondary school admissions. Fourth, while an entity may be liable under Title IX where a single school administrator with authority to take corrective action responds to harassment with deliberate indifference, an entity is liable under § 1983 only if that administrator acts pursuant to a discriminatory policy, custom, or practice.[381]

Parallel and concurrent claims frequently arise in employment discrimination actions by public employees, where discriminatory employment decisions or harassment potentially violate both the Equal Protection Clause and federal statutes prohibiting discrimination in employment because of race, sex, age, or disability. The prevailing view has long been that a constitutional claim under § 1983 can proceed alongside a parallel Title VII claim.[382] That conclusion is unquestion-

---

[377] Fitzgerald v. Barnstable School Committee, 555 U.S. 246, 255–56 (2009).

[378] *Id.* at 252–55.

[379] *Id.* at 257–59 & n.2.

[380] *Id.* at 255–56.

[381] *Id.* at 255–59; *infra* Ch. 4, Part A.

[382] Henley v. Brown, 686 F.3d 634 (8th Cir. 2012); Campbell v. Galloway, 483 F.3d 258 (4th Cir. 2007); Valentine v. City of Chicago, 452 F.3d 670 (7th Cir. 2006); Annis v. County of Westchester, 36 F.3d 251

ably correct in light of *Fitzgerald*'s new analysis and focus on divergent rights and protections. While both prohibit intentional discrimination, the scope of the rights and obligations imposed is different; a Title VII claim is available against the entity but not individual officers, Title VII protects only employees but not independent contractors,[383] and the standard for liability under Title VII is different than the standard for entity liability for constitutional claims under § 1983. Although Title VII establishes a unique remedial scheme, notably requiring plaintiffs to exhaust administrative remedies,[384] other differences between the scope of the statutory and constitutional rights allow the claims to proceed together.

By contrast, prior to *Fitzgerald* every circuit had concluded that the Age Discrimination in Employment Act precludes § 1983 equal protection claims, because Congress intended the ADEA's comprehensive statutory remedy to be exclusive.[385] But in *Levin v. Madigan*, the Seventh Circuit became the first court to rely on *Fitzgerald* to reach the opposite conclusion. While Congress did intend the ADEA to provide an exclusive remedy, that only precludes other methods of enforcing the rights created by the statute itself; it says nothing about the viability of independent claims for disability discrimination in violation of the Fourteenth Amendment. Instead, the *Fitzgerald* analysis shows that, that as with Title VII, ADEA rights and protections sufficiently diverge from Fourteenth Amendment rights and protections in terms of who can sue, who can be sued, and what conduct establishes a violation by the entity.[386]

PART D
CLAIMS AGAINST FEDERAL OFFICERS

§ 2.16   OVERVIEW

28 U.S.C. § 1346(b)

(1) Subject to . . . the district courts, together with the United States District Court for the District of the Canal Zone and the District Court of the Virgin Islands, shall have exclusive jurisdiction of civil actions on claims against the United States, for money damages, accruing on and after January 1, 1945, for injury or loss of property, or personal injury or death caused by the negligent or wrongful act or omission of any employee of the Government while acting within the scope of his office or employment, under circumstances where the United States, if a private person,

---

(2d Cir. 1994); Bradley v. Pittsburgh Bd. of Educ., 913 F.2d 1064 (3d Cir. 1990).

[383] 42 U.S.C. § 2000e(f); Farlow v. Wachovia Bank of N.C., N.A., 259 F.3d 309 (4th Cir. 2001).

[384] 42 U.S.C. § 2000e-5(b).

[385] Ahlmeyer v. Nevada. Sys. of Higher Educ., 555 F.3d 1051 (9th Cir. 2009); Tapia-Tapia v. Potter, 322 F.3d 742 (1st Cir. 2003); Lafleur v. Texas Dep't of Health, 126 F.3d 758 (5th Cir. 1997); Zombro v. Baltimore City Police Dep't, 868 F.2d 1364 (4th Cir. 1989).

[386] Levin v. Madigan, 692 F.3d 607, 621-22 (7th Cir. 2012), *cert. granted*, ___ S. Ct. ___ (2013).

would be liable to the claimant in accordance with the law of the place where the act or omission occurred.

(2) No person convicted of a felony who is incarcerated while awaiting sentencing or while serving a sentence may bring a civil action against the United States or an agency, officer, or employee of the Government, for mental or emotional injury suffered while in custody without a prior showing of physical injury.

28 U.S.C. § 2679

(b) (1) The remedy against the United States provided by section 1346(b) and 2672 of this title for injury or loss of property, or personal injury or death arising or resulting from the negligent or wrongful act or omission of any employee of the Government while acting within the scope of his office or employment is exclusive of any other civil action or proceeding for money damages by reason of the same subject matter against the employee whose act or omission gave rise to the claim or against the estate of such employee. Any other civil action or proceeding for money damages arising out of or relating to the same subject matter against the employee or the employee's estate is precluded without regard to when the act or omission occurred.

(2) Paragraph (1) does not extend or apply to a civil action against an employee of the Government—

(A) which is brought for a violation of the Constitution of the United States, or

(B) which is brought for a violation of a statute of the United States under which such action against an individual is otherwise authorized.

(c) The Attorney General shall defend any civil action or proceeding brought in any court against any employee of the Government or his estate for any such damage or injury. The employee against whom such civil action or proceeding is brought shall deliver within such time after date of service or knowledge of service as determined by the Attorney General, all process served upon him or an attested true copy thereof to his immediate superior or to whomever was designated by the head of his department to receive such papers and such person shall promptly furnish copies of the pleadings and process therein to the United States attorney for the district embracing the place wherein the proceeding is brought, to the Attorney General, and to the head of his employing Federal agency.

Section 1983 establishes claims against persons who act under color of the laws, customs, and usages "of any State or Territory or the District of Columbia."[387] It applies to officers working for state, county, and municipal governments, as well as

---

[387] 42 U.S.C. § 1983.

to officials of multi-state entities created under the Compact Clause.[388]

But § 1983 does not provide a cause of action against federal officers or those acting under color of federal law, nor is there any statutory counterpart to § 1983 creating claims against federal officers. Nevertheless, it long has been established that individuals can sue federal officers to challenge the constitutionality of federal law and seek injunctive, declaratory, or other prospective relief against its enforcement, even without statutory authorization.[389]

The problem is how to recover damages for past or completed constitutional violations by federal officers. It is widely accepted that the federal government enjoys sovereign immunity, meaning it cannot be sued *eo nomine* ("in that name" or "by name"),[390] thus there is no way to sue the federal government for damages for constitutional violations.[391] Under the Federal Tort Claims Act, a plaintiff can bring a claim for money damages against the United States for tortious acts by government employees acting within the scope of employment, applying the tort law of the state in which the tortious acts or omissions occurred;[392] the FTCA reflects an explicit waiver of sovereign immunity, with the United States consenting to suit and to liability in federal court. In the Westfall Act, Congress affirmed the exclusivity of the FTCA damages action against the United States and its preclusion of any action against federal employees.[393] More importantly, the Act also makes explicit that the substitute action against the United States is unavailable for claimed constitutional violations by federal officers.[394]

§ 2.17   *BIVENS V. SIX UNKNOWN NAMED AGENTS OF FEDERAL BUREAU OF NARCOTICS*

The solution is a right of action implied from the Constitution itself. The Court reserved this question in *Bell v. Hood* in 1946,[395] then finally recognized the cause of action in 1971 in *Bivens*.

Bivens involved facts somewhat similar to *Monroe v. Pape* — warrantless entry into a suspect's home, a search and arrest without probable cause and with excessive force, ransacking of the home, and threats directed at family members in the house. The difference is that Bivens was suspected of federal narcotics violations and the violators were federal agents of the Bureau of Narcotics purportedly acting

---

[388] *Cf.* Lake Country Estates, Inc. v. Tahoe Regional Planning Agency, 440 U.S. 391, 399–400 (1979).

[389] Bivens v. Six Unknown Named Agents of Federal Bureau of Narcotics, 403 U.S. 388, 400, 404 (1971) (Harlan, J., concurring in the judgment); Bell v. Hood, 327 U.S. 678 (1946).

[390] Louis L. Jaffe, *Suits Against Governments and Officers: Sovereign Immunity*, 77 HARV. L. REV. 1, 1 (1963).

[391] *Bivens*, 403 U.S. at 410 (Harlan, J., concurring in the judgment).

[392] 28 U.S.C. § 1346(b).

[393] 28 U.S.C. § 2679(b)(1).

[394] *Id.* § 2679(b)(2)(A).

[395] Bivens v. Six Unknown Named Agents of Federal Bureau of Narcotics, 403 U.S. 388, 389 (1971) (discussing Bell v. Hood, 327 U.S. 678 (1946)).

under color of federal law.[396] Six justices agreed that the plaintiff could bring a claim for damages directly under the Constitution — Justice Brennan writing for five and Justice Harlan concurring in the judgment. Although reaching the same conclusion, the two opinions begin from different major premises.

Justice Brennan's starting point was that the Fourth Amendment establishes an independent substantive federal right to be free from unreasonable searches and seizures. The Fourth Amendment protects different interests than state law and the latter may be inconsistent, and perhaps even hostile, to the interests protected by the former. Federal constitutional rights require protection not by ordinary state tort law, but through a different remedy that reflects the unique individual interests protected by the Fourth Amendment in the face of the popular will and the popular branches of government. Moreover, there is something different in degree and in kind about violations committed by federal officers, warranting a different right and remedy. Federal officers are difficult to resist, because, unlike with an ordinary trespass by a private individual, a homeowner cannot call the police on federal agents; rather, the claim of federal authority by the person entering is "likely to unlock the door."[397]

Having recognized the unique individual federal right established by the Fourth Amendment, Brennan cited *Marbury v. Madison* for the hoary proposition that there must also be a federal remedy, because "the very essence of civil liberty certainly consists in the right of every individual to claim the protection of the laws whenever he receives an injury."[398] An injured plaintiff must be entitled to redress for the violation of her rights through any remedy normally available; historically, the ordinary remedy for an invasion of private rights is money damages, which federal courts are empowered to award unless Congress affirmatively declares that persons may not recover.[399] Because the Fourth Amendment is an independent right, it requires an independent damages remedy, in the absence of a congressional command that such a remedy is unavailable.

Justice Harlan's concurrence begins from the grant to federal district courts of general "arising under" jurisdiction in § 1331. That jurisdictional grant gives courts the presumptive power to provide equitable remedies; it had long been recognized that a federal court can enjoin enforcement of an unconstitutional federal law, even in the absence of a statutory cause of action.[400] Once granted jurisdiction, a court also may provide all other traditional remedies necessary or appropriate to effectuate the purposes of the constitutional right. It follows that if an explicit statutory cause of action is not necessary for a federal court to provide equitable remedies, then it should not be necessary for legal remedies, such as money damages.[401]

---

[396] *Id.*; *see also* James E. Pfander, *The Story of* Bivens v. Six Unknown Named Agents of the Federal Bureau of Narcotics, *in* FEDERAL COURTS STORIES 280 (Vicki C. Jackson & Judith Resnik eds., 2010).

[397] *Bivens*, 403 U.S. at 392–95.

[398] *Id.* at 397 (citing Marbury v. Madison, 5 U.S. (1 Cranch.) 137, 163 (1803)).

[399] *Id.* at 395–96.

[400] *Id.* at 404–06 (Harlan, J., concurring in the judgment).

[401] *Id.* at 400, 405 (Harlan, J., concurring in the judgment).

Moreover, Justice Harlan emphasized the necessity of a damages remedy as the only way to assert and enforce constitutional rights. In the Fourth Amendment claim at hand, no direct action was available against the United States because it had not waived sovereign immunity; the Exclusionary Rule was irrelevant because Bivens never was prosecuted; and prospective injunctive relief would not remedy a past, completed constitutional violation. Thus, for "people in Bivens' shoes, it is damages or nothing."[402]

There were three separate dissents in *Bivens* — from Chief Justice Burger, Justice Black, and Justice Blackmun. All focused on varying themes of separation of powers, the exclusive role of Congress in creating causes of action, and the inappropriateness of courts wielding that power themselves.[403] Justice Brennan responded that the "present case involves no special factors counseling hesitation in the absence of affirmative action by Congress." Congress had not prohibited this damages action, nor had Congress provided that such claims be remitted to another, equally effective remedy, nor did the case involve unique circumstances, such as effects on the public fisc, on the relationship between government and soldiers, or on congressional employees.[404]

This hinted, however, that separation of powers concerns might in some special instances compel the Court to defer to Congress and decline a private cause action on a constitutional right. This was just not such a case.

§ 2.18 SPECIAL FACTORS AND BALANCING

In *Bivens*, Justice Brennan insisted that the action was available because there were no "special factors counseling hesitation" compelling the Court to stay its hand.[405] In *Wilkie v. Robbins*,[406] the Court converted this into a two-step analysis governing whether courts can "extend" *Bivens* into new situations.

First, the court looks to whether there are alternative existing processes for protecting the plaintiff's interests, which tell the court it should refrain from providing a new and freestanding constitutional damages remedy. In particular, courts defer to any "elaborate remedial system that has been constructed step by step, with careful attention to conflicting policy considerations."[407] Thus, the Supreme Court has rejected *Bivens* actions for a First Amendment free speech claim by a federal employee in favor of federal civil service procedures;[408] a Fifth Amendment due process claim by Social Security disability claimants in favor of the

---

[402] *Id.* at 409–10 (Harlan, J., concurring in the judgment).

[403] *Id.* at 411–12 (Burger, C.J., dissenting); *id.* at 427–28 (Black, J., dissenting); *id.* at 430 (Blackmun, J., dissenting).

[404] *Id.* at 396–97.

[405] Bivens v. Six Unknown Named Agents of Federal Bureau of Narcotics, 403 U.S. 388, 396–97 (1971).

[406] Wilkie v. Robbins, 551 U.S. 537 (2007).

[407] *Id.* at 551–554.

[408] Bush v. Lucas, 462 U.S. 367 (1983).

elaborate administrative scheme for making and challenging benefits decisions;[409] and constitutional claims by military personnel for personal injuries in favor of an elaborate system of military civil justice.[410] More recently, the Court held that the general availability of state tort claims (in that case, for medical malpractice) precludes a *Bivens* action for allegedly unconstitutional medical treatment against employees of a private company operating a federal prison.[411] Any alternative remedy need not be perfectly congruent in terms of procedures or available relief, and differences or limits in remedies do not render an alternative scheme inadequate.[412] In fact, the alternative remedial mechanism need not even be a singular remedy in a single forum from a single legal source; it may be sufficient that there is a patchwork quilt of state and federal, administrative and judicial remedies applying constitutional, legislative, common law, and administrative rules.[413]

Second, even absent an adequate alternative remedy, whether to permit a *Bivens* remedy remains subject to the court's sound judgment. Federal courts "must make the kind of remedial determination that is appropriate for a common-law tribunal, paying particular heed, however, to any special factors counseling hesitation before authorizing a new kind of federal litigation."[414] This means other special factors may preclude a *Bivens* action, even if there is no adequate alternative remedial scheme and even if the absence of a *Bivens* action leaves a plaintiff entirely without available statutory, administrative, or common-law remedies.

Consider, for example, the D.C. Circuit decision in *Wilson v. Libby*. The plaintiff, a former covert CIA operative, and her husband brought a *Bivens* action against various officials in the Office of Vice President Dick Cheney; the officials allegedly leaked the agent's identity to the press in retaliation for her husband's criticism of the George W. Bush Administration's efforts to justify going to war in Iraq. The court rejected the agent's claim because she could seek relief under the Privacy Act, a federal law prohibiting disclosure of federal employees' information and establishing a specific statutory enforcement scheme.[415] More importantly (and arguably problematically), the court also rejected the husband's constitutional claim, even though he, not being a federal employee, did not have any right or remedy under the Privacy Act or any other source of law, for the injuries he suffered as a result of the disclosure of his wife's identity.[416]

The Supreme Court has twice recognized that the unique structure, disciplinary rules, and congressional role in the military constitute special factors precluding *Bivens* actions.[417] In *Wilkie*, a case arising out of a land dispute between a Wyoming

---

[409] Schweiker v. Chilicky, 487 U.S. 412 (1988).

[410] United States v. Stanley, 483 U.S. 669 (1987); Chappell v. Wallace, 462 U.S. 296 (1983).

[411] Minneci v. Pollard, 132 S. Ct. 617 (2012).

[412] *Id.* at 625.

[413] *Wilkie*, 551 U.S. at 553–54.

[414] *Id.* at 551, 553–54.

[415] Wilson v. Libby, 535 F.3d 697, 710 (D.C. Cir. 2008).

[416] *See id.* at 720 (Rogers, J., concurring in part and dissenting in part).

[417] United States v. Stanley, 483 U.S. 669 (1987); Chappell v. Wallace, 462 U.S. 296 (1983).

ranch owner and the federal government over the owner's refusal to grant the government an easement, the Court identified two further special considerations. The first is a floodgates concern; a *Bivens* action in this context

> would invite claims in every sphere of legitimate governmental action affecting property interests . . . . Exercising any governmental authority affecting the value or enjoyment of property interests would fall within the *Bivens* regime.[418]

Second, and relatedly, is a line-drawing problem. As the *Wilkie* Court said, "across this enormous swath of potential litigation would hover the difficulty of devising a 'too much' standard that could guide an employee's conduct and a judicial factfinder's conclusion."[419] Because the federal government will (and should) engage in hard bargaining in property deals, it would be impossible for courts to clearly or accurately define the cause of action, to identify the limits to "legitimate zeal" when the government acts on the public's half, or to determine when permissible advocacy becomes a constitutional violation.[420]

The Supreme Court thus has allowed causes of action only twice since *Bivens* itself — in an Eighth Amendment claim against a federal prison official for providing insufficient medical care[421] and in a Fifth Amendment equal protection claim for sex discrimination in employment by a member of Congress.[422] Otherwise the Court has rejected or questioned the availability of the *Bivens* claim in every case in which the issue has been squarely presented,[423] while repeatedly expressing reluctance to "extend" *Bivens* to new contexts or new defendants.

While the history of *Bivens* claims is clear, the Court has split over what it means for *Bivens* going forward.

The *Wilkie* majority argued that this history demonstrates that a *Bivens* action "is not an automatic entitlement no matter what other means there may be to vindicate a protected interest," and that the Court has repeatedly found the *Bivens* remedy unjustified suggests a presumption against recognizing a claim.[424] And in several cases rejecting *Bivens* claims, Justice Scalia has concurred to insist that *Bivens* has been and should be limited to its facts — Fourth Amendment claims against federal law-enforcement officers; otherwise, *Bivens* is a "relic of the heady days in which this Court assumed Common Law powers to create causes of action."[425]

On the other hand, Justice Ginsburg has drawn the opposite default rule from this history. All the cases in which the *Bivens* remedy has been rejected arose in

---

[418] *Wilkie*, 551 U.S. at 561.

[419] *Id.*

[420] *Id.* at 554.

[421] Carlson v. Green, 446 U.S. 14 (1980).

[422] Davis v. Passman, 442 U.S. 228 (1979).

[423] *Minneci*, 132 S. Ct. at 622–34 (citing cases); *Wilkie*, 551 U.S. at 549–50 (citing cases).

[424] *Wilkie*, 551 U.S. at 550.

[425] *Minneci*, 132 S. Ct. at 626 (Scalia, J., concurring); *Wilkie*, 551 U.S. at 568 (Scalia, J., concurring); Corr. Servs. Corp. v. Malesko, 534 U.S. 61, 75 (2001) (Scalia, J., concurring).

special contexts — military, civil service and federal employment, and complex federal administrative programs, such as Social Security. But outside those special contexts, the basic default of *Bivens* should be that the constitutional action is permitted.[426] Thus, the plaintiff in *Wilkie* should not be confined to a patchwork quilt of different procedures against different parties for different remedies that provides no relief for the "relentless torment" the plaintiff has suffered.[427] Similarly, a plaintiff should have the right to seek a uniform constitutional remedy, rather than being left to the "vagaries" of varied state law.[428] This echoes Justice Harlan's *Bivens* concurrence, where he insisted that automatically (or even presumptively) closing the doors to the court expresses value judgments about federal rights.[429]

§ 2.19　PARALLELISM

In theory, there is and should be parallelism between *Bivens* and § 1983, as the Court often describes *Bivens* as the federal "analog" to § 1983,[430] with the same liability rules, the same *Screws/Monroe* "clothed with authority" standard for when a federal officer acts under color of law,[431] and the same individual defenses.[432] But the Court has undermined, if not expressly rejected, parallelism in many respects.

[1]　Rights Enforceable

The Court's recent decisions impose a retail rather than wholesale approach to determining what rights and circumstances can form the basis for a *Bivens* action. By contrast, all incorporated Bill of Rights liberties are "rights, privileges, or immunities secured" that can form the basis of a § 1983 action. As a result, some constitutional violations may be challenged and remedied when committed by state or local officers through § 1983, but not when committed by federal officers because *Bivens* is unavailable for a given right.

Again, the Supreme Court has expressly allowed a *Bivens* claim to enforce only three rights: the Fourth Amendment right against unreasonable searches and seizures in *Bivens*, the Eighth Amendment right of a prisoner to proper medical treatment in *Carlson*, and the equal protection component of Fifth Amendment due process in *Davis*. The Court has assumed but never decided that other rights

---

[426]　*Wilkie*, 551 U.S. at 574–76 (Ginsburg, J., dissenting).

[427]　*Id.* at 576 (Ginsburg, J., dissenting).

[428]　*Minneci*, 132 S. Ct. at 627 (Ginsburg, J., dissenting).

[429]　*Bivens*, 403 U.S. at 410 (Harlan, J., concurring in the judgment).

[430]　Ashcroft v. Iqbal, 556 U.S. 662, 675 (2009).

[431]　Jacob v. Curt, 721 F. Supp. 1536, 1538 (D.R.I. 1989).

[432]　Wilson v. Layne, 526 U.S. 603 (1999) (qualified immunity); Koubriti v. Convertino, 593 F.3d 459 (6th Cir. 2010) (prosecutorial immunity); Case v. Milewski, 327 F.3d 564 (7th Cir. 2003) (procedural bars). In fact, most of the Supreme Court's decisions on qualified immunity, the primary defense in actions against individual executive officers, have come in *Bivens* actions rather than § 1983 actions. Ashcroft v. al-Kidd, 131 S. Ct. 2074 (2011); Saucier v. Katz, 533 U.S. 194 (2001); Harlow v. Fitzgerald, 457 U.S. 800 (1982). These defenses are discussed at length in Chs. 4 and 5.

can be enforced via *Bivens*, including First Amendment free speech[433] and First Amendment free exercise.[434] One also could infer that a claim could be brought to enforce other Fourth Amendment rights, such as the prohibition on excessive force, where the Court has been silent on the question in rejecting claims on other grounds.[435] Lower courts have been more willing to expressly and directly enforce other Bill of Rights liberties through *Bivens*.[436]

[2] Defendants

The Court also has rejected straight parallelism as to possible defendants. A *Bivens* claim is available only against individual federal officer defendants, not against the federal government or federal agencies;[437] by contrast, local governments and their agencies are persons for § 1983 purposes and are, under certain circumstances, subject to suit.[438] A *Bivens* claim is not available against private entities,[439] while private entities may act under color of state law and be subject to a § 1983 action.[440] Most recently, the Court held that a *Bivens* claim is not available for an Eighth Amendment violation by private employees of a private entity hired to manage a federal prison;[441] by contrast, private employees of a private entity hired to manage a state prison may act under color of state law and be subject to a § 1983 action.[442]

In reaching those conclusions, neither *Minneci* nor *Malesko* discussed whether the defendant employees acted under color of federal law so as to be subject to the Constitution.[443] This potentially calls into question lower court cases accepting, or at least analyzing, whether a person can act under color of federal law, and thus be subject to *Bivens* liability, through the various "joint participation" tests.[444] That analysis is unnecessary if a private person simply is never a proper *Bivens*

---

[433] Reichle v. Howards, 132 S. Ct. 2088, 2093 n.4 (2012) (refusing to decide whether *Bivens* extends to First Amendment retaliatory arrest claim).

[434] *Iqbal*, 556 U.S. at 675.

[435] *Saucier*, 533 U.S. at 197 (excessive force claim under Fourth Amendment rejected on immunity grounds).

[436] Moss v. United States Secret Serv., 675 F.3d 1213 (9th Cir. 2012) (free speech); Marcavage v. Nat'l Park Serv., 666 F.3d 856 (3d Cir. 2012) (free speech); Rogers v. United States, 696 F. Supp. 2d 472 (W.D. Pa. 2010) (free exercise).

[437] FDIC v. Meyer, 510 U.S. 471 (1994).

[438] Monell v. Dep't of Social Servs., 436 U.S. 658 (1978); *infra* Ch. 4.

[439] Corr. Servs. Corp. v. Malesko, 534 U.S. 61 (2001).

[440] *Id.* at 75 n.5; Rosborough v. Mgmt. & Training Corp., 350 F.3d 459 (5th Cir. 2003) (per curiam); Skelton v. Pri-Cor, Inc., 963 F.2d 100 (6th Cir. 1991); *supra* § 2.04.

[441] *Minneci v. Pollard*, 132 S. Ct. 617, 620 (20120.

[442] *Rosborough*, 350 F.3d at 461; Street v. Corr. Corp. of Am., 102 F.3d 810 (6th Cir. 1996).

[443] *Minneci*, 132 S. Ct. at 627 n.* (Ginsburg, J., dissenting).

[444] Weise v. Casper, 593 F.3d 1163 (10th Cir. 2010) (action against volunteers working at presidential event); Brown v. Philip Morris, Inc., 250 F.3d 789 (3d Cir. 2001) (analyzing whether tobacco companies are federal actors under prevailing tests); Morast v. Lance, 807 F.2d 926 (11th Cir. 1987) (analyzing whether bank was federal actor); *see also* Peoples v. CCA Det. Ctrs., 422 F.3d 1090 (10th Cir. 2005) (Ebel, J., dissenting).

defendant because *Bivens* does not "extend" so far.

We perhaps can reconcile these lines according to the degree of connection between the government and the private individual in a particular case. Where, as in *Minneci*, the individual works for a company that contracts with the government to provide a service, the connection is too attenuated for *Bivens* liability, at least where alternative remedies (such as state tort law) remain available. But *Bivens* liability remains possible where a private individual works directly with or under the supervision of public officials, requiring the court to analyze the close nexus between government and individual on those facts.[445]

[3] Cause of Action or Constitutional Violation

Courts often conflate whether a cause of action exists with whether a violation of the underlying substantive right has occurred. This problem arises under the retail approach of *Bivens* but never under the wholesale approach of § 1983.

For example, the *Wilkie* Court identified as one special factor the impossibility of recognizing when legitimate zeal in representing government interests in property negotiations crosses the line into a constitutional violation, which compelled the Court to stay its hand under *Bivens*.[446] Of course, those line-drawing concerns arise in an identical action brought against state officials under § 1983.[447] But in a § 1983 action, line-drawing would be addressed as part of the constitutional analysis of whether, on these facts, the plaintiff's due process rights had been violated. They would not be considered a threshold question of whether a cause of action exists; a cause of action exists by virtue of the plain existence of § 1983.

On the other hand, in considering whether a plaintiff could bring a *Bivens* action for retaliatory prosecution, the Court in *Hartman v. Moore* discussed whether a plaintiff could "prevail" on such a claim, concluding he could only do so by showing absence of probable cause for the original arrest.[448] Notably, the Court analyzed this point not as a special factor in a threshold inquiry about the cause of action, but as a matter of substantive First Amendment law and whether the plaintiff's constitutional rights had been violated. Which is precisely how it would be analyzed in the identical § 1983 action.

[4] A Wholesale Approach to *Bivens*

James Pfander and David Baltmanis argue that Congress itself established parallelism as a statutory matter by enacting the Westfall Act in 1986. By expressly excluding from the FTCA's substitute action all claims based on violations of a constitutional right,[449] Congress implicitly confirmed that constitutional claims are

---

[445] *Weise*, 593 F.3d at 1165.

[446] *Wilkie*, 551 U.S. at 553–54.

[447] *Id.* at 581 (Ginsburg, J., dissenting) (pointing to absence of similar cases against state and local officials under § 1983).

[448] Hartman v. Moore, 547 U.S. 250 (2006).

[449] 28 U.S.C. § 2679(b)(2)(A).

to be brought through some other vehicle. That other vehicle must be *Bivens*, which was well established at the time of the Act and which Congress recognized and adopted as the appropriate vehicle for asserting constitutional damages claims against federal officers. Pfander and Baltmanis explain that, in exempting constitutional claims, the Westfall Act

> clearly recognizes and preserves the right to sue that the Court had established in *Bivens* and elaborated in subsequent cases. Moreover, by speaking in broad and unqualified terms, the statute suggests that *any* alleged violation of the Constitution will support a claim against federal officials.[450]

Although not as clear or explicit as affirmative creating a cause of action such as § 1983, the effect is the same.[451]

The Westfall Act, incorporating *Bivens*, thus becomes a genuine statutory analog to § 1983 creating true parallelism. It eliminates the retail, case-by-case analysis of whether a *Bivens* claim should lie in a particular case or for a particular right in favor of a cause of action automatically available for all constitutional rights. Liability depends only on the plaintiff establishing a violation of a substantive constitutional right and action under color of law, whether a claim is brought against federal, state, or local officials.

---

[450] James E. Pfander & David Baltmanis, *Rethinking* Bivens: *Legitimacy and Constitutional Adjudication*, 98 GEO. L.J. 117, 131–32 (2009).

[451] *Id.* at 135–36.

Chapter 3

INDIVIDUAL IMMUNITIES

§ 3.01 OVERVIEW: INDIVIDUAL IMMUNITY

The basic elements of both § 1983 and *Bivens* claims are that the defendant acted under color of law (state or federal) and that the plaintiff was deprived of a federal right (constitutional or statutory). We also see limitations on the cause of action that function as additional elements, such as the "special factors" analysis under *Bivens* or the limits on § 1983 "and laws" actions. The primary target of constitutional litigation generally is individual officer defendants, sued for their individual misconduct under color of law. We turn now to official immunities, the primary defenses for these individual defendants under both § 1983 and *Bivens*. Immunities protect defendants regardless of whether a constitutional violation occurred in the transaction or occurrence at issue.

Immunities are defined along three features. First is the "scope" of the immunity, which considers the conduct, circumstances, or functions to which immunity attaches. Second is the "application" of the immunity, which considers the persons or entities who can claim the immunity as a defense. Third is the "level" of immunity, which considers how much immunity the defendant receives and what he is immunized against. Immunity can be absolute or qualified/limited; it can be from suit or only from ultimate liability; it can be from civil suit, criminal prosecution, or both; and it can be from claims for damages, equitable relief, or both.

The default, generally available immunity for all defendants is qualified immunity, which protects those who did not violate a clearly established constitutional right.[1] Defendants receive absolute immunity for some special functions, including legislative,[2] prosecutorial,[3] and judicial[4] functions, as well as other functions related to the judicial process.[5] Having qualified immunity as a fallback prevents unnecessary or unwarranted extensions of absolute immunity.[6] Absolute immunity applies only to those functions or circumstances in which the purposes and policy goals of immunity can be served only if that protection is absolute.[7] Absolute immunity is a special exception applicable only to special functions warranting heightened protection, usually where the risk and cost of civil litigation is high and where other

---

[1] Ashcroft v. al-Kidd, 131 S. Ct. 2074, 2085 (2011); Pearson v. Callahan, 555 U.S. 223, 243 (2009).

[2] Bogan v. Scott-Harris, 523 U.S. 44 (1998).

[3] Van de Kamp v. Goldstein, 555 U.S. 335 (2009).

[4] Stump v. Sparkman, 435 U.S. 349 (1978).

[5] Rehberg v. Paulk, 132 S. Ct. 1497 (2012) (grand jury complaining witness); Briscoe v. LaHue, 460 U.S. 325 (1983) (trial witness).

[6] Burns v. Reed, 500 U.S. 478, 486–87 (1991); Forrester v. White, 484 U.S. 219, 224 (1988).

[7] *Forrester*, 484 U.S. at 224.

checks on constitutional misconduct are in place.

Absolute immunity means the question of whether the privilege applies is "stripped of all considerations of intent and motive," malice, or corruption.[8] Even corrupt and vindictive conduct is privileged,[9] as is conduct done specifically for retaliatory, personal, or other unworthy purposes.[10] There is no place for judicial or jury inquiry or speculation as to underlying motive or intent, which would undermine the separation-of-powers underpinnings of the immunity itself. Immunity obviously cannot be absolute if it can be lost because indisputably immune functions were performed for improper purposes.

Immunity is an affirmative defense, thus the burden generally is on the defendant to plead and prove it.[11] Moreover, a defendant asserting immunity bears the burden of moving a case from default qualified immunity to which all officers are entitled into one of the special and limited categories of absolute immunity.[12]

The sparse language of § 1983 makes no mention of immunities. But in enacting the Ku Klux Klan Act of 1871, Congress legislated against a common law background that recognized various forms of official immunity. Absent a clear statement to the contrary, Congress must be understood as not having "impinged on a tradition so well-grounded in history and reason" as these immunities, but instead as having preserved and incorporated them into the statute.[13] The Court first recognized legislative immunity as part of § 1983, then inevitably recognized that all other common law immunities existing in 1871 similarly survived passage of the Act. Meanwhile, it was easy to superimpose judge-made immunity defenses onto the judge-made *Bivens* cause of action, particularly to maintain the appearance that *Bivens* is the federal counterpart to § 1983 and that claims and defenses available to state and federal officials are parallel.[14]

Immunity reflects a judicial balancing of public policies. Clearly, immunity undermines § 1983's goal of compensating injured persons, as well as the ancient declaration that for every right there must be a remedy. Because immunity protects defendants even if their conduct is unconstitutional, some blatant and unquestioned constitutional violations will remain unremedied. Immunity also diminishes accountability, as government and its officers may never be called to account for their constitutional misconduct. Absent liability and accountability, there is a loss or lessening of deterrence against future violations.

---

[8] Bogan v. Scott-Harris, 523 U.S. 44, 55 (1998); Mireles v. Waco, 502 U.S. 9, 13 (1991) (per curiam); Stump v. Sparkman, 435 U.S. 349, 355–56 (1978).

[9] Gravel v. United States, 408 U.S. 606, 612–13 (1972).

[10] *Bogan*, 523 U.S. at 54; Eastland v. United States Servicemen's Fund, 421 U.S. 491, 508 (1975); Bryant v. Jones, 575 F.3d 1281 (11th Cir. 2009).

[11] Crawford-El v. Britton, 523 U.S. 574, 587 (1998); *Burns*, 500 U.S. at 486–98.

[12] Buckley v. Fitzsimmons, 509 U.S. 259, 268–69 (1993); Antoine v. Byers & Anderson, 508 U.S. 429, 432 & n.4 (1993); Archie v. Lanier, 95 F.3d 438, 441 (6th Cir. 1996).

[13] Tenney v. Brandhove, 341 U.S. 367, 376 (1951).

[14] *Antoine*, 508 U.S. at 433 n.5; Butz v. Economou, 438 U.S. 478, 504 (1978); Bolin v. Story, 225 F.3d 1234, 1242 (11th Cir. 2000).

But the twin interests in compensation and deterrence are balanced against, and often yield to, "overriding considerations of public policy" that demand protection of public officials from personal liability.[15] If § 1983 is about deterrence, immunity helps prevent over-deterrence. Immunity enables officers to vigourously perform their jobs and to carry out the public's business, without fear of suit, prosecution, or personal civil or criminal liability; the core concern is protecting officials against timidity or a "chilling effect" on performance of their public duties.[16] They must remain free to act on their own convictions, exercising discretion and independent judgment in a fearless and principled manner as to the best course of conduct in furthering the public interest. The specter of suit and liability hampers that fearless decision-making, causing officers to steer unnecessarily wide of the line between lawful and unlawful conduct. Immunity also protects officers against the distractions, costs, burdens, and harassment of defending themselves in civil litigation, especially vexatious litigation by people angered by the officers' exercise of the very independent judgment we want to protect and encourage. Officials should focus their energies and attention on performing public functions in pursuit of the common good, not on defending themselves in court or wading through civil discovery. Finally, we do not want to deter qualified people from seeking public office and public positions because they fear personal liability.[17]

At the Constitutional Convention in Philadelphia in 1787, James Wilson explained federal legislative immunity in terms applicable to all officer immunities.

> To enable and encourage the Representatives of the public to discharge their trust with the firmness and success, it is indispensably necessary that he should enjoy the fullest liberty of speech, protected from the resentment of every one to whom the exercise of that liberty may cause offense.[18]

PART A
LEGISLATIVE IMMUNITY

§ 3.02 SPEECH OR DEBATE

U.S. Const. art. I, § 5, cl. 2

Each House may determine the Rules of its Proceedings, punish its Members for disorderly Behaviour; and, with the Concurrence of two thirds, expel a Member.

---

[15] *Forrester*, 484 U.S. at 224.

[16] Filarsky v. Delia, 132 S. Ct. 1657, 1665 (2012); Burns v. Reed, 500 U.S. 478, 484 (1991).

[17] Harlow v. Fitzgerald, 457 U.S. 800, 814 (1982).

[18] United States v. Brewster, 408 U.S. 501, 548 n.9 (1972) (quoting 1 THE WORKS OF JAMES WILSON 421 (R. McCloskey ed. 1967)).

U.S. Const. art. I, § 6, cl. 1

The Senators and Representatives shall receive a Compensation for their Services, to be ascertained by Law, and paid out of the Treasury of the United States. They shall in all Cases, except Treason, Felony and Breach of the Peace, be privileged from Arrest during their Attendance at the Session of their respective Houses, and in going to and returning from the same; and for any Speech or Debate in either House, they shall not be questioned in any other Place.

The Constitution establishes legislative immunity for members of Congress. Article I, § 6 provides that "for any Speech or Debate in either House, [members of Congress] shall not be questioned in any other Place."[19] This federal immunity is uniquely grounded in separation of powers, the "historic balance of three co-equal branches," and the need to protect legislators from intimidation and harassment by the historically more powerful executive.[20] Anglo-American legislative immunity originated to protect Parliament from the King; under the Constitution, it protects Congress from the President or from the Department of Justice armed with subpoenas.

Speech or Debate immunity also ensures that legislators remain free to act proactively as to the other branches. *United States v. Gravel* arose from a federal grand jury investigation into Senator Mike Gravel and his aide, Dr. Leonard Rodberg, over their conduct with respect to a classified Department of Defense document titled "History of the United States Decision-Making Process on Viet Nam Policy," more famously known as "The Pentagon Papers." The Pentagon Papers showed that military and defense officials had exaggerated and misstated issues related to U.S. escalation in Viet Nam. Senator Gravel placed the 47-volume report in the record of a Senate committee hearing and also spoke with several publishers about publishing it.[21] Both actions can be understood as legislative oversight, as a legislator (and legislative body) attempting to expose and publicize executive misconduct.

By its terms, the Speech or Debate Clause only protects members of Congress. In *Tenney v. Brandhove*, the Supreme Court recognized that state legislators enjoyed immunity at common law in 1871, an immunity that survived passage of, and was incorporated into, § 1983.[22] It necessarily follows that all legislators at all levels of government enjoy this immunity, including states,[23] municipalities,[24] and regional authorities.[25]

---

[19] U.S. Const. art. I, § 6, cl.1.

[20] Doe v. McMillan, 412 U.S. 306 (1973).

[21] Gravel v. United States, 408 U.S. 606, 608–09 (1972).

[22] Tenney v. Brandhove, 341 U.S. 367, 376 (1951).

[23] Supreme Court v. Consumers Union of United States, 446 U.S. 719 (1980); *Tenney*, 341 U.S. at 376.

[24] Bogan v. Scott-Harris, 523 U.S. 44, 46 (1998).

[25] Lake Country Estates, Inc. v. Tahoe Regional Planning Agency, 440 U.S. 391 (1979).

§ 3.03 LEVEL OF IMMUNITY

Absolute legislative immunity is exceedingly broad. It protects against any liability — criminal[26] or civil[27], for retroactive or prospective relief[28] — based on conduct to which the privilege applies. Moreover, the language of the Speech or Debate Clause — "shall not be questioned in any other Place" — means legislators cannot be made to defend themselves as a party to a judicial proceeding over conduct to which the privilege applies.[29] It even immunizes them from being made testify or answer questions about protected activities in any judicial proceeding; in fact, the constitutional dispute in *Gravel* arose when the Senator's aide was subpoenaed to testify before a grand jury and the Senator asserted immunity on a motion to quash the subpoena.[30]

Relatedly, evidence of legislative conduct is not admissible even to prove an otherwise unprivileged violation of the law. In *United States v. Brewster*, the Court held that, in prosecuting a member of Congress for accepting bribes, the government could not offer any evidence of the defendant's legislative acts, such as votes or speeches with respect to legislation, even those done in furtherance of the corrupt promises for which he accepted those bribes.[31] This did not necessarily undermine the government's ability to prosecute legislators, since it only needed to show that the defendant accepted the bribe and promised to perform some acts in exchange for a bribe, not that he actually performed those legislative acts.[32] The Court has reaffirmed this view, insisting that the privilege precludes offering evidence that mentions legislative acts already performed, but not evidence of the offering of the promise to perform future acts.[33]

In the civil context, the evidentiary privilege often implicates employment discrimination claims under the Congressional Accountability Act of 1995, which makes most federal employment discrimination statutes applicable to members of Congress and their officers and employees.[34] The D.C. Circuit first held that the Speech or Debate Clause precluded a civil action where the plaintiff's job duties were an integral part of the legislative process.[35] But it later rejected this focus on the employee's duties as "too crude a proxy" for protected activity. Instead, speech or debate precludes admission of any evidence in support of or opposition to a discrimination claim that involves legislative acts or the motivation for legislative

---

[26] United States v. Jefferson, 546 F.3d 300, 306 (4th Cir. 2008).

[27] Hutchinson v. Proxmire, 443 U.S. 111, 126 (1979); Doe v. County of Centre, 242 F.3d 437, 453–54 (3d Cir. 2001).

[28] *Supreme Court*, 446 U.S. at 733; Cmty. House, Inc. v. City of Boise, 623 F.3d 945, 959 (9th Cir. 2010).

[29] Dombrowski v. Eastland, 387 U.S. 82 (1967) (per curiam); Powell v. Ridge, 247 F.3d 520, 525 (3d Cir. 2001).

[30] Gravel v. United States, 408 U.S. 606, 660 (1972).

[31] United States v. Brewster, 408 U.S. 501 (1972).

[32] *Id.* at 526–27.

[33] United States v. Helstoski, 442 U.S. 477, 489 (1979).

[34] 2 U.S.C. § 1302.

[35] Browning v. Clerk, United States House of Representatives, 789 F.2d 923 (D.C. Cir. 1986).

acts. And to the extent the plaintiff has no other evidence with which to prove her claim, the claim fails.[36] The Tenth Circuit has adopted a similar approach.[37]

Immunity is absolute because whether the privilege applies is "stripped of all considerations of intent and motive," malice, or corruption.[38] Even corrupt and vindictive conduct is privileged,[39] as is conduct done specifically for retaliatory, personal, or other unworthy purposes.[40] There is no place for judicial inquiry or speculation as to underlying motive or intent, which would undermine the separation-of-powers underpinnings of the immunity itself. Immunity obviously cannot be absolute if it can be lost because indisputably immune conduct was performed for improper purposes.

Speech or debate immunity shares rationales with common law immunity of state and local legislators and the two are co-extensive as applied to § 1983 civil actions against state and local legislators.[41]. But common law immunity does not protect state legislators against federal criminal prosecution. Unlike the Speech or Debate Clause, common law immunity is not grounded in separation of powers or the historic balance of power between legislators and a powerful executive. And any concerns for federalism or federal/state balance raised by a federal prosecution are overcome by the Supremacy Clause, under which the actions of state legislators must yield to the dictates of federal law.[42]

§ 3.04 APPLICATION OF IMMUNITY

In *Gravel v. United States*, the Court held that absolute legislative immunity protects not only the legislator himself, but also his aides, staffers, and assistants. In modern government, members of Congress could not function without their aides, who function as legislative "alter-egos."[43] The protection accorded by the Speech or Debate Clause would "inevitably be diminished and frustrated" if not extended to legislative aides. The privilege makes no distinction between legislator and aide; if the Senator would be immune for a particular act, then his aide is immune for performing the same act.[44]

Legislative immunity protects legislators, best defined as members of a legislature. Broadly speaking, a legislature is a government body empowered to make

---

[36] Fields v. Office of Eddie Bernice Johnson, 459 F.3d 1, 11 (D.C. Cir. 2006).

[37] Bastien v. Office of Sen. Ben Nighthorse Campbell, 390 F.3d 1301 (10th Cir. 2004).

[38] Bogan v. Scott-Harris, 523 U.S. 44, 55 (1998).

[39] *Gravel*, 408 U.S. at 612–13.

[40] *Bogan*, 523 U.S. at 54; Eastland v. United States Servicemen's Fund, 421 U.S. 491, 508 (1975); Bryant v. Jones, 575 F.3d 1281 (11th Cir. 2009).

[41] *Supreme Court*, 446 U.S. at 733.

[42] U.S. Const. art. VI; United States v. Gillock, 445 U.S. 360 (1980); *see also Supreme Court*, 446 U.S. at 733.

[43] Gravel v. United States, 408 U.S. 606, 616–17 (1972).

[44] Eastland v. United States Servicemen's Fund, 421 U.S. 491, 508 (1975) (subcommittee counsel); *Gravel*, 408 U.S. at 608–10 (Senator's aide); Jeff D. v. Otter, 643 F.3d 278, 290 (9th Cir. 2011) (legislative budget analyst).

legislation — that is, to promulgate prospective rules of general applicability. A legislature is typically designated as such by the government's constituting documents and includes the full body, as well as any committee system the body uses in performing its lawmaking functions.[45] But bodies other than the designated legislature may possess organic or inherent power to legislate in a particular area. For example, state supreme courts often exercise inherent power to regulate the state bar and bench; as the only state-created body empowered to enact legal rules in that area, the court becomes a legislature and its members legislators.[46] A legislature also may delegate power to other bodies to make prospective rules in some area and those delegatees may enjoy legislative immunity.[47]

§ 3.05   SCOPE OF IMMUNITY

The scope of legislative immunity turns not on the actor, but on the "function" performed. In other words, immunity attaches not because the actor is a legislator, but because the function he performed was legislative. Thus, an executive official, such as a city mayor, enjoys legislative immunity when performing legislative functions, such as signing legislation into law.[48] Conversely, a legislative official will not enjoy legislative immunity for performing non-legislative functions.[49]

The Court has framed several connected standards for what constitutes a legislative function, for both Speech or Debate and common law privileges. Legislative functions include "anything generally done in a session of a House by one of its members in relation to the business before it."[50] It includes anything within the legitimate sphere of legislative authority or activity.[51] It includes all acts that form an "integral part of the deliberative and communicative process by which its Members participate in committee and House proceedings with respect to the consideration and passage or rejection of proposed legislation or other matters which the Constitution places within the jurisdiction of either House."[52] Stated in the negative, immunity should not extend beyond what is "essential to foreclose executive control of legislative speech or debate or associated matters."[53]

The Court expanded this functional approach in *Bogan v. Scott-Harris*, the case formally recognizing immunity for local and municipal legislators.[54] The Court explained that immunity attaches to any function that is either legislative in form ("procedurally legislative") or legislative in substance ("substantively legislative").[55]

---

[45] Supreme Court v. Consumers Union of United States, 446 U.S. 719, 733–34 (1980).

[46] *Id.* at 731, 733.

[47] *Id.* at 734; Schmidt v. Contra Costa County, 693 F.3d 1122 (9th Cir. 2012).

[48] Bogan v. Scott-Harris, 523 U.S. 44, 55 (1998).

[49] Powell v. Ridge, 247 F.3d 520, 529 n.* (3d Cir. 2001) (Roth, J., concurring).

[50] Kilbourn v. Thompson, 103 U.S. 168, 204 (1881).

[51] Rehberg v. Paulk, 132 S. Ct. 1497, 1502 (2012); *Bogan*, 523 U.S. at 54.

[52] Gravel v. United States, 408 U.S. 606, 625 (1972).

[53] *Id.* at 620.

[54] *Bogan*, 523 U.S. at 54.

[55] *Id.* at 55–56.

Considerations for what makes an act legislative include whether it involves individual, ad hoc decisions or broad policy judgments; whether it applies to a few individuals or circumstances or to the public at large; and whether it bears the "hallmarks" of traditional legislation."[56]

The plaintiff in *Bogan* was a municipal employee who had initiated internal proceedings to terminate an underling for misconduct; the underling used her political connections with several city officials to avoid being fired and ultimately to get her sanctions reduced. While this was playing out, the mayor proposed a new budget that eliminated the department of which the plaintiff was the director and sole employee. A committee of the city council approved an ordinance adopting the budget, the ordinance passed the full council, and the mayor signed it into law.[57]

The plaintiff argued that the focus should be on the substance of her claim, which challenged what amounted to the firing of one individual, ordinarily understood as an executive or administrative act. But the defendants' actions bore all the hallmarks of legislation. Proposing a budget, introducing and voting on an ordinance, and signing an ordinance into law are "quintessentially" legislative activities, at least in form. The ordinance governed a broad field in which city legislators had the power to act. It reflected discretionary policymaking decisions implicating budget priorities and the services the city would provide to the public at large. It also did more than fire a single employee in a single administrative decision; it eliminated a position and entire department in city government, which has broader prospective implications beyond the current occupant of the office.[58]

Core legislative functions obviously include writing, discussing and debating,[59] advocating or opposing,[60] introducing, voting on, and signing or vetoing[61] legislation.[62] They also include preparing, presenting, and voting on budgets, including eliminating the funding for positions or departments.[63] They may include decisions regarding condemnation of property.[64] They include speeches, reports, and written statements on the legislative record, the house floor, and in committee proceedings and records, even if the actions are immediately damaging to a particular individual[65] and even if the presentation itself is unlawful.[66] They include investigating, gathering information, and advocating in hearings and other committee and

---

[56] *Id.* at 55; Cmty. House, Inc. v. City of Boise, 623 F.3d 945, 960 (9th Cir. 2010).

[57] *Bogan*, 523 U.S. at 46–47.

[58] *Id.* at 55–56.

[59] Almonte v. City of Long Beach, 478 F.3d 100 (2d Cir. 2007).

[60] Baraka v. McGreevey, 481 F.3d 187 (3d Cir. 2007).

[61] *Bogan*, 523 U.S. at 55; Bagley v. Blagojevich, 646 F.3d 378 (7th Cir. 2011); Torres-Rivera v. Calderon-Serra, 412 F.3d 205 (1st Cir. 2005).

[62] *Bogan*, 523 U.S. at 48–49; Gravel v. United States, 408 U.S. 606 (1972); Scott v. Taylor, 405 F.3d 1251 (11th Cir. 2005); County Concrete Corp. v. Twp. of Roxbury, 442 F.3d 159 (3d Cir. 2006).

[63] *Bogan*, 523 U.S. at 55; Kensington Volunteer Fire Dep't, Inc. v. Montgomery County, 684 F.3d 462 (4th Cir. 2012); Smith v. Jefferson County Bd. of Sch. Comm'rs, 641 F.3d 197 (6th Cir. 2011) (en banc); Bryant v. Jones, 575 F.3d 1281 (11th Cir. 2009).

[64] Sable v. Myers, 563 F.3d 1120, 1126 (10th Cir. 2009).

[65] Hutchinson v. Proxmire, 443 U.S. 111 (1979); Eastland v. United States Servicemen's Fund, 421 U.S. 491 (1975); Doe v. McMillan, 412 U.S. 306 (1973).

house proceedings, as well as the processes used in those investigations, such as issuing subpoenas; legislators inform themselves through these investigations and hearings, which in turn informs debate and ultimate passage or rejection of legislation.[67] Finally, legislative functions include organizing, participating, and voting in impeachment proceedings[68] and other public meetings and hearings at which legislative business is conducted,[69] although the actual conducting of the meeting may not necessarily be legislative.[70]

On the other hand, some functions do not qualify as legislative, even if performed by a legislator or by a legislative body. Most common is administrative functions, such as decisions regarding hiring, firing, promotion, demotion, or resignation of individual employees.[71] Communicating with constituents or other members of the public also is not privileged as legislative activity; while such communication is valuable and important and even influences the ultimate legislative and deliberative processes, these are political activities and not the integral legislative functions with which immunity is concerned.[72] At times, the line between legislative and executive functions is thin, turning on whether the defendants acted with a focus on, and desire to affect, the public at large (a mark of legislative conduct) as opposed to focusing on a particular individual or particular application of the law (a mark of administrative, non-legislative conduct).[73] If a function is deemed non-legislative, default qualified immunity still may apply.[74]

§ 3.06 CHECKING LEGISLATIVE MISCONDUCT

Granting absolute immunity for legislative functions does not eliminate all checks on legislator misconduct. One obvious check is the ballot box, as legislators must regularly stand for election. More importantly, legislatures have the power to control their members, through punishment, censure, and even expulsion.[75] This explains the "in any other Place" language in the Speech or Debate Clause; a legislative body is expected to police its own members and it is in that place, not the

---

[66] Gravel v. United States, 408 U.S. 606 (1972).

[67] *Eastland*, 421 U.S. at 494–95; *McMillan*, 412 U.S. at 308; Tenney v. Brandhove, 341 U.S. 367 (1951).

[68] Larsen v. Senate of the Commonwealth, 154 F.3d 82 (3d Cir. 1998).

[69] Kensington Volunteer Fire Dep't, Inc. v. Montgomery County, 684 F.3d 462 (4th Cir. 2012); Guindon v. Twp. of Dundee, 488 F. App'x 27, 2012 U.S. App. LEXIS 10118 (6th Cir. 2012); Hogan v. Twp. of Haddon, 278 F. App'x 98, 2008 U.S. App. LEXIS 5183 (3d Cir. 2008).

[70] Sable v. Myers, 563 F.3d 1120 (10th Cir. 2009).

[71] Bogan v. Scott-Harris, 523 U.S. 44, 55–56 (1998); Bryant v. Jones, 575 F.3d 1281 (11th Cir. 2009); Fields v. Office of Eddie Bernice Johnson, 459 F.3d 1 (D.C. Cir. 2006); Bastien v. Office of Sen. Ben Nighthorse Campbell, 390 F.3d 1301 (10th Cir. 2004); Harhay v. Town of Ellington Bd. of Educ., 323 F.3d 206 (2d Cir. 2003).

[72] *Hutchinson*, 443 U.S. at 133; *Gravel*, 408 U.S. at 625–26.

[73] Cmty. House, Inc. v. City of Boise, 623 F.3d 945 (9th Cir. 2010); Kaahumanu v. County of Maui, 315 F.3d 1215 (9th Cir. 2003); *but see* Sable v. Myers, 563 F.3d 1120 (10th Cir. 2009) (condemnation of particular property by ordinance is legislative).

[74] *Harhay*, 323 F. 3d at 210–11; *infra* Ch. 3, Part C.

[75] U.S. Const. art. I, § 5, cl. 2; Powell v. McCormack, 395 U.S. 486 (1969).

courts, that the allegedly wrongful actions of members can and will be questioned and dealt with appropriately.

Nor does the speech or debate evidentiary privilege preclude all prosecutions of federal legislators; while it makes the government's job more difficult, the very purpose of immunity is to limit the extent to which the executive can pursue legislators or inquire into their legislative conduct in the courts.[76] And prosecutors know that the prohibition extends to evidence of past legislative acts but not to the promises or guarantees of future acts,[77] which allows room for appropriate litigation.

In fact, legislative immunity may be the defense that least interferes with the goals of compensation and deterrence underlying constitutional litigation. It generally does not deprive an injured plaintiff of any judicial remedy, but in most cases simply redirects litigation to a different, more appropriate defendant performing different functions. For example, a plaintiff threatened with enforcement of an unconstitutional law or policy cannot sue the legislators who enacted the law, who enjoy legislative immunity; she instead sues the executive officer charged with executing or enforcing that unconstitutional law, policy, or legislative command.[78]

This is true even if litigation is redirected to the same person or entity performing a different function. In *Supreme Court of Virginia v. Consumers Union of the United States*, plaintiffs challenged the constitutionality of bar regulations prohibiting attorney advertising; the state supreme court was the body empowered under state law both to promulgate and to enforce those regulations. A federal court could not enjoin the court from enacting the regulations, which was a core legislative function protected by legislative immunity, but it could enjoin the state supreme court from enforcing those regulations, an executive function to which legislative immunity does not attach.[79] Similar issues often arise in zoning cases, where enactment of zoning legislation is unquestionably legislative and privileged, but decisions on use permits for particular property are not, even when the same entity performs both functions.[80]

In some cases, of course, the operation of the legislative process itself causes the injury. Although this might leave plaintiffs without a remedy in many cases, it is an inevitable consequence of the balancing inherent in legislative immunity. For example, there is no way the plaintiff in *Bogan* could get her job back or recover any monetary or other remedy in federal court; although her injury was the loss of her job, it was done not by a singular firing but through a legislative process for which all the defendants involved were absolutely immune.[81] The same is true for an

---

[76] United States v. Helstoski, 442 U.S. 477, 488–89 (1979).

[77] *Id.* at 488; United States v. Brewster, 408 U.S. 501 (1972).

[78] *Powell*, 395 U.S. at 493; Dombrowski v. Eastland, 387 U.S. 82 (1967) (per curiam); Kaahumanu v. County of Maui, 315 F.3d 1215 (9th Cir. 2003); Scott v. Taylor, 405 F.3d 1251 (11th Cir. 2005).

[79] Supreme Court v. Consumers Union of United States, 446 U.S. 719 (1980).

[80] *Kaahumanu*, 315 F.3d at 1224; Brown v. Bryan County, 219 F.3d 450 (5th Cir. 2000); Jaggers v. City of Alexandria, 2009 U.S. App. LEXIS 2048 (6th Cir. Feb. 2, 2009).

[81] *Bogan v. Scott-Harris*, 523 U.S. 44, 47, 55–56 (1998).

official removed from office via impeachment proceedings conducted by a state legislature.[82]

PART B
JUDICIAL PROCESS IMMUNITIES

§ 3.07 OVERVIEW AND CONNECTIONS

All the primary actors working within the judicial phase of the criminal justice system enjoy a similarly strong form of absolute immunity. The Supreme Court first recognized judicial immunity.[83] Lower courts then identified a derivative, quasi-judicial immunity protecting prosecutors,[84] while several justices argued for independent prosecutorial immunity, relying in part on the strong analogy between immunity for the prosecutor and immunity for the judge.[85] Ultimately, the Supreme Court firmly recognized immunity for prosecutors as prosecutors,[86] as well as for witnesses at trial[87] and before the grand jury.[88] Like non-federal legislative immunity, judicial-process immunities originate in common law and are deemed to have survived passage of, and been incorporated into, the 1871 Act. These immunities apply to § 1983 actions arising from state judicial proceedings[89] and to *Bivens* actions against actors in federal judicial proceedings.[90]

Prosecutorial and judicial immunities both are designed to protect the proper functioning of the legal system and both are justified by the existence of systemic processes for remedying constitutional violations that obviate the need for civil liability as a remedial mechanism. First, judges and prosecutors work within a self-regulating and self-correcting adjudicative system. The appellate process remains the primary means of identifying and reversing constitutional errors in litigation; the right to appeal a constitutionally erroneous ruling or constitutionally invalid litigation conduct enables individuals to protect and vindicate their rights without resorting to damages litigation.[91] Second, prosecutors (as licensed attorneys) are subject to self-regulation through ethics rules and systems of professional responsibility and discipline.[92] That bar complaints are rarely, if ever, pursued or successful in cases of prosecutorial misconduct does not change this

---

[82] Larsen v. Senate of Commonwealth, 154 F.3d 82 (3d Cir. 1998).

[83] Pierson v. Ray, 386 U.S. 547 (1967).

[84] Imbler v. Pachtman, 424 U.S. 409 (1976).

[85] *Id.* at 438 (White, J., concurring).

[86] Burns v. Reed, 500 U.S. 478 (1991); *Imbler*, 424 U.S. at 431.

[87] Briscoe v. LaHue, 460 U.S. 325 (1983).

[88] Rehberg v. Paulk, 132 S. Ct. 1497 (2012).

[89] Antoine v. Byers & Anderson, 508 U.S. 429, 433 n.5 (1993).

[90] Koubriti v. Convertino, 593 F.3d 459 (6th Cir. 2010).

[91] *See* Forrester v. White, 484 U.S. 219 (1988); Adams v. Hanson, 656 F.3d 397, 410–11 (6th Cir. 2011).

[92] Imbler v. Pachtman, 424 U.S. 409 (1976); Pierson v. Ray, 386 U.S. 547 (1967); Dawson v. Newman, 419 F.3d 656 (7th Cir. 2005).

analysis.[93] Prosecutors and judges also remain subject to state and federal criminal prosecution, even for conduct that might be immune from civil suit.[94]

Third, there is an electoral check, direct or indirect. Many state judges are elected or subject to retention elections. Lead prosecutors at the local level are generally elected, or at least are appointed by officials who are elected, allowing for some popular check on the functioning of the prosecutor's office.

Finally, concerns for the independence of the judicial system uniquely support immunity for actors within the judicial process. At least one party to a case always walks away unhappy, disgruntled, or in disagreement with an adjudicative outcome. Convicted defendants readily believe their convictions resulted from witness, jury, judicial, attorney, or prosecutorial misconduct (likely some combination of all). Civil litigation for damages by an unhappy defeated litigant is inevitable in virtually every case; even if most claims would be frivolous, § 1983 and *Bivens* litigation would become a *de facto* appellate review process. The judicial system only can function if judges, jurors, prosecutors, witnesses, and other actors exercise their best independent judgment through fearless, principled advocacy and decisionmaking, without fear or timidity from the threat or risk of later suits or personal liability.[95]

We can understand judicial process immunities as of a piece with the Court's decision that public defenders do not act under color of state law and thus cannot be liable for constitutional damages under § 1983.[96] Together they ensure that all primary actors within the criminal judicial process — judge, prosecutor, and defense counsel — exercise their best professional judgment free from fear of civil litigation and liability allowing the judicial process the space to self-correct errors.

§ 3.08 JUDICIAL IMMUNITY

[1] Scope of Immunity

The Court has adopted a functional approach to judicial immunity; immunity attaches only to "truly judicial acts,"[97] not to acts that just happen to have been performed by a judge.

---

[93] Angela J. Davis, *When Good Prosecutors Go Bad, in* INSTITUTIONAL FAILURES: DUKE LACROSSE, UNIVERSITIES, THE NEWS MEDIA, AND THE LEGAL SYSTEM 23 (Howard M. Wasserman ed., 2011); Sam Kamin, *Duke Lacrosse, Prosecutorial Misconduct, and the Limits of the Civil Justice System, in* INSTITUTIONAL FAILURES: DUKE LACROSSE, UNIVERSITIES, THE NEWS MEDIA, AND THE LEGAL SYSTEM 41 (Howard M. Wasserman ed., 2011); Fred C. Zacharias & Bruce A. Green, *The Duty to Avoid Wrongful Convictions: A Thought Experiment in the Regulation of Prosecutors*, 89 B.U. L. REV. 1 (2009).

[94] Briscoe v. LaHue, 460 U.S. 325, 345 n.32 (1983); *Imbler*, 424 U.S. at 429; Archie v. Lanier, 95 F.3d 438, 441 (6th Cir. 1996).

[95] Mireles v. Waco, 502 U.S. 9, 10 (1991) (per curiam); *Forrester*, 484 U.S. at 226–27; Stump v. Sparkman, 435 U.S. 349, 363 (1978); *Pierson*, 386 U.S. at 554; Milstein v. Cooley, 257 F.3d 1004 (9th Cir. 2001).

[96] Polk County v. Dodson, 454 U.S. 312 (1981); *supra* § 2.03[5].

[97] Forrester v. White, 484 U.S. 219, 227 (1988).

A judicial act is one normally performed by a judge as a judge in the course of resolving legal and factual disputes between parties who have invoked the court's jurisdiction.[98] It is not the act itself but the nature and function of the act that matters, meaning courts "look to the particular act's relation to a general function normally performed by a judge."[99] This considers the extent to which an act entails discretionary decisions involving independent exercise of learned legal judgment,[100] as well as the parties' expectations and whether they understand that they are dealing with a judge in her judicial capacity.[101]

We also can understand judicial acts in relation to a judge's adjudicative authority. This approach distinguishes between acts performed in excess of jurisdiction and acts committed in the clear or complete absence of jurisdiction.[102] Judges do not enjoy absolute immunity for acts performed in the complete absence of jurisdiction — acts for which there is no judicial power and no colorable claim that jurisdiction is present, such that the act is no different than if a non-judge had done the same thing. For example, a probate judge trying a criminal case acts in the clear absence of jurisdiction,[103] just as would a non-judge in trying a criminal case. On the other hand, judges do enjoy absolute immunity for acts in excess of jurisdiction, which typically involves exercising legitimate judicial authority, but in a way that goes beyond the scope of that authority. A judge convicting a defendant of a non-existent crime merely acts in excess of jurisdiction, as does a judge who violates state rules regarding procedure or recusal in the course of adjudicating a matter.[104]

Judicial functions include issuing orders and judgments granting or denying litigants' requests for relief,[105] making decisions to grant or deny motions,[106] refusing to hear or decide an issue,[107] or deciding to continue hearing a case, even where doing so violates state rules as to recusal.[108] These functions enjoy absolute immunity even when made informally or *ex parte*, without hearing from a party, or absent the formal trappings of judicial proceedings.[109] Presiding in court is a judicial function, as is issuing any orders to ensure those proceedings function appropriately.[110] So is appointing and removing counsel for indigent defendants[111]

---

[98] Mireles v. Waco, 502 U.S. 9, 12 (1991) (per curiam); Richman v. Sheahan, 270 F.3d 430, 436–37 (7th Cir. 2001).

[99] *Mireles*, 502 U.S. at 13.

[100] Stump v. Sparkman, 435 U.S. 349, 362 (1978); *Richman*, 270 F.3d at 436.

[101] *Stump*, 435 U.S. at 362.

[102] *Stump*, 435 U.S. at 356–57.

[103] *Stump*, 435 U.S. at 356–57.

[104] *Stump*, 435 U.S. at 356; Savoie v. Martin, 673 F.3d 488 (6th Cir. 2012); Gallas v. Supreme Court, 211 F.3d 760 (3d Cir. 2000).

[105] *Stump*, 435 U.S. at 362; Leech v. DeWeese, 689 F.3d 538 (6th Cir. 2012).

[106] Capogrosso v. Supreme Court of N.J., 588 F.3d 180 (3d Cir. 2009).

[107] Sherman v. Babbitt, 772 F.2d 1476 (9th Cir. 1985).

[108] Savoie v. Martin, 673 F.3d 488 (6th Cir. 2012).

[109] *Stump*, 435 U.S. at 360; Capogrosso v. Supreme Court of N.J., 588 F.3d 180 (3d Cir. 2009).

[110] Mireles v. Waco, 502 U.S. 9 (1991) (per curiam).

and awarding attorneys' fees to assigned counsel in a particular case.[112]

Judicial immunity does not protect the range of administrative, ministerial, executive, or legislative functions performed by judges that, while essential to the functioning of the judicial system, are not judicial. Judges instead might enjoy absolute legislative immunity for legislative acts they are authorized to perform[113] or, more likely, default qualified immunity for ministerial or administrative acts.[114]

Courts have identified a number of lines to demarcate judicial acts from administrative acts.

One distinguishes between acts requiring exercise of judicial discretion from purely ministerial acts that could be entrusted to a non-judge or to someone without judicial training.[115] This distinction connects with immunity's goal of preserving independent judicial decisionmaking; if the act at issue does not implicate that decisionmaking, judicial immunity is unwarranted. Most obviously, a judge acts in an administrative, thus non-judicial, capacity in making employment and supervisory decisions with respect to even essential court personnel.[116]

A second, more disputed line distinguishes decisions made in the course of resolving a single case from decisions affecting issues in a large number of cases, with only the former treated as judicial functions entitled to absolute immunity.[117]

A third category of non-judicial function to which absolute immunity should not attach involves individual, often personally motivated acts by a person who happens to be a judge but which have nothing to do with the operation or functioning of the judicial system. Importantly, however, labeling a function non-judicial does not mean a judge does not act under color of law, as broadly defined under § 1983 and *Monroe v. Pape*. Where a judge commits a non-judicial act but uses the trappings or apparent authority of the judicial office to make his misconduct possible, he acts under color of law and is subject to a § 1983 suit, but cannot claim judicial immunity.[118]

The Supreme Court's most controversial application of judicial immunity came in *Stump v. Sparkman*. As a teen, the plaintiff was sterilized pursuant to a court order obtained by her mother; the mother submitted a handwritten affidavit and petition to the judge *ex parte* in chambers, which the judge signed. No formal

---

[111] Roth v. King, 449 F.3d 1272 (D.C. Cir. 2006).

[112] Bliven v. Hunt, 579 F.3d 204 (2d Cir. 2009).

[113] Supreme Court v. Consumers Union of United States, 446 U.S. 719 (1980).

[114] Brown v. Griesenauer, 970 F.2d 431, 436 (8th Cir. 1992).

[115] Atherton v. D.C. Office of the Mayor, 567 F.3d 672, 685 (D.C. Cir. 2009).

[116] *Forrester*, 484 U.S. at 220 (judge fired probation officer); Meek v. County of Riverside, 183 F.3d 962 (9th Cir. 1999) (judge fired court commissioner).

[117] *Compare* Davis v. Tarrant County, Tex., 565 F.3d 214 (5th Cir. 2009) (refusal to include attorney on wheel for court appointments was judicial), *and* Roth v. King, 449 F.3d 1272 (D.C. Cir. 2006) (devising and implementing system for appointment of attorneys involved judges acting in "judicial capacity"), *with* Bliven v. Hunt, 579 F.3d 204 (2d Cir. 2009), *and* Mitchell v. Fishbein, 377 F.3d 157 (2d Cir. 2004) (maintenance of list of attorneys for court appointments was administrative); *infra* § 3.10[2].

[118] Archie v. Lanier, 95 F.3d 438 (6th Cir. 1996); *supra* § 2.03.

process attended the decision; there was no docket entry, no formal petition, no hearing, and no representation appointed for the daughter. The girl was told that she was going to the hospital to have her appendix removed, not to have a tubal ligation.[119] As a married adult seeking to become pregnant, the daughter and her husband brought a § 1983 action against the judge, the girl's mother, the mother's lawyer, and the doctors who performed the surgery.

The Supreme Court held that the judge was absolutely immune from suit. Taking cognizance of a legal and factual issue and making a ruling on it is what judges do as judges. The informality of the proceeding, and the absence of the ordinary attributes of a judicial proceeding, is not conclusive; judges often act *ex parte*, and the decision granting this petition was no different.[120] The Court defined the function at issue, generally as "approv[ing] petitions," which is indisputably judicial, not at the more-specific level of the specific content of the particular petition.[121] Moreover, the judge did not act in the "clear absence" of jurisdiction; although he lacked positive authority to grant a petition ordering sterilization, as a judge serving on a state court of general jurisdiction he presumptively had authority to act on any matter presented to him unless he was affirmatively divested of jurisdiction over that area of the law.[122]

The dissent's response was less about the judicial nature of the act than about its litigation context (or lack thereof). There was no case; no litigants; no notice, representation, or opportunity for the young girl to be heard; no opportunity for appeal; and "not even the pretext of principled decisionmaking,"[123] The "total absence of *any* of these normal attributes of a judicial proceeding" meant this could not be a judicial act.[124] Given this informality, none of the features justifying judicial immunity were present, because the internal systemic checks on constitutional error, particularly appellate review, were unavailable.

[2] Application of Immunity

While judicial immunity protects judges, courts also have accorded absolute quasi-judicial immunity to non-judicial actors performing judicial functions. The latter is roughly co-extensive with judicial immunity, such that a non-judicial actor is immune for performing functions for which a judge would be immune.[125]

Quasi-judicial immunity applies in two broad contexts. First it protects non-judges working within non-judicial bodies but performing functions that are "functionally comparable" to the work of judges within those bodies. The primary example is hearing officers making adjudicative decisions in executive,

---

[119] *Stump*, 435 U.S. at 351–53, 360.

[120] *Id.* at 363 n.12.

[121] *Id.* at 362 & n.11.

[122] *Id.* at 362–63.

[123] *Id.* at 368–69 (Stewart, J., dissenting).

[124] *Id.* at 369 (Stewart, J., dissenting) (emphasis in original).

[125] Butz v. Economou, 438 U.S. 478, 512–13 (1978).

administrative, and agency proceedings.[126] Such hearing officers function like judges in all respects relevant to the policies of immunity — they hear and resolve legal and factual issues through formal processes; they exercise independent judgment that must be protected against outside pressures such as fear of liability; one or both parties are likely to be disappointed with case outcomes; and the hearing system incorporates structural safeguards allowing for review and correction of error.[127] This immunity extends to decisionmakers in federal agencies[128] local zoning boards,[129] parole boards,[130] state gaming boards,[131] state bar proceedings,[132] and state medical boards.[133]

Second, quasi-judicial immunity protects the array of non-judges working alongside judges, performing functions (or helping judges perform functions) integral to the operation of the judicial system, where those functions require exercise of judicial discretion or judgment.[134] Absolute immunity thus extends to jurors and grand jurors,[135] law clerks assisting the judge in resolving cases,[136] a court-appointed special master in a probate case,[137] the clerk of court entering a default judgment under the rules of procedure,[138] or the clerk of court preparing the record on appeal.[139] It applies to guardians *ad litem* appointed by the court to investigate, gather information, and make recommendations to the judge in family and domestic matters,[140] as well as to other court-appointed experts.[141] It also protects those who perform particular acts at the express command of the judge.[142]

---

[126] *Id.* at 513.

[127] *Id.*

[128] *Id.*

[129] Dotzel v. Ashbridge, 438 F.3d 320 (3d Cir. 2006).

[130] Hart v. Hodges, 587 F.3d 1288 (11th Cir. 2009); Wilson v. Kelkhoff, 86 F.3d 1438 (7th Cir. 1996).

[131] Keystone Redevelopment Partners, LLC v. Decker, 631 F.3d 89 (3d Cir. 2011).

[132] Hirsh v. Justices of the Supreme Court, 67 F.3d 708 (9th Cir. 1995) (Bar Court adjudicating attorney disciplinary cases).

[133] Mishler v. Clift, 678 F.3d 737 (9th Cir. 2012).

[134] Antoine v. Byers & Anderson, 508 U.S. 429, 436–37 (1993); Snyder v. Nolen, 380 F.3d 279, 287–88 (7th Cir. 2004).

[135] Imbler v. Pachtman, 424 U.S. 409 (1976); DeCamp v. Douglas County Franklin Grand Jury, 978 F.2d 1047 (8th Cir.1992); Freeze v. Griffith, 849 F.2d 172 (5th Cir. 1988) (per curiam).

[136] Trackwell v. United States Gov't, 472 F.3d 1242 (10th Cir. 2007); Oliva v. Heller, 839 F.2d 37 (2d Cir. 1988).

[137] Nystedt v. Nigro, 700 F.3d 25 (1st Cir. 2012).

[138] Lundahl v. Zimmer, 296 F.3d 936 (10th Cir. 2002).

[139] Florance v. Buchmeyer, 500 F. Supp. 2d 618, 643 (N.D. Tex. 2007).

[140] Hughes v. Long, 242 F.3d 121 (3d Cir. 2001); Cok v. Consentino, 876 F.2d 1 (1st Cir. 1989); Meyers v. Contra Costa County Dep't of Social Services, 812 F.2d 1154 (9th Cir. 1987).

[141] *Hughes*, 242 F.3d at 126; McArdle v. Tronetti, 961 F.2d 1083 (3d Cir. 1992); Moses v. Parwatikar, 813 F.2d 891 (8th Cir. 1987).

[142] Stein v. Disciplinary Bd., 520 F.3d 1183 (10th Cir. 2008); Snyder v. Nolen, 380 F.3d 279, 287 (7th Cir. 2004); Richman v. Sheahan, 270 F.3d 430 (7th Cir. 2001); Gallas v. Supreme Court, 211 F.3d 760 (3d Cir. 2000); Florance v. Buchmeyer, 500 F. Supp. 2d 618 (N.D. Tex. 2007).

On the other hand, quasi-judicial immunity does not extend to non-discretionary functions which do not require exercise of judicial knowledge. This includes court reporters preparing transcripts,[143] the clerk of court filing[144] or refusing to file[145] otherwise proper papers in a legal action, and the clerk interfering with sending a formal notice of entry of judgment.[146]

[3] Level of Immunity

Where applicable, judicial (and quasi-judicial) immunity is absolute. It protects judges even when their conduct is malicious, corrupt, or done with an improper motive, and regardless of how obviously wrong or unlawful the conduct.[147] It also is deemed immunity from suit — immunity from having to be a party to litigation and from having to deal with the burdens, costs, and distractions of litigation — not merely immunity against ultimate liability.[148]

Judicial immunity protects judges from civil actions for damages,[149] but not from criminal prosecution.[150] In *Pulliam v. Allen*, the Supreme Court held that judicial immunity also did not protect judges from civil actions seeking injunctive relief.[151] Although at common law there was no such thing as an injunction against a judge, there did exist the analogous practice of the King's Bench issuing prerogative writs (such as prohibition and mandamus) to compel inferior-court judges to prospectively act or refrain from acting. This practice developed alongside common law judicial immunity. The judicial immunity incorporated into § 1 of the Ku Klux Klan Act thus was limited by judges' amenability to prospective relief of various forms.[152] And given Congress' unique concerns in 1871 with the ineffectiveness of state judges in protecting federal rights, it makes sense that judges remain subject to prospective checks on constitutional misconduct.[153]

Pulliam was limited (although not overruled) by the Federal Courts Improvement Act of 1996,[154] which added a new clause to the basic § 1983 cause of action: "except that in any action brought against a judicial officer for an act or omission taken in such officer's judicial capacity, injunctive relief shall not be granted unless a declaratory decree was violated or declaratory relief was

---

[143] Antoine v. Byers & Anderson, 508 U.S. 429 (1993).

[144] Maness v. Dist. Court, 495 F.3d 943 (8th Cir. 2007).

[145] Snyder v. Nolen, 380 F.3d 279 (7th Cir. 2004).

[146] Lowe v. Letsinger, 772 F.2d 308 (7th Cir. 1985).

[147] Forrester v. White, 484 U.S. 219, 227 (1988); Stump v. Sparkman, 435 U.S. 349, 356–57 (1978).

[148] Mireles v. Waco, 502 U.S. 9, 11 (1991) (per curiam); Keystone Redevelopment Partners, LLC v. Decker, 631 F.3d 89, 101 (3d Cir. 2011); Dawson v. Newman, 419 F.3d 656, 660–61 (7th Cir. 2005).

[149] Pulliam v. Allen, 466 U.S. 522, 543 (1984).

[150] Imbler v. Pachtman, 424 U.S. 409, 429 (1976) (citing O'Shea v. Littleton, 414 U.S. 488, 503 (1974)).

[151] *Pulliam*, 466 U.S. at 541–42. The core issue in *Pulliam* was whether, having enjoined a state court judge from continuing an unconstitutional practice, the court could award attorney's fees against the judge; the propriety of attorney's fees depended on the propriety of the injunction. *Id.* at 527–28.

[152] *Id.* at 529–30.

[153] *Id.* at 539–40.

[154] Federal Courts Improvement Act of 1996, Pub. L. No. 104-317, 110 Stat. 3847 (1996).

unavailable."[155] This statutory change means a plaintiff cannot immediately obtain injunctive relief that prohibits a judge from acting in a judicial capacity (from performing functions to which judicial immunity would otherwise attach). The plaintiff must first seek a declaration that the judge's conduct violates the Constitution; only if the declaratory judgment is obtained and ignored, or if such remedy is inadequate at the outset, will the plaintiff then be able to obtain an injunction.[156]

The new clause imposes a new burden on the plaintiff challenging judicial functions; she cannot proceed directly to injunctive relief, but must seek declaratory relief first. But this limitation does not change *Pulliam*'s underlying point that judicial immunity does not bar § 1983 actions seeking prospective relief.

[4] Shifting the focus of litigation

An act does not morph from "judicial" to "executive" because it is carried out by executive officers, since that is how most judicial orders are enforced.[157] We instead distinguish civil actions challenging the judge's order, to which judicial immunity attaches, from civil actions challenging execution of the judge's order by an executive officer, to which it does not.[158] The result is that the judge enjoys absolute immunity for issuing the order (a judicial function), but executive officers do not enjoy absolute immunity for carrying out the order (a non-judicial function).[159] As with legislative immunity, shifts the litigation focus onto the executive officers charged with carrying out the decree.

In *Mireles v. Waco*, a judge ordered police officers to " 'forcibly and with excessive force seize' " and bring to the courtroom a public defender, who was waiting to appear in another courtroom in the building. The Supreme Court held that the judge enjoyed absolute immunity because the plaintiff, brought into the courtroom for a pending case, was dealing with the defendant as a judge. Moreover, stripped of the improper direction to use excessive force, ordering court officers to bring counsel before the court to handle a pending matter is a function generally performed by a judge.[160] But the plaintiff also sued the police officers, alleging that they used excessive force in carrying out the order, including dragging him backwards from another courtroom, slamming him through the swinging doors and gates in Judge Mireles' courtroom, and swearing at him and calling him offensive names.[161] A plaintiff can pursue claims against the officers

---

[155] 42 U.S.C. § 1983 (as amended by Federal Courts Improvement Act of 1996, Pub. L. No. 104-317, 110 Stat. 3847 (1996)).

[156] Brandon E. ex rel. Listenbee v. Reynolds, 201 F.3d 194, 197–98 (3d Cir. 2000); 28 U.S.C. §§ 2201–2202. A fuller discussion of the distinctions and connections between injunctive and declaratory relief appears *infra* Ch. 6 and Ch. 7.

[157] Mireles v. Waco, 502 U.S. 9, 13 (1991) (per curiam).

[158] Snyder v. Nolen, 380 F.3d 279 (7th Cir. 2004); Richman v. Sheahan, 270 F.3d 430 (7th Cir. 2001).

[159] *Richman*, 270 F.3d at 436, 439.

[160] *Mireles*, 502 U.S. at 10, 12–13.

[161] *Id.* at 10.

who cannot assert absolute immunity.[162]

A different, albeit less successful, example of shifting litigation targets comes in the follow-up to *Stump v. Sparkman*. The district court had initially held that, if the judge was immune and thus not liable for his acts, the remaining private defendants could not be liable because they did not act under color of state law.[163] On remand from the Supreme Court's decision that the judge was immune, the Seventh Circuit affirmed that portion of the district court's original decision and ordered dismissal of the remaining claims.[164] One year later (too late to help the plaintiff, of course), the Supreme Court recognized that private actors who conspire with a judge to violate the Constitution do act under color of law and are subject to suit under § 1983, even if the judge is absolutely immune.[165]

[5] Judicial Immunity Puzzle

Judge Talmadge Littlejohn, a state chancery court judge in Mississippi, begins each session of court by requiring everyone present to stand and recite the Pledge of Allegiance. When one attorney refuses to do so, the judge holds him in contempt of court and has him jailed (by the bailiff) for several hours. Requiring the attorney to stand and recite the Pledge violates the First Amendment, thus so does the contempt order. The judge ultimately withdraws the contempt citation, recognizes that he violated the attorney's rights, and agrees to change his courtroom practices to "respect and protect the First Amendment rights of anyone who refrains from reciting the pledge in his courtroom." Judicial ethics charges also are filed; Judge Littlejohn is found to have violated state rules and is given a public reprimand and ordered to pay $100 in costs.[166]

Imagine the attorney files a § 1983 damages action against Judge Littlejohn, alleging a violation of his First Amendment rights and requesting damages. Consider whether the judge is entitled to judicial immunity under the following circumstances.

1. *The actual facts described above.*

2. *The same basic facts, except that rather than holding the attorney in contempt, the judge orders the bailiff to "do whatever you have to do — grab him, pull him, whatever — to make him stand up and recite the Pledge."*

3. *The same basic facts, except that rather than holding the attorney in contempt the judge orders the bailiff to Taser the attorney for failing stand and recite the Pledge.*

---

[162] *Richman*, 270 F.3d at 437–39 (refusing to deny remedy in action against those who enforce judicial order).

[163] Stump v. Sparkman, 435 U.S. 349, 354 (1978).

[164] Sparkman v. McFarlin, 601 F.2d 261 (7th Cir. 1979) (en banc) (per curiam).

[165] Dennis v. Sparks, 449 U.S. 24 (1980).

[166] *Inquiry Concerning a Judge*, MISSISSIPPI COMMISSION ON JUDICIAL PERFORMANCE, Nov. 30, 2010, *available at* courts.ms.gov/Images/Opinions/CO70311.pdf.

4. *The same basic facts, except that rather than holding the attorney in contempt, the judge himself Tasers the attorney for failing to stand and recite the Pledge.*

§ 3.09 PROSECUTORIAL IMMUNITY

[1] Scope of Immunity

As with all absolute immunities, prosecutorial immunity is defined by function, not actor. It protects the prosecutor acting as an "advocate for the State," performing functions "intimately associated with the judicial phase of the criminal process."[167] It protects all "acts undertaken by a prosecutor in preparing for the initiation of judicial proceedings or for trial, and which occur in the course of his role as an advocate."[168] For all other, non-advocate functions, qualified immunity affords sufficient protection, even if the actor is a prosecutor.[169] As always, the burden is on the party seeking absolute immunity to show that it is necessary to protect the function in question and that more-limited qualified immunity is insufficient.[170]

Immune prosecutorial functions include initiating and pursuing prosecution[171]and appearing in court[172] or before a grand jury[173] to present evidence or testimony, even where that testimony is perjured or otherwise false.[174] It also protects out-of-court preparation necessary for in-court presentations.[175]

Prosecutorial immunity is absolute where it applies, again without inquiry as to the prosecutor's motive or state of mind. Thus, knowingly and willfully presenting false or fabricated evidence or knowingly suborning perjury in a judicial proceeding enjoys immunity,[176] as does knowingly suppressing or failing to disclose exculpatory material to the defense when such disclosures are required in preparing for or conducting a trial.[177]

Like judicial immunity, prosecutorial immunity guards the vigorous exercise of independent prosecutorial and legal judgment within a proper functioning judicial

---

[167] Burns v. Reed, 500 U.S. 478, 486 (1991); Imbler v. Pachtman, 424 U.S. 409, 430 (1976).

[168] Buckley v. Fitzsimmons, 509 U.S. 259, 273 (1993).

[169] *Id.* at 268–69; Harris v. Bornhorst, 513 F.3d 503, 504 (6th Cir. 2008).

[170] *Buckley,* 509 U.S. at 269.

[171] *Burns,* 500 U.S. at 486.

[172] Kalina v. Fletcher, 522 U.S. 118, 125–26 (1997).

[173] *Burns,* 500 U.S. at 485.

[174] *Id.; Imbler,* 424 U.S. at 439.

[175] *Kalina,* 522 U.S. at 125; Higgason v. Stephens, 288 F.3d 868 (6th Cir. 2002).

[176] *Buckley,* 509 U.S. at 270; *Imbler,* 424 U.S. at 439.

[177] Fields v. Wharrie, 672 F.3d 505 (7th Cir. 2012); Koubriti v. Convertino, 593 F.3d 459 (6th Cir. 2010); Cousin v. Small, 325 F.3d 627 (5th Cir. 2003) (per curiam); *see also* Van de Kamp v. Goldstein, 555 U.S. 335, 343 (2009) (assuming, without deciding, that immunity applies to disclosure obligations).

process.[178] It thus protects only acts requiring professional legal judgment within the confines and protections of the prosecutorial process. For example, in *Kalina v. Fletcher*, a deputy prosecutor filed three documents in asking the court for an arrest warrant: (1) an information charging an individual with burglary; (2) a petition for an arrest warrant; and (3) a "certification for a determination of probable cause"; the last document was signed by the deputy prosecutor, summarized the evidence, and vouched for the truth of the facts asserted. The Supreme Court held that the prosecutor was absolutely immune for preparing the documents, reviewing the evidence in support, and presenting them to the Court. But she was not immune for the allegedly false statements of fact contained in the third document; in making factual assertions and vouching for their truthfulness, the prosecutor was acting as a fact witness, not a lawyer, and therefore was not exercising the professional judgment that prosecutorial immunity is designed to protect.[179]

Similarly, a prosecutor is not absolutely immune for statements made to the media during the course of an investigation or during judicial proceedings. While communicating with the press and the public is a vital public function, it is not a prosecutorial function and not a function performed as an advocate for the state within the judicial phase of the criminal process.[180]

Importantly, however, prosecutors do more than prosecute cases in court. Prosecutors also routinely work with law enforcement and police investigators in gathering, organizing, evaluating, understanding, and piecing together evidence and information, all prior to the initiation of judicial proceedings. When prosecutors perform the same investigative functions as police officers, they should receive the same immunity; because police only enjoy qualified immunity for their investigative functions, so should prosecutors.[181] This makes sense in light of prosecutorial immunity's concern with protecting legal judgment. When the officer is exercising the same judgment as police officers rather than specialized legal judgment, the need for special, heightened immunity vanishes.

Courts thus distinguish prosecutorial functions, which are unique to prosecutors, from investigative functions, which are performed by many different officers; absolute immunity attaches only to the former.[182] Prosecutors do not enjoy absolute immunity for providing advice to police about how to handle a suspect during the course of an investigation and prior to initiation of judicial proceedings.[183] Neither police nor prosecutors enjoy absolute immunity for fabricating evidence while investigating a case.[184] And while prosecutors enjoy absolute immunity for issuing subpoenas for an already-convened grand jury, they

[178] *Van de Kamp*, 555 U.S. at 343; Kalina v. Fletcher, 522 U.S. 118, 127 (1997); *Imbler*, 424 U.S. at 422–23.

[179] *Kalina*, 522 U.S. at 120–22, 130–31.

[180] *Buckley*, 509 U.S. at 278.

[181] *Id.* at 273.

[182] *Buckley*, 509 U.S. at 270; Hart v. Hodges, 587 F.3d 1288 (11th Cir. 2009).

[183] *Burns*, 500 U.S. at 491; Lacey v. Maricopa County, 693 F.3d 896 (9th Cir. 2012).

[184] Whitlock v. Brown, 596 F.3d 406, 410 (7th Cir. 2010).

do not enjoy absolute immunity for issuing subpoenas outside formal judicial processes and away from the judicial oversight and procedural checks they provide.[185]

For a prosecutor, investigation (covered by qualified immunity) ends and prosecution (covered by absolute immunity) begins at probable cause. A prosecutor does not and cannot be considered an advocate for the state or to be working in the judicial phase of the criminal process until judicial proceedings could be initiated — and that occurs only when the prosecutor has probable cause to arrest or to present the case to a grand jury.[186] The probable cause line recognizes important distinctions in what prosecutors do. As investigators, they search for and gather evidence; as advocates, they evaluate that evidence in preparation for presentation to court. In following that probable-cause line, lower courts consider facts such as whether there has been an arrest or an identified suspect and whether the prosecutor is acting with an eye towards a pending or soon-to-be pending proceeding at which he will act as an advocate.[187]

The investigative/prosecutorial line and using probable cause as the relevant turning point split the Supreme Court in *Buckley v. Fitzsimmons*. Justice Kennedy, writing for four justices in dissent, argued that even when police and prosecutors engage in the same investigative conduct, they do not necessarily perform the same functions. A prosecutor acts with a different focus; in looking for and gathering evidence or preparing witnesses, a prosecutor evaluates evidence with a special eye towards how persuasive it will be before a grand jury and a trial jury.[188] For this reason, the dissent argued, prosecutorial immunity should protect all actions by the prosecutor leading to trial, including all decisions leading to the ultimate advocate's choice of whether and how to use a particular piece of evidence.[189]

Buckley arose from a prosecutor's multiple efforts, all prior to any decision to convene a special grand jury, to locate an expert who would (falsely) link a boot print found at the crime scene with the defendant's boot. Given that timing, the prosecutor could not have been acting as an advocate for the state, and therefore was performing an investigative function to which absolute immunity did not attach.[190] The majority in *Buckley* insisted it would be "anomalous" to accord absolute immunity when the prosecutor himself participates in fabricating some evidence, when it was established that he would not receive absolute immunity for giving advice to police to do the same thing.[191] The dissent countered that in hunting for a witness, a prosecutor is, in fact, preparing for judicial proceedings, because identifying and preparing the witness who will present evidence to the

---

[185] *Lacey*, 693 F.3d at 913–14.

[186] *Buckley*, 509 U.S. at 274.

[187] Giraldo v. Kessler, 694 F.3d 161 (2d Cir. 2012); Cousin v. Small, 325 F.3d 627 (5th Cir. 2003) (per curiam).

[188] *Buckley*, 509 U.S. at 289 (Kennedy, J., concurring in part and dissenting in part).

[189] *Id.* at 284 (Kennedy, J., concurring in part and dissenting in part).

[190] *Buckley*, 509 U.S. at 274–75.

[191] *Id.* at 275; *see also Burns*, 500 U.S. at 495.

court is an essential step in those proceedings.[192]

[2] Application of Immunity: Quasi-Prosecutorial Immunity

Courts have granted quasi-prosecutorial immunity to non-prosecutors who act as advocates for the State in preparing for, initiating, and pursuing judicial proceedings. Chief among these are social workers in child custody, dependency, and welfare proceedings; like attorneys, they exercise independent professional judgment and make snap decisions within judicial proceedings.[193] Government attorneys who initiate and pursue agency proceedings also enjoy quasi-prosecutorial immunity, since they make similar decisions requiring independent professional discretion and judgment needing protection from the threat of civil litigation.[194] Probation officers also enjoy absolute immunity in preparing reports for the court.[195]

But quasi-prosecutorial immunity does not extend to acts not involving advocacy within judicial proceedings. Courts thus have declined to accord absolute immunity to social worker recommendations about placement of children that were made outside of formal proceedings,[196] investigations of family situations,[197] and decisions to take someone into custody without initiating proceedings.[198]

[3] Level of Immunity

Like judicial immunity, prosecutorial immunity accords absolute protection from civil actions for damages over alleged prosecutorial misconduct, but not from federal or state criminal prosecutions.[199] It also does not apply to civil actions seeking to enjoin prosecutors from initiating judicial proceedings. As we will see, injunctions against prosecuting officers are an essential part of constitutional litigation, although such actions may be subject to limitations other than prosecutorial immunity.[200]

---

[192] *Buckley*, 509 U.S. at 284 (Kennedy, J., concurring in part and dissenting in part).

[193] Pittman v. Cuyahoga County Dep't of Children & Family Servs., 640 F.3d 716 (6th Cir. 2011); Whisman ex rel. Whisman v. Rinehart, 119 F.3d 1303 (8th Cir. 1997); Ernst v. Child & Youth Servs., 108 F.3d 486 (3d Cir. 1997); Miller v. Livingston, 99 F.3d 1146 (9th Cir. 1996).

[194] Butz v. Economou, 438 U.S. 478, 511–12 (1978).

[195] Freeze v. Griffith, 849 F.2d 172 (5th Cir. 1988).

[196] *Miller*, 99 F.3d at 1146.

[197] *Pittman*, 640 F.3d at 726; Achterhof v. Selvaggio, 886 F.2d 826 (6th Cir. 1989).

[198] *Whisman*, 119 F.3d at 1308.

[199] Imbler v. Pachtman, 424 U.S. 409, 429 (1976).

[200] *Infra* § 4.13; *infra* §§ 6.10–6.12.

§ 3.10   RETHINKING ADMINISTRATIVE FUNCTIONS

[1] *Van de Kamp* and Prosecutorial Administration

Absolute prosecutorial immunity does not attach when the prosecutor is engaged in administrative tasks, such as "workplace hiring, payroll administration, the maintenance of physical facilities, and the like."[201] But in *Van de Kamp v. Goldstein*, the Court recognized that some administrative functions are "directly connected with the conduct of a trial" and thus are different for absolute immunity purposes than simple employment decisions.[202]

The plaintiff in *Van De Kamp* had been convicted of murder; after his conviction was overturned on federal habeas corpus, the plaintiff brought a § 1983 action alleging that prosecutors failed to disclose exculpatory material about a confidential informant. The plaintiff alleged that senior supervisors in the prosecutors' office had caused the wrongful conviction by not properly training or supervising line prosecutors on their constitutional disclosure obligations and by failing to establish proper systems, policies, and procedures through which line prosecutors could share information about informants with one another and with defense counsel.[203] While these are administrative functions involving management of a government agency, they require legal knowledge and prosecutorial discretion and judgment and therefore require the absolute protection of prosecutorial immunity.[204]

The Court illustrated its conclusion by positing a hypothetical case in which supervising attorneys provide direct advice and supervision in an individual prosecution, insisting that absolute immunity for the supervisors would be clear in that case.[205] There was, however, no difference between case-specific training and supervision and general office-wide supervision and training; "a suit charging that a supervisor made a mistake directly related to a particular trial, on the one hand, and a suit charging that a supervisor trained and supervised inadequately, on the other, would seem very much alike."[206]

Critically, either claim depends on constitutional misconduct within the judicial process. The plaintiff can prove that the supervisors failed in their policymaking only if she can show a constitutional violation by the line prosecutors. But since the line prosecutors likely enjoy absolute immunity for that conduct (in this case, failure to disclose exculpatory evidence about an informant), the claim against the supervisors also falls within the core concerns justifying prosecutorial immunity. Moreover,   treating   case-specific   supervision   differently   than   office-wide

---

[201] Van de Kamp v. Goldstein, 555 U.S. 335, 344 (2009); Lacey v. Maricopa County, 693 F.3d 896 (9th Cir. 2012); McLaughlin v. Watson, 271 F.3d 566 (3d Cir. 2001); Carter v. City of Philadelphia, 181 F.3d 339 (3d Cir. 1999); *cf.* Garcetti v. Ceballos, 547 U.S. 410 (2006) (reaching First Amendment merits, without comment, on claim by fired assistant district attorney).

[202] *Van de Kamp*, 555 U.S. at 344.

[203] *Id.* at 339–40.

[204] *Id.* at 344–46.

[205] *Id.*

[206] *Id.* at 346–48.

supervision would create disparities depending on the size of the prosecutor's office, disadvantaging large offices (such as Los Angeles County, the office involved in *Van De Kamp*) where supervisors work at the broad level of office policy manuals, as compared with small offices, where supervisors are more directly involved in individual prosecution.

[2] Other Administrative Tasks

An open issue after *Van de Kamp* is whether the sharp distinction between prosecution-related administrative tasks and more routine administrative duties makes sense. After all, one could argue that decisions on hiring, firing, case-assignment, and other routine employment matters — regularly defined as administrative — involve discretion, legal knowledge, and professional judgment in a way that ultimately affects individual judicial proceedings and thus implicates the policy concerns of immunity. For example, the Ninth Circuit held that a district attorney's decision to appoint a special prosecutor in a particular matter to avoid a conflict of interest falls within the prosecutorial function and is shielded by absolute immunity, even if general decisions about employment and conditions of employment are not.[207]

The reach of *Van de Kamp* in this regard may depended on the plaintiff and the nature of the claim, specifically whether the claim relates to, or requires proof of, misconduct in a particular judicial proceeding. In a routine employment discrimination claim, for example, the plaintiff is an adversely affected employee of the agency, who can prove her case without touching on any constitutional violations from any specific case; the only constitutional violation at issue is the discriminatory personnel decision.[208] This contrasts with cases in which the plaintiff is an individual claiming injury from the supervisor's employment or assignment decision because that decision results in a constitutional violation in a particular proceeding against the plaintiff. Consider, for example, the Ninth Circuit decision in *Lacey v. Maricopa County*. The plaintiffs, owners of an independent newspaper, alleged that the district attorney appointed a special prosecutor to pursue an investigation that violated their First Amendment rights. The district attorney enjoyed absolute immunity for making that appointment; naming a single special prosecutor to pursue a particular investigation of particular actor and conduct was a prosecutorial function requiring judgment and discretion, not an administrative one, where the § 1983 claim challenged the constitutional validity of the very investigation for which the district attorney made the appointment.[209]

Some lower courts have relied on *Van De Kamp* to reject any line between case-specific and broader administrative decisions as to other immunities. The Second Circuit has held that decisions respecting appointed counsel in a particular case are judicial, but that creating and maintaining a general list of potential appointees (and deciding who is placed on that list) is administrative.[210] But the Fifth Circuit

---

[207] *Lacey*, 693 F.3d at 930–31.

[208] *Id.* at 931.

[209] *Id.* at 930–31.

[210] Bliven v. Hunt, 579 F.3d 204 (2d Cir. 2009); Mitchell v. Fishbein, 377 F.3d 157 (2d Cir. 2004); *see*

more recently rejected that approach, citing *Van De Kamp* and concluding that both case-specific decisions and general macro decisions are judicial and entitled to absolute immunity.[211]

§ 3.11   WITNESS IMMUNITY

The final judicial-process immunity protects witnesses, both private or lay witnesses and police officers, even when they provide perjured, false, or fabricated testimony. In *Briscoe v. LaHue*, the Court rejected arguments for treating police-officer witnesses at trial different than other government actors in the judicial process or than private witnesses (who do not act under color of law and thus are not subject to suit under § 1983).[212]

Once again, immunity attaches to the function — testifying at trial — without regard to the identity of the person performing the function. As with other judicial-process immunities, witness immunity protects the effective functioning of the judicial system, particularly in light of how frequently and regularly police officers and other government officials testify. As with other immunities, the judicial process provides systemic protections against abuse that render civil liability unnecessary; police-officer witnesses are under oath, may be criminally prosecuted for perjury and other federal civil rights crimes, and, most importantly, are subject to cross-examination.

Lower courts have extended this immunity to witnesses in preliminary hearings.[213] And the Supreme Court recently extended it to all witnesses in grand jury proceedings, stating that the rationales supporting immunity for trial witnesses support identical immunity for grand-jury witnesses.[214] The Court rejected the argument that grand-jury witnesses are different because they are not subject to cross-examination by defense counsel before the grand jury; important witnesses (the ones whose testimony could cause constitutional injury by leading to a wrongful conviction) will repeat their testimony at trial, where they will be subject to cross-examination, thereby providing the structural process protections that justify absolute immunity.[215]

---

also Lacey, 693 F.3d at 930–31 (adhering to distinction as to both judicial and prosecutorial immunity).

[211]   Davis v. Tarrant County, Tex., 565 F.3d 214 (5th Cir. 2009).

[212]   Briscoe v. LaHue, 460 U.S. 325 (1983).

[213]   Brice v. Nkaru, 220 F.3d 233, 239 n.6 (4th Cir. 2000); Williams v. Hepting, 844 F.2d 138 (3d Cir. 1988).

[214]   Rehberg v. Paulk, 132 S. Ct. 1497 (2012).

[215]   *Id.* at 1509.

PART C
EXECUTIVE QUALIFIED IMMUNITY

§ 3.12   OVERVIEW

When absolute immunity is not necessary or justified for a given function, the officer still may fall back on ordinary executive qualified immunity.[216] This is the default immunity for all state and federal actors under color of law for all functions that are not legislative, judicial, or prosecutorial.[217] It covers cabinet officers;[218] presidential aides;[219] state and local elected officials;[220] all appointed and hired officers and employees working within the executive bureaucracy for all governments;[221] law enforcement officers for all governments (the most common use of qualified immunity);[222] and prison guards[223] and officials.[224] The one exception is for the President, in whom all constitutional executive authority is vested, who enjoys absolute immunity from suit for his conduct in office.[225]

Qualified immunity applies only to claims for damages, not to criminal prosecutions and not to civil actions for injunctive relief.[226] The scope of the defense is the same in § 1983 actions against state and local officers and in *Bivens* actions against federal officers;[227] in fact, most of the Supreme Court's qualified immunity jurisprudence has been established in the latter.[228]

Qualified immunity is grounded in the same policies as absolute immunity: preventing timidity and a chilling effect on executive officials' fearless and independent decision making; encouraging vigorous exercise of public authority; protecting officials from the distraction, costs, and burdens of civil litigation, thus enabling

---

[216] Buckley v. Fitzsimmons, 509 U.S. 259 (1993); Archie v. Lanier, 95 F.3d 438 (6th Cir. 1996).

[217] Antoine v. Byers & Anderson, 508 U.S. 429, 432 n.4 (1993); Burns v. Reed, 500 U.S. 478, 486–87 (1991).

[218] Ashcroft v. al-Kidd, 131 S. Ct. 2074 (2011); Butz v. Economou, 438 U.S. 478 (1978).

[219] Harlow v. Fitzgerald, 457 U.S. 800 (1982).

[220] Scheuer v. Rhodes, 416 U.S. 232 (1974); Whitney v. City of Milan, 677 F.3d 292 (6th Cir. 2012).

[221] Padilla v. Yoo, 678 F.3d 748 (9th Cir. 2012) (government attorney); Morgan v. Swanson, 659 F.3d 359 (5th Cir. 2011) (public school principal).

[222] Reichle v. Howards, 132 S. Ct. 2088 (2012); Pearson v. Callahan, 555 U.S. 223 (2009); Saucier v. Katz, 533 U.S. 194 (2001); Antoine v. Byers & Anderson, 508 U.S. 429 (1993).

[223] Procunier v. Navarette, 434 U.S. 555 (1978).

[224] Dahl v. Weber, 580 F.3d 730 (8th Cir. 2009).

[225] Nixon v. Fitzgerald, 457 U.S. 731 (1982); U.S. Const. art. II, § 1 ("The executive Power shall be vested in a President of the United States of America.").

[226] Adler v. Pataki, 185 F.3d 35, 48 (2d Cir. 1999); *see also* Morse v. Frederick, 551 U.S. 393, 432 (2007) (Breyer, J., concurring in part and dissenting in part).

[227] Harlow v. Fitzgerald, 457 U.S. 800, 818 & n.30 (1982); *but see al-Kidd*, 131 S. Ct. at 2085–86 (Kennedy, J., concurring) (arguing for different qualified immunity analysis for high-level federal officers).

[228] Reichle v. Howards, 132 S. Ct. 2088 (2012); Ashcroft v. al-Kidd, 131 S. Ct. 2074 (2011); Saucier v. Katz, 533 U.S. 194 (2001); Anderson v. Creighton, 483 U.S. 635 (1987); *Harlow*, 457 U.S. at 802.

them to focus their energies on their public functions; and not deterring capable people from entering public service through threat of personal liability.[229] Courts again must balance the need to vindicate constitutional rights, compensate injured persons, and deter future violations with the need to avoid overdeterrence and to protect effective performance of government functions.[230]

The limited scope of absolute immunity means we accord only qualified immunity to the vast majority of government functions. First, the greater power of executive officials, especially high-ranking ones, presents a greater opportunity for lawlessness. Executive officers (notably law enforcement and corrections officers) can act individually, unilaterally, and proactively in a way that causes constitutional harm; this contrasts with judges, who only act when asked to do so by litigants, or with legislators, who generally only act in concert with other legislators. Second, citizens have more regular, frequent, day-to-day contact with executive-branch officials, particularly (again) law enforcement and persons working in the government bureaucracy. Third, the alternative systemic and institutional protections that justify special absolute immunities (appellate review, professional regulation, and popular election) are absent as to ordinary, daily on-the-street interactions between citizens and law enforcement; civil litigation becomes the primary mechanism for enforcing rights and correcting constitutional error. For example, there is no appellate review of a police officer's use of force. And the electoral check is far more attenuated; that an elected mayor appoints the chief of police, or even that a county sheriff is directly elected, is not likely to deter or remedy misconduct by an individual beat cop.

On the other hand, one might argue that executive officers should receive greater immunity for their ordinary functions. High-ranking executive officers wield broad policy-making authority and discretion; like legislators, they should do so without fear of civil litigation by disappointed citizens. The President relies on aides and cabinet officers to the same degree that legislators do and they are just as much "alter-egos" without whom he could not perform public functions.[231] Police officers act on a moment's notice while often facing imminent harm in uncertain, unfriendly, dangerous surroundings. They exercise a great deal of experienced-based discretion and expertise in a rapidly developing environment that arguably demands greater protection to avoid chilling on vigorous and fearless performance of their public duties.

§ 3.13   EVOLUTION: SUBJECTIVE TO OBJECTIVE

Qualified, or "good-faith," immunity existed at 19th century common law and survived passage of the 1871 Act.[232] That immunity contained both objective and subjective components.[233] Police officers were protected if they acted in subjective

---

[229] Filarsky v. Delia, 132 S. Ct. 1657, 1665 (2012); Wyatt v. Cole, 504 U.S. 158, 167–68 (1992); *Harlow*, 457 U.S. at 814; Pinsky v. Duncan, 79 F.3d 306, 311 (2d Cir. 1996).

[230] *Reichle*, 132 S. Ct. at 2093; *Pearson*, 555 U.S. at 231.

[231] *Harlow*, 457 U.S. at 826–27 (Burger, C.J., dissenting).

[232] Scheuer v. Rhodes, 416 U.S. 232, 245 (1974); Pierson v. Ray, 386 U.S. 547, 554–55 (1967).

[233] Harlow v. Fitzgerald, 457 U.S. 800, 815 (1982).

good faith and with probable cause. For higher executive officers, the defense focused on the reasonableness of the officer's belief in the lawfulness of his actions and his subjective good faith in their lawfulness, accounting for varying degrees of discretion and responsibility in the position.[234]

Qualified immunity protects officers from suit, not merely liability.[235] It relieves defendants of the burden of having to litigate at all and from having to deal with the costs of the pre-trial process, particularly discovery, which is "peculiarly disruptive of effective government."[236] Qualified immunity is "effectively lost if a case erroneously goes to trial."[237] The defense therefore demands that the defendant have an opportunity to terminate the case and get out of litigation as early as possible; this, in turn, requires a standard that can be applied at the summary judgment or motion to dismiss stages, preferably with little or no discovery.[238] But having the defendant's subjective state of mind as part of the defense undermined that purpose; state of mind is the quintessential jury question, meaning cases under the common law standard had to proceed to trial and could not be resolved at an earlier stage.

In *Harlow v. Fitzgerald*, the Court recognized these procedural concerns and adjusted sustantive qualified immunity away from its common law roots, replacing it with a wholly objective standard that could more easily be raised and resolved prior to trial. The revised defense immunizes conduct that does not violate "clearly established constitutional rights of which a reasonable person would or should have known." Stated differently, an official has immunity if he "could not reasonably be expected to anticipate subsequent legal developments, nor could he fairly be said to 'know' that the law forbade conduct not previously identified as unlawful."[239]

This objective standard ties to a policy of ensuring that executive officers are on notice about the unlawfulness of their conduct before being subjected to damages. It would be fundamentally unfair to hold a government officer personally liable for money damages if he could not and should not have known at the time he acted that his conduct was unlawful. Tying immunity to the state of clearly established law at the time of the conduct ensures that reasonable officers are on notice as to what they can or cannot do and can reasonably anticipate when their conduct will give rise to constitutional harm and thus to liability.[240] In fact, the Supreme Court has explicitly linked qualified immunity in civil actions to § 242's requirement that a constitutional right has been "made specific" — qualified immunity protects government officers from civil liability to the same extent they are protected from prosecution under criminal statutes that are so vague as to not provide clear notice

---

[234] *Scheuer*, 416 U.S. at 245–46.

[235] Pearson v. Callahan, 555 U.S. 223, 231 (2009).

[236] Ashcroft v. Iqbal, 556 U.S. 662, 672 (2009); James v. Sadler, 909 F.2d 834, 838 (5th Cir. 1990).

[237] *Pearson*, 555 U.S. at 231.

[238] *Id.* at 232; Hunter v. Bryant, 502 U.S. 224, 227 (1991) (per curiam); *Harlow*, 457 U.S. at 814–15.

[239] *Harlow*, 457 U.S. at 818–19.

[240] Hope v. Pelzer, 536 U.S. 730, 739–40 (2002); Saucier v. Katz, 533 U.S. 194, 202 (2001); Youngbey v. March, 676 F.3d 1114, 1117 (D.C. Cir. 2012).

of what conduct is unlawful.[241]

One interesting puzzle, offered by Justice Brennan's concurring opinion in *Harlow*, is what to do about the "clever and unusually well-informed violator of constitutional rights," the officer who subjectively knows the state of the law and knows that he is violating someone's rights, even when he ordinarily should not reasonably be expected to know it.[242] Four years after *Harlow*, the Court in *Malley v. Briggs* defined qualified immunity as providing "ample protection to all but the plainly incompetent or those who knowingly violate the law."[243] This suggests that the unreasonably knowing violator could lose immunity, although the situation does not often arise.

The Court ultimately refined qualified immunity into a two-step analysis. Courts first ask whether a constitutional right was violated on the facts alleged (in the complaint) or shown on the evidence (at summary judgment); if no right was violated, the defendant prevails. If the plaintiff's rights were violated, courts then ask whether that right was "clearly established" at the time of the events, such that a reasonable officer would have known that his conduct was unconstitutional, or, stated differently, that no reasonable officer could have believed his conduct was lawful or constitutional.[244]

§ 3.14   ORDER OF BATTLE

In *Saucier v. Katz*, the Supreme Court established a rigid and mandatory "order of battle" for that two-step analysis, requiring that courts always resolve the merits question (whether the plaintiffs' rights had been violated) before determining whether the right was clearly established.[245] Over the next several years, Justice Breyer[246] and several commentators[247] criticized mandatory merits first, arguing that courts should have discretion to depart this rigid sequence. Eight years later in *Pearson v. Callahan*, the Court reversed course, stating that merits-first is not mandatory, although it frequently is the appropriate and more beneficial approach.[248]

---

[241] *Hope*, 536 U.S. at 739–41; United States v. Lanier, 520 U.S. 259, 270–71 (1997).

[242] *Harlow*, 457 U.S. at 821 (Brennan, J., concurring).

[243] Malley v. Briggs, 475 U.S. 335, 341 (1986).

[244] Reichle v. Howards, 132 S. Ct. 2088, 2093 (2012); Ashcroft v. al-Kidd, 131 S. Ct. 2074, 2080 (2011); *Pearson*, 555 U.S. at 230–33.

[245] Saucier v. Katz, 533 U.S. 194 (2001).

[246] Morse v. Frederick, 551 U.S. 393, 430 (2007) (Breyer, J., concurring in the judgment in part and dissenting in part); Scott v. Harris, 550 U.S. 372, 387 (2007) (Breyer, J., concurring); Brosseau v. Haugen, 543 U.S. 194, 201–02 (2004) (Breyer, J., concurring).

[247] Nancy Leong, *The* Saucier *Qualified Immunity Experiment: An Empirical Analysis*, 36 Pepp. L. Rev. 667 (2009); Thomas Healy, *The Rise of Unnecessary Constitutional Rulings*, 83 N.C. L. Rev. 847 (2005).

[248] Pearson v. Callahan, 555 U.S. 223, 236 (2009).

[1] Benefits to Merits-First

There are three primary identifiable benefits to resolving the merits first.

First, it allows courts to make substantive constitutional law going forward. In the course of resolving the case at hand, federal courts establish principles for determining the scope of constitutional rights, developing and refining constitutional precedent. This is particularly important with respect to those constitutional claims that only ever arise in damages actions under § 1983 or *Bivens*, such as claims of excessive force against law enforcement and corrections officers.

Second, merits-first preserves judicial resources. Courts need not waste time determining whether a right is clearly established if no rights have been violated.

Third, addressing the merits enables government to shift resources to preventing future wrongs. By first and always identifying whether a violation occurred in this case, the court's opinion compels changes in government policies, training, and practices to prevent future similar misconduct, even if the defendant officer is not ultimately held liable.[249]

[2] Problems with Merits-First

While there are some benefits to considering the merits first, *Pearson* acknowledged a number of reasons that a court might not do so in a given case, justifying the departure from a mandatory order of battle.

First, the judicial resources concern runs in both directions. It is just as much a waste of party and judicial resources to unnecessarily litigate and resolve the merits as to unnecessarily litigate and resolve the clearly established question. Second, many constitutional claims and issues are highly fact-bound particularly when arising in damages actions; any precedent the court creates will be of limited value in developing and elaborating on constitutional law because it will be linked to the present facts. Indeed, many merits decisions confuse more than clarify.[250]

Third, the same or similar constitutional issues often are pending before a higher court, thus any merits decision, especially by a district court, may quickly be rendered incorrect. Fourth, merits-first may be unworkable at the pleading stage. The scope of the right at issue, and thus whether it was violated, is not necessarily clear from the pleadings. On the other hand, a court can determine from the pleadings that an asserted right is not clearly established. This means the defense actually can be litigated and resolved more quickly (as we want with a defense to suit) without having to await discovery and later elaboration of the claim.[251]

Mandating merits-first also may result in bad constitutional decisionmaking and thus bad precedent. The parties do not always do a good job litigating these claims

---

[249] *Id.*

[250] *Id.* at 236–37.

[251] *Id.* at 237–39.

and cases often suffer from "woefully inadequate" briefing. They also may suffer from inadequate judging. The order in which a judge writes her opinion is not always the same as the order in which she reasons the case. Courts often can quickly and easily decide that a right is not clearly established and that the defendant is entitled to qualified immunity, but a rigid order of battle forces the judge to go back and analyze the merits issue, often without sufficient care and in a way that does not produce good or well thought-out constitutional rules.[252]

Mandatory merits-first also contradicts two prudential rules of judging. The first is the rule of constitutional avoidance, which states that courts should not pass on questions of constitutionality unless there is no other way to resolve the case. If a right is obviously not clearly established, constitutional avoidance compels courts not to address constitutional meaning or to determine whether the Constitution was violated in the events in question.[253] The second is the rule against advisory opinions, which arguably is violated by any unnecessary merits ruling that declares that the conduct at issue violates the Constitution, but accords no legal relief for that violation. Instead, the opinion does nothing more than advise persons, entities, and courts going forward, clearly establishing (or at least helping to clearly establish) a constitutional right that someone else may violate and for which someone else may recover next time. But it has no effect on the plaintiff presently before the court.[254] It also appears to give government officers one (or several) freebies — a court essentially is announcing that these officers could and did violate constitutional rights with impunity.

Finally, a rigid order of battle is not necessary to make and develop constitutional law. Constitutional rights can be litigated and constitutional rules declared in other contexts in which qualified immunity is not in play — in civil actions for injunctive relief, in civil actions against government entities (which do not enjoy immunity), in § 242 prosecutions and other proceedings brought by the federal government, and as a defense in a criminal proceeding against the right-holder.[255]

[3]   Order of Battle after *Pearson*

Pearson vests courts with discretion as to whether to consider the merits and in what order, depending on the needs and posture of the case. We can expect courts to skip the merits where that question is particularly difficult or fact-bound or where the unclear state of the law and the lack of a clearly established right is so obvious and easily announced.[256] Otherwise, courts (especially district courts) may

---

[252] *Id.* at 239–40.

[253] *Id.* at 241.

[254] Thomas Healy, *The Rise of Unnecessary Constitutional Rulings*, 83 N.C. L. Rev. 847, 920 (2005).

[255] *Pearson*, 555 U.S. at 242–43.

[256] *Compare* Ashcroft v. al-Kidd, 131 S. Ct. 2074 (2011), *with* Reichle v. Howards, 132 S. Ct. 2088 (2012). For lower courts, *compare* Rees v. Office of Children and Youth, 437 F. App'x 139, 2012 U.S. App. LEXIS 6447 (3d Cir. 2012) (exercising discretion to pretermit merits), *and* Morgan v. Swanson, 659 F.3d 359 (5th Cir. 2011) (same), *with* Atkins v. City of Chicago, 631 F.3d 823, 838 (7th Cir. 2011) (Hamilton, J., concurring in part and concurring in the judgment), *and* Ontiveros v. City of Rosenberg, 564 F.3d 379

find it best to reach the merits first simply to create a full record and render a complete decision.[257]

§ 3.15 CLEARLY ESTABLISHED RIGHTS

Qualified immunity necessarily centers on what it means for a constitutional right to be clearly established, how rights become clearly established, and how courts decide.

[1] Defining Rights

In determining whether a constitutional right is clearly established, courts must identify the right at issue with the appropriate level of specificity; the right cannot be defined too generally or be based on broad discussions of history or constitutional principles.[258] It is not enough to say that the Fourth Amendment prohibits unreasonable searches and seizures or even that the Fourth Amendment prohibits warrantless entry absent exigent circumstances; while these broad principles are clearly established, rights must be defined with reference to the particular facts in the case. The question is what a reasonable officer would have known about the lawfulness of his conduct in light of broad constitutional principles, preexisting law, and the facts and information at hand in that case.[259]

The "'contours of the right must be sufficiently clear' that every 'reasonable official would have understood that what he is doing violates that right.'"[260] The Supreme Court has often insisted that the very action in question need not have been held unlawful in a prior judicial decision, nor must the plaintiff be able to find a case directly on point with fundamentally or materially similar facts; an official can be on notice that even novel factual circumstances violate a right.[261] But "existing precedent must have placed the statutory or constitutional question beyond debate."[262] It must be "so obvious" in light of pre-existing general rules and principles that the defendant's conduct is unlawful.[263] The "relevant, dispositive inquiry in determining whether a right is clearly established is whether it would be clear to a reasonable officer that his conduct was unlawful in the situation he confronted."[264] Moreover, the right must be defined by the same source of law — that some conduct runs afoul of an administrative regulation does not clearly

---

(5th Cir. 2009); Beckinger v. Twp. of Elizabeth, 697 F. Supp. 2d 610 (W.D. Pa. 2010) (following original sequence of *Saucier*); Bailey v. Robinson, 2009 U.S. Dist. LEXIS 19666 (W.D. Wash. Mar. 12, 2009).

[257] Colin Rolfs, *Qualified Immunity After* Pearson v. Callahan, 59 UCLA L. Rev. 468 (2011) (empirical study finding that courts of appeals are avoiding merits at a higher rate, while district courts continued to adhere to merits-first order).

[258] Anderson v. Creighton, 483 U.S. 635, 639–40 (1987).

[259] Ashcroft v. al-Kidd, 131 S. Ct. 2074, 2083 (2011); Saucier v. Katz, 533 U.S. 194, 200–01 (2001); *Anderson*, 483 U.S. at 639–40.

[260] Reichle v. Howards, 132 S. Ct. 2088, 2094 (2012); *al-Kidd*, 131 S. Ct. at 2083.

[261] Hope v. Pelzer, 536 U.S. 730, 740–41 (2002); United States v. Lanier, 520 U.S. 259, 269–70 (1997).

[262] *al-Kidd*, 131 S. Ct. at 2083.

[263] *Hope*, 536 U.S. at 739.

[264] Brosseau v. Haugen, 543 U.S. 194, 198–99 (2004) (quoting *Saucier*, 533 U.S. at 201–02).

establish the right under the Constitution.[265]

Thus, in a *Bivens* action alleging that an arrest supported by probable cause was effected in retaliation for the plaintiff's speech, the right at issue (and thus the right that must be clearly established) is not the general right to be free from retaliation for protected speech, but a more specific right to be free from a First-Amendment based retaliatory arrest otherwise supported by probable cause.[266] Similarly, a plaintiff cannot rely on the general First Amendment prohibition on viewpoint discrimination, but must show prior case law prohibiting government officials from excluding people from an official presidential event on private property because of their viewpoint.[267] Similarly, in a challenge to media members entering the plaintiff's home as part of a police ride-along where the media is not mentioned in the warrant, the plaintiff's right is not to be free of searches exceeding the scope of a warrant, but a more specific right against media entering the home without a warrant as part of a ride-along with police.[268] And the question is not whether it is clearly established that shooting a fleeing suspect constitutes excessive force in violation of the Fourth Amendment, but whether it is clearly established that shooting this fleeing suspect is excessive given the facts at hand.[269]

The resulting analytical inconsistency and variance relates both to the level of specificity at which the right will be defined and the degree of factual overlap courts demand from prior precedent. Some distinctions always can be drawn between precedent and the current case; the issue then becomes whether the distinctions are sufficiently material that the precedent does not clearly establish unlawfulness of the conduct at issue on the current facts.[270]

More problematically, the easiest and most extreme cases likely never arise, meaning there will be no prior case law to clearly establish the right. As Judge Richard Posner famously argued, there "has never been a § 1983 case accusing welfare officials of selling foster children into slavery; it does not follow that if such a case arose, the officials would be immune from damages liability because no previous case had found liability in those circumstances."[271] Similarly, a prior judicial opinion should not be necessary to provide fair notice to a judge that he violates the Constitutional by using his official power to extort sexual favors from potential litigants.[272]

The Supreme Court has recognized some violations that are obvious in light of general constitutional principles,[273] but lower courts have been more mixed on

---

[265] Elder v. Holloway, 510 U.S. 510, 515 (1994).

[266] *Reichle*, 132 S. Ct. at 2094.

[267] Weise v. Casper, 593 F.3d 1163, 1167–68 (10th Cir. 2010).

[268] Wilson v. Layne, 526 U.S. 603, 615 (1999).

[269] *Brosseau*, 543 U.S. at 200–01.

[270] *Cf.* Youngbey v. March, 676 F.3d 1114, 1124 (D.C. Cir. 2012); Purcell ex rel. Estate of Morgan v. Toombs County, 400 F.3d 1313, 1324 n.25 (11th Cir. 2005).

[271] K.H. ex rel. Murphy v. Morgan, 914 F.2d 846, 851 (7th Cir. 1990) (Posner, J.).

[272] *Wilson*, 526 U.S. at 621 (Stevens, J., concurring and dissenting).

[273] *Hope*, 536 U.S. at 741–42.

this.[274]

[2]   Clearly Establishing Rights

The primary means of clearly establishing a right is through prior case law. A right is clearly established by one binding judicial decision — from the Supreme Court of the United States, the circuit court of appeals in which the events occur, or the state supreme court in which the events occur — subject to some level of factual specificity and similarity to the present case. Alternatively, a "robust" consensus of persuasive authority, notably from other circuits or from district courts within one circuit, may clearly establish the right, at least in the absence of binding contrary authority.[275]

By contrast, a split of judicial authority often demonstrates that the law is not clearly established, even if the split develops after the events at issue. If "judges thus disagree on a constitutional question, it is unfair to subject police to money damages for picking the losing side of the controversy."[276] As one court of appeals explains it, "[o]fficials are not liable for bad guesses in gray areas; they are liable for transgressing bright lines."[277] Outside the extreme or obvious case, officers may expect that their conduct is constitutional in the absence of case law specifically holding their conduct, in its factual context and details, unconstitutional.[278]

Justice Kennedy recently argued that the question of what legal sources can clearly establish a right must account for the nature and responsibilities of the defendant. Kennedy would distinguish high-ranking federal officers working at the national level, such as the Attorney General, from officers (federal or state) who operate within a single state or judicial district. National officeholders working across multiple jurisdictions should not have to adjust their conduct to the most stringent standard anywhere in the United States, nor should they lose immunity in the face of disagreement among the lower courts. Absent strong consensus, the views of a small number of regional circuits should not establish a binding national rule.[279] The effect of such an approach would be that, at least for some high-level

---

[274] *Compare* Shekleton v. Eichenberger, 677 F.3d 361 (8th Cir. 2012) (right to be free from excessive force obvious on general principles), *with* Terrell v. Smith, 668 F.3d 1244 (11th Cir. 2012) (finding factual distinctions with prior suspect-shooting cases); Priester v. City of Riviera Beach, 208 F.3d 919 (11th Cir. 2000) (qualified immunity denied where officers ordered police dog to attack non-resisting arrestee), *with* Buckley v. Haddock, 2008 U.S. App. LEXIS 19482 (11th Cir. Sept. 9, 2008) (officer tasered peacefully non-compliant suspect, but force not "so excessive as obviously to violate the Fourth Amendment"); Surita v. Hyde, 665 F.3d 860 (7th Cir. 2011) (right to speak at public meeting clearly established on general First Amendment principles), *with* Fields v. Prater, 566 F.3d 381 (4th Cir. 2009) (general law regarding First Amendment limits on political patronage not enough where differences are "often matters of degree"), *and* Weise, 593 F.3d at 1167–68 (general First Amendment prohibition on viewpoint discrimination not sufficient to clearly establish right not to be removed from event because of opinion expressed away from event).

[275] *al-Kidd*, 131 S. Ct. at 2084; *Wilson*, 526 U.S. at 616–17; *Youngbey*, 676 F.3d at 1117.

[276] *Wilson*, 526 U.S. at 617–18.

[277] *Fields*, 566 F.3d at 389.

[278] *Id.* at 389–90.

[279] *al-Kidd*, 131 S. Ct. at 2085–86 (Kennedy, J., concurring).

officers or some issues, only Supreme Court precedent could clearly establish a right,[280] a proposition the Court has rejected elsewhere.[281]

Constitutional rules also can be clearly established via regulations, rules, policies, and training manuals of the relevant executive or government agency. An officer should be able to rely on departmental policies and training to guide his conduct without fear of liability, at least so long as those regulations are not directly and obviously violative of developed case law.[282] On the other hand, a violation of a clearly established regulation or policy is not a violation of a clearly established constitutional right.[283]

Finally, the nature and closeness of the constitutional question matters, as does whether the court can identify good reason for the official conduct. Unlawfulness will be apparent and the right clearly established, even without much or any prior case law, in the most-blatant cases, where these can be no good reason for the officer's conduct. On the other hand, close constitutional issues require a greater amount of binding or consistent precedent to clearly establish the right.

In *Wilson v. Layne*, the Court considered the constitutionality of media members, on a ride-along with law-enforcement, entering a home, where the reporters were not mentioned in the warrant; it held that the Fourth Amendment was violated by their entering the plaintiff's home, but the right was not clearly established. The Court emphasized the important public purposes behind media ride-alongs, such as publicizing the work of law enforcement and educating the public about their efforts.[284] While not enough to establish the constitutionality of ride-alongs, these legitimate government purposes suggested that the validity of the conduct was at least an open question at the time, requiring specific case law to clearly establish its constitutional invalidity.

One commentator suggested that qualified immunity should be reformulated to ask not whether the right was clearly established, but whether the defendant's actions were "clearly unconstitutional." This rhetorical alteration would leave immunity in place where the law is evolving or unsettled or where the case is "genuinely borderline." But it would curtail the scope of qualified immunity by focusing less on the precise technical sources of law or the presence of specific case precedent in favor of looking at an officer's "common social duty," taking account of the outrageousness or egregiousness of the misconduct.[285]

---

[280] *Compare* 28 U.S.C. § 2254(d)(1) (writ of habeas corpus permissible only if state court produced decision "that was contrary to, or involved an unreasonable application, of clearly established Federal law, as determined by the Supreme Court of the United States").

[281] *Lanier*, 520 U.S. at 268–69.

[282] *Hope*, 536 U.S. at 742; *Wilson*, 526 U.S. at 617.

[283] *Elder*, 510 U.S. at 515.

[284] *Wilson*, 526 U.S. at 612–14.

[285] John C. Jeffries, Jr., *The Liability Rule for Constitutional Torts*, 99 VA. L. REV. ___ (forthcoming 2013).

[3]   Qualified Immunity Puzzless

1. *Police arrest the plaintiff on an outstanding traffic warrant from the neighboring county. When the neighboring county is unable to effect a formal transfer of custody that evening, the arresting officers drive the plaintiff to a shopping center, tie him to a metal pole with flex-cuffs, place a note explaining that there were outstanding warrants for him in that county, and leave the scene. The officers also call police in the transferee county to report the situation, but do not identify themselves or explain how the plaintiff came to be tied to the pole. Officers from the second county arrive to untie the plaintiff 10 to 15 minutes later.*[286] *Plaintiff sues the arresting officers and the arresting county, alleging violations of the U.S. Constitution; the officers assert qualified immunity.*

Consider whether the defense should succeed, under the two-step, non-mandatory approach to qualified immunity. How is your analysis affected by the fact that the Fourth Circuit had not decided a factually similar case?

2. *Return to the Puzzle of the judge who held an attorney in contempt and had him arrested and jailed for failing to stand and recite the Pledge of Allegiance at the beginning of court proceedings.*[287] *The attorney brings a § 1983 damages action against the bailiff who carried out the judge's commands. Accept that, on the basic facts described in § 3.08[5], compelling the attorney to stand and recite the Pledge and punishing him for failing to do so violates the First Amendment.*

One of the Supreme Court's canonical First Amendment cases is West Virginia Board of Education v. Barnette, *which held that a school cannot make a student participate in the Pledge and included the famous assertion that "[i]f there is any fixed star in our constitutional constellation, it is that no official, high or petty, can prescribe what shall be orthodox in politics, nationalism, religion, or other matters of opinion or force citizens to confess by word or act their faith therein."* [288]*Another is* Wooley v. Maynard, *where the Court held that a person cannot be compelled to display the state's "Live Free or Die" motto on his license plate, because the "First Amendment protects the right of individuals to hold a point of view different from the majority and to refuse to foster . . . an idea they find morally objectionable.*[289]*Finally, bailiffs, who are Deputy County Sheriffs, are trained and instructed only to use Tasers in response to "forceful resistance to a lawful command."*

Consider whether the bailiff can successfully assert qualified immunity, using the two-step, non-mandatory analysis, in the following circumstances:

1. *After the judge holds the attorney in contempt of court, the bailiff obeys the judge's order and handcuffs the attorney, takes him into custody, and places him in the courthouse holding cell.*

---

[286]   Robles v. Prince George's County, 302 F.3d 262 (4th Cir. 2002).

[287]   *supra* § 3.08[5].

[288]   W. Va. Board of Educ. v. Barnette, 319 U.S. 624, 642 (1943).

[289]   Wooley v. Maynard, 430 U.S. 705, 715 (1977).

2. When the attorney fails to stand and recite the Pledge, the judge orders the bailiff to Taser the attorney and the bailiff does as ordered.

§ 3.16 PRIVATE ACTORS AND IMMUNITY

A final consideration is whether private actors who act under color of law so as to come within § 1983 (or, to the extent it remains possible, *Bivens*) may assert immunity as a defense. It is clear that private actors cannot claim any absolute immunities.[290] It is less clear with respect to qualified immunity. Lower courts facing this issue often ask whether there is a history of according qualified immunity to this private party and whether doing so is consistent with its underlying purposes and policies.[291] Two considerations might guide this question.

First is the presence of a profit-making and profit-motivated private entity, which operates without regard to the incentives that qualified immunity seeks to promote. On two occasions, the Supreme Court has rejected qualified immunity defenses by economically motivated private companies. The concerns for officer timidity do not translate to private companies operating in competitive markets, focusing on private goals, and subject to competitive market pressures.[292] Such entities (and their employees) do not need qualified immunity because other market incentives sufficiently serve the same purposes and functions.[293] A private company operating a state prison responds to market-created pressures that provide strong incentives to avoid timid, fearful, or insufficiently vigorous performance; they are economically motivated to continue to operate prisons even in the face of liability and they can offset risks to employees with higher pay or increased benefits.[294] Similarly lower courts have found that qualified immunity does not protect a private bail bonds-man[295] or a community development organization,[296] also work under similar economic incentives overriding any benefits of qualified immunity.

Second is the presence of a direct connection between the private actor and the government itself. A private individual functionally operating as a government employee needs the same protections as a regular employee; it is equally necessary for him to avoid timidity in performing public functions and for the law to avoid deterring private individuals from agreeing to cooperate with and assist govern-ment. In *Filarsky v. Delia*, the Court held that a private lawyer who contracted with a municipality to conduct an internal affairs investigation could assert qualified immunity. Critically, the Court saw no difference between the defendant, also worked for the city on a short-term contractual basis, and someone working for the city as a full-time employee. In light of the purposes of qualified immunity, it makes no sense not to accord immunity to all officers performing identical public functions

---

[290] Wyatt v. Cole, 504 U.S. 158 (1992); Dennis v. Higgins, 498 U.S. 439 (1991).

[291] McCullum v. Tepe, 693 F.3d 696, 700 (6th Cir. 2012); Gregg v. Ham, 678 F.3d 333, 340 (4th Cir. 2012).

[292] Richardson v. McKnight, 521 U.S. 399 (1997); *Wyatt*, 504 U.S. at 167–68.

[293] *Richardson*, 521 U.S. at 410–11.

[294] *Id.* at 410.

[295] *Gregg*, 678 F.3d at 340–41.

[296] Rosewood Servs., Inc. v. Sunflower Diversified Servs., 413 F.3d 1163 (10th Cir. 2005).

on the government's behalf and under the government's control, regardless of formal employee status.[297]

This also holds where a private (or non-government) individual is working for the government at the direction and control of government officials.[298] Indeed, it seems perverse to accord qualified immunity to the government officials directing the conduct and not to the private individuals following those directions.

---

[297] Filarsky v. Delia, 132 S. Ct. 1657 (2012) (independent contractor performing investigation); West v. Atkins, 487 U.S. 42 (1988) (privately contracted prison physician).

[298] Weise v. Casper, 593 F.3d 1163, 1166 (10th Cir. 2010) (volunteers working at presidential event, under close supervision of government officers).

Chapter 4

GOVERNMENT ENTITY LIABILITY

PART C   SUPERVISORY LIABILITY

§ 4.14   **Supervisory Liability**

§ 4.15   **Supervisory Liability Meets Entity Liability**

§ 4.01   OVERVIEW

The primary defendants to this point have been government officers and other individuals, the primary "person[s]" liable under § 1983, the only persons subject to *Bivens* suit, and the defendants to whom individual immunity defenses (absolute legislative, prosecutorial, and judicial, and qualified) may be available.

But focusing solely on individual litigation and liability may be inconsistent with § 1983's twin aims of compensating injured plaintiffs and deterring future constitutional violations. A plaintiff is not guaranteed compensation from an individual officer who may be unable to pay a large judgment. Of course, virtually all governments indemnify their officers against suit and damages liability,[1] which resolves, or at least minimizes, this concern.

More importantly, individual litigation, which focuses on individual instances of misconduct, may not ensure full or maximum deterrence. Constitutional violations often result from systemic wrongdoing tied to government policies, customs, practices, training, and supervision of its employees, rather than isolated individual bad acts. Courts may not be able to get at and remedy systemic misconduct through individual litigation, and the government itself may not be inclined to change its policies in response to a single case against a single officer.

We thus turn to whether and when a government entity, as well as its agencies and "arms," can be made a formal party to a case and held liable, for damages or equitable relief, for constitutional violations. At the federal level, the answer is never. *Bivens* claims are available only against individual officers, never against government agencies,[2] and the Westfall Act expressly excludes constitutional claims against the United States as a replacement defendant.[3]

At the state and local levels, the availability of litigation against a government entity has both a statutory and constitutional component. The statutory issue is whether a government entity or arm is a "person" within the meaning of § 1983 that Congress made subject to suit and liability. The constitutional issue is whether Congress can subject that government entity to suit or whether the entity instead enjoys some constitutional or common law immunity.

---

[1] Cornelia T.L. Pillard, *Taking Fiction Seriously: The Strange Results of Public Officials' Individual Liability Under* Bivens, 88 GEO. L.J. 65, 76 (1999); John C. Jefferies, Jr., *In Praise of the Eleventh Amendment and Section 1983*, 84 VA. L. REV. 47, 50 & n.16 (1998).

[2] FDIC v. Meyer, 510 U.S. 471 (1994).

[3] 28 U.S.C. § 2679(b)(2)(A); *supra* § 2.16.

PART A
MUNICIPAL LIABILITY

§ 4.02 *MONELL*: PERMITTING MUNICIPAL LIABILITY

In *Monroe v. Pape*, after broadly defining "under color of law" to allow the claims against the police officers, and creating modern constitutional and civil rights litigation,[4] the Supreme Court held that the City of Chicago could not be sued for damages under § 1983 because a municipality is not a "person" within the meaning of the statute.[5] That understanding lasted for 17 years, until *Monell v. Department of Social Services*[6] overruled *Monroe* on this point and established that a municipality is a person and is subject to an action for damages. The Court conducted a "fresh analysis" of both statutory text and the history of the Ku Klux Klan to reach this conclusion.

As a textual matter, the Court held that the statutory phrase "every person" includes all legal persons. It found support for this in the Dictionary Act, which in 1871 defined persons to include "bodies corporate and politic," a term that included local governments as well as private corporate entities.[7] The Court also emphasized that § 1983 is a "remedial statute," which must be construed broadly, liberally, and beneficially to serve its remedial purposes; § 1983 establishes a broad federal remedy for violations of federally protected rights and it is more consistent with that purpose to have the statute reach as many potential defendants, and allow a plaintiff as many potential sources of recovery, as possible.[8]

The Court's historical analysis centered on the fate of the Sherman Amendment, a proposal that would have been § 7 of the 1871 Act. The Sherman Amendment would have made municipalities liable for damages for injuries caused by persons "riotously and tumultuously assembled," language clearly aimed at lynch mobs and other Klan rioting. The statute created a cause of action primarily against the rioters, but it also subject the municipality to suit and made it responsible for any unsatisfied judgments. Municipal liability would have attached regardless of whether the municipality had notice of the riots, whether it took reasonable efforts to prevent or control the riots, whether the rioters were punished under state law, and whether the municipality even possessed police power to keep and maintain order (power which it only could obtain from the state).[9]

The Amendment passed the Senate but failed in the House,[10] due in part to explicitly constitutional objections. The main argument against the Amendment was

---

[4] *Supra* § 2.03[2].

[5] Monroe v. Pape, 365 U.S. 167, 187 (1961).

[6] Monell v. Dep't of Soc. Servs., 436 U.S. 658 (1978).

[7] *Id.* at 688–89.

[8] *Id.* at 685–86.

[9] *Id.* at 666–67.

[10] The municipal liability provision was dropped and the revised version of the Sherman Amendment was passed and codified at 42 U.S.C. § 1986.

that it imposed, as a matter of federal law, an obligation on municipalities to keep the peace, even though state law might not grant them police powers. But the scope of municipal power was a matter exclusively for the state and only the state could give local governments power to establish a police force and keep the peace. Congress had no authority under § 5 of the Fourteenth Amendment (the power source for the 1871 Act) to impose on local government the obligation to create and maintain a law-enforcement mechanism that would prevent or halt riots. And Congress could not do indirectly, through the threat of damages, what it could not order directly; it could not put municipalities to a Hobson's choice — establish law-enforcement that will keep the peace or pay civil damages for the misconduct of private individuals.[11]

For § 1983 purposes, the issue is what lesson to draw from these constitutional objections and the defeat of § 7. The *Monroe* Court concluded that this history showed Congress rejecting all municipal liability under all of the Ku Klux Klan Act.[12] But the *Monell* Court drew a different conclusion. The Sherman Amendment had been proposed as an additional section to the statute, not as an amendment to § 1 (§ 1983), thus the two provisions must be considered independently. In fact, for all the constitutional debate over § 7, there was only limited discussion of § 1.[13] Moreover, the liability scheme in § 1 is very different than the one that § 7 would have created, such that the former did not create the same Hobson's choice. Section 1983 did not impose peacekeeping obligations on the municipality; it only imposed liability when the defendant failed to properly exercise power it already possessed under state. Section 1 created no obligations other than to exercise whatever powers a municipality had been granted (by the state) in a way that comported with the Fourteenth Amendment and did not deprive persons of their federal rights.[14] And the debates over § 1 reflect that understanding.[15] The history of the congressional rejection of § 7 thus did not override the textual conclusion in § 1 that municipalities could be statutory persons.

While *Monell* established that municipalities can be named defendants and can be liable for all remedies in a § 1983 action, it also held that they could not be liable merely because an employee violated someone's rights; in other words, there could be no *respondeat superior*, or vicarious, municipal liability. This at least nominally is dictated by the "subjects or causes to be subjected" language of § 1983, which suggests that the government entity itself, not merely its employee, must cause the deprivation of the right, privilege, or immunity secured.[16] Government only "causes" violations through its policies, ordinances, regulations, and official decisions and the guidance they give to government officials. It also can cause deprivations via customs, those consistent and widespread practices that have become so permanently established as to have the practical force of policies,

---

[11] *Monell*, 436 U.S. at 679.

[12] *Monroe*, 365 U.S. at 191.

[13] *Monell*, 436 U.S. at 665.

[14] *Id.* at 679–80.

[15] *Id.* at 680.

[16] *Id.* at 690–92.

ordinances, or regulations, even if they have not been formally enacted into law.[17] A municipality thus can be liable only when it's actual or functionally formal and official rules and regulations dictate or control the offending officer's unlawful actions.

The defeat of the Sherman Amendment also influenced rejection of vicarious liability. While it did not undermine the possibility of municipal liability under a different provision of the 1871 Act, the constitutional arguments made against it suggested broad congressional rejection of vicarious municipal liability under federal law. *Respondeat superior* liability under § 1 would raise the same constitutional concerns that drove § 7 to defeat — it would impose on governments an obligation to control actors and conduct not fully subject to municipal control and make governments liable even if they have done nothing to create or enable the misconduct and even if they did everything they could to halt that misconduct.[18]

§ 4.03   SCOPE OF MUNICIPAL LIABILITY

Monell thus establishes that a municipality can be liable only when the individual misconduct was performed pursuant to municipal policy or custom established or known by a lawmaker whose edicts may "fairly be said to represent official policy."[19] The difference between individual and government liability maps onto the earlier framework of the legalist and governmental models of § 1983 liability.[20] Individual liability functions on the governmental model; an officer is liable for lawless action if his apparent governmental authority enabled or facilitated his misconduct. Government-entity liability functions on the legalist model; the government is liable only if its actual, formal legal rules compelled, approved, accepted, or enabled the unconstitutional behavior. Importantly, however, individual liability remains essential to any claim of governmental liability; if the individual officer does not violate the plaintiff's rights, then the government's policies and practices do not violate those rights.[21]

Moreover, a municipality only creates formal rules (or their functional equivalent) through officers possessing final policymaking authority. Municipal liability thus attaches only if the challenged acts were pursuant to policy adopted or known about by city officials responsible for making policy in that particular area of city business.[22] Whether someone is a policymaker is a question of state law to be decided by the court, not a question of fact for the jury.[23] A municipality can have different policymakers for different areas of city business; an individual can be a

---

[17] *Id.* at 690–91.

[18] *Id.* at 693–94.

[19] Monell v. Dep't of Soc. Servs., 436 U.S. 658, 694 (1978).

[20] Larry Alexander, *Constitutional Torts, the Supreme Court, and the Law of Noncontradiction: An Essay on* Zinermon v. Burch, 87 Nw. U. L. Rev. 576 (1993); *supra* § 2.08[4].

[21] Moore v. City of Desloge, 647 F.3d 841 (8th Cir. 2011).

[22] McMillian v. Monroe County, 520 U.S. 781, 785 (1997); St. Louis v. Praprotnik, 485 U.S. 112, 123 (1988) (plurality opinion).

[23] *Praprotnik*, 485 U.S. at 124; Brammer-Hoelter v. Twin Peaks Charter Acad., 602 F.3d 1175 (10th Cir. 2010).

policymaker for some areas and purposes and not for others and the municipality is liable only if some actor is the policymaker on the relevant areas and issues.[24]

Only a policymaker, someone with final policymaking authority, can establish formal municipal policy; an official wielding delegated policy-implementing authority, even discretionary authority cannot make policy. The line between the two often depends on whether a decisionmaker's determination is subject to review and ratification by another official. Someone is a policymaker so long as he retains authority to review and approve or reject another's discretionary choices; someone is not a policymaker if his discretionary decisions remain subject to review by someone else. That remains true even if review is circumscribed and highly deferential, even if review is not exercised in the case at hand, and even if that review is never exercised at all.[25]

Moreover, the municipality is not liable merely because a policymaker goes along with his subordinate's conduct; it is liable only if the policymaker expressly ratifies or approves, converting that subordinate decision into formal policy. Thus, a former municipal employee could not establish entity liability as to his transfer and termination, when his allegations demonstrated only misconduct by non-policymaking supervisors, when other final policymakers retained review authority and did not exercise it to expressly approve or ratify the challenged decisions.[26]

§ 4.04   ESTABLISHING MUNICIPAL LIABILITY

A municipal liability claim under *Monell* contains three elements. The plaintiff must plead and prove: (1) that she was deprived of a right, privilege, or immunity secured by the Constitution and laws, (2) that the municipality acted under color of state law (always the case with a government entity defendant), and (3) one of four basic circumstances in which a municipality may be liable.

[1]   Officers Acts Pursuant to Formal Policy

The most direct way to establish municipal liability is to show that individual officers acted pursuant to or in accordance with clear, formal, official government rules or policies established by a final policymaker. Even under this stricter standard, municipal liability was obvious and unquestionable in *Monell* itself. The plaintiffs were placed on maternity leave in the fifth month of pregnancy, although they were medically able to keep working and wanted to do so; leave was mandated by formal city policy (enacted by appropriate policymakers) and the plaintiffs were challenging the formal policy as violating equal protection.[27]

---

[24] *McMillian*, 520 U.S. at 785–86; Vodak v. City of Chicago, 639 F.3d 738 (7th Cir. 2011); Vives v. City of New York, 524 F.3d 346 (2d Cir. 2008).

[25] *Praprotnik*, 485 U.S. at 128–30; *but see id.* at 144–45 (Brennan, J., concurring in the judgment) (criticizing reliance on availability of review, where review not exercised and highly deferential).

[26] *Id.* at 128, 130–31.

[27] Monell v. Dep't of Soc. Servs., 436 U.S. 658, 660–61 & n.2, 694–95 (1978).

[2] Acts of Policymakers

A municipality can be liable for unconstitutional acts directly committed by its final policymaker,[28] even if the policymaker's acts are unlawful and even if they involve single or isolated actions rather than the formation of official policy.[29] There must be "a deliberate choice to follow a course of action . . . made from among various alternatives by the official or officials responsible for establishing final policy with respect to the subject matter in question."[30] In an extreme example, a municipality may be liable for a single sexual assault committed under color of law by the sheriff, who wields final policymaking authority as to law enforcement.[31] As the ultimate repository of power in a given area, all of the policymaker's on-duty actions, even unlawful ones, are the actions of the municipality and thus subject it to liability.[32] By contrast, the plaintiff in *Praprotnik* tried to meet this standard by challenging the allegedly unlawful employment decision; the claim failed because he was unable to show either that the supervisor who made the decision was the final policymaker or that final policymakers were involved in the decision.[33] A plaintiff can succeed only by showing direct involvement or active agreement, ratification, or acquiescence in the non-policymaker's decisions.[34]

[3] Persistent and Widespread Practices

Municipalities also may be liable under the "custom" language of § 1983 for practices that are so persistent and widespread as to practically have the force of law.[35] This prevents municipalities from insulating themselves from liability by delegating decision-making authority to non-policymakers; government still may be liable for a series of unlawful decisions by a non-policymaking subordinate, even if the policymaker does not review or ratify these decisions.[36] By acquiescing in these customs, the policymaker (as defined in state law) allows them to continue and to functionally take on the force of policy. Critically, the policymaker must be aware that these persistent and widespread practices exist and must acquiesce in them with deliberate indifference to the people whose rights may be violated by disregarding the known or obvious unconstitutional consequences of those practices.[37]

---

[28] Welch v. Ciampa, 542 F.3d 927 (1st Cir. 2008).

[29] Board of the County Comm'rs v. Brown, 520 U.S. 397 (1997); Newport v. Fact Concerts, Inc., 453 U.S. 247 (1981); Valle v. City of Houston, 613 F.3d 536 (5th Cir. 2010).

[30] Pembaur v. City of Cincinnati, 475 U.S. 469 (1986) (plurality opinion); Teesdale v. City of Chicago, 690 F.3d 829 (7th Cir. 2012).

[31] Bennett v. Pippin, 74 F.3d 578 (5th Cir. 1996); Turner v. Upton County, 915 F.2d 133 (5th Cir. 1990).

[32] *Turner*, 915 F.2d at 137.

[33] *Praprotnik*, 485 U.S. at 127–30.

[34] Jones v. Town of E. Haven, 691 F.3d 72 (2d Cir. 2012); Jeffes v. Barnes, 208 F.3d 49 (2d Cir. 2000).

[35] *Praprotnik*, 485 U.S. at 127.

[36] *Id.* at 130–31.

[37] Connick v. Thompson, 131 S. Ct. 1350 (2011); Amnesty Am. v. Town of W. Hartford, 361 F.3d 113 (2d Cir. 2004).

[4]　Failure to [Blank]

The final way to establish municipal liability is to show a "failure to [blank]" — a municipal failure (through a policymaker) to train,[38] supervise,[39] discipline,[40] or otherwise control individual officers who then engage in misconduct. One way of thinking about this is that the municipality's failure to [blank] reflects a "policy of inaction," functionally equivalent to an affirmative decision by the municipality that causes the plaintiff to be subject to the deprivation of his rights.[41] Another way is to think of it as a form of custom liability — the failure to [blank] indicates acceptance of individual unconstitutional practices and imbues them with some force. Either way, the Court recently described this as the "most tenuous" basis for municipal liability, applicable only in "limited circumstances."[42]

Failure-to-[blank] liability contains three strands. First, there must be a direct causal link between the municipality's failure and the deprivation of rights, such that the municipality can be said to be the "moving force" behind the violation.[43] The plaintiff must identify defects in the training or supervision programs and show how they contributed to the violation.[44] Liability will not attach where proper conduct should be obvious to the individual officer without training or supervision; in such a case the failure to train or supervise cannot be said to have caused the constitutional violation.[45] Moreover, it is not enough to show that better or more training could have helped avoid the injury or accident, because other factors may have a causal connection.[46]

Second is a foreseeability requirement. The constitutional injury must be a "highly predictable consequence" of the municipality's acts or failures to act.[47]

Third, there is a stringent standard of fault. The municipality must have acted with deliberate indifference to individual rights and to the risk that untrained or poorly trained or poorly supervised officers would violate rights. It must have disregarded known or obvious unconstitutional consequences of its failures, after being on actual or constructive notice that omissions in training, supervision, discipline, or control may cause individual officers to violate constitutional rights.[48]

---

[38] *Connick*, 131 S. Ct. at 1359; *Board of the County Comm'rs*, 520 U.S. at 410; City of Canton v. Harris, 489 U.S. 378 (1989).

[39] *Amnesty Am.*, 361 F.3d at 127.

[40] Batista v. Rodriguez, 702 F.2d 393 (2d Cir. 1983); Montgomery v. De Simone, 159 F.3d 120 (3d Cir. 1998).

[41] *Connick*, 131 S. Ct. at 1360; *City of Canton*, 489 U.S. at 395.

[42] *Connick*, 131 S. Ct. at 1359; Oklahoma City v. Tuttle, 471 U.S. 808, 822 (1985) (labeling such a policy "nebulous"); Mize v. Tedford, 2010 U.S. App. LEXIS 8650 (6th Cir. Apr. 26, 2010) (calling such cases "rare").

[43] *Board of the County Comm'rs*, 520 U.S. at 400; *City of Canton*, 489 U.S. at 389.

[44] *Amnesty America*, 361 F.3d at 127 n.8, 129–30.

[45] Walker v. New York, 974 F.2d 293, 300 (2d Cir. 1992).

[46] *City of Canton*, 489 U.S. at 390–91; *Amnesty Am.*, 361 F.3d at 130–31.

[47] *Connick*, 131 S. Ct. at 1361; *Board of the County Comm'rs*, 520 U.S. at 409.

[48] *Connick*, 131 S. Ct. at 1359; *Board of the County Comm'rs*, 520 U.S. at 409–10; *City of Canton*, 489 U.S. at 388.

Predictability and fault are linked — the more predictable or obvious the violation resulting from the failure, the more likely that failure is a product of deliberate indifference. Courts must "carefully test the link" between the policymaker's inadequate decisions (as to training, supervision, discipline, etc.) and the particular injury and also find the requisite high degree of fault, lest this all "collapse" into *de facto respondeat superior* liability.[49] As always, a final policymaker (as defined by state law) must be involved in the failure to [blank] in order to bind the municipality.

Predictability and fault can be shown in either of two ways. First, and ordinarily, there must be a pattern of repeated similar constitutional violations by untrained/unsupervised/undisciplined employees of which the final policymaker has notice and to which he did not respond.[50] Much of the action in litigation, and much of the "extraordinary unpredictability"[51] in this area, is over what constitutes a sufficient pattern of past violations, how similar the past instances must be, whether the policymaker in the relevant area was on notice, and the amount of knowledge or notice the policymaker must have of the prior incidents.[52]

Second, the Supreme Court has hypothesized that failure-to-[blank] liability may be possible on a "single incident," without a pattern of prior misconduct, "in a narrow range of circumstances" — recurring situations in which the need for more, better, or detailed training is "so obvious," and the potential for violations so predictable.[53] *City of Canton* suggested the obvious situation — an untrained police officer using deadly force against a fleeing suspect. Given the known frequency with which armed police officers come into contact and attempt to arrest fleeing suspects and the predictability that an officer untrained in the use of deadly force will misuse force in a way that violates citizens' rights, policymakers know to a "moral certainty" that officers will encounter that situation and the decision not to train its officers in the use of deadly force shows deliberate indifference to a highly predictable consequence of the absence of training.[54] Single-incident liability remains academic, however, as the Supreme Court has rejected both prior attempts to establish it.

In *Connick v. Thompson*, the Court held that line prosecutors' violations of their obligations to disclose exculpatory evidence[55] could not form the basis for single-incident failure-to-train municipal liability. Attorneys do not require the same training as police officers, because they come to their jobs equipped (from law school) with the tools to figure out their constitutional obligations, such that the absence of training does not make a future violation obvious. Moreover, disclosure

---

[49] *Connick*, 131 S. Ct. at 1360; *Board of the County Comm'rs*, 520 U.S. at 410.

[50] *Connick*, 131 S. Ct. at 1360.

[51] *Board of the County Comm'rs*, 520 U.S. at 435 (Breyer, J., dissenting); Peter Schuck, *Municipal Liability Under Section 1983: Some Lessons from Tort Law and Organization Theory*, 77 Geo. L.J. 1753, 1783 (1989).

[52] Vann v. City of New York, 72 F.3d 1040 (2d Cir. 1995).

[53] *Connick*, 131 S. Ct. at 1361; *City of Canton*, 489 U.S. at 390 & n.10.

[54] *City of Canton*, 489 U.S. at 390 n.10.

[55] Brady v. Maryland, 373 U.S. 83 (1963).

obligations are more nuanced than the rules governing deadly force, such that formal training beyond the basics is neither feasible nor necessary.[56] Thus, despite record evidence that the district attorney (the final policymaker for the office and thus for the municipality) himself did not fully understand disclosure rules and despite an alleged "culture of inattention"[57] to these obligations that was created by the DA and ran throughout the office, single-incident municipal liability was not established because the failure in this sort of training did not create such an obvious risk that the specific constitutional violation at issue would occur.[58] Instead, the plaintiff only could prevail by showing a pattern of past similar violations, a conclusion not supported by the record.

In *Board of County Commissioners of Bryan County v. Brown*, the municipality was sued over a single instance of excessive force by a deputy sheriff. The county's policies and training on the use of force were adequate, the deputy had no prior history of on-the-job misconduct and certainly not of excessive force so there was no failure to supervise or discipline, and the sheriff (the county's policymaker on law-enforcement matters) did not authorize or know about the deputy's misconduct. With failure to train and supervise cut off, the plaintiff tried to frame a claim around the policymaker's failure to scrutinize the responsible deputy prior to hiring him, arguing that the sheriff did not examine the applicant's background closely enough in search of something suggesting that the deputy might use excessive force. The Court rejected this argument, however. The hiring decision itself was lawful. And, further scrutiny of the deputy's background likely would not have revealed anything; the only violent incident that might have been discovered was a single bar fight in college, which would not have established the necessary "strong" causal connection between the deputy's background and the risk that he would use excessive force once on the job.[59] The sheriff thus did not act with deliberate indifference to a known risk that he was hiring someone likely to engage in this misconduct.

§ 4.05 THE FUTURE OF MUNICIPAL LIABILITY

The past two decades have revealed a deep divide within the Supreme Court about the future of municipal liability, especially under the failure-to-[blank] theory. This divide shows itself in sharp dissents in the two cases rejecting single-incident municipal liability.

In *Bryan County*, Justice Souter (writing for Justices Stevens, Ginsburg, and Breyer) criticized the majority's "deep skepticism" and "inhospitality" to municipal liability and the "skeptical hurdles" it kept raising to those claims.[60] The result is that many avenues of municipal liability are, as a practical matter, cut off — a plaintiff likely can recover only where the policy itself is unconstitutional. Souter insisted, however, that a facially constitutional policy or supervisory act sometimes

---

[56] *Connick*, 131 S. Ct. at 1361–64.

[57] *Id.* at 1382 (Ginsburg, J., dissenting).

[58] *Id.* at 1363–64.

[59] *Board of the County Comm'rs*, 520 U.S. at 405, 408–11, 412–14.

[60] *Id.* at 416, 421.

presents substantial risks of constitutional injury.[61] In *Connick*, Justice Ginsburg (joined by Justice Breyer and now by Justices Sotomayor and Kagan) insisted that the line prosecutors' non-disclosure was "no momentary oversight," but reflected a pervasive and persistent disregard of their constitutional obligations,[62] which pervaded the entire office.

The point of departure may be competing visions of whether constitutional cases typically involve a "single incident of a lone officer's misconduct" or whether they really hide more systemic and systematic misconduct.[63] The current approach reflects a strong preference for individual liability, leaving entity liability limited and rare by demanding so much to prove a *Monell* claim.

Of course, *Monell* identified § 1983's broad remedial purposes as one reason that liability should be genuinely available against the full range of potential wrongdoers and government misconduct. Narrowing municipal liability undermines deterrence, especially when combined with widespread indemnification of individual officers. There, arguably there is no true individual deterrence because the indemnified officer does not pay and no true governmental deterrence because government liability is so rare. The deliberate indifference requirement removes policymakers' incentive to closely monitor their underlings, at least outside the very narrow circumstances in which obviousness alone establishes liability (a category that may consist only of deadly force against a fleeing felon, as hypothesized in *City of Canton*). The standard also creates a conflict between the municipality and its officers, particularly when they are co-defendants in a damages action; government can avoid entity liability by relying on a "bad apple" or "rogue officer" defense, shifting blame entirely to the officer by arguing that policymakers did nothing to enable or encourage the individual misconduct. A rogue officer is just that — he does not act pursuant to policy or custom and no additional training, supervision, or discipline could change his behavior or avoid the constitutional harm.

In *Bryan County*, Justice Breyer (joined by Justices Stevens and Ginsburg, although not Souter) expressly urged the Court to reconsider *Monell's* rejection of municipal liability. Breyer argued that the history of the Sherman Amendment, on which *Monell* relied, showed Congress rejecting vicarious municipal liability for the acts of private citizens, which reveals nothing about congressional intent as to vicarious municipal liability for the acts of municipal employees. Stripped of that history, § 1983's "subject[] or cause[] to be subjected" is not inconsistent with *respondeat superior.* A municipality acts through its employees, thus it is linguistically proper to say it "causes" a constitutional violation whenever a municipal employee acts within the scope (or apparent scope) of his employment.[64] Moreover, a move to vicarious liability brings municipal liability in line with individual liability by adhering to a governmental rather than legalist, liability model.

Instead, Breyer argued, we are left with a body of law that is "neither readily understandable nor easy to apply" and that turns on some very fine and uncertain

---

[61] *Id.* at 416–21 (Souter, J., dissenting).

[62] *Connick*, 131 S. Ct. at 1370 (Ginsburg, J., dissenting).

[63] *Id.* (Ginsburg, J., dissenting).

[64] *Board of the County Comm'rs*, 520 U.S. at 431–32 (Breyer, J., dissenting).

distinctions. A legal principle — the supposed line between municipal liability and vicarious liability — that depends on so many ethereal distinctions "may not deserve such longevity."[65]

§ 4.06 REMEDIES AND MUNICIPAL LIABILITY

Difficult issues of municipal liability typically arise in damages actions, such as *Monell* and all of the cases discussed above. Claims for retrospective relief require courts to determine what happened in a past transaction or occurrence, whether and how it connected to municipal policy, custom, or failures to [blank], and whether any policymaker knew of or was involved in the past misconduct.

In *Los Angeles County v. Humphries*, the Court held that *Monell*'s policy-or-custom requirement also applies to claims for prospective relief, such as injunctions. In light of the plain language of § 1983 and the logic and reasoning of *Monell*, there is no "relief-based bifurcation" and no different requirements for different remedies.[66] The Court rejected the argument that *Monell* was concerned only with protecting the government from large damage awards for employee misconduct it did not cause, a concern not present with claims for injunctive relief; *Monell* was not about the city's economic needs, but about not imposing liability where the municipality does not cause the injury through official policy or custom.[67] That concern remains, regardless of the remedy sought.

§ 4.07 MUNICIPALITIES AND IMMUNITY

Municipalities do not enjoy any of the absolute or qualified immunities available to their officers. In *Owen v. City of Independence*, decided two years after *Monell*, the Court explained that the twin aims of § 1983 — compensation of victims of past abuses and deterrence of future constitutional violations — meant that qualified immunity does not extend to municipalities. The threat of entity, not merely individual, liability provides special deterrence of government misconduct. It would be "uniquely amiss" to allow government to escape liability for harms it causes, particularly where an injured plaintiff is otherwise left with no remedy because the responsible officer is entitled to immunity. Moreover, the overriding public policy considerations that justify immunizing individual officers do not justify similarly immunizing the municipality. In particular, the Court doubted that the risk of municipal (as opposed to personal) liability would chill any officer in performing his public duties. And even if it did final policymaking officials (those whose conduct triggers municipal liability) already consider the public fisc in deciding whether their policy-making conduct comports with constitutional mandates, so the additional consideration associated with entity liability does not change much.[68] The Supreme Court unanimously reaffirmed the inapplicability of immunity to munici-

---

[65] *Id.* at 433, 435 (Breyer, J., dissenting).

[66] Los Angeles County v. Humphries, 131 S. Ct. 447, 452–53 (2010).

[67] *Id.*

[68] Owen v. Independence, 445 U.S. 622, 651–52, 653 & n.37, 655–56 (1980).

palities, although without further explanation,[69] and lower courts have followed suit as to all immunity defenses.[70]

The combination of individual immunity and no municipal immunity means it is possible that an entity can be liable even if the individual officers are not. The elements for municipal liability are independent of any immunity defenses the individual officers may assert.[71] On the other hand, municipal liability will not attach if the claim against the individual officer fails because there was no predicate constitutional violation.[72]

§ 4.08　MUNICIPAL LIABILITY PUZZLES

1. *In July 2008, a church pastor is arrested for trespass when he and members of his church attempt to preach and distribute literature at a street festival. One year later, in July 2009, the pastor and four church members file a § 1983 action against the city and the officers who effected the 2008 arrest; among the relief sought is injunctive relief safeguarding their right to attend and engage in expressive activity at all future festivals, including the 2009 festival that is three days away. In opposing the injunction, the attorney for the city argues that under controlling Supreme Court case law the plaintiffs have no First Amendment right to attend and preach at a street festival and that police can remove them from the grounds at any time; this argument is legally erroneous, although the attorney does not disavow it during litigation in the district court. The parties twice (in 2009 and again in 2010) enter "standby orders" allowing the pastor and a small contingent of church members to attend, preach, and distribute literature at that year's festival, while the litigation moves forward. The case is now in the court of appeals, with the plaintiffs arguing that a permanent injunction should be entered against the city (not individual police officers).*[73]

Consider whether the city can be held liable and subject to an injunction based on the erroneous litigation position taken by its attorney.

2. *At two separate protests (approximately two months apart) at an abortion clinic, protesters entered and remained in the clinic reception area, chaining themselves together to block access to the area in which medical services are provided. When police come on the scene and seek to remove the protesters from the clinic, protesters utilize "passive-resistance" techniques; while not actively fighting back, they make it difficult to arrest and remove them from the premises. Police necessarily use "some degree of physical coercion" to get the protesters out of the*

---

[69] Leatherman v. Tarrant County Narcotics Intelligence & Coordination Unit, 507 U.S. 163, 166–67 (1993).

[70] Lore v. City of Syracuse, 670 F.3d 127 (2d Cir. 2012) (qualified immunity); Berkley v. Common Council, 63 F.3d 295 (4th Cir. 1995) (en banc) (legislative immunity); Singletary v. District of Columbia, 685 F. Supp. 2d 81 (D.D.C. 2010) (prosecutorial immunity).

[71] Gibson v. County of Washoe, 290 F.3d 1175, 1185 n.6 (9th Cir. 2002); Glenn v. City of Tyler, 242 F.3d 307 (5th Cir. 2001); Joyce v. Town of Tewksbury, 112 F.3d 19 (1st Cir. 1997) (en banc).

[72] Los Angeles v. Heller, 475 U.S. 796 (1986); Evans v. Chalmers, 703 F.3d 636 (4th Cir. 2012); Marion v. City of Corydon, 559 F.3d 700 (7th Cir. 2009); Green v. Post, 574 F.3d 1294 (10th Cir. 2009).

[73] Teesdale v. City of Chicago, 690 F.3d 829 (7th Cir. 2012).

building. But the protesters allege that the amount of force went beyond what was necessary under the circumstances; they offer evidence that officers inflicted pain on the protesters and made comments revealing an intent to inflict pain. They also offer evidence that many protesters were screaming in pain throughout the events and many suffered injuries.

The chief of police — the city's final policymaker on law enforcement matters — is present during both protests and supervises the officers making the arrests; plaintiffs allege that people repeatedly informed him that excessive force was being used. In between the two protests, the department establishes a new policy for handling abortion-clinic protests; the policy provides for video recording of all protests, photographing of all arrestees at the scene, and stationing of ambulances on the scene, along with a reminder to officers to act in a professional manner.[74]

Consider whether the protesters can establish municipal liability under either a failure to train or failure to supervise theory. Consider what facts are necessary for the plaintiffs to prevail.

PART B
STATE LIABILITY AND SOVEREIGN IMMUNITY

§ 4.09 SOVEREIGNTY

Liability of states under § 1983 for constitutional violations must begin with an account of the concepts of sovereignty and sovereign immunity. A detailed and thorough discussion of the theory and doctrine of sovereignty and the Eleventh Amendment to the United States Constitution is beyond the scope of this book. But general principles of sovereignty provide a necessary foundation for discussing how constitutional rights can be enforced and what civil rights Congress can create and vindicate.

Sovereignty refers to a political entity's authority or power to govern and to apply its law within a territory.[75] An entity is sovereign when it possesses political authority independent of any other person, entity, or body. The United States is sovereign under the Constitution. The several states are regarded as sovereign, in that they do not owe their origins, existence, or powers to the United States or the United States Constitution; they exercise inviolable power derived from The People of that state and would continue to exist as legal entities even without the federal government, the U.S. Constitution, or federal law. By contrast, municipalities are not sovereign, in that they draw their existence and authority not organically and not directly from The People, but instead from the states that establish them as municipal corporations and determine the powers they possess.[76]

---

[74] Amnesty Am. v. Town of W. Hartford, 361 F.3d 113 (2d Cir. 2004) (Sotomayor, J.).

[75] Boumediene v. Bush, 553 U.S. 723, 754–55 (2008); Steven G. Gey, *The Myth of State Sovereignty*, 63 Ohio St. L.J. 1601, 1631 (2002).

[76] Mt. Healthy City Sch. Dist. Bd. of Educ. v. Doyle, 429 U.S. 274 (1977).

Immunity from suit is "inherent in the nature of sovereignty."[77] Derived from European monarchies and the idea that "The King can do no wrong,"[78] immunity means that the sovereign cannot, without his consent, be sued *eo nomine* (by that name or in his own name) and made to answer and be held to account in his courts. The King, as the sovereign source of law, could not logically enforce the laws against himself.[79]

Sovereign immunity does not necessarily translate to republican government in the United States, where, at least theoretically, The People are sovereign. No government entity is truly sovereign because the entity must obtain its authority from those who consent to the exercise of authority over them; the public is the organic source of lawful political authority, government exercises only that authority delegated by the public so government can act on the public's behalf, and the expectation is that government should be accountable to the public for its conduct.[80] Moreover, immunity derives from ideals of royal divinity, of "the sovereign as divinely commissioned, and of the citizen as lacking power and agency,"[81] hailing the sovereign prince into court without his consent is an affront to his dignity. But that idea fits poorly with founding-generation conceptions of democratic accountability. It also is incoherent to ascribe dignity to a legal entity such as a government or for a government entity to suffer an affront to dignity.

Nevertheless, early on the Supreme Court identified the sovereign immunity of the United States government as a "universally received opinion."[82] The federal government is not subject to suit in its own name (or the name of its agencies or arms) in federal court for any remedy unless it consents to suit, as Congress did in the Federal Tort Claims Act and the Westfall Act.[83] Indeed, the development of, and confusion surrounding, the *Bivens* cause of action stems in part from the United States expressly declining to waive sovereign immunity as to constitutional claims against federal officers.[84] Every state recognizes its own immunity from suit, without its consent, in its own courts and under its own laws.[85]

---

[77] The Federalist No. 81 (Alexander Hamilton) (Clinton Rossiter ed., 1961).

[78] Louis L. Jaffe, *Suits Against Governments and Officers: Sovereign Immunity*, 77 Harv. L. Rev. 1, 4 (1963).

[79] *Id.* at 1, 2–4.

[80] John T. Noonan, Jr., Narrowing The Nation's Power: The Supreme Court Sides with The States (2002); Erwin Chemerinsky, *Against Sovereign Immunity*, 53 Stan. L. Rev. 1201 (2001); Steven G. Gey, *The Myth of State Sovereignty*, 63 Ohio St. L.J. 1601 (2002); Lauren K. Robel, *Sovereignty and Democracy: The States' Obligations to Their Citizens Under Federal Statutory Law*, 78 Ind. L.J. 543 (2003); Howard M. Wasserman, *Rejecting Sovereign Immunity in Public Law Litigation*, 80 Fordham L. Rev. Res Gestae 76 (2012).

[81] Lauren K. Robel, *Sovereignty and Democracy: The States' Obligations to Their Citizens Under Federal Statutory Law*, 78 Ind. L.J. 543, 553 (2003).

[82] Cohens v. Virginia, 19 U.S. (6 Wheat.) 264, 411–12 (1821).

[83] 28 U.S.C. §§ 1346(b), 2679; *see* Sosa v. Alvarez-Machain, 542 U.S. 692, 700 (2004) (quoting Richards v. United States, 369 U.S. 1, 6 (1962)).

[84] 28 U.S.C. § 2679(b)(2)(A); James E. Pfander & David Baltmanis, *Rethinking* Bivens: *Legitimacy and Constitutional Adjudication*, 98 Geo. L.J. 117, 121–22 (2009); *supra* § 2.19[4].

[85] *See, e.g.*, Am. Home Assurance Co. v. Nat'l R.R. Passenger Corp., 908 So. 2d 459 (Fla. 2005); Alston v. State, 762 N.E.2d 923 (N.Y. 2001).

§ 4.10 ELEVENTH AMENDMENT AND STATE SOVEREIGN IMMUNITY

U.S. Const. amend XI (1795)

The Judicial power of the United States shall not be construed to extend to any suit in law or equity, commenced or prosecuted against one of the United States by Citizens of another State, or by Citizens or Subjects of any Foreign State.

The more complex question is the extent to which states can be subject to suit in federal court and/or under federal law.

[1] Origins and Development of the Eleventh Amendment

Just four years into the new Constitution, the Supreme Court held in *Chisholm v. Georgia* that it had original jurisdiction over an action by a South Carolina citizen against the state of Georgia to recover on Revolutionary War bonds. Article III § 2's enumeration of the cases federal courts could hear included controversies "between a state and citizens of another state,"[86] language which plainly encompassed that case. And principles of sovereign immunity did not override that constitutional language.[87]

At its first meeting following the Court's decision, Congress proposed, and the states quickly ratified, a constitutional amendment providing that:

> The Judicial power of the United States shall not be construed to extend to any suit in law or equity, commenced or prosecuted against one of the United States by Citizens of another State, or by Citizens or Subjects of any Foreign State.[88]

In *Hans v. Louisiana*, the Court considered the effect of the Eleventh Amendment on an action in federal district court against a state by a citizen of that state. The plaintiff, a Louisiana citizen, held Civil War bonds and claimed that certain changes to Louisiana law unconstitutionally impaired the state's contractual obligations as to the bonds.[89] He argued that the federal court had jurisdiction because the claim arose under the Constitution of the United States and that the Eleventh Amendment was inapplicable because it deprived federal courts of jurisdiction only over claims against a state by citizens of another state, not claims against a state by its own citizens. The Court rejected this argument, insisting that a plaintiff's ability to sue a state in federal court depended not on the language of Article III (where the justices had mistakenly focused in *Chisholm*) or the Eleventh Amendment, but on general principles of sovereign immunity. States enjoy the same broad immunity from being haled into federal court as they do from being

---

[86] U.S. Const. art. III, § 2.

[87] Chisholm v. Georgia, 2 U.S. 419 (1793).

[88] U.S. Const. amend. XI (1795).

[89] U.S. Const. art. I, § 10.

haled into their own courts, subject only to their consent or their waiver of immunity.[90]

[2]   Possible Meanings of the Eleventh Amendment

Three competing theories of the meaning of the Eleventh Amendment have developed in the federal courts and in the scholarly literature.

First is the "plain meaning" approach, which posits that the Eleventh Amendment means precisely what it says: Federal courts do not have subject-matter jurisdiction over actions against a state by a citizen of another state. But the amendment does not bar jurisdiction over actions against a state by its own citizen (assuming some other basis for federal jurisdiction). States in such cases perhaps enjoy a sub-constitutional common law immunity, which Congress may abrogate. Individuals thus can sue their own states in federal court in federal-question cases (such as constitutional claims), but they cannot sue other states.[91] In other words, *Hans* was simply wrong.

Second is the "diversity" theory, most commonly associated with Justices Stevens and Brennan. It holds that the Eleventh Amendment prohibits only suits against a state by a citizen of another state where the basis for subject-matter jurisdiction is the identities of the parties. The language of the Eleventh Amendment tracks the language of the citizen-state diversity provision in Article III, § 2, carving out one narrow exception from that jurisdictional grant. But the Eleventh Amendment does not speak to suits enjoying some other basis of federal jurisdiction that does not depend on the identity of the parties, namely that the action arises under the Constitution or laws of the United States.[92]The Eleventh Amendment does not protect a state from suit as to federal constitutional or statutory claims, whether by its own citizens or by citizens of another state.

The third view has prevailed — states enjoy in federal court a broad constitutionally based sovereign immunity, recognized in *Hans* and reaffirmed by the Court in its recent federalism cases.[93] The Eleventh Amendment's text does not control the inquiry and is somewhat beside the point. In amending the Constitution, Congress wanted to do nothing more than overturn *Chisholm*; to do this, it only had to address the citizen-state diversity provision of Article III, § 2 on which the *Chisholm* Court had relied in finding jurisdiction. It was unnecessary for Congress to do anything more or to paint with any broader brush. And it certainly was unnecessary for Congress to specify that states could not be sued by their own

---

[90]   Hans v. Louisiana, 134 U.S. 1 (1890).

[91]   Lawrence C. Marshall, *Fighting the Words of the Eleventh Amendment*, 102 HARV. L. REV. 1342 (1989).

[92]   Seminole Tribe v. Florida, 517 U.S. 44, 110–11 (1996) (Stevens, J., dissenting); Atascadero State Hospital v. Scanlon, 473 U.S. 234, 294 (1985) (Brennan, J., dissenting); Akhil Reed Amar, *Of Sovereignty and Federalism*, 96 YALE L.J. 1425 (1987); William A. Fletcher, *A Historical Interpretation of the Eleventh Amendment: A Narrow Construction of an Affirmative Grant of Jurisdiction Rather than a Prohibition Against Jurisdiction*, 35 STAN. L. REV. 1033 (1983).

[93]   Coleman v. Court of Appeals, 132 S. Ct. 1327 (2012); Alden v. Maine, 527 U.S. 706 (1999); *Seminole Tribe*, 517 U.S. at 54.

citizens — no one thought they could be. At the Founding, the nation knew that states enjoyed immunity as sovereigns and the Framers would not have undone such traditional and historic protections without saying so in more explicit and concrete terms.[94]

Alden v. Maine marks the apotheosis of the move from the Eleventh Amendment's text to this freestanding sovereign immunity, because the action was brought under federal law in state court. The Eleventh Amendment, which speaks of the "judicial power of the United States," is by its terms inapplicable in state court. Nevertheless, *Alden* insisted that what is colloquially called "Eleventh Amendment immunity" is merely "convenient shorthand" for broad notions of state sovereign immunity, derived from the fundamental nature of sovereignty, not from the Constitution.[95] This immunity applies to all private lawsuits against the state, regardless of the source of law and regardless of forum.[96] And regardless of remedy sought. Although courts sometimes loosely state that immunity prohibits claims for damages against states,[97] the doctrinal reality is that sovereign immunity prohibits all private suits against states *eo nomine* for any remedy, prospective, or retroactive.[98]

[3] Goals of State Sovereign Immunity

Sovereign immunity serves two primary goals.

First, as discussed, it protects the dignity of states as sovereigns, insulating them from coercive process of judicial tribunals, which carries with it the obligation to respond and to comply with court orders. The affront to state dignity was even greater in *Alden*, when the sovereign state was subject to suit and coercive process in its own courts.[99]

Second, sovereign immunity protects the state treasury and the financial integrity of the states, ensuring that states, not Congress or federal courts, control the state fisc.[100] Having to pay court judgments leaves the state with less money available to serve public needs. Choices of how public funds should be spent should not be determined by federal judicial decree, but should remain in the hands of the state's elected representatives, who are publicly charged with balancing competing financial demands. This concern for the public treasury is particularly salient in the Eleventh Amendment's history. Both *Chisholm*, which prompted the amendment, and *Hans*, which introduced the broad immunity theory that has carried the doctrinal day, arose out of private suits against states to recover on war debts, in immediate post-war periods in which states were genuinely concerned with the

---

[94] *Alden*, 527 U.S. at 724–25.

[95] *Id.* at 712–13, 730–31.

[96] *Id.* at 712.

[97] *Coleman*, 132 S. Ct. at 1333.

[98] Howard M. Wasserman, *Rejecting Sovereign Immunity in Public Law Litigation*, 80 FORDHAM L. REV. RES GESTAE 76, 79 (2012).

[99] *Alden*, 527 U.S. at 709, 749–51.

[100] *Id.* at 751; Hess v. Port Auth. Trans-Hudson Corp., 513 U.S. 30 (1994).

pressure such debts were putting on their treasuries.[101]

[4] Limits of State Sovereign Immunity

There are several limits on state sovereign immunity.

First, sovereign immunity applies only to states, state agencies, and other "arms of the state."[102] It does not protect cities, counties, or other local government entities, which are not sovereign; municipal governments originate, exist, and exercise power by virtue of state law and state delegation, not of their own force and not directly by power granted by The People.[103] Whether sovereign immunity applies in a given case depends on whether a particular defendant is the state or an arm of the state, a question of state law on which the defendant bears the burden of persuasion.[104] One might question whether this frees a state to manipulate the titles and structure of its municipalities and local officials, making everything an arm of the state and everyone a state officer, shielding local government thereby, but the Court has rejected those arguments.[105]

Second, even arms of the state are not left unchecked and free to ignore obligations under federal law. There is a distinction between "regulatory" immunity (immunity from legal regulation of one's conduct) and "remedial" immunity (immunity from private litigation and privately enforced judicial remedies); states enjoy only the latter. Federal law remains valid as regulation of state conduct and Congress can obligate states to follow otherwise-valid federal laws. States are immunized only against private enforcement of federal law, but not from the reach of the laws themselves.[106] Because states remain subject to the obligations of federal law they remain subject to enforcement mechanisms other than suit *eo nomine* by private individuals. States can be sued by the United States; by subjecting themselves to the dictates of federal law, states also subject themselves to the power of the national government to enforce federal law in federal court.[107]

Two final alternatives will be discussed in detail in the following sections: (1) Congress can abrogate sovereign immunity and subject states to private suit under federal law and (2) private plaintiffs can sue individual state officers, who do not enjoy sovereign immunity, in their individual capacities for both legal and equitable relief.

---

[101] Thomas H. Lee, *Making Sense of the Eleventh Amendment: International Law and State Sovereignty*, 96 Nw. U. L. Rev. 1027, 1043 (2002).

[102] McMillian v. Monroe County, 520 U.S. 781 (1997).

[103] Mt. Healthy City Sch. Dist. Bd. of Educ. v. Doyle, 429 U.S. 274 (1977).

[104] Gorton v. Gettel, 554 F.3d 60 (2d Cir. 2009).

[105] *McMillian*, 520 U.S. at 796.

[106] *Alden*, 527 U.S. at 754–55; Louis D. Bilionis, *Conservative Reformation, Popularization, and the Lessons of Reading Criminal Justice as Constitutional Law*, 52 UCLA L. Rev. 979, 1022 (2005).

[107] *Alden*, 527 U.S. at 755–57.

§ 4.11   OVERCOMING STATE SOVEREIGN IMMUNITY: CONGRESSIONAL ABROGATION

[1]   Abrogation

Congress may enact legislation abrogating sovereign immunity and subjecting states or arms of the state to private suit. Abrogation is consistent with the idea that states surrendered portions of their sovereignty as part of the "Plan of the Convention" at which they created and ratified the Constitution; states ceded to Congress authority to legislate on certain matters, agreed that federal law would prevail over conflicting state law, and agreed to be bound by Congress' exercise of its enumerated legislative powers.[108] Congressional power to abrogate also is consistent with the so-called "political safeguards of federalism"; because states are represented in Congress and play a role in the creation of federal legislation, state interests and state burdens, already have been considered in creating federal law.[109] Federalism interests otherwise served by state sovereign immunity will be taken into account in the federal legislative process itself; if Congress nevertheless subjects states to suit, it has done so conscious and respectful of those state interests. While the Court has declined to rely exclusively on those structural safeguards,[110] the possibility of abrogation in some circumstances under some powers has been accepted in part because state interests are protected in the legislative process. Finally, as a matter of separation of powers and democratic theory, it is significant that the popularly elected and democratically accountable Congress, not unelected courts, is the institution making abrogation choices and altering the federal-state balance.

Abrogation entails a two-step inquiry. First, Congress must include an unequivocal and unmistakably clear statutory statement that immunity has been abrogated, that states are subject to the new legislation, and that state are subject to private suit for its enforcement.[111] In other words, Congress must, in fact, clearly have abrogated sovereign immunity in that legislation. Second, if Congress did abrogate through the necessary clear statement, it must have the constitutional power to subject states to private suit; that is, it must have enacted the legislation under an enumerated power that permits abrogation.[112] In other words, Congress must be able to abrogate.

The analysis typically centers on the second question. Congress generally knows how to provide a clear statement that states are subject to suit under a law, although it must be careful to specify not only that states can be sued, but also

---

[108] Alden v. Maine, 527 U.S. 706, 755–56 (1999).

[109] Kimel v. Florida Bd. of Regents, 528 U.S. 62, 93 (2000) (Stevens, J., dissenting in part and concurring in part); Seminole Tribe v. Florida, 517 U.S. 44, 184 (1996) (Souter, J., dissenting); *see also* Michael E. Solimine, *Formalism, Pragmatism, and the Conservative Critique of the Eleventh Amendment*, 101 MICH. L. REV. 1463, 1482 (2003).

[110] Anthony J. Bellia, Jr., *Federalism Doctrines and Abortion Cases: A Response to Professor Fallon*, 51 ST. LOUIS U. L.J. 767, 794 (2007).

[111] *Kimel*, 528 U.S. at 73; *Seminole Tribe*, 517 U.S. at 55.

[112] *Kimel*, 528 U.S. at 73; *Seminole Tribe*, 517 U.S. at 55.

what remedies they can be sued for.[113] The more controversial question is whether that abrogation is constitutional, which depends on what power Congress exercised in enacting a particular piece of legislation.

[2]   Article I, § 8

The first source of legislative power is Article I, § 8, which contains a laundry list of subjects and areas on which Congress may legislate.

Congress cannot abrogate state sovereign immunity when acting under many of its Article I powers, including its power to regulate commerce with Indian tribes,[114] to regulate commerce among the several states,[115] and to establish systems of intellectual property.[116] Moreover, a state does not constructively waive sovereign immunity and subject itself to suit under federal laws regulating interstate commerce simply by engaging in a particular lawful market activity.[117]

On the other hand, Congress can abrogate in creating uniform laws on bankruptcy, in light of the unique history and nature of bankruptcy and the Bankruptcy Clause.[118] It also can abrogate under the Spending Clause; it may condition federal funds on states agreeing to private suit, so long as it makes sufficiently clear that by accepting federal funds states are waiving immunity, agreeing to private suit, and aware of precisely what they are agreeing to private suit for.[119]

[3]   Fourteenth Amendment § 5

The second source of legislative power is § 5 of the Fourteenth Amendment, which empowers Congress to "enforce" the provisions of the Fourteenth Amendment, particularly the substantive provisions of § 1, via "appropriate legislation."[120] Starting with *Fitzpatrick v. Bitzer*,[121] the Court has repeatedly stated that Congress can abrogate sovereign immunity when acting pursuant to that enforcement power. The Fourteenth Amendment "fundamentally altered the balance of federal/state power"; § 5 is a grant of plenary authority to enforce a constitutional provision that, by its terms, limits the power of the states.[122] That necessarily limits state sovereignty, as well, by empowering Congress to ensure that federal interests remain paramount and that states adhere to their federal obligations; subjecting states to private litigation is one means of ensuring state

---

[113] Sossamon v. Texas, 131 S. Ct. 1651 (2011).

[114] *Seminole Tribe*, 517 U.S. at 47.

[115] Board of Trustees v. Garrett, 531 U.S. 356 (2001); College Sav. Bank v. Florida Prepaid Postsecondary Educ. Expense Bd., 527 U.S. 666 (1999).

[116] College Sav. Bank v. Florida Prepaid Postsecondary Educ. Expense Bd., 527 U.S. 666 (1999).

[117] *Id.* at 680–83.

[118] Cent. Va. Cmty. College v. Katz, 546 U.S. 356 (2006).

[119] *Sossamon*, 131 S. Ct. at 1655.

[120] U.S. Const. amend. XIV, § 5 (1868).

[121] Fitzpatrick v. Bitzer, 427 U.S. 445 (1976).

[122] Alden v. Maine, 527 U.S. 706, 756 (1999); *Fitzpatrick*, 427 U.S. at 453–56.

adherence. Justice Scalia has explained *Fitzpatrick* in terms of the timing of various constitutional provisions. The Constitution of 1787 embodies prevailing notions of state sovereign immunity and the Eleventh Amendment, ratified eight years later, reaffirms that consensus. The Fourteenth Amendment, by contrast, postdates that reaffirmation and marks a change in the federal/state balance and in the scope of congressional power; it reflects a subsequent limitation on sovereign immunity justifying the power to abrogate.[123]

But Congress is limited in § 5 to enacting only "appropriate legislation" that "enforce[s]" the Fourteenth Amendment. This means it only can enact "corrective" or "prophylactic" legislation that will "remedy" or "deter" constitutional violations by states.[124] The point of debate is what that means. The Court at one point held that § 5 incorporates the forgiving standard for Article I's Necessary and Proper Clause as elaborated in *McCulloch v. Maryland.*[125] And Justice Brennan once proposed what scholars label the "ratchet theory," under which § 5 functions as a one-way power ratchet; § 1 establishes a floor below which Congress cannot drop individual rights, but Congress through § 5 can ratchet statutory rights above that floor.[126] Thus, for example, while the Constitution does not prohibit states from using literacy tests as a condition on voting, it would be appropriate remedial legislation for Congress to prohibit literacy tests through the Voting Rights Act, enacted under its powers to enforce the Fourteenth and Fifteenth Amendments.[127]

But in *City of Boerne v. Flores*, the Court narrowed that enforcement power. "Appropriate legislation" must be congruent and proportionate to the legitimate ends Congress is trying to serve (correcting some constitutional violations) — or, stated differently, there must be congruence and proportionality between the statutory right created and the constitutional right being enforced.[128] This standard limits the scope of the statutory rights Congress can create through its § 5 power, linking them to the scope of the constitutional rights established in § 1 of the Fourteenth Amendment (including the incorporated Bill of Rights).[129] Congress can by statute regulate more than what the Constitution actually prohibits of its own force, but not too far — the statutory right must be congruent and proportional to the constitutional right. Moreover, *Boerne* and its progeny make federal courts, particularly the Supreme Court, final arbiter of § 1 constitutional meaning and the scope of constitutional rights, requiring Congress to yield to that interpretation. In other words, statutory rights must be congruent and proportionate to constitutional rights as interpreted and established by the

---

[123] Pennsylvania v. Union Gas Co., 491 U.S. 1, 41–42 (1989) (Scalia, J., concurring in part and dissenting in part).

[124] City of Boerne v. Flores, 521 U.S. 507 (1997); Civil Rights Cases, 109 U.S. 3 (1883).

[125] South Carolina v. Katzenbach, 383 U.S. 301, 326 (1966) (quoting McCulloch v. Maryland, 17 U.S. (4 Wheat.) 316, 421 (1819)).

[126] Katzenbach v. Morgan, 384 U.S. 641, 651 n.10 (1966); William Cohen, *Congressional Power to Interpret Due Process and Equal Protection*, 27 STAN. L. REV. 603 (1975).

[127] *Katzenbach*, 384 U.S. at 649–50. The Fifteenth Amendment contains an identical enforcement provision. U.S. CONST. AMEND. XV § 2 (1870).

[128] *City of Boerne*, 521 U.S. at 519–20, 529–30, 533–34.

[129] *Id.* at 519.

federal courts.[130] To show congruence and proportionality, Congress must build a legislative record of a pattern or history of unconstitutional laws, practices, and conduct by states and state agencies; societal, private, or municipal misconduct is not sufficient,[131] nor is misconduct targeting a group different than the one protected by the legislation.[132]

After *Boerne*, state sovereign immunity can be abrogated, and states can be subject to suit *eo nomine* under federal law, only if the statute qualifies as valid enforcement legislation under § 5 — that is, only if the statute is congruent and proportional to the constitutional right (as construed by the federal courts) being enforced. This has produced a mixed bag as to modern civil rights legislation in the past two decades. Congress can subject states to suit under Title VII of the Civil Rights Act of 1964,[133] the family care provisions of the Family and Medical Leave Act ("FMLA"),[134] and the public accommodations provisions of the Americans with Disabilities Act ("ADA") as applied to the fundamental right of access to the courts.[135] Congress cannot subject states to private suit under the employment provisions of the ADA,[136] the Age Discrimination in Employment Act,[137] or the self-care provisions of the FMLA.[138]

Importantly, these statutes all remain valid and enforceable as legislation enacted under the Commerce Clause, the source of authority for most modern civil rights legislation. Private actors and municipalities remain subject to private suit under these laws as regulations of interstate commerce; because neither enjoys sovereign immunity, there is no need for Congress to abrogate sovereign immunity through Article I. States do enjoy sovereign immunity, however, so they cannot be subject to private suit under a Commerce Clause enactment; they can be sued only if the law is also valid as § 5 legislation, requiring the congruence-and-proportionality assessment.

One way of understanding congruence and proportionality is that it links the statutory right to the standard of scrutiny for the underlying constitutional right being "enforced." The more the statutory right looks like the constitutional right, the more congruent and proportionate it is. Moreover, there is a longer history of state misconduct as to those rights that receive higher scrutiny, thus Congress likely can build a stronger legislative record of past state discrimination. The statutes upheld as valid § 5 abrogations all enforce rights subject to strict or heightened scrutiny — race discrimination, gender discrimination, and discrimination affecting fundamental rights. By contrast, statutory rights have been found not congruent and proportionate where the underlying constitutional

---

[130]   *Kimel*, 528 U.S. at 83; *City of Boerne*, 521 U.S. at 519.

[131]   Board of Trustees v. Garrett, 531 U.S. 356, 368–69 (2001).

[132]   Coleman v. Court of Appeals, 132 S. Ct. 1327, 1335 (2012).

[133]   *Fitzpatrick*, 427 U.S. at 456–57.

[134]   Nev. Dep't of Human Res. v. Hibbs, 538 U.S. 721 (2003).

[135]   Tennessee v. Lane, 541 U.S. 509 (2004).

[136]   Board of Trustees v. Garrett, 531 U.S. 356 (2001).

[137]   *Kimel*, 528 U.S. at 66–67.

[138]   *Coleman*, 132 S. Ct. at 1332.

right is subject to rational basis review (age discrimination or disability discrimination), because the statute prohibits significantly more conduct than does the Constitution of its own force.[139] In fact, this analysis plays out in the Court's most recent § 5 case, which held that states cannot be sued for damages under the FMLA's self-care provisions. The majority understood the statute as remedying discrimination because of pregnancy or illness, which receives only rational-basis review, while Justice Ginsburg's dissent argued that the statute remedies sex discrimination, which receives heightened scrutiny.[140]

Justice Scalia has urged the Court to drop the congruence-and-proportionality test. Congress only "enforces" the Fourteenth Amendment if the conduct it prohibits by statute is already prohibited by the Constitution; whenever Congress regulates more than the Fourteenth Amendment prohibits, even if it is still proportionate, it no longer is enforcing the Constitution. Section 5 thus only empowers Congress to create statutory rights equivalent to existing constitutional rights, as well as to create statutory causes of action and remedies for actual constitutional violations.[141]

An example of the Scalia approach in action is *United States v. Georgia*, a suit against a state challenging prison conditions under the ADA's public accommodations provisions. Writing for the Court, Justice Scalia concluded that the ADA validly abrogated sovereign immunity in that case by reading the complaint as challenging conduct that actually violated the Eighth Amendment (as incorporated in § 1 of the Fourteenth Amendment). The ADA simply provided a private statutory remedy against a state for conduct that independently violated the Constitution.[142]

§ 4.12 ABROGATION AND § 1983

Justice Scalia has cited § 1983 as an example of a statute that validly abrogates sovereign immunity under his narrower approach to § 5.[143] Section 1983 does not create rights, prohibit conduct, or impose duties; it merely provides a private cause of action and a remedy to enforce rights existing under § 1 itself. A plaintiff prevails on a § 1983 constitutional claim only by establishing that the defendant's conduct, in fact, violates the Constitution. In *City of Boerne* terms, there is perfect congruence and proportionality between § 1983 and the Constitution, at least as to constitutional claims. As far as the Eleventh Amendment is concerned, therefore, Congress could subject states to suit under § 1983.

In *Edelman v. Jordan* in 1974 and its 1979 sequel, *Quern v. Jordan*, however, the Court held that § 1983 did not abrogate state sovereign immunity, given the absence of any discussion of sovereign immunity in the history of the Ku Klux Klan Act of

---

[139] *Garrett*, 531 U.S. at 372–73.

[140] *Compare Coleman*, 132 S. Ct. at 1335 *with id.* at 1339–40 (Ginsburg, J., dissenting).

[141] *Id.* at 1338–39 (Scalia, J., concurring in the judgment); Tennessee v. Lane, 541 U.S. 509, 557–59 (2004) (Scalia, J., dissenting).

[142] United States v. Georgia, 546 U.S. 151, 158–59 (2006).

[143] Tennessee v. Lane, 541 U.S. 509, 559–60 (2004) (Scalia, J., dissenting).

1871 or any clear statutory indications of congressional intent to subject states to suit.[144] It was unclear, however, whether this conclusion was a product of statutory interpretation or the limits of the Eleventh Amendment.

In *Will v. Michigan Department of State Police*, the Court squarely confronted the issue and concluded it was the former. *Will* involved a § 1983 action brought in state court, where the Eleventh Amendment was not (at least at the time) thought applicable; the Court formally held what it insisted had been implicit in *Quern* — a state is not a "person" for purposes of § 1983 and thus is not subject to suit as a statutory matter.[145]

Several statutory arguments supported this conclusion. First, if states are included within the meaning of "person," it would mean the statute reaches "any [state]" acting "under color of any [law] of any State," which is awkward drafting. Second, the ordinary meaning of "person" does not include sovereigns, so that word does not make "unmistakably clear" that Congress intended to subject sovereign entities to private suit. Third, the Court relied on the Dictionary Act (as it did in recognizing municipal liability under § 1983 in *Monell*[146]), which in 1871 defined persons as bodies corporate and politic, a term construed not to include states.[147]

Will also turned on evolving case law. In *Fitzpatrick v. Bitzer* in 1976, the Court pointed out that Title VII used the word "person" to identify potential defendants, but that the statute did not originally reach state employers; it took amendments expressly defining person to include "governments, governmental agencies, [and] political subdivisions."[148] The conclusion, for which the *Fitzpatrick* Court had cited *Monroe v. Pape*, was that the unmodified "person" does not include states unless the statute explicitly includes states in the definition.[149] But two years after *Fitzpatrick*, *Monell* overturned the municipal-liability holding of *Monroe* and held that "person" under § 1983 could include local governments; this implied that *Fitzpatrick* no longer controlled the point and the door was open to the conclusion that "person," unmodified, could include all government entities, including states. But the Court rejected this argument. *Monell* was about municipalities only, while the Eleventh Amendment and sovereign immunity are about states and arms of the states; that "person" includes municipalities says nothing about whether it includes states and state agencies.[150]

The inability to sue arms of the state under § 1983 therefore is not about the Eleventh Amendment at all, but about statutory interpretation. Stated differently, states cannot be sued under § 1983 because of the first prong of the abrogation analysis, not the second. Although regularly overlooked, the point is significant in two respects. First, federal courts actually misapply the law by repeatedly discussing these cases in terms of sovereign immunity and the Eleventh Amend-

---

[144] Quern v. Jordan, 440 U.S. 332 (1979); Edelman v. Jordan, 415 U.S. 651 (1974).

[145] Will v. Michigan Dep't of State Police, 491 U.S. 58 (1989).

[146] Monell v. Dep't of Soc. Servs., 436 U.S. 658 (1978); *supra* § 2.03[2].

[147] *Will*, 491 U.S. at 64–70.

[148] Fitzpatrick v. Bitzer, 427 U.S. 445, 449 n.2 (1976).

[149] *Id.* at 451–52.

[150] *Will*, 491 U.S. at 70; *Quern*, 440 U.S. at 341.

ment rather than the text of § 1983 and the meaning of "person."[151] Second, the amenability of states to suit under § 1983 is entirely in Congress' hands; Congress could amend the statute to clearly and explicitly define states as persons (as it did in amending Title VII), thereby allowing private suits against states *eo nomine* on constitutional claims.

§ 4.13 OVERCOMING STATE SOVEREIGN IMMUNITY: *EX PARTE YOUNG*

[1] *Ex Parte Young*

The second method of privately enforcing federal rights in the face of sovereign immunity or the textual limits of § 1983 is to pursue litigation not against the state or state agency, but against state officials. This brings us to the doctrine of *Ex parte Young*.[152]

The state of Minnesota, at the urging of state Attorney General Young, imposed sharp limits on the rates that railroads could charge in the state; those limits were enforceable through "drastic" criminal penalties against railroad shareholders, officers, and employees. Shareholders brought suit in federal court against Young, who as attorney general was the executive-branch officer charged with enforcing state law; the lawsuit argued that the rate laws violated Substantive Due Process and the Contracts Clause and sought an injunction preventing Young from initiating any prosecutions or making any other attempts to enforce the rates. The district court agreed that the law was unconstitutional and entered the injunction. Young ignored it and initiated enforcement proceedings in state court, and the district court held him in contempt. Young then argued that the contempt citation was improper because the injunction was improper under the Eleventh Amendment.[153]

The Supreme Court rejected Young's argument, holding that the contempt order was permissible because the injunction was permissible. The underlying lawsuit was a valid action against a responsible executive officer (the attorney general) for prospective relief from an ongoing violation of the federal Constitution by state officials and state law.[154] The ongoing violation was the continued threat of enforcement of an unconstitutional state law; the prospective relief was the injunction prohibiting Young from prosecuting or otherwise enforcing the statute. Although the state law remains on the books, the injunction means it cannot be

---

[151] McMillian v. Monroe County, 520 U.S. 781 (1997); Lewis v. Univ. of Texas Med. Branch, 665 F.3d 625 (5th Cir. 2011); Carter v. City of Philadelphia, 181 F.3d 339 (3d Cir. 1999).

[152] Ex parte Young, 209 U.S. 123 (1908); Barry Friedman, *The Story of* Ex Parte Young: *Once Controversial, Now Canon, in* Federal Courts Stories 247 (Vicki C. Jackson & Judith Resnik eds., 2010); John Harrison, Ex Parte Young, 60 Stan. L. Rev. 989 (2008).

[153] *Young*, 209 U.S. at 145–46; Barry Friedman, *The Story of* Ex Parte Young: *Once Controversial, Now Canon, in* Federal Courts Stories 247, 259–64 (Vicki C. Jackson & Judith Resnik eds., 2010); John Harrison, Ex Parte Young, 60 Stan. L. Rev. 989, 991–92 (2008).

[154] *Young*, 209 U.S. at 159–60; Barry Friedman, *The Story of* Ex Parte Young: *Once Controversial, Now Canon, in* Federal Courts Stories 247, 266–67 (Vicki C. Jackson & Judith Resnik eds., 2010).

enforced as to the plaintiffs, thus preventing continuance or reoccurrence of the harm to the railroad and its agents and shareholders of being subject to enforcement of an unconstitutional law.

The common way of asserting constitutional rights and challenging unconstitutional state laws is by raising unconstitutionality as a defense once a prosecution or other enforcement proceeding is initiated in state court. *Young* establishes an alternative approach — an anticipatory or preemptive federal action. A would-be defendant goes to federal court, before state proceedings have been initiated, asserting as a federal claim what would be a constitutional defense in the state enforcement action.

Under historical equity principles, a court can issue an injunction only if the claimant has no adequate remedy at law. Arguably, of course, the shareholder plaintiffs in *Young* had one — the company could have disobeyed the law by charging higher rates, allowed shareholders, officers, or agents to be prosecuted in state court (an action at law), and then argued the unconstitutionality of the rate laws as a defense. But the Court held that this did not qualify as an adequate remedy, given the loss to the railroad companies and the risk to its agents from state enforcement. It might be impossible to find someone willing to take the risk of violating the law and facing prosecution, given the long jail terms involved and the long time it may take for the prosecution to be resolved. Meanwhile, the company is losing money because it is unable to charge its desired rates. Alternatively, the company might violate the law but not be prosecuted, leaving the ultimate constitutional issue unresolved.[155]

The remaining issue in *Young* was the Eleventh Amendment; after all, Young would have been acting as state attorney general in enforcing state law on behalf of the state, which should bring him within the protections of sovereign immunity. But the Court held that because the statute he was enforcing was unconstitutional, he was not acting as or on behalf of the state. He had been "stripped" of his official or representative capacity and instead was acting in an individual capacity, as an individual who does not hold and cannot assert sovereign immunity.[156]

[2]   *Ex Parte Young* as Fiction or Not

Young is regularly described (or derided) as a legal fiction.[157] Actually, it is two fictions. First, the federal action appears to really be against the officer in his official capacity and not as an individual; after all, any injunction barring enforcement continues to run against the new holder of that office, even after the named defendant (who is subject to the injunction) moves on. Second, while the officer enforcing an allegedly unconstitutional law is stripped of his state or representative capacity for Eleventh Amendment purposes, he remains a state

---

[155] *Young*, 209 U.S. at 163–64; John Harrison, Ex Parte Young, 60 Stan. L. Rev. 989, 994 (2008).

[156] *Young*, 209 U.S. at 159–60.

[157] Va. Office for Prot. & Advocacy v. Stewart, 131 S. Ct. 1632, 1638 (2011); Barry Friedman, *The Story of* Ex Parte Young: *Once Controversial, Now Canon, in* Federal Courts Stories 247, 271 (Vicki C. Jackson & Judith Resnik eds., 2010); John Harrison, Ex Parte Young, 60 Stan. L. Rev. 989, 990 (2008).

actor for Fourteenth Amendment purposes, otherwise he could not act in a way that violates the Constitution.

In fact, *Young* arguably is not a fiction at all, nor is it an exception to sovereign immunity. Rather, *Young* reflects an integral part of sovereign immunity itself. Under English common law, while the King could not be sued *eo nomine* given divine right and royal dignity, the King's men could be; the King's ministers and officers all were subject to a full range of prerogative writs, including injunctions, in the Courts of Common Law and the Chancery Courts.[158] *Young* imports these officer suits into the sovereignty and sovereign immunity of republican government; the lawsuit runs against the sovereign's officer, Attorney General Young, rather than the sovereign itself, the State of Minnesota.

Young also fits within the historical divide between courts of law and courts of equity in England. One common use of equity was the anti-suit injunction; a potential defendant in a threatened action at law brings suit in the equity court, asserting as a claim what would be a defense in the action at law and asking the equity court to enjoin the opposing party (the defendant in equity) from proceeding with the action at law. At bottom, *Young* was just such an action in equity for an anti-suit injunction. Young was threatening to initiate a legal proceeding (the criminal prosecution against the railroad's shareholders or agents); the shareholders, who would be defendants in the state legal proceeding, went to a federal court of equity; their claim in the equitable action was the unconstitutionality of state law, which would have been a defense in that action at law; and they asked the federal court of equity to enjoin Young from initiating or prosecuting the state action in law. Importantly, sovereign immunity plays no role on this understanding. Immunity does not protect the sovereign against the assertion of defenses in its enforcement actions; it follows that the sovereign is also not immune when those defenses are converted to claims in equity in an anticipatory anti-suit injunction action.[159]

One remaining consideration is identifying *Ex parte Young*'s precise source. In constitutional cases, it arguably is a gloss on § 1983; the responsible executive officer is a "person" acting under color of state law, is depriving the plaintiff of federal rights through threatened (or actual) enforcement of an unconstitutional state law, and is subject to a suit in equity. What courts and parties occasionally label an *Ex parte Young* action thus really is a § 1983 action for equitable relief, with *Young* defining the proper "person" to be sued (the responsible executive officer). *Young* thus comports with the *Monell* model of § 1983, which focuses litigation primarily on individual officers and away from the government entity itself.[160]

---

[158] Louis L. Jaffe, *Suits Against Governments and Officers: Sovereign Immunity*, 77 HARV. L. REV. 1, 1–2 (1963).

[159] John Harrison, Ex Parte Young, 60 STAN. L. REV. 989, 996 (2008); *see also Stewart*, 131 S. Ct. at 1643 (2011) (Kennedy, J., concurring).

[160] John C. Jefferies, Jr., *In Praise of the Eleventh Amendment and Section 1983*, 84 VA. L. REV. 47, 50, 68 (1998).

[3]   Current Scope of *Ex Parte Young*

Fiction or otherwise, *Young* is "accepted as necessary to permit federal courts to vindicate federal rights."[161] It is woven into the fabric of the Court's sovereign immunity jurisprudence. In fact, the theory of *Young* has been silently accepted and applied beyond its precise terms. It allows similar anticipatory pre-enforcement constitutional challenges to federal laws, through suits against the President, attorney general, or other responsible federal executive officers.[162]

More importantly, *Young* has been extended beyond the precise procedural posture of *Young* itself — an anticipatory anti-suit action to enjoin threatened judicial enforcement of state law, raising as a claim in equity a defense that would have been available in the state enforcement proceeding. It now is used to permit all suits to enjoin all state conduct in the administration and enforcement of its laws and policies; the relief sought need only be described as "prospective," targeting ongoing or future constitutional violations, and not retroactive, seeking monetary compensation for past violations.[163] John Harrison has argued, and Justices Kennedy and Thomas have hinted, however, that this extension beyond anti-suit injunctions is unwarranted.[164]

The line between prospective or retroactive relief "will not in many instances be that between day and night."[165] In *Edelman v. Jordan*, plaintiffs challenged state administration of federal welfare programs, seeking to recover moneys improperly withheld from them. Although the lawsuit named as defendant the director of the state Department of Public Aid — the responsible executive officer — the Court held that the state was the real and substantial party in interest, making it an action against the state that is not permitted under § 1983 or the Eleventh Amendment.[166] In essence, the action sought to recover money from the state; the remedy, if granted, would have required a "substantial expenditure" of state funds, a practical effect "indistinguishable" from an award of retroactive compensatory damages against the state.[167] *Young* is limited only to an action and remedy that would not "expend itself on the public treasury," the domain of the state at the heart of Eleventh Amendment policy.[168]

---

[161] *Stewart*, 131 S. Ct. at 1638; Barry Friedman, *The Story of* Ex Parte Young: *Once Controversial, Now Canon, in* FEDERAL COURTS STORIES 247, 271 (Vicki C. Jackson & Judith Resnik eds., 2010).

[162] Alexander A. Reinert, *Measuring the Success of* Bivens *Litigation and Its Consequences for the Individual Liability Model*, 62 STAN. L. REV. 809, 811 n.2 (2010); *see, e.g.*, Nat'l Fed'n of Indep. Bus. v. Sebelius, 132 S. Ct. 2566 (2012) (naming Secretary of Health and Human Services in challenge to federal health-care law); Ashcroft v. ACLU, 542 U.S. 656 (2004) (naming Attorney General in challenge to criminal statute); Skinner v. Railway Labor Executives' Ass'n, 489 U.S. 602 (1989) (naming Secretary of Transportation in challenge to federal regulation of railroad workers).

[163] Chester Bros. Const. Co. v. Schneider, 886 F. Supp. 2d 896 (C.D. Ill. 2012).

[164] *Stewart*, 131 S. Ct. at 1642–43 (Kennedy, J., joined by Thomas, J., concurring); John Harrison, Ex Parte Young, 60 STAN. L. REV. 989, 1009 (2008); John Harrison, *Jurisdiction, Congressional Power, and Constitutional Remedies*, 86 GEO. L.J. 2513, 2519–20 (1998).

[165] Edelman v. Jordan, 415 U.S. 651, 667 (1974).

[166] *Id.* at 663.

[167] *Id.* at 665, 668

[168] *Stewart*, 131 S. Ct. at 1638.

Of course, most injunctions cost money, as state efforts to conform to federal requirements often require expenditure of funds from the state treasury in order to comply with a federal court order. *Edelman* thus recognized what has come to be called the "prospective compliance exception"[169] to the Eleventh Amendment, which permits merely "ancillary effects" on the state treasury as an inevitable consequence of injunctions under *Young*.[170] A claim is not barred simply because the state must bear costs that are the "necessary result of compliance with decrees which by their terms were prospective in nature."[171] And the Court insists that manageable distinctions are possible. Prohibited retroactive relief compensates those injured before the state official was obligated by a court to act a certain way and involves money paid because of a past breach of legal duty owed by the defendant; permissible prospective relief imposes only the cost of preventing future breaches of a newly imposed legal duty.[172]

These distinctions make some sense, given sovereign immunity's concerns for ensuring state control over the public fisc. A state possesses a definable pool of funds for its known obligations, and it can allocate and control its own budgetary affairs for known future obligations to comply with already-entered judicial orders. But the state loses full control over the public treasury, and it suffers a decrease in available funds, when it must subsequently order (or reorder) its financial affairs to comply with new court decrees ordering financial remedies for past conduct and harms.

In *Edelman*, the Court held that the Eleventh Amendment precludes a claim to recover past federal welfare payments unlawfully withheld.[173] On remand, the lower courts ordered state officials to send notices to all potential claimants, informing them of their entitlement to future payments and of the process for claiming benefits. This would impose two costs on the state: the cost of sending out the notices and the cost of increased welfare payments, as more people were likely to file, and thus recover benefits, if they knew of their eligibility and of the process.[174] In *Quern v. Jordan*, the follow-up in the Supreme Court (with the new head of the state agency as the responsible executive-officer defendant), the Court held that both orders were permissible prospective orders under *Young* and not barred by sovereign immunity. As to the first, the cost of providing notice is an ancillary effect of ongoing and future compliance with federal law; as to the second, any effect on the treasury is not a direct product of the court's order but of the state-run hearings themselves that find more people entitled to benefits.[175]

---

[169] Milliken v. Bradley, 433 U.S. 267 (1977).

[170] *Edelman*, 415 U.S. at 668.

[171] Quern v. Jordan, 440 U.S. 332, 337 (1979); *Edelman*, 415 U.S. at 667–68.

[172] *Edelman*, 415 U.S. at 668.

[173] *Id.* at 659.

[174] *Quern*, 440 U.S. at 334–35.

[175] *Id.* at 349.

[4]   Responses to *Ex Parte Young*

Ex parte Young triggered a "storm of controversy" over the power it vested in a single district judge to enjoin enforcement of state law.[176] It produced two congressional responses — one immediate, the other more distant in time but still motivated by the potential problems of *Young*.[177]

The immediate response was the creation of three-judge district courts for all civil actions challenging the constitutionality, and seeking to enjoin enforcement of, state[178] or federal[179] laws. Its explicit purpose was to limit the power of a single federal judge to halt enforcement of state law. Three-judge panels also make it, theoretically, more difficult for courts to enjoin state or federal law, since plaintiffs now must convince at least two judges in order to obtain the injunction, often including a judge from outside the state or the immediate area of controversy.[180] Congress also provided for direct mandatory review of three-judge panel decisions to the Supreme Court, fast-tracking ultimate national resolution of constitutional issues and further limiting the power of the individual judge to make a constitutional decision that would control for long.[181]

Ironically, given the procedure's origins, three-judge courts became a major weapon for plaintiffs during the Civil Rights Era and the late Warren Court years, as Jim Crow and restrictive state laws were challenged in a long series of § 1983 *Ex parte Young* actions.[182] Civil rights plaintiffs actually found three-judge panels more receptive to their arguments and more willing to enjoin state laws, since the two additional judges often came from outside the district and thus were immune to the local passions and prejudices that weighed against plaintiffs appearing before a single local judge. In other words, civil rights plaintiffs benefitted from the decreased power of the individual district judge. At the same time, judges in the southern districts and circuits engaged in a certain amount of maneuvering to get onto panels or to keep certain judges off.

The plaintiffs also engaged in their own maneuvering with three-judge courts. A three-judge court was required only if the action sought to enjoin state law, but not if the challenge was to local laws or to executive actions or decisions, which followed

---

[176] Steffel v. Thompson, 415 U.S. 452, 465 (1974); Barry Friedman, *The Story of* Ex Parte Young: *Once Controversial, Now Canon, in* FEDERAL COURTS STORIES 247, 269 (Vicki C. Jackson & Judith Resnik eds., 2010); Michael E. Solimine, *Congress,* Ex Parte Young, *and the Fate of the Three-Judge District Court*, 70 U. PITT. L. REV. 101 (2008).

[177] *Steffel*, 415 U.S. at 466.

[178] 28 U.S.C. § 2281 (repealed).

[179] 28 U.S.C. § 2282 (repealed).

[180] Barry Friedman, *The Story of* Ex Parte Young: *Once Controversial, Now Canon, in* FEDERAL COURTS STORIES 247, 269–71 (Vicki C. Jackson & Judith Resnik eds., 2010); Michael E. Solimine, *Congress,* Ex Parte Young, *and the Fate of the Three-Judge District Court*, 70 U. PITT. L. REV. 101, 114–15 (2008).

[181] 28 U.S.C. § 2253; Barry Friedman, *The Story of* Ex Parte Young: *Once Controversial, Now Canon, in* FEDERAL COURTS STORIES 247, 272 (Vicki C. Jackson & Judith Resnik eds., 2010); Michael E. Solimine, *Congress,* Ex Parte Young, *and the Fate of the Three-Judge District Court*, 70 U. PITT. L. REV. 101, 114–15 (2008).

[182] Moody v. Flowers, 387 U.S. 97 (1967); Michael E. Solimine, *Congress,* Ex Parte Young, *and the Fate of the Three-Judge District Court*, 70 U. PITT. L. REV. 101, 126 (2008).

ordinary 3-stage litigation processes. By the statutory terms, three-judge courts only were required as to claims for injunctions. This created strategic choices for the plaintiffs as to how to frame their cases, whom to name as defendants, and what relief to seek, depending on how they viewed the original district judge to whom the case had been assigned and whether they believed they were better or worse off before the single judge.[183]

Congress eliminated mandatory three-judge courts in 1976.[184] Instead, three-judge courts, still with direct review in the Supreme Court, are used in apportionment and voting cases and when Congress requires by law,[185] usually by providing in a piece of legislation that all constitutional challenges to that legislation must be heard by a three-judge court.[186] Otherwise, actions seeking to enjoin unconstitutional state laws proceed as any other litigation, arguably demonstrating wide judicial and congressional acceptance of *Young*.[187]

The second, although more delayed, response to *Ex parte Young* was enactment in 1934 of the federal Declaratory Judgment Act, which empowers courts to "declare the rights and other legal relations of any interested party."[188] A federal court may simply declare that a state law is unconstitutional and thus unenforceable in a procedurally similar action against the responsible executive officer (and not the state). Unlike an injunction, a federal declaratory judgment does not directly prohibit or compel the state officer's conduct and the judgment is not immediately coercively enforceable through the court's contempt power.[189] Declaratory relief is a "milder alternative" to the "strong medicine" of an injunction against state officers.[190] It is less intrusive on the state and state authority because it is not coercive; declaratory judgments function instead through persuasion, seeking to convince state officers to decline to enforce a constitutionally suspect state law.[191] A request for a declaratory judgment may, but need not, be accompanied by a request for other relief, including an injunction.[192] And if the declaratory judgment does not succeed in convincing state officials that the law is unconstitutional and should not be enforced, it may become the basis for obtaining a later injunction.[193]

---

[183] Michael E. Solimine, *Congress*, Ex Parte Young, *and the Fate of the Three-Judge District Court*, 70 U. Pitt. L. Rev. 101, 127–30 (2008).

[184] Act of Aug. 12, 1976, Pub. L. No. 94-381, 90 Stat. 1119 (1976).

[185] 28 U.S.C. § 2284(a).

[186] *See, e.g.*, Communications Decency Act of 1996, Pub. L. No. 104-104, § 561, 110 Stat. 133 (1996).

[187] *Infra* Ch.7, Part B.

[188] 28 U.S.C. § 2201

[189] *Steffel*, 415 U.S. at 470–71.

[190] *Id.* at 466–67.

[191] *Id.* at 470–71.

[192] 28 U.S.C. § 2201.

[193] 28 U.S.C. § 2202. Recall the 1996 amendment to § 1983, under which a plaintiff cannot obtain an injunction against a state judge for conduct in her judicial capacity unless the plaintiff first obtains a declaratory judgment. *Supra* § 3.08[3].

Interestingly, these two efforts to limit the force of *Ex parte Young* overlapped. A plaintiff could avoid a three-judge district court by seeking only declaratory relief and waiting to pursue an injunction (and to face a three-judge court) only if the declaratory judgment proved unsuccessful in halting the prospective constitutional violation.

PART C
SUPERVISORY LIABILITY

§ 4.14   SUPERVISORY LIABILITY

Midway between individual liability and entity liability is supervisory liability — the liability not of the officers who violated the Constitution on the ground in the encounter with a plaintiff, but of the higher-up government officials who oversaw, directed, or controlled the officers directly involved. Given the "subjects or causes to be subjected" language of § 1983, supervisory liability, like municipal liability, cannot be available on vicarious or *respondeat superior* liability.[194]

Instead, lower courts allowed liability where a supervisory official was personally involved in the misconduct, had taken some action to cause the violation, and had acted with the requisite state of mind. Every circuit had recognized supervisory liability in some form, typically in any of five situations: (1) the supervisor personally participated in the wrongdoing; (2) the supervisor controlled or directed his underlings in their wrongdoing; (3) the supervisor failed to supervise or control his underlings; (4) the supervisor had knowledge of past misconduct and did nothing to correct it, thus acquiescing in it; or (5) the supervisor created, implemented, or enforced policies that underlings followed in engaging in their misconduct.[195] Different lower courts also employed slightly different language as to state of mind, speaking of actual knowledge of misconduct, recklessness in supervision, or deliberate indifference to the rights of the people with whom their underlings came in contact.[196] But most regarded supervisory liability as essentially aligning with municipal liability — the supervisory officer must have been deliberately indifferent to the risk to the public from his creation or enforcement of policy or from an underling's misconduct of which the supervisor had notice and did nothing to prevent or correct.[197]

In *Ashcroft v. Iqbal*, however, the Supreme Court questioned supervisory liability as at least a misnomer, given the prohibition on vicarious liability.[198] *Iqbal* involved a *Bivens* action by a post-9/11 detainee against the former Attorney General and

---

[194] Bistrian v. Levi, 696 F.3d 352 (3d Cir. 2012); Briscoe v. Cnty. of St. Louis, 690 F.3d 1004 (8th Cir. 2012).

[195] Dodds v. Richardson, 614 F.3d 1185, 1194–96 (10th Cir. 2010).

[196] Ashcroft v. Iqbal, 556 U.S. 662, 693–94 (2009) (Souter, J., dissenting) (discussing range of standards in lower-courts).

[197] Hartley by Hartley v. Parnell, 193 F.3d 1263 (11th Cir. 1999); Colon v. Coughlin, 58 F.3d 865 (2d Cir. 1995).

[198] *Iqbal*, 556 U.S. at 667.

former Director of the FBI, alleging that federal officers had detained them and mistreated them while in detention because of their race, religion, and national origin, pursuant to policies that the two high-level officers had created and implemented. The Court held that the high-ranking defendants' mere knowledge of or deliberate indifference to their underlings' unconstitutional behavior on the ground was not sufficient to establish their liability. Rather, plaintiffs had to establish that the defendants created and implemented the challenged detention policies with the intent or purpose of discriminating against the plaintiffs on account of race, religion, or national origin.[199]

Lower courts have criticized *Iqbal* for clouding already muddy waters,[200] as they struggle to determine what effect it had on supervisory liability and on lower-court precedent. Three possibilities have emerged. One is that *Iqbal* eliminates supervisory liability entirely, a fear that Justice Souter expressed in his *Iqbal* dissent.[201] But no lower court has adopted that view, which would require them to read *Iqbal* as having silently overturned a host of Supreme Court, as well as lower-court, precedents.[202]

A second possibility is that *Iqbal* tightens the causation requirements, requiring a clearer showing that the supervisor acted in some way and that those acts were the proximate cause of the plaintiff's injuries.[203]

A third possibility is that *Iqbal*'s requirement of a showing of intent or purpose for supervisory liability applies only where the underlying constitutional right requires intent or purpose (as was the case for the equal protection and free exercise claims in *Iqbal*). But where the underlying right requires a lesser state of mind, supervisory liability attaches on a lesser state of mind.[204]

To be sure, even the third marks a significant change in law. Prior to *Iqbal*, a plaintiff trying to establish supervisory liability on an underlying claim of race discrimination would have had to show that the officer on the ground intended to discriminate on the basis of race and that the supervisor knew of and was deliberately indifferent to the risk that the officer might intentionally discriminate. After *Iqbal*, that supervisor's misconduct (lack of supervision or creation of a policy) must have been done with the intent that his underlings would discriminate. On the other hand, where the underlying right does not require intent or purpose (for example, excessive force or catch-all substantive due process), pre-*Iqbal* principles of supervisory liability from the lower courts continue unchanged. Thus, a supervisor can be liable where he has actual knowledge of past violations and fails to stop them, where he fails to [blank] with deliberate indifference, and where he creates or

---

[199] *Id.*

[200] *Dodds*, 614 F.3d at 1209 (Tymkovich, J., concurring).

[201] *Iqbal*, 556 U.S. at 693 (Souter, J., dissenting); *Dodds*, 614 F.3d at 1198; *id.* at 1210 (Tymkovich, J., concurring).

[202] Starr v. Baca, 652 F.3d 1202, 1207 (9th Cir. 2011); *Dodds*, 614 F. 3d at 1200-01.

[203] Starr v. Cnty. of Los Angeles, 659 F.3d 850 (9th Cir. 2011) (O'Scannlain, J., dissenting from order denying rehearing en banc); *Dodds*, 614 F.3d at 1199.

[204] Lacey v. Maricopa County, 693 F.3d 896 (9th Cir. 2012); Starr v. Baca, 652 F.3d 1202 (9th Cir. 2011); *Dodds*, 614 F.3d at 1199–1200; Sandra T.E. v. Grindle, 599 F.3d 583 (7th Cir. 2010).

implements policies with deliberate indifference to the constitutional harm they might cause when carried out.[205]

In *Dodds v. Richardson*, the Tenth Circuit considered a damages claim against the county sheriff over a department policy of not allowing arrestees to post bail until they had a hearing the following business morning, a policy that resulted in the plaintiff having to spend a weekend in jail. *Dodds* held that the plaintiff stated a supervisory-liability claim against the sheriff. The sheriff had personally acted by creating and maintaining the bail policy; the policy caused the plaintiff not to get bail for several days, which was the complained-of constitutional harm; and because the plaintiff alleged a violation of substantive due process[206], in which deliberate indifference is the applicable state of mind, the plaintiff only needed to show that the supervisor created and maintained the no-bail policy with deliberate indifference to the risk that the plaintiff would unconstitutionally remain in jail for too long a period.[207]

§ 4.15   SUPERVISORY LIABILITY MEETS ENTITY LIABILITY

If supervisory liability is the midpoint between individual liability and entity liability, it also may be the bridge. At some point, the liability of the supervisory officer may trigger liability for the entity. Two things must happen.

First, the liable supervising officer must be the final policymaker for the entity, as defined by state law. A plaintiff essentially can sue her way up the chain of command, establishing individual liability against the responsible officer and supervisory liability against his supervisors and higher-ups until she finds the supervisor who is the final policymaker. And if she can establish that policymaker's liability (through the supervisory-liability analysis), she establishes the municipality's liability.[208]

Second, the entity must be subject to suit and liability. In a *Bivens* action, the United States cannot be liable, so liability ends with individual supervisory liability, even if the supervisor could be characterized as a policymaker for the entity (as the defendants in *Iqbal* arguably were). In a § 1983 action, entity liability depends on what entity is sued — states cannot be liable under § 1983[209] while municipalities can be. Having identified a policymaker to whom supervisory liability attaches, the court then must determine for whom that policymaker works — whether he is policymaker for the state or an arm of the state or whether he is a policymaker for a municipality. The entity can be sued and held liable for the supervisor's

---

[205] *Starr*, 652 F.3d at 1207–08; *Dodds*, 614 F.3d 1211 (Tymkovich, J., concurring).

[206] *Supra* § 2.07[1].

[207] *Id.* at 1189, 1202–03.

[208] Connick v. Thompson, 131 S. Ct. 1350 (2011); McMillian v. Monroe County, 520 U.S. 781 (1997); *supra* § 4.04.

[209] Again, courts unfortunately speak about this in Eleventh Amendment term rather than in terms of the text of § 1983 and the limited statutory meaning of "person" after *Will* and *Quern. See* Carter v. City of Philadelphia, 181 F.3d 339, 347 (3d Cir. 1999); *supra* § 4.12.

misconduct only in the latter circumstance but not the former.

Whether a policymaker works for state or local government is an issue of state constitutional and statutory law.[210] The defendant bears the burden of proving that he works for the state and thus that the government is not subject to suit.[211] This turns on the functions performed and how state law labels those functions. Courts consider a combination of overlapping factors, including how state law defines the office and the officer in performing the function at issue; the degree of control the state wields over the entity and its officers or, stated differently, the degree of autonomy the entity and its officers have from state control; the nature of the officer's conduct as uniquely state or local; the source of funding for the entity; and who bears financial responsibility for paying any judgment entered.[212] Courts balance these factors, with the final two often carrying substantial weight, given the Eleventh Amendment's concerns with protecting the treasury and state control over the treasury.[213]

The need to distinguish state from municipal bodies, and thus state from municipal policymakers, arises most frequently in actions against sheriff's departments,[214] county prosecutors' offices,[215] school boards,[216] and municipal and county courts.[217] These agencies uniquely combine state and local responsibilities — they may be local parts of a broader statewide structure, they may perform statewide functions (such as law enforcement or adjudication) at a local level, or they may enforce both state and local law at a local level. Characterizing an office and an officer will be highly fact-intensive; the analysis depends on the laws of the particular state and on the particular areas, functions, or issues on which the policymaker was acting in the particular case.[218] A policymaker may be a state officer in performing some functions and a municipal officer in performing others.[219]

---

[210] *McMillian*, 520 U.S. at 786.

[211] Betts v. New Castle Youth Dev. Ctr., 621 F.3d 249 (3d Cir. 2010); Gorton v. Gettel, 554 F.3d 60 (2d Cir. 2009).

[212] *McMillian*, 520 U.S. at 787–93; Pucci v. Nineteenth Dist. Court, 628 F.3d 752 (6th Cir. 2010); Carter v. City of Philadelphia, 181 F.3d 339 (3d Cir. 1999).

[213] Black v. N. Panola Sch. Dist., 461 F.3d 584 (5th Cir. 2006).

[214] *McMillian*, 520 U.S. at 783 (arm of state under Alabama law); Manders v. Lee, 338 F.3d 1304 (11th Cir. 2003) (arm of state under Georgia law).

[215] Nielander v. Bd. of County Comm'rs, 582 F.3d 1155 (10th Cir. 2009) (arm of state under Kansas law); Hudson v. City of New Orleans, 174 F.3d 677 (5th Cir. 1999) (not arm of state under Louisiana law); *Carter*, 181 F.3d at 354 (not arm of state under Pennsylvania law as to some decisions).

[216] Mt. Healthy City Sch. Dist. Bd. of Educ. v. Doyle, 429 U.S. 274 (1977) (not arm of state under Ohio law); Woods v. Rondout Valley Cent. Sch. Dist. Bd. of Educ., 466 F.3d 232 (2d Cir. 2006) (same under New York law); *Black*, 461 F.3d at 598 (same under Mississippi law).

[217] Gollomp v. Spitzer, 568 F.3d 355 (2d Cir. 2009) (unified state court system is arm of state under New York law); Kelly v. Municipal Courts, 97 F.3d 902 (7th Cir. 1996) (arms of the state under Indiana law); Franceschi v. Schwartz, 57 F.3d 828 (9th Cir. 1995) (per curiam) (arms of the state under California law); Dolan v. City of Ann Arbor, 666 F. Supp. 2d 754 (E.D. Mich. 2009) (arms of state under Michigan law).

[218] *McMillian*, 520 U.S. at 785–86; *Manders*, 338 F.3d at 1308; Owens v. Fulton County, 877 F.2d 947 (11th Cir. 1989).

[219] *See, e.g.*, Coleman v. Kaye, 87 F.3d 1491, 1499–1505 (3d Cir. 1996) (distinguishing law enforcement

And the person performing some function may be a state officer in one state and a local officer in another.

Chapter 5

CIVIL RIGHTS PROCEDURE

PART A
JURISDICTION AND PROCEDURE

§ 5.01   SUBJECT MATTER JURISDICTION IN THE FEDERAL DISTRICT COURTS

28 U.S.C. § 1331

The district courts shall have original jurisdiction of all civil actions arising under the Constitution, laws, or treaties of the United States.

28 U.S.C. § 1343

(a) The district courts shall have original jurisdiction of any civil action authorized by law to be commenced by any person:

* * *

(3) To redress the deprivation, under color of any State law, statute, ordinance, regulation, custom or usage, of any right, privilege or immunity secured by the Constitution of the United States or by any Act of Congress providing for equal rights of citizens or of all persons within the jurisdiction of the United States.

28 U.S.C. § 1367

(a) Except as provided * * *, in any civil action of which the district courts have original jurisdiction, the district courts shall have supplemental jurisdiction over all other claims that are so related to claims in the action within such original jurisdiction that they form part of the same case or controversy under Article III of the United States Constitution. Such supplemental jurisdiction shall include claims that involve the joinder or intervention of additional parties.

Federal courts and state courts exercise concurrent original jurisdiction over § 1983 actions; a plaintiff can bring the action in the first instance in federal district court or in a state trial court.[1]

In federal court, the plaintiff must identify a statutory source of jurisdiction,[2] pointing to either of two possible provisions. The first is 28 U.S.C. § 1331, which grants district courts original jurisdiction over "all civil actions arising under the Constitution, laws, or treaties of the United States"; at its core, this means cases in which the cause of action and the substantive right (or rule of decision) asserted are created by federal law.[3] Section 1983 actions plainly satisfy that standard — § 1983 is a federal cause of action and the action seeks to enforce rights created by the federal Constitution or federal statutes.

The second source of jurisdiction is 28 U.S.C. § 1343(a)(3), which is the jurisdictional counterpart to the § 1983 cause of action, both part of the Ku Klux Klan Act of 1871. It grants district courts original jurisdiction "of any civil action

---

[1] Haywood v. Drown, 556 U.S. 729, 734–35 (2009); Maine v. Thiboutot, 448 U.S. 1, 3 n.1 (1980).

[2] Fed. R. Civ. P. 8(a)(1).

[3] 28 U.S.C. § 1331; Mims v. Arrow Fin. Servs., LLC, 132 S. Ct. 740, 748–49 (2012).

authorized by law to be commenced by any person . . . [t]o redress the deprivation, under color of any State law, statute, ordinance, regulation, custom or usage, of any right, privilege or immunity secured by the Constitution of the United States or by any Act of Congress providing for equal rights of citizens."[4] Stated more succinctly, it grants district courts jurisdiction over any civil action asserting a § 1983 claim seeking to vindicate rights under the Constitution and some federal statutes designed to provide for equal rights. In 1871, district courts lacked general "arising under" federal question jurisdiction; this provision thus provided the only basis for jurisdiction over the now constitutional actions created by the 1871 Act. Congress granted district courts general "arising under" federal-question jurisdiction (in the precursor to § 1331) four years later, as part of a different Reconstruction effort to protect the rights of freedmen and others by opening the federal district courts and making them the primary forum for protecting and vindicating all federal rights under all sources of federal law.[5]

Moreover, until 1980, § 1331 included an amount-in-controversy requirement.[6] The statute-specific grant in § 1343(a)(3) thus remained necessary to ensure that smaller-value § 1983 actions could be brought in federal court. As discussed in *Maine v. Thiboutot*, this left a potential jurisdictional gap — small-value actions to enforce non-equal-protection statutes could be brought under § 1983, but the district court would not have jurisdiction under either § 1331 or § 1343(a)(3), pushing those claims into state court.[7] Eliminating § 1331's amount-in-controversy requirement eliminates that gap. But it instead renders § 1343(a)(3) largely superfluous, as there will never be a § 1983 action over which § 1331 does not provide jurisdiction or in which § 1343(a)(3) will be the sole source of jurisdiction.[8] Section 1331 now provides jurisdiction over all § 1983 actions, regardless of amount in controversy, for all constitutional claims and all "and laws" claims. Section 1343(a)(3) provides an additional (although strictly speaking unnecessary) basis for jurisdiction, regardless of amount in controversy, for all constitutional claims and for "and laws" claims involving equality-enforcing statutes.[9] As a practical matter, plaintiffs should and will identify both provisions as the basis for jurisdiction, where applicable.

The other significant jurisdictional provision in constitutional litigation is supplemental jurisdiction, which authorizes federal district courts to hear state law claims that are so factually related to a federal claim (such one under § 1983) as to form one

---

[4] 28 U.S.C. § 1343(a)(3).

[5] Judiciary Act of Mar. 3, 1875, § 1, 18 Stat. 470 (1875); Steffel v. Thompson, 415 U.S. 452, 464 (1974). The 1875 Act actually marked the second time Congress had granted district courts general federal question jurisdiction. The first time was in the infamous Midnight Judges Act of 1801, Midnight Judges Act, 2 Stat. 92 (1801), enacted in the waning days of John Adams' presidency; that jurisdictional grant was repealed one year later. Act of Mar. 8, 1802, § 1, 2 Stat. 132 (1802). The Midnight Judges Act, of course, provided the factual predicate for *Marbury v. Madison*, 5 U.S. (1 Cranch.) 137 (1803).

[6] Federal Question Jurisdictional Amendments Act of 1980, Pub. L. No. 96-486, 94 Stat. 2369 (1980).

[7] *Thiboutot*, 448 U.S. at 8 n.6.

[8] Kulick v. Pocono Downs Racing Ass'n, 816 F.2d 895, 898 n.4 (3d Cir. 1987) (labeling § 1343(a)(3) an "anachronism" in light of amendments to § 1331).

[9] *Supra* § 2.12.

"case or controversy" for Article III purposes.[10] Because the Constitution creates rights independent of, and different from, state statutes or common law,[11] the facts, conduct, transactions, or occurrences providing the basis for a federal constitutional claim also might support a range of state tort claims against the same or related defendants. Because all these claims arise from the same basic set of operative real-world facts, § 1367 allows the court to hear (and thus the plaintiff to bring) all claims against all possible defendants in a single action in federal court and to obtain relief in a single action. For example, the use of excessive force by a police officer may form the basis for a Fourth Amendment unreasonable seizure claim, as well as for state law claims for assault, battery, and negligence.[12] Similarly, a municipal employee subject to on-the-job sexual harassment can allege violations of: Fourteenth Amendment equal protection by the municipality (in a *Monell* claim) and by her harassing co-workers (as individuals acting under color of state law), Title VII of the Civil Rights Act of 1964 by the municipal employer, a state employment-discrimination statute (against the municipality and the individuals), and state torts such as intentional infliction of emotional distress and assault against the individuals and against the municipality under *respondeat superior*. As for jurisdiction over those claims: both § 1331 and § 1343(a)(3) provide jurisdiction over the federal constitutional claims; both § 1331 and a statute-specific jurisdictional grant in Title VII itself[13]provide jurisdiction over the federal statutory claims; and § 1367(a) provides jurisdiction over all the state statutory and tort claims.[14]

§ 5.02   SUBJECT MATTER JURISDICTION ON APPEAL

28 U.S.C. § 1291

The courts of appeals (other than the United States Court of Appeals for the Federal Circuit) shall have jurisdiction of appeals from all final decisions of the district courts of the United States.

28 U.S.C. § 1292

(a) Except as provided in subsections (c) and (d) of this section, the courts of appeals shall have jurisdiction of appeals from:

    (1) Interlocutory orders of the district courts of the United States, the United States District Court for the District of the Canal Zone, the District Court of Guam, and the District Court of the Virgin Islands, or of the judges thereof, granting, continuing, modifying, refusing or dissolving injunctions, or refusing to dissolve or modify

---

[10] 28 U.S.C. § 1367(a); Exxon Mobil Corp. v. Allapattah Servs., 545 U.S. 546, 580 (2005).

[11] Bivens v. Six Unknown Named Agents of Federal Bureau of Narcotics, 403 U.S. 388, 392–93 (1971); *id.* at 403 (Harlan, J., concurring in the judgment); Monroe v. Pape, 365 U.S. 167, 171 (1961); *id.* at 196 (Harlan, J., concurring).

[12] King v. Taylor, 694 F.3d 650 (6th Cir. 2012).

[13] 42 U.S.C. § 2000e-5(f)(3) (granting district court jurisdiction over civil actions "brought under" Title VII).

[14] Valentine v. City of Chicago, 452 F.3d 670 (7th Cir. 2006).

injunctions, except where a direct review may be had in the Supreme Court;

* * *

(b) When a district judge, in making in a civil action an order not otherwise appealable under this section, shall be of the opinion that such order involves a controlling question of law as to which there is substantial ground for difference of opinion and that an immediate appeal from the order may materially advance the ultimate termination of the litigation, he shall so state in writing in such order. The Court of Appeals which would have jurisdiction of an appeal of such action may thereupon, in its discretion, permit an appeal to be taken from such order, if application is made to it within ten days after the entry of the order: Provided, however, That application for an appeal hereunder shall not stay proceedings in the district court unless the district judge or the Court of Appeals or a judge thereof shall so order.

28 U.S.C. § 1254

Cases in the courts of appeals may be reviewed by the Supreme Court by the following methods:

(1) By writ of certiorari granted upon the petition of any party to any civil or criminal case, before or after rendition of judgment or decree;

(2) By certification at any time by a court of appeals of any question of law in any civil or criminal case as to which instructions are desired, and upon such certification the Supreme Court may give binding instructions or require the entire record to be sent up for decision of the entire matter in controversy.

[1] Final Judgment Rule

The ordinary rule in federal court is that only final decisions of a district court are appealable to the regional circuit court of appeals.[15] The Supreme Court can assert appellate jurisdiction over a case once it has reached the court of appeals, either by writ of *certiorari* before or after judgment by the court of appeals, or by certification from the court of appeals.[16] Finality thus triggers two layers of potential appellate review, but neither can happen until finality; a decision must be final to move from the district court to the court of appeals and the Supreme Court can review the case only once it is properly in the court of appeals on review of a final district court judgment.

---

[15] 28 U.S.C. § 1291.

[16] 28 U.S.C. § 1254.

A final decision generally is one "by which a district court disassociates itself from a case,"[17] one that "ends the litigation on the merits and leaves nothing for the court to do but execute the judgment."[18] Finality serves important efficiency interests; it avoids piecemeal litigation and cases yo-yoing among levels of the federal judiciary after each individual decision or order. It also helps reviewing courts avoid unnecessarily deciding interlocutory issues that may go away with the ultimate resolution of the litigation in the trial court.[19] Finality also respects the relative competencies of appellate and trial courts; appellate courts should not act where the trial court's work remains open, unfinished, or inconclusive, instead awaiting the creation of a full record in the lower court.[20]

Under the doctrine of "merger," interlocutory (non-final) orders in the district court merge with the final judgment and can be reviewed as part of the appeal from the district court's final order.[21] A party often must litigate around a possibly erroneous early ruling, only able to challenge and have it reversed at the end of the case. Of course, if the party successfully litigates around the erroneous ruling and prevails in the case despite the error, it obviates the need for appeal.

Appeal of final district court orders is of right; the losing party need not seek leave to appeal and the court of appeals cannot decline to hear a timely and properly filed appeal of a final decision. On the other hand, Supreme Court review of cases from the court of appeals is always by discretionary writ of *certiorari*.[22]

[2] Statutory Exceptions to Finality

There are a number of exceptions to the finality requirement, statutory and otherwise; two statutory exceptions are especially relevant to constitutional and civil rights litigation.

The first permits immediate appeal of all decisions involving preliminary and permanent injunctions — all orders granting, continuing, modifying, refusing or dissolving injunctions, or refusing to dissolve or modify.[23] Section 1983 allows for a "suit in equity," meaning a suit seeking preliminary and permanent injunctive relief; these cases comprise a significant portion of constitutional litigation. In fact, many actions seeking injunctive relief do not reach final judgment in the district court, at least initially. Instead, the district court either grants or denies a preliminary injunction and the adversely affected party immediately appeals to the regional court of appeals and then to the Supreme Court. To the extent constitutional law is often made in the Supreme Court and the courts of appeals in injunctive actions, it often is on review of a decision on a preliminary, rather than

---

[17] Mohawk Indus. v. Carpenter, 558 U.S. 100, 130 S. Ct. 599, 600 (2009).

[18] Riley v. Kennedy, 553 U.S. 406 (2008); Catlin v. United States, 324 U.S. 229, 233 (1945).

[19] *Mohawk Indus.*, 130 S. Ct. at 605.

[20] *Id.*

[21] Pineda v. Ford Motor Co., 520 F.3d 237, 243 (3d Cir. 2008).

[22] Compare § 1291 with § 1254.

[23] 28 U.S.C. § 1292(a)(1); Salazar v. District of Columbia, 671 F.3d 1258 (D.C. Cir. 2012).

permanent, injunction.[24]

The second exception allows district courts to certify individual interlocutory decisions for immediate appellate review. This is limited to decisions involving a "controlling question of law as to which there is substantial ground for difference of opinion" where an "immediate appeal from the order may materially advance the ultimate termination of the litigation."[25] These appeals typically are limited to purely legal issues that are novel or on which clear guidance from the courts of appeals is lacking and that are sufficiently controversial or uncertain to justify immediate review.[26] If the district court certifies the issue, the adversely affected party may seek review in the court of appeals, subject to the appellate court's discretionary determination that the order does, in fact, satisfy the statute and warrant immediate review.[27]

[3] Immunity and Appealability: The Collateral Order Doctrine

One judge-made, non-statutory departure from the seeming rigidity of the Final Judgment Rule is the "Collateral Order Doctrine," first recognized in *Cohen v. Beneficial Industrial Loan.*[28] *Cohen* allows for immediate review of a "small class" of orders that "finally determine claims of right separate from, and collateral to, rights asserted in the action, too important to be denied review and too independent of the cause itself to require" review to be deferred.[29] While sometimes described as an "exception" to the finality requirement,[30] the collateral order doctrine is more accurately viewed as a "practical construction" of finality[31] — the seemingly interlocutory order is, in fact, a final judgment on that collateral issue and the court of appeals has jurisdiction under § 1291, as construed. And unlike case-by-case interlocutory appeals under § 1292(b), collateral order review is categorical; all cases falling within a category may be reviewed immediately, with no consideration of whether immediate review is warranted in the specific case.[32]

To fall within *Cohen*, the order to be reviewed: (1) must conclusively determine the disputed question; (2) must resolve an important issue "completely separate from the merits of the action"; and (3) must be "effectively unreviewable on appeal from final judgment."[33] Much of the action centers on the third prong, which considers whether the legal right sought to be protected on appeal, or the policies

---

[24] Doran v. Salem Inn, Inc., 422 U.S. 922 (1975); Jones v. Caruso, 569 F.3d 258 (6th Cir. 2009).

[25] 28 U.S.C. § 1292(b).

[26] Caraballo-Seda v. Municipality of Hormigueros, 395 F.3d 7 (1st Cir. 2005); S.B.L. by & through T.B. v. Evans, 80 F.3d 307 (8th Cir. 1996).

[27] 28 U.S.C. § 1292(b).

[28] Cohen v. Beneficial Industrial Loan Corp., 337 U.S. 541 (1949).

[29] *Mohawk Indus.*, 130 S. Ct. at 603; Ashcroft v. Iqbal, 556 U.S. 662, 671 (2009).

[30] Finigan v. Marshall, 574 F.3d 57, 60–61 n.2 (2d Cir. 2009).

[31] Will v. Hallock, 546 U.S. 345, 349 (2006).

[32] *Mohawk Indus.*, 130 S. Ct. at 605.

[33] *Will*, 546 U.S. at 349 (quoting Puerto Rico Aqueduct & Sewer Auth. v. Metcalf & Eddy, Inc., 506 U.S. 139, 144 (1993)).

and values underlying that right, would be lost or undermined if the party seeking to vindicate the right must wait until final judgment before obtaining appellate review. In making that determination, courts sometimes distinguish between a right not to be made to stand trial (or to face the other burdens of being a party to litigation) and a right not to ultimately be held liable. The former right is lost if the holder cannot immediately appeal; if a party must wait until final judgment in the district court to appeal an adverse ruling affecting a right against standing trial, he has been made to litigate and to stand trial, defeating the right itself.[34] This is especially problematic where the district court ruling is erroneous and reversal on appeal would, in fact, have end the litigation at an earlier stage. Alternatively, courts can consider whether delaying review and making a party continue to litigate would "imperil a substantial public interest" or endanger "some particular value of a high order," all of which outweighs the ordinary benefits of finality.[35]

Defendants in constitutional actions can seek immediate collateral-order review of decisions denying absolute presidential immunity,[36] absolute legislative immunity,[37] absolute judicial immunity,[38] qualified immunity,[39] and state sovereign immunity.[40] Immunity defenses have been conceptualized as according a right not to stand trial and not to be subject to continued litigation, not just as protection against ultimate liability.[41] Alternatively, all are grounded in substantial public values — separation of powers, federalism, state dignity, avoiding disruption and overdeterrence of government functions — that are denigrated if a defendant must wait to obtain review and remain in the case longer than necessary. Immediate reversal of an erroneous district court decision on any of these issues would end the litigation for the defendant.

In theory, immediate collateral-order review is available only if the district court's immunity decision was based on purely legal, as opposed to factual, issues.[42] For example, a defendant moves for summary judgment on qualified immunity grounds and the motion is denied. The defendant can immediately appeal that decision where the court determines that no right was violated on the facts at issue or that the right is not clearly established,[43] but not where the motion is denied because there are factual disputes as to what happened in the events at issue and whether it constitutes a violation.[44] This distinction flows from the nature of appellate review and the respective fact-finding capacities of trial and appellate

---

[34] Digital Equip. Corp. v. Desktop Direct, 511 U.S. 863, 868–69 (1994).

[35] *Will*, 546 U.S. at 352–53.

[36] Nixon v. Fitzgerald, 457 U.S. 731 (1982).

[37] Larsen v. Senate of Commonwealth, 152 F.3d 240 (3d Cir. 1998); Roberson v. Mullins, 29 F.3d 132 (4th Cir. 1994).

[38] Roland v. Phillips, 19 F.3d 552 (11th Cir. 1994).

[39] Ortiz v. Jordan, 131 S. Ct. 884 (2011); *Iqbal*, 556 U.S. at 672–74; Johnson v. Jones, 515 U.S. 304 (1995); Mitchell v. Forsyth, 472 U.S. 511 (1985).

[40] Puerto Rico Aqueduct & Sewer Auth. v. Metcalf & Eddy, Inc., 506 U.S. 139 (1993).

[41] *Ortiz*, 131 S. Ct. at 891; *Iqbal*, 556 U.S. at 672; *supra* Ch.3.

[42] *Ortiz*, 131 S. Ct. at 891 (discussing *Johnson*, 515 U.S. at 313).

[43] *Ortiz*, 131 S. Ct. at 891–92.

[44] *Id.*

courts. Courts of appeals are best able to review "neat abstract issues of law"; they thus should be able to act immediately on those pure legal issues where there is no need for further factual development at the trial court, but not on more fact-bound issues.[45]

In reality, however, courts have applied the doctrine far more broadly than the rhetoric suggests. Courts have broadly defined what constitutes an abstract issue of law, such that most denials of motions to dismiss or for summary judgment are immediately appealable where qualified immunity might be in play.[46] This includes determinations of whether a *Bivens* cause of action is even available in the case,[47] and whether the plaintiff has successfully pled the elements of a constitutional claim.[48] Courts also have created pendent appellate jurisdiction, allowing review over otherwise-not-immediately-reviewable issues that are "inextricably intertwined" with the immunity issue over which they have collateral order jurisdiction.[49]

[4] Immunity and Appealability: Prevailing Parties

Standard federal appellate practice in both the Supreme Court and the courts of appeals is that only the party aggrieved by a lower court order may appeal.[50] Courts review judgments, not the dicta, statements, reasoning, or words that underlie or justify those judgments. Judicial resources are not well spent having reviewing courts "superintend" the words leading to a judgment that ultimately goes in the would-be appellant's favor. Courts also are wary of issuing what appears to be an advisory opinion, altering the basis for a judgment without actually changing the practical effect of that judgment. But this rule is one of prudential appellate procedure, not appellate jurisdiction, meaning courts may depart where justified by policy reasons of sufficient importance.[51]

In *Camreta v. Greene*, the Supreme Court held that the important policy reasons underlying qualified immunity place it in a special category, allowing for appeals by prevailing parties. In that case, the court of appeals granted the qualified immunity defense, finding that the defendants had violated the plaintiffs' rights (by seizing and questioning a minor without a warrant and without parental permission), but that the right was not clearly established.[52] The defendants sought to appeal the adverse merits determinations, even though they ultimately prevailed in the case and thus were not adversely affected by the court order.

---

[45] *Johnson*, 515 U.S. at 317.

[46] Stephen I. Vladeck, *Pendent Appellate Bootstrapping*, 16 GREEN BAG 2D 199 (2013).

[47] Wilkie v. Robbins, 551 U.S. 537 (2007); Vance v. Rumsfeld, 701 F.3d 193 (D.C. Cir. 2012) (en banc).

[48] *Iqbal*, 556 U.S. at 674-75; Hartman v. Moore, 647 U.S. 250 (2006).

[49] Evans v. Chalmers, 703 F.3d 636, 658 (4th Cir. 2012); Stephen I. Vladeck, *Pendent Appellate Bootstrapping*, 16 GREEN BAG 2D 199, 205 (2013).

[50] Camreta v. Greene, 131 S. Ct. 2020 (2011); IPSCO Steel (Ala.), Inc. v. Blaine Constr. Corp., 371 F.3d 150 (3d Cir. 2004).

[51] *Camreta*, 131 S. Ct. at 2030.

[52] *Id.* at 2027.

In allowing defendants to seek review, *Camreta* identified two reasons for special treatment for appeals of a qualified immunity order. First, the court of appeals decision announcing or defining the scope of the constitutional right creates binding law as to that right, clearly establishing it going forward and defeating qualified immunity in future cases. This has significant future effect on government policy and on the conduct of governments and officials — from this entity and others — who must adjust their behavior and policies to conform to the binding pronouncement of the court of appeals. Second, and related, Supreme Court review of winners' appeals furthers the goal of clarifying and developing substantive constitutional law by offering the Court additional opportunities to step-in and resolve disputed questions of the scope and meaning of constitutional rights.[53] Recall that the opportunity for law development is one of the benefits to the merits-first approach to qualified immunity.[54] If law development constitutes a good reason for courts of appeals to consider the merits in qualified immunity cases even where the right ultimately is not clearly established, it also constitutes a good reason to provide an additional opportunity for the Supreme Court to review those merits decisions.

Ironically, *Pearson* specifically highlighted this very problem — the non-appealability by the prevailing defendant of a grant of qualified immunity where a lower-court finds that a right has been violated but is not clearly established — as one basis for rejecting mandatory order of battle.[55] *Pearson* expressed concern that a prevailing defendant would be deprived of any opportunity to appeal the lower court's constitutional interpretation and construction, while also remaining bound by the merits decision clearly establishing that right. But in highlighting this as a situation in which mandatory merits first creates problems, the *Pearson* Court never considered the possibility that the prevailing defendant might be able to appeal that merits ruling, an issue it addressed just two years later. *Camreta* thus arguably undermines at least one in *Pearson*'s laundry list of reasons for abandoning mandatory order-of-battle in qualified immunity.[56]

Camreta limits these prevailing-party appeals in two important ways. First, winners' appeals are allowed from the court of appeals to the Supreme Court, not necessarily from the district court to the court of appeals. While leaving the question undecided, the Court emphasized that the same policy concerns are not implicated by district court decisions finding a right to have been violated, since district courts do not create binding precedent, rarely settle constitutional standards, and rarely are the basis for clearly establishing rights for qualified immunity purposes. Second, winners' appeals to the Supreme Court remain subject to the Court's discretion whether to grant *certiorari*, with the Court understanding that, even if it has jurisdiction, it should accept winners' petitions only in "sufficiently important cases."[57] Courts of appeals do not exercise the same (or,

---

[53] *Id.* at 2032.

[54] Pearson v. Callahan, 555 U.S. 223, 237 (2009); *supra* § 3.14[1].

[55] *Id.* at 240–41 & n.2 (discussing Mellen v. Bunting, 327 F.3d 355 (4th Cir. 2003), *cert. denied*, 541 U.S. 1019 (2004)).

[56] *Supra* § 3.14[2].

[57] *Camreta*, 131 S. Ct. at 2033; 28 U.S.C. § 1254(a).

indeed, any) discretion over their docket as to final judgments under § 1291 and the collateral order doctrine, thus it should remain more difficult for prevailing parties to appeal there.

§ 5.03   SECTION 1983 IN STATE COURT

As noted earlier, state courts exercise concurrent jurisdiction over § 1983 actions.[58] Concurrent jurisdiction is the default in a federalist system; Congress may divest state courts of jurisdiction only by an explicit statement that jurisdiction is exclusively federal or that state courts are divested of their usual jurisdiction.[59] On the other hand, state courts generally may not decline to exercise jurisdiction over federal claims, except through a "neutral state rule regarding the administration of the courts."[60] But that neutral rule cannot be grounded in state disagreement with the content or underlying policies of federal law. States cannot effectively nullify a federal right or cause of action solely because it is inconsistent with local policies.

In *Haywood v. Drown*, the Supreme Court considered a state rule that divested state trial courts of jurisdiction over claims by prisoners against corrections officers for money damages; such claims would proceed as actions against the state in the state court of claims.[61] The law was unique in that the state divested its own courts of jurisdiction over apparently disfavored federal claims. While state law treated federal and state claims equally and thus did not discriminate against federal claims, the absence of discrimination is not the end of the inquiry. Even an evenhanded state rule can undermine federal interests. Having created courts of general jurisdiction, the state cannot shut the door to those courts for federal claims from which it wishes to dissent or which it believes are at odds with its local policies. Moreover, the Court found it significant that the state rule left state courts to hear the lion's share of § 1983 actions — all of them, in fact, except for claims for damages by prisoners against corrections officers. The uniqueness of that scheme was significant to the Court's conclusion that it undermined the federal interests served by § 1983.[62]

§ 5.04   JURY TRIAL

Amendment VII (1791)

In Suits at common law, where the value in controversy shall exceed twenty dollars, the right of trial by jury shall be preserved, and no fact tried by a jury, shall be otherwise re-examined in any Court of the United

---

[58] Haywood v. Drown, 556 U.S. 729, 734–35 (2009); Maine v. Thiboutot, 448 U.S. 1, 3 n.1 (1980).

[59] Mims v. Arrow Fin. Servs., LLC, 132 S. Ct. 740, 748 (2012).

[60] *Haywood*, 556 U.S. at 735 (citing Howlett v. Rose, 496 U.S. 356 (1990)).

[61] *Id.* at 733–34. State law functioned much like the Federal Tort Claims Act, taking away jurisdiction over actions against the officer and allowing an action against the state in its stead. *See* 28 U.S.C. § 1346(b).

[62] *Haywood*, 556 U.S. at 737–39.

States, than according to the rules of the common law.

Although § 1983 does not specifically provide for a jury trial, an action for damages (an "action at law" under the statute) is treated as a "Suit at common law" for purposes of the Seventh Amendment right to a civil jury.[63] Parties also have a jury right in *Bivens* actions; in fact, the Supreme Court pointed to the availability of a jury in a *Bivens* action, but not in a claim against the United States under the Federal Tort Claims Act, as one reason to allow *Bivens* claims by federal prisoners against federal prison officials.[64] Section 1983 actions do remain subject to all ordinary procedures through which federal courts resolve cases prior to trial and without a jury, such as by summary judgment or dismissal for failure to state a claim.[65]

On the other hand, there is no jury right in a § 1983 action seeking equitable relief (a "suit in equity" under the statute); an action seeking injunctive relief is not a "Suit at common law" to which the jury right attaches, so the court serves as fact-finder.[66] Where a § 1983 plaintiff seeks both damages (legal) and injunctive (equitable) relief, the court in resolving the equitable claims is bound by the jury's findings on any facts common to both forms of relief.[67]

A third common remedy under § 1983 is a declaratory judgment, in which a federal court issues an order declaring the rights of, and legal relations between, parties.[68] A court can determine the constitutional validity of a law or government conduct and whether a plaintiff's rights have been violated, but without also issuing any coercive order.[69] Declaratory judgments are neither legal nor equitable.[70] But where (as is typically the case in § 1983 litigation) the request for declaratory relief is closely tied to a request for injunctive relief, the declaratory claim is treated as equitable, the Seventh Amendment does not apply, and the court serves as fact-finder.[71]

---

[63] City of Monterey v. Del Monte Dunes, Ltd., 526 U.S. 687 (1999); *id.* at 723 (Scalia, J., concurring in part and concurring in the judgment) (insisting a jury should be available in all § 1983 actions seeking monetary damages); Dillon v. Rogers, 596 F.3d 260 (5th Cir. 2010).

[64] Carlson v. Green, 446 U.S. 14 (1980).

[65] *Dillon*, 596 F.3d at 271–72; Fed. R. Civ. P. 12(b)(6), 56(a).

[66] *Del Monte Dunes*, 526 U.S. at 729; Wilson v. Bailey, 934 F.2d 301, 305 (11th Cir. 1991).

[67] Burton v. Armontrout, 975 F.2d 543 (8th Cir. 1992).

[68] 28 U.S.C. § 2201.

[69] Steffel v. Thompson, 415 U.S. 452, 471 (1974).

[70] Douglas Laycock, Modern American Remedies: Cases and Materials 6 (4th ed. 2010).

[71] Johnson v. Randle, 2012 U.S. Dist. LEXIS 75080 (S.D. Ill. May 31, 2012); DL v. District of Columbia, 845 F. Supp. 2d 1 (D.D.C. 2011).

PART B
COMPETING VEHICLES FOR ENFORCING
CONSTITUTIONAL RIGHTS

§ 5.05   OVERVIEW

Individuals can litigate federal constitutional rights in any of three ways. One way is defensive — where a right-holder asserts constitutional rights as a defense to criminal or civil litigation in federal or state court. Two others are offensive — the right-holder initiates an action in court against the government or government officials, seeking resolution of the constitutional issue and requesting affirmative relief from the court. There are two vehicles for offensively asserting constitutional rights. One is civil litigation — through a § 1983 action for damages or for equitable relief against state law and state officials, through a direct action for injunctive relief against federal officers, or through a *Bivens* action for damages against federal officers. The other offensive vehicle is a petition for a Writ of Habeas Corpus, a request to a federal court by a prisoner seeking release from state or federal custody.

The issue is establishing the proper domain for these two offensive vehicles for constitutional relief and identifying the appropriate approach for doing so.

§ 5.06   HABEAS CORPUS: A PRIMER

28 U.S.C. § 2241

(a) *Writs of habeas corpus may be granted by the Supreme Court, any justice thereof, the district courts and any circuit judge within their respective jurisdictions. The order of a circuit judge shall be entered in the records of the district court of the district wherein the restraint complained of is had.*

(b) *The Supreme Court, any justice thereof, and any circuit judge may decline to entertain an application for a writ of habeas corpus and may transfer the application for hearing and determination to the district court having jurisdiction to entertain it.*

(c) *The writ of habeas corpus shall not extend to a prisoner unless—*

(1) *He is in custody under or by color of the authority of the United States or is committed for trial before some court thereof; or*

(2) *He is in custody for an act done or omitted in pursuance of an Act of Congress, or an order, process, judgment or decree of a court or judge of the United States; or*

(3) *He is in custody in violation of the Constitution or laws or treaties of the United States; or*

(4) He, being a citizen of a foreign state and domiciled therein is in custody for an act done or omitted under any alleged right, title, authority, privilege, protection, or exemption claimed under the commission, order or sanction of any foreign state, or under color thereof, the validity and effect of which depend upon the law of nations; or

(5) It is necessary to bring him into court to testify or for trial.

28 U.S.C. § 2254

(a) The Supreme Court, a Justice thereof, a circuit judge, or a district court shall entertain an application for a writ of habeas corpus in behalf of a person in custody pursuant to the judgment of a State court only on the ground that he is in custody in violation of the Constitution or laws or treaties of the United States.

(b) (1) An application for a writ of habeas corpus on behalf of a person in custody pursuant to the judgment of a State court shall not be granted unless it appears that—

(A) the applicant has exhausted the remedies available in the courts of the State; or

(B) (i) there is an absence of available State corrective process; or

(ii) circumstances exist that render such process ineffective to protect the rights of the applicant.

(c) An applicant shall not be deemed to have exhausted the remedies available in the courts of the State, within the meaning of this section, if he has the right under the law of the State to raise, by any available procedure, the question presented.

(d) An application for a writ of habeas corpus on behalf of a person in custody pursuant to the judgment of a State court shall not be granted with respect to any claim that was adjudicated on the merits in State court proceedings unless the adjudication of the claim—

(1) resulted in a decision that was contrary to, or involved an unreasonable application of, clearly established Federal law, as determined by the Supreme Court of the United States; or

(2) resulted in a decision that was based on an unreasonable determination of the facts in light of the evidence presented in the State court proceeding.

[1] Habeas Corpus: The Basics

The Writ of Habeas Corpus, the "Great Writ," dates to medieval England. Literally meaning "you have the body," it empowered courts to order the King's officers (not the King, of course, in light of sovereign immunity) to present a prisoner to the court for a judicial determination of the lawfulness of the detention or custody. The writ was carried to the United States and protected against "suspension" in the Constitution.[72] All justices and federal judges are authorized to entertain habeas corpus petitions to adjudicate federal constitutional and statutory challenges to custody or detention by the United States[73] or by a state pursuant to a state-court conviction and sentence.[74]

Habeas relief is defined by several features. The applicant must be in custody,[75] broadly defined to include not only imprisonment, but also probation[76] or parole or supervised release.[77] Custody does not include the ongoing collateral consequences of a conviction (for example loss of the right to vote, hold public office, or hold certain jobs; placement in immigration detention; or mandatory sex-offender registration) once the sentence imposed for the conviction has been fully served and has expired.[78] Because of sovereign immunity, a habeas action must be brought against the executive officer responsible for placing or holding the applicant in custody — the President, Attorney General, or, in actions by state prisoners, the warden or state superintendent of prisons.[79] A habeas petition can challenge constitutional defects in either the substantive law under which the petitioner was convicted or in the process that resulted in his being convicted and placed in custody; constitutional defects as to either means he is in custody in violation of the Constitution or laws of the United States. The typical remedy in habeas is vacatur of the state conviction and sentence and conditional release from custody, unless the government reinitiates prosecution or other procedures with any federal constitutional defects corrected.[80]

The most common habeas corpus activity involves petitions in federal district court under § 2254 by state prisoners challenging state convictions and sentences. These cases raise a host of unique procedural and substantive issues. State prisoners can assert violations of all constitutional rights except the Fourth

---

[72] U.S. Const. art. I, § 9, cl. 2; Boumediene v. Bush, 553 U.S. 723 (2008).

[73] 28 U.S.C. § 2241.

[74] *Id.* § 2254.

[75] *Id.* § 2241(c); *id.* § 2254(a).

[76] Lee v. Stickman, 357 F.3d 338 (3d Cir. 2004).

[77] Maleng v. Cook, 490 U.S. 488 (1989); Jones v. Cunningham, 371 U.S. 236 (1963).

[78] Wilson v. Flaherty, 689 F.3d 332 (4th Cir. 2012) (requirement of registration as sex offender did not place person in custody); Ogunwomoju v. United States, 512 F.3d 69 (2d Cir. 2008) (placement in immigration detention not custody); Virsnieks v. Smith, 521 F.3d 707 (7th Cir. 2008) (requirement to register as sexual offender does not render person in custody); Leslie v. Randle, 296 F.3d 518 (6th Cir. 2002).

[79] *Supra* § 4.09.

[80] Foxworth v. Maloney, 515 F.3d 1 (1st Cir. 2008).

Amendment.[81] A general claim of actual innocence, disconnected from any violation of an identified constitutional right, cannot provide a basis for overturning a conviction.[82] A prisoner on a habeas petition is typically bound by the law in effect at the time his conviction became final; the court will not apply "new law" (law established subsequent to the conviction) on habeas review, subject to certain limited exceptions.[83]

Several significant limitations on habeas petition by state petitioners were originally judicially imposed, then codified in § 2254.

First, a state prisoner must exhaust available state judicial remedies, meaning he must challenge the constitutionality of his conviction and sentence in state court prior to bringing constitutional claims in a federal habeas action.[84] Exhaustion in state court generally proceeds in two stages. First, the prisoner pursues direct review of the conviction through all levels of the state judicial system (and perhaps to the Supreme Court of the United States); at the end of that process, the state conviction is final. All states then provide post-conviction relief processes, in which the prisoner again challenges the conviction through the state judicial process, beginning in the trial court that imposed the original conviction and sentence and working through all levels of state review (with review by the Supreme Court again possible, although less likely). At each step in each round of state-court litigation, the prisoner must "fairly present"[85] all federal constitutional issues and give the state court an opportunity to consider and address those issues. Only after going fully through both available rounds of state review can a prisoner go to federal court on habeas,[86] and then only with the federal constitutional issues that have been fairly presented to the state court. Failure to present and exhaust a constitutional issue in state court means it cannot be raised in federal court, although default may be excused in limited circumstances.[87]

The exhaustion requirement makes sense as a matter of federalism and judicial process. A federal habeas court functionally acts as an appellate court, reviewing the state court's constitutional analysis and rulings; basic principles of appellate review require that a lower court (the state court in these cases) be given an opportunity to redress any constitutional violations before the reviewing court (the federal court in these cases) will overturn its decision. Exhaustion also furthers critical values of comity and federalism by giving the state court an opportunity to correct its own errors before a federal court does it for them; it "would be unseemly in our dual system of government for a federal district court to upset a state court conviction without an opportunity to the state courts to correct a constitutional violation."[88]

---

[81] Stone v. Powell, 428 U.S. 465 (1976).

[82] Herrera v. Collins, 506 U.S. 390 (1993).

[83] Chaidez v. U.S., 133 S. Ct. 1103 (2013); Teague v. Lane, 489 U.S. 288 (1989).

[84] 28 U.S.C. § 2254(b); Granberry v. Greer, 481 U.S. 129 (1987).

[85] Baldwin v. Reese, 541 U.S. 27 (2004).

[86] 28 U.S.C. § 2254(c).

[87] Maples v. Thomas, 132 S. Ct. 912 (2012).

[88] Rose v. Lundy, 455 U.S. 509, 518 (1982).

Second, a federal court can grant a § 2254 petition only if the state court's decision was "contrary to, or involved an unreasonable application of, clearly established Federal law, as determined by the Supreme Court of the United States" or was "based on an unreasonable determination of the facts in light of the evidence presented in the State court proceeding."[89] Such highly deferential review again furthers important values of comity and federalism in respecting state courts, state processes, and state decision-making. It also respects the value of finality; a state-court order entered and appealed to a final judgment in the state system (including possible review by the U.S. Supreme Court) is entitled to respect and deference, in the interest of preserving and ensuring the predictability and certainty of state decisions, even if the federal court might have resolved the constitutional issues differently.[90]

The final statutory limitation on federal habeas relief by state prisoners is the absence of the ordinary appeal as of right from a federal district court to the court of appeals. A habeas petitioner can appeal only if he obtains a certification of appealability from the circuit court, which requires a "substantial showing of the denial of a constitutional right."[91]

[2] Habeas Corpus and § 1983, Compared and Contrasted

Petitions for a writ of habeas corpus under § 2254 and civil actions under § 1983 perform overlapping functions — providing a federal vehicle for a federal court to review the constitutionality of the actions of states and state officers. But these distinct vehicles for enforcing federal rights diverge in three important respects.

The first, and obvious one, is the available remedy. The remedy for a habeas petition is vacatur of the conviction and release from custody, or at least a new state-court proceeding free from constitutional defect. Section 1983 provides civil remedies such as damages, injunctive relief, and declaratory judgments.

Second is the scope of review. A federal court on habeas reviews the state court decision for error, under a highly deferential standard of review. On the other hand, a federal court in a § 1983 action decides the constitutional issue in the first instance; it merely must conclude that state officers caused a "deprivation" of a right, privilege, or immunity secured by federal law, according no formal decisional deference to the conduct or decisions of state actors. Section 2254(d)(1)'s requirement that federal law be clearly established does parallel the qualified immunity defense to § 1983. Importantly, however, law can be clearly established for habeas purposes only through a decision of the Supreme Court of the United States, while law can be clearly established for qualified immunity purposes by a binding decision of the courts of appeals or by a strong consensus of other courts of appeals and district courts.[92]

---

[89] 28 U.S.C. § 2254(d); Lafler v. Cooper, 132 S. Ct. 1376 (2012).

[90] Williams v. Taylor, 529 U.S. 420 (2000); Frazier v. Bouchard, 661 F.3d 519 (11th Cir. 2011).

[91] 28 U.S.C. §§ 2253(c)(1), (2).

[92] *Compare* 28 U.S.C. § 2254(d)(1), *with* United States v. Lanier, 520 U.S. 259, 269 (1997); *supra* § 3.15[2].

Third, unlike habeas, § 1983 contains no exhaustion requirement. In recognizing § 1983 as a "supplementary" remedy to state tort litigation, *Monroe v. Pape* implicitly rejected any requirement that a plaintiff first go to the state court or that she show that state remedies were inadequate or unavailable in that case as a condition of going to federal court.[93] Subsequently, in *Patsy v. Board of Regents*, the Court rejected a state requirement that a public employee exhaust state administrative remedies prior to initiating a § 1983 equal protection action challenging her dismissal. Section 1983 is grounded on mistrust of state institutions and state fact-finding and it therefore makes federal courts the paramount enforcers of federal rights; requiring a plaintiff to go through state proceedings as a condition precedent to federal litigation contradicts § 1983's broad statutory purpose to "throw open the courthouse doors" to civil rights plaintiffs.[94]

§ 5.07   SEPARATING HABEAS CORPUS AND § 1983: *HECK v. HUMPHREY*

Given the procedural hurdles built into habeas corpus but not into § 1983, federal claimants given a choice obviously would gravitate toward the latter vehicle, undermining the legislative policy choices behind habeas procedures and thus the vibrancy of habeas as a unique remedial scheme. Habeas would become a dead letter if a plaintiff could use § 1983 to bypass its limitations. It thus becomes necessary to define a distinct realm for each federal litigation vehicle and to keep each safely in its own sphere.

In *Preiser v. Rodriguez*, several state prisoners brought a § 1983 action seeking injunctions ordering restoration of their good-time credits toward early release, arguing that prison officials had withdrawn the credits without due process; the effect of the injunction restoring those credits would have been that the plaintiffs would be released from prison earlier than they would be under current circumstances. The Supreme Court held that the claim to recover the credits was not cognizable under § 1983. A habeas petition under § 2254 is the exclusive remedy for all state prisoners challenging the fact or duration of their confinement and seeking any federal judicial order compelling immediate or speedier release from state custody.[95] In dicta, the Court allowed that a § 1983 action might be available if the prisoner seeks damages rather than an injunction compelling immediate or speedier release from custody or if the prisoner attacks something other than the fact or length of confinement.[96]

In *Heck v. Humphrey*, the Court directly confronted that dicta. The plaintiff had been convicted in state court and brought a § 1983 action alleging that police and prosecutors had jointly destroyed evidence, gathered and admitted illegal evidence, and unlawfully targeted him for prosecution. He did not seek an injunction overturning the conviction or ordering immediate or earlier release; he only sought

---

[93]   Monroe v. Pape, 365 U.S. 167 (1961); *supra* § 2.03[2].

[94]   Patsy v. Bd. of Regents, 457 U.S. 496, 503–04 (1982).

[95]   Preiser v. Rodriguez, 411 U.S. 475 (1973).

[96]   *Id.* at 507.

damages for the misconduct that lead to his conviction and incarceration.[97]

The analytical starting point is whether, in establishing the basis for his damages claim, the plaintiff must prove that the conviction, the sentence, or the duration of the sentence is constitutionally invalid. If the answer is no, the § 1983 damages action can proceed. If the answer is yes, the damages claim is not cognizable under § 1983 unless the conviction has been invalidated; invalidation means the conviction has been reversed on appeal, set aside on post-conviction review, impugned by the federal grant of a writ of habeas corpus, or eliminated by an executive grant of a pardon or clemency.[98] This additional element on the plaintiff's § 1983 or *Bivens*[99] action imports into constitutional litigation the "favorable termination" requirement from the tort of malicious prosecution, under which a plaintiff must show that the prosecution alleged to be malicious has been resolved in his favor.[100] In effect, if a federal action would directly or by implication invalidate a conviction, habeas corpus is the only appropriate federal remedial vehicle for challenging that conviction.

What courts label the "*Heck* bar" (or what the Supreme Court subsequently referred to as the "implicit habeas exception to § 1983"[101]) obviously applies to claims seeking damages for injuries caused by the unconstitutional conviction or sentence itself. But it also reaches damages claims "for other harm caused by actions whose unlawfulness would render a conviction or sentence invalid."[102] As an example of the latter, the majority hypothesized a person convicted and sentenced for resisting arrest (generally defined as intentionally preventing a peace officer from effecting a lawful arrest) who brings a damages action against the arresting officer for an unreasonable seizure. To prevail on that Fourth Amendment claim, the § 1983 plaintiff must demonstrate that the seizure (the arrest) was unreasonable or without probable cause, which negates an element ("lawful arrest") of the crime for which he was convicted and sentenced.[103]

On the other hand, if a constitutional claim by a prisoner would not *necessarily* (emphasis intentional) demonstrate or imply the invalidity of the fact of conviction or the fact or duration of a sentence it may proceed under § 1983. In footnote 7, for example, the *Heck* majority suggested that a prisoner may be able to bring a Fourth Amendment unreasonable-search claim through § 1983, even if evidence obtained from that search has been used in the criminal proceeding. A finding that the search was unreasonable does not necessarily imply the invalidity of the conviction. The unlawfully discovered evidence may have been found and used and the person convicted in any event. Or the conviction might have been upheld, even if the search was unlawful, under harmless error analysis. The Court emphasized, however, that the plaintiff can prevail only if he suffers an actual, compensable injury, other than

---

[97] Heck v. Humphrey, 512 U.S. 477, 478–81 (1994).

[98] *Id.* at 486–87.

[99] Crow v. Penry, 102 F.3d 1086 (10th Cir. 1996); Tavarez v. Reno, 54 F.3d 109 (2d Cir. 1995).

[100] *Heck*, 512 U.S. at 484.

[101] Wilkinson v. Dotson, 544 U.S. 74, 82 (2005).

[102] *Heck*, 512 U.S. at 486.

[103] *Id.* at 486–87 n.6.

the "injury" of being convicted and imprisoned unless the conviction has been overturned or invalidated.[104]

Heck's Footnote 7 has created a split in the lower courts. The Seventh Circuit reads that language to mean *Heck* is entirely inapplicable to Fourth Amendment search claims, because the challenged misconduct (the unlawful search) is unrelated to the judicial process resulting in the conviction and incarceration; unreasonable-search claims thus can proceed under § 1983 without showing favorable termination of criminal proceedings.[105] This separate treatment of Fourth Amendment claims also makes sense, given that such claims cannot be raised through habeas.[106] Other courts hold that *Heck* applies to any search that produces evidence actually used in the criminal procedure to obtain a conviction.[107]

Justice Souter, joined by three other justices, concurred only in the judgment in *Heck*. While agreeing that the instant claim was barred, Souter argued that the favorable termination requirement should not be imposed in all cases, but only in cases truly at the intersection of § 1983 and habeas corpus — where the § 1983 plaintiff remains in custody and thus would be able to assert his constitutional right through habeas.[108] Souter offered a hypothetical of an individual framed and convicted by a Klan-dominated state judicial system who did not discover that he had been framed until after he no longer was in custody.[109] Habeas no longer is available to a person not in custody. But under the majority's approach, neither is § 1983 unless his conviction has been invalidated, because his claim necessarily implies the invalidity of the conviction. The only option is to pursue state remedies to invalidate the conviction — asking the state court to reopen the case and vacate or overturn the conviction or asking the state governor for a pardon. Functionally, Justice Souter argued, this requires the plaintiff to exhaust state judicial and political remedies, which is inconsistent with the ordinary requirements and core purposes of § 1983 (as reflected in *Patsy*), particularly the historical suspicion of state institutions and officials that motivated enactment of the 1871 Act in the first place.[110] The claimant in such a case might be entirely denied a federal forum in which to assert his federal rights by the whims of, at least historically, distrusted state institutions and officials.

At the end of the day, *Heck* and its progeny establish "that a state prisoner's § 1983 action is barred (absent prior invalidation) — no matter the relief sought (damages or equitable relief), no matter the target of the prisoner's suit (state conduct leading to conviction or internal prison proceedings) — *if* success in that action would necessarily demonstrate the invalidity of confinement or its dura-

---

[104] *Id.* at 487 n.7.

[105] Copus v. City of Edgerton, 151 F.3d 646 (7th Cir. 1998); Antonelli v. Foster, 104 F.3d 899 (7th Cir. 1997).

[106] Stone v. Powell, 428 U.S. 465 (1976).

[107] Szajer v. City of Los Angeles, 632 F.3d 607 (9th Cir. 2011); Whitaker v. Garcetti, 486 F.3d 572 (9th Cir. 2007); Schilling v. White, 58 F.3d 1081 (6th Cir. 1995).

[108] *Heck*, 512 U.S. at 498–501 (Souter, J., concurring in the judgment).

[109] *Id.* at 501–02 (Souter, J., concurring in the judgment).

[110] *Id.* at 501–02 (Souter, J., concurring in the judgment).

tion."[111] Such a claim must be brought to federal court through habeas. Moreover, *Heck* is an all-or-nothing bar to a claim, not an exhaustion requirement. A court ordinarily should not stay a § 1983 action pending the plaintiff's efforts to resolve *Heck* issues.[112] If the claim would not necessarily imply invalidity when filed, it proceeds; if it would necessarily imply invalidity at the time of filing, it must be dismissed. And the importance of the word "necessarily" cannot be overstated.[113]

§ 5.08 *HECK* AND PRISON ADMINISTRATION

[1] Administrative Punishments and Credit Toward Release

Beyond the core situation of seeking damages resulting from a conviction or conduct made in securing the conviction, *Heck* issues frequently arise in actions challenging decisions made through prison administrative processes that affect sentences and the timing of release for people already convicted and in custody.

Preiser establishes that § 1983 is not the proper vehicle for overturning prison administrative decisions withdrawing good-time credits toward release. The Supreme Court subsequently extended this to bar to claims seeking damages for those lost credits. A finding of unconstitutionality in the prison administrative process (such as deceit and bias) used to cancel credits and the awarding of damages for their loss necessarily implies the invalidity of the loss, which in turn necessarily suggests that the plaintiff's sentence should be shorter and that he should be released sooner than he otherwise will be.[114] On the other hand, a § 1983 action can be brought to enjoin prospective use of those same unconstitutional procedures.[115] A request for prospective relief, applicable only to future disciplinary actions, does not speak to the validity of past cancellation of good-time credits.

In *Wilkinson v. Dotson*, the Court considered two cases on the applicability of *Heck* to the slightly different context of parole determinations. One case challenged procedures used to determine a prisoner's parole eligibility (whether he should get a parole hearing), while the other challenged the procedures used to determine a prisoner's parole suitability (whether he should receive parole and be released from prison); both plaintiffs sought new hearings.[116] These federal claims were not *Heck*-barred because success would not compel the plaintiffs' immediate release or "necessarily spell speedier release"; it only would get them a new parole hearing or a new eligibility hearing (and perhaps new consideration for parole).[117] The practical possibility that they might prevail in these procedurally proper new hearings, and thus obtain speedier release from custody, results from the state

---

[111] Wilkinson v. Dotson, 544 U.S. 74, 81–82 (2005) (emphasis in original).

[112] Edwards v. Balisok, 520 U.S. 641, 649 (1997).

[113] Nelson v. Campbell, 541 U.S. 637, 647 (2004).

[114] *Edwards*, 520 U.S. at 647.

[115] *Id.* at 648.

[116] *Wilkinson*, 544 U.S. at 76–77.

[117] *Id.* at 82.

proceedings themselves, not from the federal court's judgment and order.

The Court in *Wilkinson* also suggested the need to limit *Heck* only to cases in which the federal relief sought would be available through habeas if § 1983 were foreclosed. The claims in *Wilkinson*, which only would result in new procedurally proper state proceedings, lay far from the "core" of habeas, which ordinarily produces a federal court order directly ordering immediate or speedier release.[118] A claim that "neither terminates custody, accelerates the future date of release from custody, nor reduces the level of custody" is not properly brought through habeas and therefore must remain cognizable under § 1983.[119]

[2] Methods and Procedures of Execution

Heck considerations also have arisen in Eighth Amendment challenges to a state's methods of executing an inmate, with the Court twice holding that § 1983 is the proper vehicle for challenging the manner of execution and for enjoining unconstitutional means of executing by lethal injection.[120] Critical to both cases was that any federal injunction would not bar the execution or even the use of lethal injection as the means execution, as ordered by the state judgment; it only would bar the state from utilizing certain prerequisite procedures (a particular drug cocktail or an invasive procedure to overcome the prisoner's compromised veins) in carrying out the execution, forcing the state to find alternative ways to perform lethal injection.[121]

Hill did consider the government's argument that a ban on the prerequisites of lethal injection would, as a practical matter, ban the execution altogether, because the plaintiff did not identify any combination and sequence of drugs that would satisfy the Eighth Amendment. It thus really became a challenge to the constitutionality of lethal injection itself, a claim properly brought in habeas and not § 1983. But the Court again emphasized the centrality of the word "necessary" in the *Heck* analysis — absent a showing that the injunction necessarily forecloses the state entirely from implementing a capital sentence and thus necessarily reduces the sentence from death, *Heck* does not bar a § 1983 action.[122]

§ 5.09 *HECK*, WRONGFUL CONVICTIONS, AND DNA TESTING

Heck poses a significant limitation on using § 1983 to recover damages for unlawful convictions, since the § 1983 claim cannot be brought until the conviction has been invalidated through habeas or some other process.[123] A different *Heck* problem involves prisoners using § 1983 to obtain DNA evidence or DNA testing in

---

[118] *Id.*; *id.* at 86 (Scalia, J., concurring).

[119] *Id.* at 86 (Scalia, J., concurring).

[120] Hill v. McDonough, 547 U.S. 573 (2006); Nelson v. Campbell, 541 U.S. 637 (2004).

[121] *Hill*, 547 U.S. at 580; *Nelson*, 541 U.S. at 645–46.

[122] *Hill*, 547 U.S. at 581–82.

[123] Brandon L. Garrett, *Innocence, Harmless Error, and Federal Wrongful Conviction Law*, 2005 WIS. L. REV. 35.

order to show that the conviction is wrongful and should be invalidated in state proceedings or in habeas.

In *District Attorney's Office v. Osborne*, the Court avoided the *Heck* question, holding instead that a prisoner does not have a substantive due process right to obtain DNA evidence or testing, so the constitutional claims fail regardless of the litigation vehicle used.[124] Justice Alito concurred (writing only for himself) to insist that *Heck* did bar the § 1983 action and that such a claim even, if substantively feasible, only can be brought in habeas. Alito argued that the plaintiff was attempting to use § 1983 as a discovery tool to lay the foundation for a future challenge to his conviction. That strategy implicated the comity and federalism concerns underlying limits on habeas, including limits on habeas discovery, that *Heck* is designed to protect.[125] A claim for DNA testing is functionally a due process claim for disclosure of exculpatory evidence under *Brady v. Maryland*,[126] a claim regularly asserted through habeas. In particular, a *Brady* claim requires a showing that the evidence, if disclosed, would have affected the judgment in the criminal case and might have produced an acquittal — which is functionally the same as necessarily implying invalidity of the conviction.[127]

Two years later, in *Skinner v. Switzer*, the Court addressed the *Heck* question in a slightly different context. The plaintiff did not assert a substantive due process right to DNA testing (the claim foreclosed by *Osborne*). Instead, he alleged that the state statute governing DNA testing, as authoritatively construed by the state courts, violated procedural due process. The majority held that this claim was cognizable under § 1983 and not *Heck*-barred; while "test results might prove exculpatory, that outcome is hardly inevitable; . . . results might prove inconclusive or they might further incriminate" the prisoner.[128] A *Brady* claim, by definition, seeks only exculpatory evidence that necessarily undermines or calls into question the validity of the conviction or sentence. By contrast, the uncertainty of what DNA testing might show means it is not certain that this claim would undermine the conviction, a relevant distinction given the import of the word "necessarily" under *Heck*.[129] The majority did emphasize the difficulty of such a claim in light of *Osborne* and thus the likely limited effect of its decision.[130] But the possibility at least remains open.

---

[124] DA's Office v. Osborne, 557 U.S. 52 (2009).

[125] *Id.* at 75–79 (Alito, J., concurring).

[126] Brady v. Maryland, 373 U.S. 83 (1963).

[127] *Osborne*, 557 U.S. at 77–78 (Alito, J., concurring).

[128] Skinner v. Switzer, 131 S. Ct. 1289, 1298 (2011).

[129] *Id.* at 1300.

[130] *Id.* at 1293.

PART C
SECTION 1983 AND PRECLUSION

§ 5.10   PRECLUSION

28 U.S.C. § 1738

* * *

Such Acts, records and judicial proceedings or copies thereof, so authenticated, shall have the same full faith and credit in every court within the United States and its Territories and Possessions as they have by law or usage in the courts of such State, Territory or Possession from which they are taken.

The Full Faith and Credit Act provides that state judgments shall have "the same full faith and credit in every court within the United States and its Territories and Possessions as they have by law or usage in the courts of such State, Territory or Possession from which they are taken."[131] In other words, if a judgment is valid in the issuing state, it must be treated as valid in federal court and other state courts and accorded binding and preclusive effect. The statute incorporates common law doctrines of *res judicata*, or preclusion, prohibiting re-litigation of claims and of legal and factual issues already litigated and resolved in state court.

Although Congress can override § 1738 by statute, it did not do so through § 1983. "Nothing in the language of § 1983 remotely expresses any congressional intent to contravene the common-law rules of preclusion or to repeal the express statutory requirements" of the Full Faith and Credit Act. Section 1983 creates a new federal cause of action, but "says nothing about the preclusive effect of state-court judgments."[132] Nor does § 1983's legislative history "in any clear way suggest that Congress intended to repeal or restrict the traditional doctrines of preclusion."[133]

While § 1983 unquestionably alters the historic balance of responsibility between federal and state courts, it does so by increasing the authority of federal courts, not by decreasing the authority of state courts or the respect and credit owed to their judgments. And while the primary goal of the 1871 Act was to override the influence of the Klan on state institutions amid "grave congressional concern that the state courts had been deficient in protecting federal rights," that purpose does not provide clear enough support that § 1738 and historical preclusion principles are entirely inapplicable to § 1983 actions .[134] Thus, a federal court adjudicating a § 1983 claim must adhere to principles of preclusion with respect to any prior state court litigation.

---

[131] 28 U.S.C. § 1738.

[132] Allen v. McCurry, 449 U.S. 90, 97–98 (1980).

[133] *Id.* at 98.

[134] *Id.* at 98–99.

§ 5.11   ISSUE PRECLUSION

While the precise elements vary across jurisdictions, issue preclusion (formerly collateral estoppel) generally applies to: (1) an issue of law or fact that was (2) necessary to the prior judgment and was (3) actually litigated and resolved in the earlier litigation by giving a party a "full and fair opportunity to litigate." Historically, a fourth element had been "mutuality," meaning both parties to the second case in which issue preclusion was being asserted, were parties in the prior case. But courts have moved away from a strict mutuality requirement; a party to the second case may avail itself of issue preclusion even if not a party to the first case, although the party against whom preclusion is asserted must have been party to the first case.[135] The effect of issue preclusion is that a party and the court are bound by the earlier court's legal and factual conclusions. The second case then is adjudicated in light of already-established law and fact.

In *Allen v. McCurry*, the defendant in a state criminal prosecution filed a motion to suppress evidence as having been seized in violation of the Fourth Amendment; the state court denied the motion and the defendant was convicted. Now in prison, he brought a § 1983 damages action against, among others, the officers who allegedly entered his home without a warrant and seized evidence in violation of the Fourth Amendment.[136] The federal court was bound by the state court's conclusion that the Fourth Amendment had not been violated, a conclusion that in turn defeated the § 1983 damages claim. Critically, the state court had recognized and heard the defendant's Fourth Amendment arguments and had provided fair procedures for adjudicating them. While § 1983 might offer an exception to preclusion had that not been the case, this merely incorporates the general rule that the party against whom preclusion is being used must have had a "full and fair opportunity to litigate" the issue in the prior case.[137]

The dissent in *Allen* tried to focus on § 1983's historical purposes. Section 1983 is not just about ensuring procedural regularity in state court, but about ensuring substantive justice generally unavailable in post bellum state courts because of Klan influence. As the Court held in *Monroe*, § 1983's federal remedy should be available regardless of the precise circumstances of state law or state litigation. Section 1983 therefore only can be given its necessary full breadth if it overrides § 1738 and issue preclusion as a blanket matter.[138] Moreover, raising the Fourth Amendment issues on a motion to suppress in the state criminal prosecution is not equivalent to raising them in a § 1983 damages action, because the decision-making processes are not the same. A state trial court faces institutional pressures when asked to suppress evidence that give a different shape to its Fourth Amendment analysis and thus to constitutional rights; consciously or not, the judge weighs the potential damage to the truth-finding process from the exclusion of relevant evidence in deciding the

---

[135] Allen v. McCurry, 449 U.S. 90, 94–95 (1980); *see* Parklane Hosiery Co., Inc. v. Shore, 439 U.S. 322 (1979).

[136] *Id.* at 92–93.

[137] *Id.* at 100–01.

[138] *Id.* at 105–10 (Blackmun, J., dissenting).

constitutional issue. Those pressures are absent in a § 1983 action, in which the only consequence is an award of damages.[139]

Allen also creates a problem of how parties ever can obtain a federal forum to vindicate certain federal constitutional rights. Fourth Amendment rights cannot be asserted on habeas corpus,[140] so the defendant cannot challenge the state court's rejection of the motion to suppress through a later federal habeas petition and under *Allen*, the state court decision is preclusive in any § 1983 action. Thus, the only way for a state criminal defendant to obtain a federal forum on a Fourth Amendment issue is through direct review of the state court judgment (including the decision on the motion to suppress) through the state court system and to the Supreme Court of the United States, review which is entirely discretionary with the Court.[141] In other words, there is no guarantee that a state criminal defendant ever will get a federal forum adjudicating his federal rights. This was not a significant concern for the majority in *Allen*, however, which insisted that a party has no right to one opportunity to litigate all federal issues in a federal forum.[142]

Nevertheless, *Allen* puts state defendants to a Hobson's Choice — bring the federal constitutional claim in state court, knowing that the state decision is preclusive and could deprive him of any federal forum (subject to the rare possibility of Supreme Court direct review), or forego the federal defense in state court, which preserves the issue for a § 1983 action, but at the risk of conviction.

Finally, issue preclusion does not work in the opposite direction. Had the state court in *Allen* found that the search did violate the Fourth Amendment and granted the motion to suppress, the plaintiff could not use issue preclusion in the subsequent § 1983 action to establish that the Fourth Amendment had been violated. He instead would have to convince the federal court anew that his constitutional rights had been violated. Because the officers and the police department (the defendants in the § 1983 action) were not parties to the state prosecution (the State is the "plaintiff"), they never had that "full and fair opportunity to litigate" the Fourth Amendment and thus cannot have issue preclusion asserted against them.[143]

---

[139] *Id.* at 115 (Blackmun, J., dissenting).

[140] Stone v. Powell, 428 U.S. 465 (1976).

[141] 28 U.S.C. § 1257(a). The version of § 1257 in effect when *Allen* was decided in 1980 provided for mandatory Supreme Court review of some state court decisions, notably those that considered and rejected a federal constitutional challenge to a state statute and upheld the statute as valid. 28 U.S.C. § 1257(2) (pre-1988). But cases such as *Allen*, which involved assertions of a "title, right, privilege, or immunity" under the Constitution, were subject only to *certiorari* review. 28 U.S.C. § 1257(3) (pre-1988). So even in 1980, Supreme Court review of state Fourth Amendment exclusionary decisions would have been discretionary. Congress amended § 1257 in 1988, making all Supreme Court review of state court decisions by *certiorari*. Supreme Court Case Selections Act, Pub. L. No. 100-352, 102 Stat. 662 (1988).

[142] *Allen*, 449 U.S. at 103.

[143] *Allen*, 449 U.S. at 95.

§ 5.12   CLAIM PRECLUSION

Claim preclusion (formerly *res judicata*) requires (1) a prior civil action that proceeded to a final judgment on the merits, (2) that involved the same parties as in the current action or parties in privity with them, (3) that was part of the same cause of action as the present case (typically defined to mean that the claims in the second case arise out of the same transaction or occurrence as the claims in the first case), and (4) that the claims in the current case either were brought and litigated in the first action or could have been brought and litigated. Claim preclusion bars parties from relitigating a single basic set of events, facts, or conduct in multiple lawsuits; parties have only one shot at proving their case and whatever distinct claims of right may arise against a particular party from those events, facts, or conduct. Claim preclusion entirely defeats the subsequent case and requires the second court to dismiss the claims in that second action.

There is no distinction between issue preclusion and claim preclusion for purposes of § 1983 or its relationship to § 1738, since § 1738 does not distinguish the two forms of preclusion. Because, under *Allen* § 1983 does not override issue preclusion, it follows that § 1983 does not override claim preclusion.[144]

The plaintiff in *Migra v. Warren City School District* was terminated from her position as supervisor of elementary education in a public school district. She sued in state court alleging state claims of breach of contract and tortious interference with contractual relations; after she prevailed on those claims, she brought a § 1983 action in federal court, alleging violations of the freedom of speech and due process. The Supreme Court held that the second, federal action could be claim-precluded if state law so required (the preclusive effect of a state judgment in federal court depends on the effect the issuing state courts would give the judgment).[145] The Court emphasized that a plaintiff such as Migra easily could avoid preclusion — either by litigating the § 1983 claim in her state-court action or by bringing the § 1983 claim in federal court first,[146] perhaps along with her state claims.[147]

Tellingly, *Migra* was a unanimous decision authored by Justice Blackmun, who had written the dissent in *Allen*. He explained his seemingly inconsistent positions in a footnote in *Migra*. The § 1983 plaintiff in *Allen* had not voluntarily taken his federal issues to state court; as a defendant in the state criminal proceeding, he was forced by the state to litigate there and to make litigation choices such as whether to raise his Fourth Amendment defense there or hold it for federal court. In *Migra*, by contrast, the same plaintiff was in an offensive posture in both state court and federal court, exercising full control over when and where to litigate and what claims to assert. She thus was less at risk of losing a federal forum because of involuntary litigation options; the litigation options remained hers at all times.[148]

---

[144] Migra v. Warren City School Dist. Bd. of Education, 465 U.S. 75, 83–84 (1984).

[145] *Id.* at 77–79, 85.

[146] *Id.* at 84–85.

[147] 28 U.S.C. § 1367(a); Valentine v. City of Chicago, 452 F.3d 670 (7th Cir. 2006); *supra* § 5.01.

[148] *Migra*, 465 U.S. at 85 n.7.

PART D

LIMITATIONS AND ACCRUAL

§ 5.13   SECTION 1988 AND STATUTES OF LIMITATIONS

42 U.S.C. § 1988

(a) Applicability of statutory and common law

The jurisdiction in civil and criminal matters conferred on the district courts by the provisions of titles 13, 24, and 70 of the Revised Statutes for the protection of all persons in the United States in their civil rights, and for their vindication, shall be exercised and enforced in conformity with the laws of the United States, so far as such laws are suitable to carry the same into effect; but in all cases where they are not adapted to the object, or are deficient in the provisions necessary to furnish suitable remedies and punish offenses against law, the common law, as modified and changed by the constitution and statutes of the State wherein the court having jurisdiction of such civil or criminal cause is held, so far as the same is not inconsistent with the Constitution and laws of the United States, shall be extended to and govern the said courts in the trial and disposition of the cause, and, if it is of a criminal nature, in the infliction of punishment on the party found guilty.

Section 1988(a) requires federal courts to use state law as "gap-filler" where federal law on underlying substantive and procedural matters is otherwise silent. A prominent use of § 1988(a) is to establish the statute of limitations for § 1983 claims.

Section 1983 contains no limitations period. In 1990, Congress enacted a four-year catch-all federal limitations period, applicable to civil actions arising under an act of Congress enacted after the establishment of the new statute of limitations (i.e., after 1990).[149] But this federal period does not affect § 1983 actions, since § 1983 was enacted well before 1990.[150] And while § 1983 was amended post-1990 (in the add-on provision prohibiting injunctions against judges unless the plaintiff first obtains a declaratory judgment[151]), the amendment did not create a new cause of action or expand the cause of action so as to make possible new claims not available prior to the amendment.[152]

---

[149]   28 U.S.C. § 1658(a).

[150]   Laurino v. Tate, 220 F.3d 1213, 1217 (10th Cir. 2000).

[151]   42 U.S.C. § 1983; *supra* § 3.08[3].

[152]   *Laurino*, 220 F.3d at 1218.

Federal courts are divided over how to handle a § 1981 claim against a municipality brought as an "and laws" action through § 1983 — whether it should be treated under § 1981 as amended in 1991, thus subject to § 1658's four-year period or as a § 1983 claim not subject to that period. Robinson v. City of Arkansas, Kan., 2012 U.S. Dist. LEXIS 124753 (D. Kan. Sept. 4, 2012); *cf.* Jones v. R. R. Donnelley & Sons Co., 541 U.S. 369 (2004) (§ 1658 applies to § 1981 claims, because the § 1981 cause of action was expanded post-1990).

Federal courts thus apply § 1988(a) and fill the gap by adopting the limitations period of the state in which the action is brought; more specifically, courts look to the state period for tort claims of negligence or personal injury, which are most analogous to § 1983 damages claims.[153] This does mean the statute of limitations will vary from state to state; states typically have periods of one,[154] two,[155] or three years.[156] In addition, federal courts must borrow state tolling rules.[157]

§ 5.14 ACCRUAL OF CLAIMS

By contrast, the point at which a § 1983 claim accrues — when it becomes a complete cause of action on which the plaintiff can file suit and obtain relief — and at which the borrowed limitations period begins to run is a matter of federal law.[158] The time of accrual depends on the right at issue. Typically, a constitutional claim accrues when the wrongful act occurs and the plaintiff suffers damages,[159] although some claims accrue only when the plaintiff becomes aware of the harm.[160] Other rights are violated, and therefore claims accrue, only at some later point in time, where some subsequent act or event is a necessary part of the claim. For example, a *Miranda* claim accrues not at the time of the unwarned questioning, but when the evidence is subsequently used at trial.[161] It follows that the limitations period begins to run only if and when evidence is used at trial (at which point, of course, the potential § 1983 plaintiff may have to worry about preclusion or *Heck*).

With some constitutional rights, accrual depends on first identifying an appropriate common law tort to which to analogize the constitutional right for accrual purposes. In *Wallace v. Kato*, the plaintiff, whose murder conviction had been reversed, sought damages for his original arrest, arguing that the police arrested him and took him into custody without probable cause. In trying to determine whether the limitations period had expired on the § 1983 action, the Court first had to decide when the claim accrued, which in turn required the Court to find an appropriate analogue for a Fourth Amendment unreasonable seizure claim based on an arrest without probable cause. It could be analogous to false arrest, false imprisonment, or malicious prosecution; the Court chose false imprisonment. A false imprisonment, defined as imprisonment without process, begins when the

---

[153] Owens v. Okure, 488 U.S. 235 (1989); Wilson v. Garcia, 471 U.S. 261 (1985).

[154] Rodríguez v. Municipality of San Juan, 659 F.3d 168 (1st Cir. 2011) (Puerto Rico); Hughes v. Vanderbilt Univ., 215 F.3d 543 (6th Cir. 2000) (Tennessee).

[155] Alexander v. McKinney, 692 F.3d 553 (7th Cir. 2012) (Indiana); Jones v. Blanas, 393 F.3d 918 (9th Cir. 2004) (California); Ahmed v. Dragovich, 297 F.3d 201 (3d Cir. 2002) (Pennsylvania); Meade v. Grubbs, 841 F.2d 1512 (10th Cir. 1988) (Oklahoma).

[156] Harrington v. City of Nashua, 610 F.3d 24 (1st Cir. 2010) (New Hampshire).

[157] Wallace v. Kato, 549 U.S. 384, 394 (2007).

[158] *Wallace v. Kato*, 549 U.S. 394, 388 (2007); Dique v. N.J. State Police, 603 F.3d 181 (3d Cir. 2010).

[159] *Wallace*, 549 U.S. at 391; *Dique*, 603 F.3d at 185.

[160] Sameric Corp. v. City of Philadelphia, 142 F.3d 582, 599 (3d Cir. 1998); New Port Largo v. Monroe County, 985 F.2d 1488 (11th Cir. 1993).

[161] Chavez v. Martinez, 538 U.S. 760 (2003) (opinion of Thomas, J., for four justices) (no violation of Fifth Amendment protection against self-incrimination unless and until statements used against individual at trial); Hanson v. Dane County, 608 F.3d 335 (7th Cir. 2010).

plaintiff is taken into custody and continues until the false imprisonment ends. The accrual point of the false imprisonment claim is the entire period of false custody; because a falsely imprisoned person cannot bring a claim while still imprisoned, however the clock begins running when the false imprisonment ends that occurs when the plaintiff no longer is held without process — either because he has been released (the imprisonment ends) or because he receives process (the falseness ends).[162]

The plaintiff in *Wallace* was arrested in January 1994, and he was brought before a state magistrate and bound over for trial a few days later. At that point, his unlawful seizure/false imprisonment ended because he now was held pursuant to process; his Fourth Amendment claim accrued and the two-year state statute of limitations began to run, expiring sometime in January 1996. His § 1983 action, not filed until March 2003, therefore was untimely.[163]

§ 5.15 LIMITATIONS, ACCRUAL, AND THE INTERSECTIONS OF § 1983 PROCEDURES

The plaintiff in *Wallace* was arrested in January 1994 and convicted in January 1996. His conviction was reversed on appeal and on remand to the state trial court, it was determined that his conviction (obtained following the allegedly unlawful arrest) was inadmissible. The charges against him were dropped in April 2002, and although he filed the § 1983 action less than one year later,[164] that was too late, given the point at which the claim accrued.[165]

One question is why the plaintiff waited so long to file his federal action. The answer, it appears, is that the plaintiff anticipated or expected a *Heck* bar had he filed prior to resolution of the state prosecution or once he was convicted.

There is, of course, a nice question, in light of *Heck*'s footnote 7, whether his Fourth Amendment false-arrest claim necessarily renders the fact of conviction invalid. If lack of probable cause to arrest renders the confession invalid, it perhaps renders the conviction invalid, depending on whether the state otherwise could have gotten the confession and what other evidence the state had to support the conviction. And *Wallace* arose in the Seventh Circuit, one of the courts that reads footnote 7 as making the bar entirely inapplicable to Fourth Amendment claims.[166]

In any event, the plaintiff in *Wallace* argued that the Fourth Amendment claim should not accrue, and the statute of limitations should not begin to run, until the possibility of a *Heck* bar has been removed through acquittal or other favorable termination of the state criminal proceedings. Prior to that, he need not file a federal action that could even potentially be *Heck*-barred. But the Court held that *Heck* applies only to existing convictions; the bar does not come into play at all until

---

[162] *Wallace*, 549 U.S. at 388–92.

[163] *Id.* at 391–92.

[164] Wallace v. Kato, 549 U.S. 384, 386–87 (2007).

[165] *Id.* at 391–92.

[166] Copus v. City of Edgerton, 151 F.3d 646 (7th Cir. 1998); Antonelli v. Foster, 104 F.3d 899 (7th Cir. 1997); *supra* § 5.07.

the plaintiff is actually convicted. Prior to that, *Heck* does not affect the running of the statute of limitations and does not excuse a plaintiff for not bringing a claim prior to being convicted.[167]

The onus thus is on plaintiffs to bring § 1983 actions immediately, even while state criminal proceedings remain pending. This triggers two procedural possibilities. One is that the criminal and civil proceedings will be litigated simultaneously. As Justice Breyer argued in dissent in *Wallace*, however, this requires the litigant to divide his time, attention, and energy between dueling cases.[168]

More likely, the federal court will exercise its inherent discretion to stay the § 1983 actions pending resolution of the state prosecution. If the defendant is acquitted, the federal court simply lifts the stay and the § 1983 action proceeds. If the defendant is convicted, the federal district court determines whether the claim is *Heck*-barred. If the federal constitutional claim does not necessarily imply invalidity of the conviction, the court lifts the stay and the § 1983 action proceeds. If the § 1983 constitutional claim does necessarily imply the invalidity of the conviction, the *Heck* bar kicks in and the federal court dismisses the claim without prejudice; the plaintiff can refile when and if he obtains a favorable termination. Of course, this still puts the constitutional claimant in an awkward position of having to manage concurrent criminal and civil proceedings and produces an "uncertain system of stays, dismissals, and possible refiling."[169]

---

[167] *Wallace*, 549 U.S. at 393–95.

[168] *Id.* at 400 (Breyer, J., dissenting).

[169] *Id.* (Breyer, J., dissenting). Justice Breyer proposed equitable tolling as the solution — the limitations period on the § 1983 claim is equitably tolled while state criminal proceedings are pending, so long as the rights holder continues to challenge his conviction and the unconstitutional conduct in the state proceedings. *Id.* at 400–01 (Breyer, J., dissenting).

Chapter 6

ABSTENTION

§ 6.16   *Rooker-Feldman* Puzzles

PART E   ABSTENTION REVIEW

§ 6.17   Abstention Review Puzzle

§ 6.01   INTRODUCTION TO ABSTENTION

If a federal district court has original jurisdiction over an action under § 1331 (or any other statutory grant), it still must consider whether to exercise that jurisdiction or whether to abstain pursuant to any of several primarily judge-made doctrines. In abstaining, a district court may either abdicate or postpone jurisdiction, with different abstention doctrines taking different forms. Abdication means the court surrenders jurisdiction and never will hear the claim (at least in its current form and procedural posture), while postponement means the court declines to hear the case for the moment, but might hear it in the same posture at a future time. Abstention generally applies only in actions seeking equitable relief, because the power and choice to abstain reflects the discretion inherent in a court exercising equitable power.[1] Courts do not abstain in actions for damages, although a court might stay a damages action for certain discretionary reasons.[2]

Abstention is problematic if we conceive of federal jurisdiction as mandatory — Article III empowers Congress to determine the jurisdiction of the federal courts and the courts must exercise the jurisdiction that has been statutorily granted them.[3] The Supreme Court long ago appeared to accept this conception, stating that federal courts had "no more right to decline the exercise of jurisdiction which is given than to usurp jurisdiction which has not been given. One or the other would be treason to the Constitution."[4] That dictum never has been taken literally. Even after recognizing abstention, however, the Court insists it is the exception rather than the rule and that federal courts have a "virtually unflagging obligation" to exercise the jurisdiction Congress has vested in them.[5]

One question is how to reconcile abstention with separation of powers. If Congress has chosen to grant federal jurisdiction in some class of cases and if federal courts would otherwise have authority to hear a given case, courts ignore jurisdictional commands and act in a way not authorized by Congress. Abstention thus is "judicial lawmaking of the most sweeping nature."[6] Alternatively, it might be argued that abstention furthers separation of powers; while courts are ignoring congressional enactments, they are restraining their authority to act rather than

---

[1] Quackenbush v. Allstate Ins. Co., 517 U.S. 706 (1996); Potrero Hills Landfill, Inc. v. County of Solano, 657 F.3d 876 (9th Cir. 2011).

[2] *Quackenbush*, 517 U.S. at 719–20.

[3] U.S. Const. art. III, § 2; Martin H. Redish, *Abstention, Separation of Powers, and the Limits of the Judicial Function*, 94 Yale L.J. 71 (1984).

[4] Cohens v. Virginia, 19 U.S. 264, 404 (1821).

[5] Colorado River Water Conservation Dist. v. United States, 424 U.S. 800, 817 (1976).

[6] Martin H. Redish, *Abstention, Separation of Powers, and the Limits of the Judicial Function*, 94 Yale L.J. 71, 84 (1984).

aggrandizing their own power at the expense of Congress.[7]

These competing views reflect competing conceptions of separation of powers. On one conception, separation of powers is about choice allocation, focusing on who decides how power is allocated. On a different conception, separation of powers is about the exercise of power and on whether the courts may act in some way. If the federal courts truly are the "least dangerous" branch,[8] abstention is justified under the latter conception, because constraining on the courts' exercise of power is beneficial, even if constraints on judicial authority are self-imposed rather than legislatively imposed.

Three abstention doctrines are particularly relevant to § 1983 litigation and are considered in detail below.[9]

§ 6.02   EQUITABLE RELIEF: AN OVERVIEW

Because abstention arises only in equitable actions, a brief overview of equitable or prospective relief is appropriate.[10]

The primary equitable remedy is an injunction, a court order prohibiting the defendant from taking some action or compelling it to take some action. In constitutional litigation, this commonly involves a judicial determination that a law or policy violates the Constitution and an order prohibiting government officials from enforcing the law or policy at issue, leaving the plaintiff free of the burden of the unconstitutional law and free to engage in what she believes is constitutionally protected conduct. A court retains ongoing jurisdiction to ensure that parties comply with the injunction, notably by holding in contempt a party who disregards its obligations under the injunction.[11]

Injunctive relief consists of three distinct remedies considered at three stages of the case. First is a Temporary Restraining Order. Typically issued *ex parte*, this order lasts for a brief, defined period (in federal court, not to exceed 14 days[12]) and preserves the status quo until all parties can receive notice and the court can hold a fuller adversarial hearing. Second is a Preliminary Injunction. Issued following an adversarial hearing fairly early in the case, this order makes a preliminary determination on the merits of the claim and preserves the status quo during the pendency of litigation and until a final decision is made on the claim.[13] Third is a

---

[7] Michael Wells, *Why Professor Redish Is Wrong About Abstention*, 19 GA. L. REV. 1097 (1985).

[8] ALEXANDER HAMILTON, THE FEDERALIST No. 78, at 433 (Clinton Rossiter ed., 1961).

[9] Two others could arise in a range of federal litigation, including constitutional cases, although comparably infrequently. One is *Colorado River* abstention, in which federal courts abstain in deference to parallel and concurrent state proceedings. Colorado River Water Conservation Dist. v. United States, 424 U.S. 800 (1976). The other is *Burford* abstention, in which federal courts abstain in deference to a complex state regulatory system. Burford v. Sun Oil Co., 319 U.S. 315 (1943).

[10] A more detailed discussion of equitable relief and the processes surrounding equitable relief is in Ch. 7.

[11] *Cf.* Ex parte Young, 209 U.S. 123 (1908).

[12] FED. R. CIV. P. 65(b)(2).

[13] Sole v. Wyner, 551 U.S. 74 (2007); Doran v. Salem Inn, Inc., 422 U.S. 922 (1975).

Permanent Injunction. This is a final judgment on the merits, usually issued following a full trial on the merits of the claim, in which the court makes a final, conclusive decision on the constitutionality of the challenged law.

The test for all three forms of injunctive relief consists of five conjunctive elements, with sliding levels of proof depending on the stage of proceedings.[14] First, and most importantly, a plaintiff must show a substantial likelihood of success on the merits (at the TRO and preliminary stages) or actual success on the merits of the claim (for a permanent injunction); in other words, the plaintiff must persuade the court that the challenged law or policy violates the Constitution. The showing a plaintiff must make on this prong particularly depends on the stage of the case; the proof of unconstitutionality necessary for a permanent injunction is greater than the showing necessary for a TRO.[15] Because there historically was no jury in courts of equity and the Seventh Amendment civil jury right applies only to claims for legal relief, the court, rather than a jury, acts as fact-finder on the merits of the constitutional issues.[16]

Second, a plaintiff must show that she will suffer irreparable injury unless the injunction is issued, with irreparable injury presumed where a plaintiff's constitutional rights are involved.[17] Third, the plaintiff must show that she has no adequate remedy at law. This harkens to the historic divide in England between Courts of Common Law and Chancery Courts, a divide brought to the United States; equity was established as an alternative adjudicative system to which a party can and should turn only when resort to the common law courts (and common law remedies) would not properly provide relief for the injury. Fourth, the court balances whether the injury to the movant from not obtaining an injunction is greater than the injury or harm to the non-movant if the injunction is issued. Fifth, the court considers whether an injunction is in the public interest. The first and third are the primary elements in play in constitutional injunction litigation with the second generally presumed.

A second form of functionally equitable relief[18] is a declaratory judgment — a federal court order declaring the rights of, and legal relations between, parties.[19] Declaratory judgments allow federal courts to pronounce that some law infringes on a plaintiff's constitutional rights, that the government cannot enforce that law, and that the plaintiff remains free to engage in some conduct. And like injunctions, declaratory judgments are used preemptively to halt potential future enforcement of an unconstitutional law. Unlike injunctions, however, declaratory judgments

---

[14] Winter v. NRDC, Inc., 555 U.S. 7 (2008); Salazar v. Buono, 559 U.S. 700 (2010).

[15] *Sole*, 551 U.S. at 84.

[16] City of Monterey v. Del Monte Dunes, Ltd., 526 U.S. 687, 719 (1999); Wilson v. Bailey, 934 F.2d 301, 305 (11th Cir. 1991).

[17] Obama for Am. v. Husted, 697 F.3d 423 (6th Cir. 2012).

[18] Declaratory relief post-dates the old law/equity divide and thus is neither legal nor equitable in nature. DOUGLAS LAYCOCK, MODERN AMERICAN REMEDIES: CASES AND MATERIALS 6 (4th ed. 2010). But declaratory judgments typically accompany claims for injunctive relief. Johnson v. Randle, 2012 Ill. App. Unpub. LEXIS 1305 (June 5, 2012); DL v. District of Columbia, 845 F. Supp. 2d 1 (D.D.C. 2011).

[19] 28 U.S.C. § 2201; DOUGLAS LAYCOCK, MODERN AMERICAN REMEDIES: CASES AND MATERIALS 6 (4th ed. 2010).

impose no formal restrictions on government officials; they are not coercive and are not enforceable via contempt.[20] They instead function by persuading state or federal officers of their constitutional obligations, of the constitutional deficiencies in the target law, and of the need to reconsider and change their policies or plans for enforcement.[21] A declaratory judgment also can form the basis for future injunctive relief.[22]

A typical constitutional claim for equitable relief proceeds roughly as follows. A law, regulation, or policy is on the books and allegedly violates some constitutional right; the plaintiff wants to halt its enforcement and be able to continue engaging in constitutionally protected conduct. She brings a § 1983 action[23] in federal court against the executive officer responsible for enforcing that law (under the theory of *Ex Parte Young*). The officer acts under color of state law in enforcing (or threatening to enforce) the law or policy; the plaintiff is deprived of a right, privilege, or immunity secured by the Constitution because of enforcement or threatened enforcement and the chill on her constitutionally protected activity; and the remedy sought is a declaratory judgment that the law is unconstitutional and that the plaintiff can continue engaging in protected conduct, an injunction prohibiting enforcement of the law, or (most likely) both. Along with the complaint, the plaintiff may file a motion for a TRO and/or Preliminary Injunction in order to freeze the status quo pending the outcome of litigation. Prior to 1976, an action alleging that a state[24] or federal[25] law was unconstitutional and seeking to enjoin its enforcement was heard by a three-judge district court, although current law leaves most cases before a single district judge.[26]

PART A
PULLMAN ABSTENTION

§ 6.03 *PULLMAN* ABSTENTION

The Supreme Court established the first judge-made abstention doctrine in 1941 in *Railroad Commission of Texas v. Pullman Co.* The state railroad commission issued a regulation requiring that all trains traveling through Texas must be staffed by Pullman conductors rather than Pullman porters; the former group consisted entirely of whites who were paid more, while the latter group was comprised of African-Americans who generally earned less. The railroad and the porters

---

[20] Steffel v. Thompson, 415 U.S. 452, 471 (1974).

[21] *Id.* at 470–71.

[22] 28 U.S.C. § 2202; Samuels v. Mackell, 401 U.S. 66 (1971).

[23] Against state or local officers with respect to state and local law. As to federal officers enforcing federals, the action is brought directly under the Constitution itself. Bivens v. Six Unknown Named Agents of Federal Bureau of Narcotics, 403 U.S. 388, 400, 405 (1971) (Harlan, J., concurring in the judgment).

[24] 28 U.S.C. § 2281 (repealed).

[25] 28 U.S.C. § 2282 (repealed).

[26] Act of Aug. 12, 1976, Pub. L. No. 94-381, 90 Stat. 1119 (1976) (codified at 28 U.S.C. § 2284).

challenged the regulation on both equal protection and due process grounds; the porters argued that the regulation deprived them of the opportunity to work because of their race, while the railroad wanted to save costs on staffing by using porters.[27]

Although the complaint "undoubtedly tendered a substantial constitutional issue," it also "touches a sensitive area of social policy upon which the federal courts ought not to enter unless no alternative to its adjudication is open." This "constitutional adjudication plainly can be avoided if a definitive ruling on the state issue would terminate the controversy."[28] The Court had to first consider whether the case could be resolved on the open sub-constitutional issue of whether the Railroad Commission had the state-law authority to issue orders regarding staffing of trains. If it did not, the regulation was invalid and plaintiffs obtain the relief they sought — the regulation is unenforceable, the company is free to staff trains as it chooses, and the porters are free to work — but without the federal court having to resolve a difficult federal constitutional issue.[29]

This preference for sub-constitutional state-law resolution rests on several considerations. It is consistent with the sound exercise of discretion that historically guides courts of equity; in particular, courts must balance the equities before granting an injunction, including acting with due "regard for public consequences in employing the extraordinary remedy of the injunction."[30] It is consistent with the need to avoid "needless friction" with state policy that arises when a federal court tells a state that its policies violate the Constitution or when a federal court prohibits a state from enforcing its policies. This hesitancy is particularly appropriate when the constitutional determination is premature or unnecessary; deference on possible state-law issues contributes to the "harmonious relation" between federal and state authority.[31] Finally, it is consistent with the "avoidance canon," under which courts should not reach or resolve constitutional questions unless and until it is necessary to decide them.[32]

But final responsibility and authority for resolving state law questions rests not with the federal court but with the state supreme court. A federal court can do no more than "forecast" state law in a tentative decision that may quickly be rendered incorrect by a subsequent state court decisions. Such a tentative decision is as wasteful of federal judicial resources as an unnecessary constitutional decision.[33] State courts therefore must have an initial opportunity to make a definitive ruling as to the validity of the regulation as a matter of state law.

The way to enable that state-court review is for the federal court to postpone its jurisdiction to decide the federal constitutional issues so the parties can litigate and

---

[27] Railroad Com. of Texas v. Pullman Co., 312 U.S. 496, 497–98 (1941).

[28] *Id.* at 498.

[29] *Id.* at 500.

[30] *Id.* at 501.

[31] *Id.* at 500–01.

[32] Camreta v. Greene, 131 S. Ct. 2020, 2031 (2011); Ashwander v. TVA, 297 U.S. 288, 346-47 (1936) (Brandeis, J., concurring).

[33] *Id.* at 499–500.

finally resolve the state-law issues in state court. The plaintiff will file suit in state court and the parties will litigate all the way through the state system, perhaps to the state supreme court, which has the final, definitive word on the meaning of state law. In *Pullman*, for example, if the state courts finally decided the Commission lacked authority to issue the regulation, the regulation would be invalid and unenforceable, the plaintiffs would prevail, and there would be no need for further adjudication in federal court. If the state court decided the Commission possessed the state-law authority to issue the regulation, the plaintiff then could return to federal court for a full determination of the validity of state law, as now authoritatively construed and interpreted by the state courts. Federal judicial resolution of the federal constitutional issues now is necessary and there is no alternative to the federal court deciding the case on federal grounds.

§ 6.04   AMBIGUOUS AND UNCLEAR STATE LAW

Although courts define *Pullman* in slightly different terms, courts generally abstain where (1) the constitutional challenge touches on a sensitive area of state social policy into which federal courts should not enter unless there is no alternative; (2) the meaning of state law is unclear or uncertain; and (3) the state court's resolution of the state law issues will or might obviate or preclude the need for a federal constitutional ruling.[34] The decision to abstain under *Pullman* is vested in the sound discretion of the district court, although appellate courts review abstention decisions under a "modified," more searching abuse of discretion standard, given the connection between abstention and subject matter jurisdiction.[35]

Abstention is appropriate only when there is an unresolved question of state law that only a state tribunal can authoritatively construe and decide.[36] State law must be "ambiguous," "unclear," or "unintelligible."[37] A federal court should abstain only if state law is "fairly subject to an interpretation which will render unnecessary or substantially modify the federal constitutional question."[38] This links the second and third prongs of the *Pullman* analysis. The federal court abstains to avoid having to decide the federal constitutional issue. Abstention is appropriate only if a state court ruling on state law can, in fact, obviate federal constitutional adjudication, which only happens if state law is susceptible to some limiting construction that avoids any constitutional defect. On the other hand, if state law is clear or unambiguous or if no interpretation or construction of state law is possible that will eliminate the federal constitutional issue, then abstention is pointless; the federal constitutional issue never disappears and the case inevitably must return to federal

---

[34] Wis. Right to Life State PAC v. Barland, 664 F.3d 139 (7th Cir. 2011); Hunter v. Hamilton County Bd. of Elections, 635 F.3d 219 (6th Cir. 2011); Barr v. Galvin, 626 F.3d 99 (1st Cir. 2010); Moore v. Hosemann, 591 F.3d 741 (5th Cir. 2009); Kan. Judicial Review v. Stout, 562 F.3d 1240 (10th Cir. 2009); Smelt v. County of Orange, California, 447 F.3d 673 (9th Cir. 2006).

[35] *Smelt*, 447 F.3d at 678; Hartford Courant Co. v. Pellegrino, 380 F.3d 83 (2d Cir. 2004).

[36] Wisconsin v. Constantineau, 400 U.S. 433 (1971).

[37] Houston v. Hill, 482 U.S. 451 (1987); Handberry v. Thompson, 446 F.3d 335, 356 (2d Cir. 2006).

[38] *Houston*, 482 U.S. at 468.

court.[39] The Supreme Court has expressed particular reluctance to abstain in First Amendment cases, given the chilling effect on the plaintiff's speech that occurs with the delay in having to wait for state-court proceedings to resolve themselves.[40]

Moreover, *Pullman* should not function as an exhaustion requirement. Federal courts are not obligated to abstain merely to give the state courts a first crack at interpreting or applying the statute as an automatic prerequisite to federal constitutional analysis. Nor is state law unclear or unintelligible simply because a state court has not yet construed it.[41]

A potentially confounding issue under *Pullman* is the effect of the state constitution on the ambiguity of state law. One might argue that there is an unresolved, unclear, and uncertain question where an unambiguous state statute might be unconstitutional under the state constitution; the federal court therefore should abstain to allow a state court to first address the validity of its law under its constitution. But this functionally imposes exhaustion — a plaintiff must first go to state court to challenge the law under the state constitution, only reaching federal court to challenge it under the federal constitution if the state challenge fails.[42]

The Supreme Court appeared to reject this approach to *Pullman* in *Wisconsin v. Constantineau*, refusing to require abstention in a case challenging an unambiguous state statute and presenting only the "naked question" of whether the statute on its face is constitutional under substantive due process. That the statute might be invalid under the state constitution does not routinely create an issue of "unresolved state law."[43] *Constantineau* distinguishes unique issue-specific state constitutional provisions governing unique state-specific subjects from general state parallels to federal constitutional provisions. *Pullman* abstention thus may be appropriate to allow state-court consideration under targeted, subject-specific provisions of the state constitution,[44] which presents a genuinely open state law issue that can obviate federal constitutional analysis. But abstention is not required in deference to adjudication under parallel state constitutional provisions (such as the due process challenge in *Constantineau*), because state constitutional adjudication is not preferred over federal constitutional adjudication.

§ 6.05 *PULLMAN* PUZZLE

In 2007, the Supreme of California held that state law limiting marriage to a union between one man and one woman violates the equal protection and due process provisions of the state constitution. In the next statewide election, the voters approved an initiative adding a new provision to the state constitution stating "Only marriage between a man and a woman is valid or recognized in this state."

---

[39] *Id.*; *Wis. Right to Life*, 664 F.3d at 151.

[40] *Houston*, 482 U.S. at 468.

[41] *Handberry*, 446 F.3d at 356.

[42] Patsy v. Bd. of Regents, 457 U.S. 496 (1982); *supra* § 5.06[2].

[43] Wisconsin v. Constantineau, 400 U.S. 433, 439 (1971); *but see id.* at 440 (Burger, C.J., dissenting).

[44] Reetz v. Bozanich, 397 U.S. 82 (1970) (state constitutional provisions relating to regulation of fisheries).

Plaintiffs bring a § 1983 action, arguing that the new state constitutional provision violates the Equal Protection Clause and Due Process Clause of the Fourteenth Amendment. Defendants argue that the federal court should abstain under Pullman, *in light of two potential state constitutional issues. The first is a provision limiting the use of direct democracy to change the state constitution; voters can "amend" the state constitution by popular initiative but cannot "revise" the state constitution by popular initiative. There is an argument that the newly approved provision is a revision rather than an amendment, which is a question of state law. The second issue is the equal protection and due process provisions of the state constitution, which could be construed by the state court to render invalid a discriminatory constitutional amendment.*[45]

Consider whether the federal court should abstain under Pullman *in deference to either state constitutional issue.*

§ 6.06   *ENGLAND* RESERVATION

Pullman involves postponement rather than abdication of federal jurisdiction; the court is not surrendering its authority over the federal constitutional claims for all purposes and all time.[46] While *Pullman* sends the plaintiff to state court for an authoritative determination of ambiguous or unclear state law, it does not force the plaintiff to accept state-court determination of those federal constitutional issues. The expectation under *Pullman* is that the plaintiff will return to federal court unless the state judgment eliminates the threat of enforcement of the challenged state law. But if the federal constitutional issues remain alive even after state adjudication, the federal court remains ready to exercise jurisdiction to finally decide them.

The problem is the claim-preclusive effect of any state-court judgment. Claim preclusion typically prohibits re-litigation of all claims actually brought in a prior action against a defendant, as well as claims that could have been litigated in the prior action but were not. Because the § 1983 constitutional claim could be brought in state court along with the state-law claims, the state court judgment ordinarily would preclude subsequent federal litigation of those related federal claims.[47] But this functionally means the federal court is abdicating, not merely postponing, jurisdiction over federal constitutional claims. It also deprives the plaintiff of the general opportunity to choose a preferred judicial forum, particularly a federal forum.

In *England v. Louisiana Board of Medical Examiners*, the Court found a solution. When a federal court abstains under *Pullman* and the plaintiff commences litigation in state court, she may "reserve" the federal issues in her state court pleadings; this informs the state courts of the background constitutional arguments and identifies the federal claims and arguments that she will bring if and when the

---

[45] Perry v. Brown, 671 F.3d 1052 (9th Cir. 2012); In re Marriage Cases, 43 Cal. 4th 757 (2008); *but cf.* Smelt v. County of Orange, California, 447 F.3d 673 (9th Cir. 2006).

[46] Georgevich v. Strauss, 772 F.2d 1078 (3d Cir. 1985).

[47] Migra v. Warren City School Dist. Bd. of Education, 465 U.S. 75 (1984); *supra* § 5.12.

case returns to federal court. While not asking the state court to decide the federal issues, the reservation permits the state court to consider and resolve state law "in light of" those lurking federal constitutional concerns; knowing of the federal constitutional context enables the state court to interpret state law in a way that avoids a potential federal bind.[48] The plaintiff may, of course, forego the federal forum and present the full case, federal and state issues, to the state court, with the opportunity to obtain federal review of the federal issues in the Supreme Court of the United States.[49] But the reservation ensures that she need not do so; a plaintiff can choose to pursue the § 1983 claim in federal court if the federal issues remain alive and their resolution necessary, without having to overcome claim preclusion.

§ 6.07 CERTIFICATION

An obvious problem with *Pullman* is the delay and cost associated with abstention. The parties must undertake full-scale, sometimes protracted litigation through multiple levels of state court review before the case then starts over in federal district court.[50] Courts thus have begun using certification to "cover[] territory once dominated"[51] by *Pullman*.[52] Under certification procedures in most states, a federal court (the Supreme Court, a court of appeals, or a district court) can refer a particular question of state law directly to the state's highest court, then decide the federal constitutional issue as appropriate in light of the state court's answer. By sending the state legal issue directly to the state's highest court while otherwise keeping the case in federal court, certification builds and enhances cooperative judicial federalism, while reducing costs and delays associated with *Pullman* and assuring that the federal court will receive an authoritative and immediate determination of state law by its final arbiter.[53]

As with abstention, the decision whether to certify a question is vested in the sound discretion of the federal court.[54] Courts have incorporated into the certification question many of the concerns reflected in *Pullman*, such that the analysis on whether to certify and whether to abstain largely overlap. Thus, certification is appropriate where *Pullman* abstention might be appropriate — only if state law is reasonably susceptible of a limiting construction and only if the answer to the certified question will avoid or modify the federal constitutional inquiry.[55] Certification also is more appropriate where state law is novel, complex, or vague, as well as where important state public policy interests are implicated in the statutory

---

[48] England v. Louisiana State Bd. of Medical Examiners, 375 U.S. 411, 420–21 (1964).

[49] *Id.* at 418, 420–21; 28 U.S.C. § 1257(a).

[50] Arizonans for Official English v. Arizona, 520 U.S. 43, 76 (1997).

[51] *Id.* at 75–76.

[52] Kan. Judicial Review v. Stout, 519 F.3d 1107 (10th Cir. 2008); Pittman v. Cole, 267 F.3d 1269 (11th Cir. 2001).

[53] *Arizonans for Official English*, 520 U.S. at 76–77.

[54] *Kan. Judicial Review*, 519 F.3d at 1120; *Pittman*, 267 F.3d at 1290–91.

[55] Houston v. Hill, 482 U.S. 451, 468 (1987); Doyle v. City of Medford, 565 F.3d 536, 543–44 (9th Cir. 2009); *Kan. Judicial Review*, 519 F.3d at 1119–20; *Pittman*, 267 F.3d at 1285.

scheme.[56]

PART B
STATUTORY ABSTENTION

§ 6.08 THE ANTI-INJUNCTION ACT

28 U.S.C. § 2283

A court of the United States may not grant an injunction to stay proceedings in a State court except as expressly authorized by Act of Congress, or where necessary in aid of its jurisdiction, or to protect or effectuate its judgments.

Historically, a common use of courts of equity was the anti-suit injunction, in which a court of equity would enjoin a pending or threatened suit in a common law court, prohibiting the parties from pursuing the suit at law (and functionally staying it). The Anti-Injunction Act[57] prohibits federal courts from enjoining state judicial proceedings, except in three enumerated situations. It limits one class of anti-suit injunctions — a federal court of equity cannot enjoin a suit at law in state court. The underlying theory and message of § 2283 is that a dual system of courts with concurrent jurisdiction means federal and state courts should not fight each other for jurisdiction (historically a common problem between law and equity). States retain power to establish distinct legal systems and to operate them largely free from most interference by federal courts.

Originally enacted as § 5 of the Judiciary Act of 1793, the original provision absolutely barred federal courts from enjoining state proceedings. A number of judge-made exceptions developed over the years, until Congress re-enacted the provision in 1948, codifying three of those judicially created exceptions.[58] These represent firm, absolute exceptions rather than general principles of comity or federalism. They are narrow, not to be enlarged by loose construction. All doubts should be resolved in favor of the statute's baseline — the federal injunction is barred and the state court action proceeds; that is, close cases are resolved against the exception and the federal court being able to enjoin state proceedings.[59]

One exception allows a federal court to enjoin a state proceeding to "protect or effectuate its judgments;"[60] this includes a "relitigation exception," under which a federal court can, in rare circumstances, enjoin a state proceeding that should be

---

[56] *Arizonans for Official English*, 520 U.S. at 79–80; *Kan. Judicial Review*, 519 F.3d at 1119–20; *Pittman*, 267 F.3d at 1285.

[57] 28 U.S.C. § 2283.

[58] Act of Mar. 6, 1948, Pub. L. No. 62 Stat. 968 (1948).

[59] Smith v. Bayer Corp., 131 S. Ct. 2368 (2011); Mitchum v. Foster, 407 U.S. 225 (1972); Toucey v. New York Life Ins. Co., 314 U.S. 118 (1941).

[60] Atlantic C. L. R. Co. v. Brotherhood of Locomotive Eng'rs, 398 U.S. 281 (1970); 28 U.S.C. § 2283.

claim-precluded by a prior federal judgment.[61] A second exception allows a federal court to enjoin state proceedings where "necessary in aid of its jurisdiction," to prevent a state court from "so interfering with the consideration or disposition of a case as to seriously impair the federal court's flexibility and authority to decide a case."[62] The third exception is most applicable to constitutional and civil rights litigation: where some other federal statute supersedes § 2283 and "expressly authorizes" the federal court to issue an injunction staying state proceedings.[63]

In *Mitchum v. Foster*, the Supreme Court held that Congress expressly authorized injunctions against state proceedings through § 1983. The statute constitutes an exception to § 2283, meaning a federal court hearing a § 1983 claim can issue injunctions staying state proceedings.

Although § 1983 authorizes a "suit in equity," which means an action seeking equitable relief such as an injunction, the statute does not specifically mention stays of pending state proceedings, explicitly authorize injunctions staying state proceedings, or expressly reference or supersede § 2283. But § 2283 does not require such specificity. The question instead is whether an Act of Congress creates a "specific and uniquely federal right or remedy, enforceable in a federal court of equity, that could be frustrated if the federal court were not empowered to enjoin a state court proceeding."[64] Section § 1983 satisfies that standard, in light of its legislative history and statutory purpose; Congress created a unique remedial mechanism for enforcing federal rights that cannot fully serve its intended purpose unless federal courts can halt state proceedings. Section 1983 worked a "vast transformation" of federalism as part of Reconstruction; its "very purpose" is to "interpose the federal courts between the States and the people." And federal injunctive relief against a state court proceeding is essential to protect against the loss of constitutional rights at the heads of state institutions.[65]

A federal court hearing a § 1983 action thus possesses broad authority to issue anti-suit injunctions blocking state litigation to enforce state law. It can enjoin threatened state enforcement under *Ex parte Young*, where § 2283 imposes no hurdle because there are no "proceedings" to be enjoined. It also can enjoin an actual pending state proceeding, at least as a statutory matter, because § 1983 authorizes the court to do so as an exception to § 2283's general prohibition.

§ 6.09 TAX INJUNCTION ACT

28 U.S.C. § 1341

The district courts shall not enjoin, suspend or restrain the assessment, levy or collection of any tax under State law where a plain, speedy and efficient remedy may be had in the courts of such State.

---

[61] *Smith*, 131 S. Ct. at 2375–76.

[62] *Atlantic C. L. R. Co.*, 398 U.S. at 294–95; 28 U.S.C. § 2283.

[63] 28 U.S.C. § 2283.

[64] *Mitchum*, 407 U.S. at 237.

[65] *Id.* at 242.

26 U.S.C. § 7421

(a) Except as provided . . . no suit for the purpose of restraining the assessment or collection of any tax shall be maintained in any court by any person, whether or not such person is the person against whom such tax was assessed.

Federal courts also are prohibited from hearing claims for injunctions restraining or interfering with the imposition, assessment, or collection of federal[66] or state and local[67] taxes, even when the challenge is to the constitutional validity of the statute imposing the tax obligation. Prohibiting federal courts from interfering with the collection of taxes ensures a steady stream of consistent revenue for government; any challenges to the validity of a tax occur in post-payment actions by taxpayers seeking a refund for taxes already paid, through remedial procedures dedicated to litigating tax claims.[68]

With respect to federal taxes, § 7421 prohibits federal courts from issuing injunctions,[69] while the Declaratory Judgment Act itself expressly excludes cases or controversies "with respect to federal taxes."[70] With respect to state and local taxes, § 1341 by its terms precludes actions for injunctions and has been interpreted to also preclude declaratory judgment actions.[71] Principles of comity, as opposed to the text of § 1341, also preclude § 1983 actions for damages based on imposition of taxes,[72] although the Court subsequently explained this as an interpretation of, and limitation on, the § 1983 cause of action itself, rather than as a product of § 1341's jurisdictional bar.[73]

Whether an action is barred by either tax injunction act depends on two considerations. The first, of course, will be whether the statute challenged as unconstitutional imposes a tax on the plaintiff. A challenge to a law that imposes a non-tax compelled payment from citizen to government is not barred.[74] Nor is an action in which the plaintiff challenges the tax liabilities of others (rather than his own) in a way that will enrich government coffers by invalidating a law granting others a tax break, requiring them to pay more in taxes.[75]

The second issue, applicable to state and local taxes implicating § 1341, is whether state courts provide some other "plain, speedy, and efficient remedy" for

---

[66]   26 U.S.C. § 7421.

[67]   28 U.S.C. § 1341.

[68]   Nat'l Fed'n of Indep. Bus. v. Sebelius, 132 S. Ct. 2566 (2012); Folio v. City of Clarksburg, 134 F.3d 1211 (4th Cir. 1998).

[69]   26 U.S.C. § 7421(a).

[70]   28 U.S.C. § 2201(a).

[71]   Levin v. Commerce Energy, Inc., 130 S. Ct. 2323, 2331 n.4 (2010); ANR Pipeline Co. v. La. Tax Comm'n, 646 F.3d 940 (5th Cir. 2011).

[72]   Fair Assessment in Real Estate Ass'n v. McNary, 454 U.S. 100 (1981).

[73]   Quackenbush v. Allstate Ins. Co., 517 U.S. 706 (1996).

[74]   *Nat'l Fed'n of Indep. Bus.*, 132 S. Ct. at 2583–84; Kathrein v. City of Evanston, 636 F.3d 906 (7th Cir. 2011).

[75]   Hibbs v. Winn, 542 U.S. 88 (2004); Henderson v. Stalder, 407 F.3d 351 (5th Cir. 2005).

challenging the tax post-payment. An injunction is barred only if state procedures allow for post-payment adjudication of all issues related to the validity of a tax, including federal constitutional objections, provide for a full hearing, and allow for ultimate review of the constitutional issues in the Supreme Court of the United States.[76]

PART C
"OUR FEDERALISM" ABSTENTION

§ 6.10   *YOUNGER* ABSTENTION

[1]   *Younger v. Harris,* Our Federalism, and Injunctive Relief

Harris was indicted in state court in California for violating the state Criminal Syndicalism Statute, an anti-Communist law prohibiting written and oral communication advocating, teaching, or promoting unlawful or violent means of social or political change. Following the indictment, Harris filed a § 1983 action, referred to a three-judge district court, seeking to enjoin the District Attorney (Younger) from pursuing the state prosecution on the ground that the state statute violated the First Amendment; that injunction would functionally stay the state proceedings.[77]

The Supreme Court held that a federal injunction was improper, but without considering or relying on § 2283. Rather, the injunction was barred by principles of "Our Federalism," a "national policy" forbidding federal courts to enjoin or stay state court proceedings except under special circumstances.[78] Our Federalism consists of three prongs.

The first is equity and the fundamental need to contain equity within narrow limits. This both protects the jury's traditional fact-finding role (recall that the judge finds facts in injunctive actions) and avoids duplication of proceedings in multiple courts. The policy against staying proceedings informs two elements of the historic injunction analysis. One is the requirement that the equity plaintiff lacks an adequate remedy at law; Harris had an adequate remedy by virtue of being party to a pending state proceeding at which he could assert his First Amendment arguments in defense. The other is the requirement that the plaintiff will suffer irreparable harm absent the injunction; the only harm Harris was suffering was "solely 'that incidental to every criminal proceeding brought lawfully' " and in presumptive good faith.[79]

---

[76]   ANR Pipeline Co. v. La. Tax Comm'n, 646 F.3d 940 (5th Cir. 2011); Pleasures of San Patricio, Inc. v. Mendez-Torres, 596 F.3d 1 (1st Cir. 2010); Colonial Pipeline Co. v. Morgan, 474 F.3d 211 (6th Cir. 2007).

[77]   Younger v. Harris, 401 U.S. 37, 38–40 (1971). Two others intervened as plaintiffs in the federal action, alleging they were chilled in their speech by the threat of prosecution, although neither had not been indicted. *Id.* at 39.

[78]   *Id.* at 44.

[79]   *Id.* at 45–47.

The second and as vital, prong is comity, defined as a "proper respect for state functions" and the "belief that the National Government will fare best if the States and their institutions are left free to perform their separate functions in their separate ways."[80] Comity acknowledges that the state has established an independent judicial system, one capable of considering and vindicating federal claims of right, and that a federal court should allow that system to function without undue interference. Later cases have suggested that comity, understood broadly as respect for state processes, is the "more vital consideration" in *Younger* analysis.[81]

The third prong is federalism. The *Younger* Court insisted that federalism does not require "blind deference" to state rights or power. Rather, federalism reflects "sensitivity to the legitimate interests of both State and National Governments, and in which the National Government, anxious though it may be to vindicate and protect federal rights and federal interests, always endeavors to do so in ways that will not unduly interfere with the legitimate activities of the States."[82]

The Court did recognize three situations where Our Federalism does not require abstention. One is if the prosecution is brought in bad faith — that is, undertaken with no hope of obtaining a valid conviction. Second is where the prosecution is taken for purposes of harassment, such as in a pattern of repeated prosecutions. Third is in other "extraordinary circumstances," as where the statute being enforced is "flagrantly and patently violative of express constitutional prohibitions in every clause, sentence and paragraph, and in whatever manner and against whomever an effort might be made to apply it."[83] None of those exceptions applied in this case.

One problem for the Court in holding that the federal court was categorically barred from granting the injunction was *Dombrowski v. Pfister*, decided just six years earlier, in which the Court approved an injunction prohibiting the state of Louisiana from enforcing certain criminal laws against officers of a civil rights organization.[84] The plaintiff in *Younger* argued (and the lower court accepted) that *Dombrowski* meant than an injunction was proper where the state law to be enforced was facially unconstitutional and where its enforcement would chill constitutionally protected speech.[85] The *Younger* Court rejected this reading, insisting that a chilling effect, without more, did not justify federal interference with state processes. Instead, *Younger* appears to have read *Dombrowski* as justified by particular allegations of multiple, repeated prosecutions or threats of prosecution and that southern state officials had no hope of obtaining a conviction under these laws, but were instead acting to harass civil rights workers and organizations.[86] There were no similar evidence or allegations here.

---

[80] *Id.* at 44.

[81] Juidice v. Vail, 430 U.S. 327, 334 (1977) (quoting Huffman v. Pursue, Ltd., 420 U.S. 592, 601 (1975)).

[82] *Younger*, 401 U.S. at 44.

[83] *Id.* at 53–54.

[84] Dombrowski v. Pfister, 380 U.S. 479 (1965).

[85] *Younger*, 401 U.S. at 53.

[86] *Id.* at 48–49.

[2] Our Federalism and Declaratory Judgments

Samuels v. Mackell was one companion case to *Younger*, similarly involving a pending state indictment (this time for criminal anarchy) and a federal § 1983 action challenging the statute on First Amendment grounds. But the federal plaintiff in *Samuels* did not seek to enjoin the state prosecution; he sought only a federal declaratory judgment that the state criminal anarchy statute was unconstitutional, an order that would not formally stay state proceedings, unless the prosecutor was persuaded by the federal court's decision and dropped the charges.[87]

Nevertheless, the Court held that "Our Federalism" compelled abstention. A declaratory judgment has the same "practical impact" as an injunction. It is enforceable through a future injunction, so it marks a substantial step towards or disruption of state proceedings. The federal declaratory judgment on the First Amendment issue also might have an issue-preclusive effect on the state court considering the same constitutional issues raised as a defense. At a minimum, it chills the state prosecutor in his willingness to continue the prosecution in light of a federal judgment pronouncing the law unconstitutional; as a practical matter, this is an identical limitation on the authority of state officials and state courts in enforcing state law.[88]

[3] Connecting Our Federalism and § 2283

One year after *Younger* established that Our Federalism generally precludes federal injunctions staying state proceedings in § 1983 actions as a matter of national policy, the Court held in *Mitchum v. Foster* that § 1983 qualifies for the "expressly authorized" exception to the Anti-Injunction Act, meaning a § 1983 action to stay a pending state proceeding is not statutorily barred.[89] The key was the history and purpose of § 1983 and the need for federal injunctive relief against state court proceedings to protect constitutional rights and to give § 1983 its intended scope and function.[90]

In holding that § 2283 did not bar the action, *Mitchum* emphasized that it was not questioning *Younger* or any of the prior cases discussed in *Younger*, the Court remanded for the district court to determine whether, § 2283 aside, *Younger* barred the federal action.[91]

But *Mitchum* makes § 2283 a necessary part of the analysis in § 1983 actions to enjoin state enforcement of state law ensuring the viability of the *Younger* exceptions without undermining Our Federalism. If Our Federalism is not

---

[87] Recall that at this time, all claims seeking injunctions against enforcement of unconstitutional state laws were heard by three-judge district courts with immediate review to the Supreme Court. 28 U.S.C. § 2281 (repealed); 28 U.S.C. § 2253. By only seeking a declaratory judgment, a plaintiff could avoid a three-judge court. *Supra* §§ 4.13[4], 6.02.

[88] Samuels v. Mackell, 401 U.S. 66 (1971).

[89] Mitchum v. Foster, 407 U.S. 225 (1972).

[90] *Id.* at 242; *supra* § 6.08.

[91] *Mitchum*, 407 U.S. at 231, 243.

triggered or if the case falls within a *Younger* exception, the action is not barred because § 1983 is a congressionally authorized exception to § 2283. Stated differently, an injunction staying state proceedings is statutorily authorized (by § 1983) and thus permissible as long as the case is not barred by Our Federalism and *Younger*'s national policy against such injunctions.

[4] Federal Forums and Federal Rights

Unlike *Pullman*, *Younger* abstention entails complete abdication of federal jurisdiction over the federal claim, not mere postponement.[92] The already-pending state prosecution continues with the expectation that the defendant will raise and litigate his federal constitutional arguments (*e.g.*, that state law violates the First Amendment) in order avoid conviction in state court.[93] Indeed, the defendant's ability to litigate his federal rights in the state proceeding is essential to *Younger*'s rationale.

But *Younger* abstention marks the end of federal review of the constitutional issues in that case through the § 1983 vehicle. If the defendant is acquitted in state court, of course, his federal rights have been vindicated and he has no need for federal review. If convicted, he has two opportunities to obtain a federal forum on his federal issues. First, he can appeal the state conviction through the state judicial system and to the Supreme Court of the United States, arguing that the statute of conviction is unconstitutional under federal law.[94] In fact, at the time of *Younger* and the early abstention cases, Supreme Court review was likely, because the Court had appellate (mandatory) jurisdiction over appeals from final decisions of a state's highest court in which a state statute was challenged as violating the federal Constitution and the state court rejected the federal constitutional arguments and upheld the state law.[95] Second, if convicted, the defendant can return to federal district court on a petition for a writ of habeas corpus, once he exhausts his state judicial remedies; a state prisoner is in custody in violation of the laws of the United States for habeas purposes if the substantive law under which he was convicted is unconstitutional.[96]

But the § 1983 action is over and will not come back. If the defendant asserts his constitutional rights as a defense in the state proceedings and the state court rejects his arguments, the state court determination has issue-preclusive effect, defeating any subsequent § 1983 action.[97] And if the defendant is convicted, any § 1983 action challenging the underlying substantive law would be *Heck*-barred,

---

[92] Ivy Club v. Edwards, 943 F.2d 270 (3d Cir. 1991).

[93] Gibson v. Berryhill, 411 U.S. 564 (1973).

[94] 28 U.S.C. § 1257(a). The Supreme Court's jurisdiction extends only to federal issues in the case. *Cf.* Murdock v. City of Memphis, 87 U.S. 590 (1875).

[95] 28 U.S.C. § 1257(2) (pre-1988 version). Congress amended § 1257 in 1988, making all Supreme Court review of decisions of state courts by (discretionary) certiorari. *See* Supreme Court Case Selections Act, Pub. L. No. 100-352, 102 Stat. 662 (1988).

[96] 28 U.S.C. § 2254(a); Huffman v. Pursue, Ltd., 420 U.S. 592, 605 (1975); Teague v. Lane, 489 U.S. 288, 311 (1989); *supra* § 5.06.

[97] *Supra* § 5.11.

since a federal determination that the substantive law of conviction violates the First Amendment would necessarily imply the invalidity of the conviction.[98]

This also means an *England* reservation should have no place when a federal court abstains under *Younger*.[99] *Pullman* is about allowing state courts to resolve state law issues that might obviate federal constitutional issues, but leaving those federal issues for ultimate federal-court resolution, if necessary. *England* reservations merely help preserve those federal issues for future federal review. *Younger*, on the other hand, is about federal courts surrendering jurisdiction to allow state processes to function and to resolve all issues they are authorized to resolve, including issues based in the federal Constitution.

Younger abstention necessarily presumes that the opportunity to litigate federal constitutional issues in state court provides sufficient protection for those rights. It marks a high point for the concept of "parity," the presumption that state courts are equivalent to federal courts in their ability and willingness to protect and vindicate federal rights.[100] State courts act in good faith and follow Supreme Court precedent, and federal courts should not act in a way reflecting negatively on state judges' willingness and ability to enforce federal principles and ideals.[101] In fact, *Younger* is a parity watershed. The Court rejected a working presumption that courts of the Jim Crow South were systemically broken and always acting in blatant disregard for federal rights, a view reflected in *Dombrowski* and other constitutional jurisprudence arising from the civil rights movement.[102] Tellingly, the Court first heard argument in *Younger* in April 1969, during the final term of the Warren Court; the case was reargued in November 1970 and decided in February 1971, after Warren Burger had become Chief Justice.

Shortly after *Younger*, Burt Neuborne wrote that even if we accept that state courts and state prosecutors act in good faith and even if the pathology of the Jim Crow South no longer holds, parity between state and federal courts nevertheless remains "at best, a dangerous myth."[103] Neuborne identifies three reasons that federal courts remain the preferable and necessary forum for resolving federal rights. First, federal judges enjoy structural protections under Article III — life tenure and guaranteed salary[104] — that insulate them from public political preferences, leaving them freer to vindicate individual rights in the face of majoritarian opposition, protections that state judges — often elected and subject to re-election — often lack. Second, federal judges possess "technical competence" in handling federal law because federal law is primarily what federal judges do.

---

[98] *Supra* § 5.07.

[99] United Parcel Service, Inc. v. California Pub. Utils. Comm'n, 77 F.3d 1178, 1184 n.5 (9th Cir. 1996).

[100] Burt Neuborne, *The Myth of Parity*, 90 Harv. L. Rev. 1105 (1977).

[101] Huffman v. Pursue, Ltd., 420 U.S. 592 (1975).

[102] Dombrowski v. Pfister, 380 U.S. 479 (1965); Cox v. Louisiana, 379 U.S. 536 (1965); Henry v. Mississippi, 379 U.S. 443 (1965); New York Times Co. v. Sullivan, 376 U.S. 254 (1964); Burt Neuborne, *The Gravitational Pull of Race on the Warren Court*, 2010 Sup. Ct. Rev. 59.

[103] Burt Neuborne, *The Myth of Parity*, 90 Harv. L. Rev. 1105, 1105 (1977).

[104] U.S. Const. art. III, § 1.

Third, federal judges possess a unique "psychological set" that comes with being part of an elite federal bureaucracy.[105]

On the other hand, as one scholar put it, federal courts are just as likely to be wrong about the federal Constitution as state courts.[106] Moreover, parity (or lack of it) is not empirically verifiable or disprovable,[107] at least outside periods of blatant systemic revolt and dysfunction, as in the South during Reconstruction, Jim Crow, or the civil rights movement. Some commentators have recently questioned Neuborne's faith in federal courts over state courts, especially as state courts have come to show a greater willingness to protect minority rights, especially on questions of equal protection.[108]

§ 6.11   EXTENDING *YOUNGER* AND OUR FEDERALISM

At its core and in its earliest cases, *Younger* is about federal court deference to state criminal prosecutions; in fact, the Court was in general agreement on the propriety of abstention, with only Justice Douglas arguing that federal courts should not abstain in deference to state criminal enforcement.[109] Criminal prosecutions are, Justice Brennan argued later, the "paradigm cases of paramount state interest" to which a federal court should defer.[110] States have the highest interest in enforcing their criminal laws and state sovereignty is at its highest point when it does so.[111]

[1]   Civil Proceedings

The Court fractured when it extended abstention to non-criminal proceedings. In *Huffman v. Pursue, Ltd.*, the Court held that *Younger* requires abstention in deference to a state public nuisance action to enjoin operation of an adult theatre allegedly showing obscene films. The Court described the action as "more akin to a criminal proceeding than to a civil action," a suit "in aid of and closely related to" criminal proceedings.[112] The same concerns for comity and federalism that motivate *Younger* as to criminal prosecutions apply in this quasi-criminal proceeding — the state was a party to the case; the rights-holder/state defendant/federal plaintiff was in a defensive posture; and the state defendant had the same adequate remedies at law of raising the First Amendment as a defense in the state action and ultimately appealing that decision to the Supreme Court of the United States.[113]

---

[105]   Burt Neuborne, *The Myth of Parity*, 90 Harv. L. Rev. 1105, 1120–27 (1977).

[106]   Owen Fiss, Dombrowski, 86 Yale L.J. 1103 (1977).

[107]   Michael E. Solimine, *The Future of Parity*, 46 Wm. & Mary L. Rev. 1457 (2005).

[108]   William B. Rubenstein, *The Myth of Superiority*, 16 Const. Comment. 599 (1999).

[109]   Perez v. Ledesma, 401 U.S. 82 (1971) (Douglas, J., dissenting in part); Younger v. Harris, 401 U.S. 37, 58 (1971) (Douglas, J., dissenting).

[110]   Trainor v. Hernandez, 431 U.S. 434, 454 (1977) (Brennan, J., dissenting).

[111]   Kelly v. Robinson, 479 U.S. 36 (1986).

[112]   Huffman v. Pursue, Ltd., 420 U.S. 592, 604 (1975).

[113]   *Id.* at 604–05.

In *Juidice v. Vail*, the Court held that *Younger* requires abstention in deference to state civil contempt proceedings because the contempt process affords the opportunity to pursue federal issues. The contempt power lies at the core of the administration of a State's judicial system it provides; the only way state courts can ensure compliance with their orders and therefore the only way they can ensure that state processes function properly. The state has a "surely . . . important interest" in vindicating the regular operation of its judicial system; while that interest might not be as important as enforcing criminal laws or even quasi-criminal laws, it is of sufficiently great import to warrant abstention. Once again, federal judicial action would interfere with the legitimate activities of the state and negatively reflect on the state court's willingness or ability to protect federal interests.[114]

Juidice places comity at the forefront of *Younger*, focusing Our Federalism on protecting the state's systemic or administrative interests in functional court processes for their own sake, distinct from concerns for enforcing substantive law.[115] The label placed on a proceeding — civil, criminal, quasi-criminal — does not matter; what matters is that states be allowed to protect their processes *qua* processes and to enforce and vindicate state policies and laws however they best see fit.[116]

Of course, civil proceedings arguably are different than criminal proceedings in one way — the opportunities for federal review of the federal issues if the § 1983 action is dismissed. As discussed, criminal prosecutions allow two paths into federal court — direct appeal of the conviction to the Supreme Court from the state's highest court (mandatory at the time of the early *Younger* cases) and habeas corpus in the district court (following exhaustion). But habeas corpus is not available for review of a civil proceeding, even one labeled as quasi-criminal, such as public nuisance or contempt, since it does not result in the claimant being placed "in custody." Because only direct review to the Supreme Court through § 1257 is available, it is likely that many federal claimants never will get a federal forum for their federal claims, particularly with the subsequent elimination of mandatory appellate jurisdiction and the move to entirely discretionary Supreme Court review.[117] The *Huffman* Court's response, again reflecting that presumption of parity, is that there is no absolute right to a federal forum for federal rights and, even if there were, the appropriate time to raise it is when seeking to relitigate federal issues already decided in state court.[118]

---

[114] Juidice v. Vail, 430 U.S. 327, 335–36 (1977).

[115] *Id.* at 334 (quoting *Huffman*, 420 U.S. at 601).

[116] *Trainor*, 431 U.S. at 444.

[117] 28 U.S.C. § 1257(a); Supreme Court Case Selections Act, Pub. L. No. 100-352, 102 Stat. 662 (1988).

[118] *Huffman*, 420 U.S. at 606 & n.18. The latter part of the argument ultimately was foreclosed by the Court's recognition that preclusion applies to § 1983. Allen v. McCurry, 449 U.S. 90 (1980); *supra* §§ 5.10–5.11.

[2] Administrative Proceedings

The final extension takes *Younger* and Our Federalism into state (and local) administrative processes.

In *Middlesex County Ethics Committee*, the Supreme Court held that *Younger* requires federal abstention in deference to proceedings of a county-level bar investigation committee. First, the proceedings at issue were sufficiently judicial in character to justify abstention. Although the hearing was before a county-level committee, the committee was established by, and treated as an arm of, the state supreme court, the state body vested with authority to regulate the legal profession. The committee exercised delegated authority to receive and investigate complaints and hold preliminary hearings — all of which is precisely what courts do. Second, the committee's determination was appealable to the state supreme court. Finally, there was a significant state and public interest in maintaining and assuring the professional conduct of licensed attorneys in the state, in turn establishing a significant state interest in all proceedings through which professional conduct is regulated.[119] That state interest triggers Our Federalism's policy considerations. Lower courts have abstained under *Younger* in favor of proceedings of various state professional licensing and regulatory bodies,[120] insisting only that the body's proceedings be sufficiently formal as to qualify as judicial in character.[121]

Younger also compels federal abstention in deference to coercive investigation and enforcement actions initiated by government agencies and resolved in administrative proceedings.[122] Most prominently, Our Federalism compels abstention in deference to state-initiated proceedings before a state civil rights commission against a religious school for firing a teacher on allegedly discriminatory grounds. The elimination of prohibited sex discrimination in employment was a sufficiently important state interest, as was the ability to establish proceedings to enforce state laws prohibiting and remedying discrimination. As in *Middlesex*, the school could assert its First Amendment rights as a defense in the administrative proceeding and seek review of that defense in the state courts, making the administrative proceeding sufficiently judicial in nature and providing the school with an adequate remedy at law.[123]

One question is how to reconcile *Dayton Christian*'s insistence that the court abstain in deference to administrative proceedings with the Court's earlier holding in Patsy that a plaintiff need not exhaust state administrative procedures prior to

---

[119] Middlesex County Ethics Committee v. Garden State Bar Ass'n, 457 U.S. 423 (1982).

[120] Majors v. Engelbrecht, 149 F.3d 709 (7th Cir. 1998) (nursing board); Hirsh v. Justices of Supreme Court, 67 F.3d 708 (9th Cir. 1995) (attorney discipline); Maymo-Melendez v. Alvarez-Ramirez, 364 F.3d 27 (1st Cir. 2004) (horse trainer licensing); Squire v. Coughlan, 469 F.3d 551 (6th Cir. 2006) (judicial discipline); Stroman Realty, Inc. v. Martinez, 505 F.3d 658 (7th Cir. 2007) (real estate licensing); Fieger v. Thomas, 74 F.3d 740 (6th Cir. 1996) (attorney discipline).

[121] Guillemard-Ginorio v. Contreras-Gomez, 585 F.3d 508 (1st Cir. 2009); *Maymo-Melendez*, 364 F.3d at 35.

[122] Moore v. City of Asheville, 396 F.3d 385 (4th Cir. 2005).

[123] Ohio Civil Rights Comm'n v. Dayton Christian Sch., Inc., 477 U.S. 619 (1986).

filing a § 1983 action.[124] The answer lies in a distinction between coercive and remedial state administrative proceedings. An individual seeking to initiate federal claims, as the plaintiff in *Patsy* was doing, cannot be forced into state remedial proceedings as a prerequisite to seeking a federal remedy through a § 1983 action, given the text and historical purposes of the 1871 Act.[125] But where the state coercively enforces its laws by initiating proceedings against an alleged wrong-doer, it may choose from all available coercive enforcement procedures and forums — criminal, civil, or administrative. *Younger* requires abstention in deference to any state coercive enforcement efforts, so long as those proceedings implicate state interests, are sufficiently judicial in nature, and allow the defending party to assert and have resolved his federal constitutional rights. Lower courts hew closely to this coercive/remedial line.[126]

§ 6.12 AVOIDING ABSTENTION

Middlesex County established what has become the prevailing three-part test for *Younger* abstention: (1) there must be an ongoing or pending state proceeding that is judicial in character, whether the proceeding is formally civil, criminal, or administrative; (2) the proceedings must implicate important state interests that would be interfered with by a grant of federal declaratory or injunctive relief; and (3) the state proceedings must afford an adequate opportunity to raise constitutional challenges, including through state judicial review of any administrative proceeding.[127] Implicit in this test is that abstention is appropriate only if the federal proceeding would create "undue interference" with that pending state proceeding;[128] absent interference, both actions should proceed independently and concurrently.[129]

As to the first prong, a state proceeding remains ongoing from its initiation. A "necessary concomitant" of *Younger* is that once a party is involved in state proceedings, it must pursue those proceedings to the end, including exhausting state judicial remedies; the state proceeding does not cease at the end of the first stage in the proceedings simply because the plaintiff does not seek further state-court review.[130] A state proceeding is defined by the full scope of state processes, including judicial review of administrative proceedings and appellate

---

[124] *Compare Ohio Civil Rights*, 477 U.S. at 627 n.2, *with* Patsy v. Fla. Bd. of Regents, 457 U.S. 496 (1982); *supra* § 5.06[2].

[125] *Patsy*, 457 U.S. at 506–07, 513–14.

[126] SKS & Assocs. v. Dart, 619 F.3d 674 (7th Cir. 2010); Majors v. Engelbrecht, 149 F.3d 709 (7th Cir. 1998); *Guillemard*, 585 F.3d at 522; *cf.* Doe v. Virginia Dept. of State Police 713 F.3d 745 (4th Cir. 2013) (King, J., dissenting).

[127] Middlesex County Ethics Committee v. Garden State Bar Ass'n, 457 U.S. 423, 432 (1982); Sprint Communs. Co., L.P. v. Jacobs, 690 F.3d 864 (8th Cir. 2012).

[128] Quackenbush v. Allstate Ins. Co., 517 U.S. 706, 719–20 (1996); New Orleans Pub. Serv., Inc. v. Council of New Orleans, 491 U.S. 350, 359 (1989); Wexler v. Lepore, 385 F.3d 1336, 1339 (11th Cir. 2004).

[129] *But cf.* Colorado River Water Conservation Dist. v. United States, 424 U.S. 800 (1976) (providing for federal abstention in deference to some concurrent state proceedings).

[130] Hicks v. Miranda, 422 U.S. 332 (1975); Huffman v. Pursue, Ltd., 420 U.S. 592 (1975); Hudson v. Campbell, 663 F.3d 985 (8th Cir. 2011); Moore v. City of Asheville, 396 F.3d 385 (4th Cir. 2005).

review of lower courts; thus, even if the opening stage of a proceeding would be too informal, standing alone, to qualify as judicial in character for *Younger* purposes, its nature changes when all appeal and review opportunities are considered.[131] Once state proceedings, including all state appeals,[132] have been fully resolved and no longer are pending, *Younger* abstention ceases to be appropriate (although other jurisdictional and procedural bars then are triggered).

As to the second prong, the ongoing state proceeding must implicate sovereign power such that exercise of federal jurisdiction disregards comity, understood as respect for state institutions enforcement of state law, and state processes *qua* processes. Moreover, courts must consider the importance of the state interest in a generic proceeding of the type at hand, not the state interest in the outcome of any particular case.[133] Finally, the state proceeding typically must be, in some manner, a coercive action to enforce state law against the right-holder.[134]

As to the third prong, federal courts presume that state courts provide an adequate opportunity to raise the issue — that is, they provide an adequate remedy at law — absent a clear showing to the contrary.[135] Importantly, however, that requirement is not satisfied simply because the plaintiff could file the § 1983 action in state rather than federal court. A party has adequate state-court remedies only if the federal issue will or could be raised and resolved in the case-in-chief or as an affirmative defense in the ongoing underlying state proceeding to which he is a party.[136] *Younger* does not extend so far as to require plaintiffs to only pursue § 1983 claims in state court.

While the previous section considered when *Younger* and Our Federalism requires abstention, we now consider when, applying the three-part test established in *Middlesex*, Our Federalism will not require abstention.

[1] No Pending Proceeding Involving This Party

Most obviously, abstention is not warranted if there is no pending state proceeding.[137] Our Federalism does not have the same vitality until prosecution (or other state enforcement proceeding) is pending; there is no disregard for comity and no disrespect for or interference with state institutions and processes if no state processes are ongoing.[138] More significantly, absent an ongoing state proceeding, the federal plaintiff lacks an adequate opportunity to assert his federal

---

[131] Maymo-Melendez v. Alvarez-Ramirez, 364 F.3d 27 (1st Cir. 2004).

[132] Taliaferro v. Darby Twp. Zoning Bd., 458 F.3d 181 (3d Cir. 2006).

[133] Ohio Civil Rights Comm'n v. Dayton Christian Sch., Inc., 477 U.S. 619 (1986).

[134] Majors v. Engelbrecht, 149 F.3d 709 (7th Cir. 1998); Guillemard-Ginorio v. Contreras-Gomez, 585 F.3d 508 (1st Cir. 2009); *see also* Doe v. Virginia Dept. of State Police 713 F.3d 745 (4th Cir. 2013) (King, J., dissenting).

[135] *Guillemard-Ginorio*, 585 F.3d at 521; FreeEats.com, Inc. v. Indiana, 502 F.3d 590, 598 (7th Cir. 2007) (citing Pennzoil Co. v. Texaco, Inc., 481 U.S. 1 (1987)).

[136] Habich v. City of Dearborn, 331 F.3d 524 (6th Cir. 2003).

[137] Doran v. Salem Inn, Inc., 422 U.S. 922 (1975); Miller v. Mitchell, 598 F.3d 139 (3d Cir. 2010); *Guillemard-Ginorio*, 585 F.3d at 519.

[138] Steffel v. Thompson, 415 U.S. 452, 462 (1974).

claims and thus lacks equity's necessary adequate remedy at law.

This ongoing-proceeding line explains why the federal court could enjoin enforcement of the state criminal law in *Ex parte Young* but not in *Younger*. Because Minnesota had not initiated state proceedings to enforce the new rate laws and might not have done so, the railroad shareholders had no other opportunity to obtain a judicial ruling on their federal constitutional arguments other than from the federal court of equity and therefore had no adequate remedy at law.[139] In *Younger*, by contrast, Harris was party to a known ongoing legal action in which he could litigate his constitutional defense.[140]

Individuals seeking to enjoin enforcement of unconstitutional state laws through § 1983 must hit a precise timing window. The threat of state enforcement of the law against them must be sufficiently genuine and imminent for the plaintiff to have standing to assert her own constitutional rights[141] and for the case to be ripe for judicial resolution.[142] Once the threat of state enforcement becomes genuine and imminent, the individual can bring her § 1983 action — but only until state proceedings actually are initiated, at which point *Younger* potentially is triggered and the federal court must abstain.

Moreover, the federal plaintiff must be a party to the ongoing state proceeding. Federal courts typically will not abstain from a federal action brought by a non-party to the state proceeding; that non-party is not compelled to intervene or otherwise insert herself into a state proceeding in which she is not otherwise involved, making federal court the only forum in which she could assert her federal rights.[143] This holds even if the party to the state action and the non-state-party/potential federal plaintiff share overlapping or even identical legal interests and problems or want to make identical legal and factual arguments; courts should not automatically throw distinct, albeit similarly situated, persons into the same hopper for *Younger* purposes.[144]

Nor does it matter that the federal court decision might indirectly affect the state adjudication, either by persuading state officials not to initiate or continue enforcement proceedings or by persuading the state tribunal that the state law is unconstitutional. Nor does it matter that the state and federal courts might reach different conclusions on the constitutional issues. While courts may prefer unified litigation to avoid conflicting decisions on similar issues, that preference yields for concurrent jurisdiction, which may on occasion result in duplicating and

---

[139] Ex parte Young, 209 U.S. 123 (1908); *supra* § 4.13.

[140] Younger v. Harris, 401 U.S. 37, 38–39 (1971).

[141] Houston v. Hill, 482 U.S. 451, 459 n.7 (1987); Babbitt v. United Farm Workers Nat'l Union, 442 U.S. 289, 298 (1979); Nichols v. Brown, 859 F. Supp. 2d 1118 (C.D. Cal. 2012).

[142] National Org. for Marriage, Inc. v. Walsh, 714 F.3d 682 (2d Cir. 2013); Maldonado v. Morales, 556 F.3d 1037, 1044 (9th Cir. 2009); *cf. Younger*, 401 U.S. at 57–58 (Brennan, J., concurring in the result) (arguing that state of California had no ripe dispute with two additional plaintiffs who were not subject to an ongoing state prosecution).

[143] *Steffel*, 415 U.S. at 472–73; Allen v. Allen, 48 F.3d 259 (7th Cir. 1995).

[144] Doran v. Salem Inn, Inc., 422 U.S. 922, 928–29 (1975); Mass. Delivery Ass'n v. Coakley, 671 F.3d 33 (1st Cir. 2012).

overlapping litigation of issues that are similar in content, time, and location but involve different parties.[145] In any event, short-term disuniformity among lower courts is inherent in a common law system; uniformity comes with eventual Supreme Court review and resolution.

Three Supreme Court decisions illustrate the broad parameters of this analysis.

The first is *Steffel v. Thompson*. Steffel and a companion were distributing anti-war handbills on the sidewalks of a shopping mall; when police ordered them to cease their activities, Steffel left but his companion continued handbilling and was arrested and arraigned on state charges of criminal trespass. Steffel then brought a § 1983 action seeking a declaratory judgment that the criminal trespass statute was unconstitutional as applied to his future plans to distribute handbills. While no one believe Steffel's prosecuted companion could pursue federal litigation in light of *Younger*, the Court held that abstention from Steffel's claim was not warranted. That Steffel and his companion shared identical interests — both sought to exercise their First Amendment liberties to distribute anti-war handbills at a particular location — did not justify abstention when no state proceeding was pending against Steffel himself.[146]

Second is *Doran v. Salem Inn, Inc.* Three companies — M & L Restaurant, Inc.; Tim-Rob Bar, Inc.; and Salem Inn, Inc. — operated bars in a town that had just passed an ordinance prohibiting topless dancing. All three companies initially complied by having dancers wear bikini tops, then together filed a § 1983 action in federal court seeking a preliminary injunction and declaratory judgment that the law violated the First Amendment. The day after the federal action was filed, M & L resumed topless dancing and was served with criminal summonses for violating the ordinance; the other two restaurants continued complying with the ordinance until the district court entered the preliminary injunction prohibiting enforcement of the law until the case could be resolved.[147]

The Court held that abstention had to be considered as to each plaintiff individually, as if each stood alone. *Younger* and *Samuels* required abstention as to M & L's claims because state proceedings had been initiated and were pending against it. It did not matter that M & L filed the federal lawsuit before the state prosecution was initiated; the federal action was "in an embryonic stage and no contested matter had been decided" at the time the state proceeding began.[148] But the pending state action against M & L and federal abstention as to M&L did not affect the federal claims by Tim-Rob and Salem who were not parties to any state proceeding. That they shared counsel, had overlapping legal and business interests, and were making identical constitutional and factual arguments did not change the analysis; they remained unrelated to M & L (and to each other) in terms of ownership, control, and management, and thus unrelated for *Younger* purposes.[149]

---

[145] *Doran*, 422 U.S. at 928.

[146] Steffel v. Thompson, 415 U.S. 452 (1974).

[147] Doran v. Salem Inn, Inc., 422 U.S. 922, 924–26 (1975).

[148] *Id.* at 929.

[149] *Id.* at 928–29.

The third, and most factually and procedurally complicated, is *Hicks v. Miranda*. Miranda controlled companies operating the Pussycat Theatre, which was showing the movie "Deep Throat." On November 23-24, 1973, police seized four copies of the film in successive raids on the theatre. On November 26, two theatre employees were charged with misdemeanors for displaying obscenity; that same day, the state court issued an order to Miranda and his companies to show cause why the films should not be found obscene. On November 27, the state trial court declared the movie obscene, and ordered all copies of the film seized. On November 29, Miranda filed a § 1983 action in federal court claiming that the film was protected under the First Amendment; he sought return of the films and an injunction prohibiting the state from prosecuting him. Miranda's request for a TRO was denied and the case was referred for a three-judge district court. On January 14, 1974, the federal defendants answered the complaint and filed motions to dismiss and for summary judgment; Miranda filed a motion for a preliminary injunction. On January 15 — the day after the government officers responded to the federal pleading — the state criminal complaint was amended to add obscenity charges against Miranda and the company under which he was doing business. Ultimately, the three-judge district held that the state obscenity statute was unconstitutional as applied to the films (because the movie was not obscene and thus constitutionally protected) and ordered the films returned to Miranda and his businesses.[150]

The Supreme Court held that the district court should have abstained in deference to the state proceedings. The Court first rejected the argument that there was no pending proceeding as to Miranda. While it was true that he and his companies were not named parties to state proceedings when the federal action was filed — only the employees had been criminally charged and the state civil action formally was an *in rem* action running against the film itself — Miranda had a "substantial stake" in both pending proceedings; his legal interests were "intertwined" with the films (which he owned) being shown in his theatre and with the legal interests of his employees, who were represented by counsel paid for by Miranda. This established privity among Miranda, his employees, and the films, giving him a direct stake and interest in the pending state proceedings, well beyond the stake held by the federal plaintiffs in *Steffel* and *Doran*.[151]

Second, the Court rejected the argument that *Younger* could not apply simply because no state proceedings were pending on the day he filed his federal action. *Younger* does not set up a simple race to the courthouse. Rather, it applies in full force "where state criminal proceedings are begun against the federal plaintiffs after the federal complaint is filed but before any proceedings of substance on the merits have taken place in the federal court."[152] The filing of pleadings and motions

---

[150] Hicks v. Miranda, 422 U.S. 332, 334–41 (1975). *Hicks* demonstrates one interesting aspect of the interactions between federal and state courts. The federal court ordered the state executive officer defendant to return the films. But at that point, the films actually were in custody of the municipal court that had seized them (at the state's request) and declared them obscene. Because the federal court could not direct an order at the municipal court, it instead ordered the state officials to "in good faith" petition the municipal court for return of the films. *Id.* at 342.

[151] *Id.* at 348–49.

[152] *Id.* at 350.

that either have been denied or not yet ruled upon is not of sufficient substance to preclude abstention.[153] Nor has a federal case progressed sufficiently where the federal defendants have not yet responded to the complaint or where there has been no discovery.[154] On the other hand, a federal action is beyond embryonic — and abstention is improper — where the federal court has issued a preliminary injunction,[155] where the federal court has held multiple status conferences and weighed in on the likely constitutionality of the challenged ordinance,[156] and where the government has answered, the parties have briefed issues, and the court has held detailed evidentiary hearings and arguments.[157]

This timing mechanism theoretically empowers and incentivizes prosecutors to trigger *Younger* strategically, by initiating state proceedings in direct response to the filing or litigating of a federal suit.[158] Some courts thus are "circumspect" in applying *Hicks* and the "proceedings of substance" requirement, precisely to ensure that state prosecutors cannot routinely halt pending federal litigation or defend a federal complaint with state litigation. Such a strategy overrides the plaintiff's choice of forum and effectively creates "reverse removal" of a pending federal claim back into state court.[159]

[2] No Interference With State Proceedings

Our Federalism does not require abstention where the federal injunction would not halt or otherwise interfere with a pending state proceeding, even one to which the federal § 1983 plaintiff is a party. To the extent the state and federal cases can proceed independently and concurrently without the latter interfering with or dictating the former, there are no comity concerns. We again can think of this as absence of an adequate remedy at law. If the constitutional issue in play in federal court is not part of the state proceeding, there will be no opportunity to litigate it there and no opportunity for an alternative remedy. Whether a federal injunction interferes with ongoing state proceedings depends on the precise nature and scope of the state proceedings and of the injunction sought in federal court.

A classic illustration is *Gerstein v. Pugh*. Individual criminal defendants had been arrested without a warrant on a police determination of probable cause and were in detention awaiting trial. They filed a § 1983 action in federal court, arguing that all criminal defendants were constitutionally entitled to a judicial determination of probable cause in order to be detained for trial. Ordinarily, that judicial determination came prior to arrest, by a judge issuing an arrest warrant on her finding of probable cause. To the extent these individuals already had been arrested without that, they instead were entitled to a post-arrest judicial

---

[153] *Id.* at 349–50; *see also Doran*, 422 U.S. at 925; Forty One News, Inc. v. County of Lake, 491 F.3d 662 (7th Cir. 2007); JMM Corp. v. District of Columbia, 378 F.3d 1117 (D.C. Cir. 2004).

[154] Stroman Realty, Inc. v. Martinez, 505 F.3d 658 (7th Cir. 2007).

[155] Hawaii Housing Authority v. Midkiff, 467 U.S. 229 (1984).

[156] Hoye v. City of Oakland, 653 F.3d 835 (9th Cir. 2011).

[157] For Your Eyes Only, Inc. v. City of Columbus, Ga., 281 F.3d 1209 (11th Cir. 2002).

[158] *Hicks*, 422 U.S. at 354 (Stewart, J., dissenting).

[159] *For Your Eyes Only*, 281 F.3d at 1219–20.

determination of probable cause in order for the state to continue detaining them before trial. The plaintiffs thus sought a federal injunction ordering the state to provide that post-arrest probable cause hearing.[160] The *Gerstein* Court held that *Younger* abstention was not warranted, because the federal injunction did not interfere with the pending state prosecution itself or the trial on the merits of that prosecution. The relief the federal plaintiffs sought — a state judicial hearing to determine probable cause — affected only their continued pre-trial detention. It did not affect the ongoing prosecution, the constitutional validity of the law being enforced, or the power of the state to prosecute them. Moreover, the state trial did not provide the necessary adequate remedy at law, since the federal issue (a judicial determination of probable cause to arrest) was not something that could be raised as a defense in the state prosecution itself.[161]

Younger does not require abstention where the federal § 1983 claim focuses on constitutional issues that are "collateral" to the primary state proceeding. For example, the Sixth Circuit considered a case in which the federal litigation involved three distinct disputes between a homeowner and the city: (1) the city refused to sell the owner an adjacent strip of property, allegedly in violation of equal protection; (2) the city padlocked her property without notice or hearing, in violation of procedural due process; and (3) the city wanted to inspect the property and issue a certificate of occupancy because the owner was renting the property. The property owner filed a § 1983 action challenging only the first few, while a hearing was being held before a city agency to determine the third. The federal court did not have to abstain because the two constitutional issues raised in the federal action were collateral to the issue in the state proceeding and likely would not arise or be litigated there.[162]

[3] Opportunity to Raise Federal Issues

Federal courts considering whether to abstain must account for the particular type of state proceeding and whether it is on appropriate forum for litigating constitutional issues. The proceeding must be "judicial in character," which suggests a level of formality and an opportunity to make legal arguments, present evidence, and obtain a reasoned and explained decision.[163] Informal stand-alone proceedings are not sufficiently formal to warrant abstention,[164] unless the state body has authority to entertain federal constitutional arguments at some point, whether in that proceeding or in later levels of state review.[165]

---

[160] Gerstein v. Pugh, 420 U.S. 103, 105–07 (1975); Hirsh v. Justices of Supreme Court, 67 F.3d 708 (9th Cir. 1995).

[161] *Id.* at 108 n.9.

[162] Habich v. City of Dearborn, 331 F.3d 524, 531–32 (6th Cir. 2003).

[163] Esso Standard Oil Co. (P.R.) v. Mujica Cotto, 389 F.3d 212 (1st Cir. 2004).

[164] Guillemard-Ginorio v. Contreras-Gomez, 585 F.3d 508 (1st Cir. 2009); Telco Commc'ns, Inc. v. Carbaugh, 885 F.2d 1225 (4th Cir. 1989).

[165] Middlesex County Ethics Committee v. Garden State Bar Ass'n, 457 U.S. 423, 429–30, 434–36 (1982); *Esso Standard*, 389 F.3d at 222.

[4] Wholly Prospective Relief

Because federal courts must abstain only where the federal injunction interferes with an ongoing state proceeding, Our Federalism does not apply where the federal plaintiff seeks wholly prospective relief — namely, a prohibition on future enforcement of an unconstitutional state law, unconnected to any ongoing proceedings or to efforts to annul or undo the results of past proceedings. In *Wooley v. Maynard*, the plaintiff had been convicted three times of a traffic offense (without ever appealing the conviction) for covering the "Live Free or Die" motto on his New Hampshire license plate. *Younger* did not bar the federal claim seeking a "wholly prospective" injunction prohibiting future prosecutions under the same statute, where the plaintiff left unchallenged and unaffected the results or consequences of his prior convictions.[166] On the other hand, a plaintiff cannot avoid *Younger* and Our Federalism where the claim seeks a declaratory judgment that past citations under a city noise ordinance are unconstitutional.[167]

[5] Narrow exceptions

Younger recognized exceptions to abstention in cases of (1) bad faith, where the state prosecution has been undertaken with no hope or expectation of securing a valid conviction; (2) harassment, where the state prosecution is one of a series of repeated prosecutions; or (3) in "extraordinary circumstances," where the statute is "flagrantly and patently violative of express constitutional prohibitions in every clause, sentence and paragraph, and in whatever manner and against whomever an effort might be made to apply it."[168] *Younger* also recognized the possibility of other "unusual situations calling for federal intervention," but found it unnecessary to specify what those might be.[169] The Court later identified one such situation, where this is institutional bias in the state decision maker.[170] On the other hand, the Seventh Circuit declined to accept a fast-approaching election as an extraordinary circumstance justifying an exception to *Younger.*[171]

Importantly, however, these exceptions are extremely narrow, intentionally limited, and rarely used as a basis for a federal court refusing to abstain.[172] The federal plaintiff bears the burden of establishing that one of the exceptions applies[173] and must offer more than conclusory allegations to support the exception.[174] The plaintiff must overcome a presumption of honesty and integrity in

---

[166] Wooley v. Maynard, 430 U.S. 705, 707–08, 709–12 (1977).

[167] Moore v. City of Asheville, 396 F.3d 385, 396–97 (4th Cir. 2005).

[168] Younger v. Harris, 401 U.S. 37, 53–54 (1971).

[169] *Id.* at 54.

[170] Gibson v. Berryhill, 411 U.S. 564 (1973).

[171] FreeEats.com, Inc. v. Indiana, 502 F.3d 590 (7th Cir. 2007).

[172] Zalman v. Armstrong, 802 F.2d 199, 205 & n.8 (6th Cir. 1986).

[173] Kern v. Clark, 331 F.3d 9 (2d Cir. 2003).

[174] Tony & Susan Alamo Found. v. Secretary of Labor, 471 U.S. 290 (1985).

state adjudicators.[175] Allegations of selective prosecution (that the state prosecuted one individual while refusing to pursue others) are not sufficient; the plaintiff must show that the decision to prosecute him was affirmatively motivated by subjective bad faith or intention to harass.[176]

At best, the *Younger* exceptions can be seen as *ex post* explanations for some of the Supreme Court's past decisions rejecting abstention. For example, *Dombrowski* can be reframed as a case of bad faith and harassment, given the circumstances and social context of the case, several prior arrests of the plaintiffs, and repeated public statements by government officials accusing the civil rights organization of subversive activities and threatening prosecution.[177] Similarly, *Wooley* can be explained as a case of harassment, considering that the plaintiff had been cited three separate times for violating the same traffic law.[178]

§ 6.13   *YOUNGER* PUZZLES

1. *A number of sexually explicit or suggestive text messages and photos of three minor high-school girls are found on the phones of a number of male high school students. The county prosecutor threatens to charge seventeen students (the three girls and fourteen boys) with felony possession or dissemination of child pornography, unless they (and their parents) agree to probation and to participation in an informal adjustment education program. The program would split the boys and girls into separate classes; the girl program is designed to help them "gain an understanding of what it means to be a girl in today's society," and includes writing a report on what they did and why it was wrong. The three girls refuse to participate in the diversion program (which requires parental permission and approval), instead filing a § 1983 action against the prosecutor, claiming that enforcement of child pornography laws against them and forcing them into the diversion program would violate the First Amendment.[179]*

Consider whether the court must abstain under Younger *and why. Consider the prosecutor's strategic options.*

2. *State law permits initiation of criminal proceedings via warrantless arrest on a finding of probable cause by police. A person arrested without a warrant must be brought before a neutral magistrate within 48 hours for a determination of probable cause and within ten days for a preliminary hearing at which the state must establish a "prima facie" case of guilt. If the judge dismisses the charges at the preliminary hearing, state law permits the district attorney to immediately reinstitute them. One local prosecutors' office, pursuant to that authority, establishes a "re-arrest" policy. When charges are dismissed at a preliminary hearing, the district attorney, acting on a continued belief that there is probable cause, can*

---

[175] Hirsh v. Justices of the Supreme Court, 67 F.3d 708 (9th Cir. 1995); Miller v. Tony & Susan Alamo Found., 924 F.2d 143 (8th Cir. 1991).

[176] Fieger v. Thomas, 74 F.3d 740 (6th Cir. 1996).

[177] *Younger*, 401 U.S. at 48 (discussing *Dombrowski*).

[178] *Wooley*, 430 U.S. at 707–08.

[179] Miller v. Mitchell, 598 F.3d 139 (3d Cir. 2010).

order that the defendant be immediately arrested and taken back into custody. The defendant must then wait another 48 hours for a new probable cause hearing and approximately two more weeks for a new preliminary hearing.

Stewart is arrested and charged with felony aggravated assault, along with several misdemeanor counts. The judge at the preliminary hearing dismisses the charges, finding that the state has not shown a prima facie case of guilt. Pursuant to the re-arrest policy, the line prosecutor immediately refiles the identical felony charge and has Stewart arrested. Because Stewart is unable to make bail, he remains in jail for almost two weeks until the next preliminary hearing.

Stewart files a § 1983 action in federal district court, arguing that the re-arrest policy, which applies without a judicial finding of probable cause, constitutes an unreasonable seizure without a warrant, in violation of the Fourth Amendment.[180]

Consider whether the district court must abstain under Younger.

PART D
ROOKER-FELDMAN

§ 6.14 *ROOKER* AND *FELDMAN*

The *Rooker-Feldman* Doctrine, sometimes labeled as abstention[181] and other times defined (more accurately) as an internal limitation on district court jurisdiction,[182] originates with two Supreme Court cases.

In *Rooker v. Fidelity Trust Co.*, the losing parties to a state proceeding asked the federal court to declare a state court judgment, which had been affirmed on appeal, null and void. The Supreme Court held that the state court had jurisdiction over the parties and issues in the first case and it was the province and duty of the state court to decide them. That the state decision might have been wrong did not render the judgment void; it remained an effective and conclusive adjudication unless reversed or modified in an appropriate and timely appellate proceeding. The only federal court statutorily authorized to reverse or modify that state judgment is the Supreme Court.[183] The federal district court, having only original jurisdiction over civil actions alleging constitutional violations,[184] does not have the authority to review or reverse a state court decision.[185]

Sixty years later, in *District of Columbia Court of Appeals v. Feldman*, the Court reiterated that federal review of final judicial determinations by a state supreme court (which includes the District of Columbia Court of Appeals, the highest court

---

[180] Stewart v. Abraham, 275 F.3d 220 (3d Cir. 2001).

[181] Brown v. Bowman, 668 F.3d 437, 442 (7th Cir. 2012).

[182] Berry v. Schmitt, 688 F.3d 290, 299 (6th Cir. 2012).

[183] 28 U.S.C. § 1257(a).

[184] 28 U.S.C. § 1331; 28 U.S.C. § 1343(a)(3).

[185] Rooker v. Fidelity Trust Co., 263 U.S. 413 (1923).

for the District of Columbia[186]) rests exclusively with the Supreme Court and not the district court. The plaintiffs in *Feldman* had been denied admission to the District of Columbia Bar pursuant to a rule requiring that bar applicants graduate from an ABA-accredited law school. The federal district court lacked jurisdiction to the extent plaintiffs challenged (as arbitrary and capricious) the refusal to waive the legal-education rule; any challenge to the validity of a decision or judgment already made by a highest state court must be made to the Supreme Court of the United States.[187] On the other hand, the federal district court did have jurisdiction to the extent the plaintiffs attacked the constitutionality of the legal-education rule generally; those claims did not require review of a court judgment and thus fell within the district court's original jurisdiction.[188]

Rooker-Feldman is grounded in the first instance in the text of the various statutory grants of federal jurisdiction and the congressional division of federal jurisdiction. The Supreme Court has exclusive appellate jurisdiction over final state-court judgments involving federal issues.[189] Federal district courts possess original, but not appellate, jurisdiction over civil actions arising under the Constitution of the United States.[190]

Rooker-Feldman applies only in "limited circumstances" to prevent a state court loser from running to federal district court claiming a constitutional injury caused by a state court judgment itself,[191] where the purported federal constitutional claim functionally asks the federal district court to review and reverse the state court judgment.[192] This involves a three-prong test: (1) A state court entered a final judgment on a matter prior to initiation of federal proceedings;[193] (2) the federal claim is brought by the state-court loser, who was party to the state proceeding; and (3) the federal claim alleges an injury caused by the state judgment itself and invites its review and rejection.[194]

The critical point is the source of the alleged injury. *Rooker-Feldman* bars federal claims that explicitly seek to overturn an adverse state court judgment or that are "inextricably intertwined" with a state court judgment. That is, the federal claim identifies the judgment as the source of constitutional injury, functionally seeks its review, and succeeds only if the state court decision was erroneous.[195] The

---

[186] 28 U.S.C. § 1257(b).

[187] District of Columbia Court of Appeals v. Feldman, 460 U.S. 462, 465–66, 482–83 (1983).

[188] *Id.* at 482–83. And because there was no pending state proceeding to enforce that rule, *Younger* and Our Federalism were not implicated.

[189] 28 U.S.C. § 1257(a); Murdock v. Memphis, 87 U.S. 590 (1875).

[190] 28 U.S.C. § 1331; *see also* 28 U.S.C. § 1343(a)(3).

[191] Lance v. Dennis, 546 U.S. 459, 466 (2006) (per curiam); Exxon Mobil Corp. v. Saudi Basic Indus. Corp., 544 U.S. 280, 291 (2005).

[192] *Brown*, 668 F.3d at 442.

[193] Hunter v. Hamilton County Bd. of Elections, 635 F.3d 219 (6th Cir. 2011) (*Rooker-Feldman* does not apply where state-court judgment issued nearly seven weeks after federal complaint filed).

[194] *Exxon Mobil*, 544 U.S. at 284; *Berry*, 688 F.3d at 298–98; Gary v. Braddock Cemetery, 517 F.3d 195 (3d Cir. 2008); Hoblock v. Albany County Bd. of Elections, 422 F.3d 77 (2d Cir. 2005).

[195] *Brown*, 668 F.3d at 442; Robins v. Ritchie, 631 F.3d 919, 925 (8th Cir. 2011).

federal action must seek to remedy an injury allegedly caused by the state judgment itself, by the process leading to the state judgment, or by conduct taken pursuant to, or under compulsion of, the state judgment.[196] On the other hand, *Rooker-Feldman* does not bar claims challenging the constitutionality of state statutes or rules, even as construed by a state judgment,[197] and seeking only to enjoin future enforcement but not to undo a prior disposition.[198] It also does not apply to challenges to actions and events independent of any state court orders.[199]

Lower courts are divided on whether *Rooker-Feldman* is limited only to final judgments from a state's highest court or whether it also bars federal challenges to interlocutory decisions and decisions of lower state courts; the majority of circuits take the latter position.[200] On one hand, there arguably is no "state court loser," as required under *Rooker-Feldman*, until entry of final judgment from the state judiciary as a whole, including reviewing courts. And to the extent *Rooker-Feldman* is grounded in the Supreme Court exclusive jurisdiction to review state-court judgments, its authority is limited only to reviewing "[f]inal judgments or decrees rendered by the highest court of a State in which a decision could be had,"[201]; there is no interference with that jurisdiction if a district court hears a federal case involving a non-final order from a court other than the state's highest court. On the other hand the fundamental policy underlying *Rooker-Feldman* — not having federal district courts hearing cases that functionally require them to review state court decisions and not subjecting state judgments to collateral attack in federal district court — holds as much for interlocutory as final decisions and as much for decisions of state trial and intermediate appellate courts as to the highest court.[202] Neither can be described as the district court exercising "original" jurisdiction so as to fall within the jurisdictional grant of § 1331.

The Second Circuit posited the following as the paradigm § 1983 action barred by *Rooker-Feldman*: A state court terminates a father's custody rights based purely on state law; the father (the state-court loser) sues in federal court, asking for an injunction ordering the restoration of custody and arguing that the state judgment

---

[196] *Hoblock*, 422 F.3d at 88 (plaintiff cannot plead around *Rooker-Feldman* where defendant's unconstitutional conduct compelled by state court order).

[197] Skinner v. Switzer, 131 S. Ct. 1289 (2011); District of Columbia Court of Appeals v. Feldman, 460 U.S. 462, 483–84 (1983); *but see* Alvarez v. AG for Fla., 679 F.3d 1257, 1262 (11th Cir. 2012) (*Rooker-Feldman* bars due process challenge to way Florida courts apply state procedures).

[198] *Berry*, 688 F.3d at 300.

[199] Great Western Mining & Mineral Co. v. Fox Rothschild LLP, 615 F.3d 159 (3d Cir. 2010); Green v. Mattingly, 585 F.3d 97 (2d Cir. 2009); McCormick v. Braverman, 451 F.3d 382 (6th Cir. 2006); Reguli v. Guffee, 2010 U.S. App. LEXIS 6767 (6th Cir. Mar. 31, 2010); Drees v. Ferguson, 2010 U.S. App. LEXIS 19631 (11th Cir. Sept. 21, 2010).

[200] *Compare* TruServ Corp. v. Flegles, Inc., 419 F.3d 584, 591 (7th Cir. 2005), *with* Pieper v. Am. Arbitration Ass'n, 336 F.3d 458, 462 (6th Cir. 2003) *and* Brown & Root, Inc. v. Breckenridge, 211 F.3d 194, 199 (4th Cir. 2000).

[201] 28 U.S.C. § 1257(a).

[202] *Pieper*, 336 F.3d at 462-63; *Cf.* SKS & Assocs. v. Dart, 619 F.3d 674 (7th Cir. 2010) (abstaining based on *Younger* from action challenging constitutionality of general court order applicable to all pending actions in state court).

violates substantive due process.[203] Common *Rooker-Feldman* situations include challenges to state court decisions over child custody or child support,[204] bar admission and disciplinary determinations,[205] election disputes,[206] and decisions over takings and just compensation for takings.[207]

The statutory nature of *Rooker-Feldman* means that Congress can override it and vest district courts with appellate jurisdiction over state-court decisions. Of course, this is functionally what habeas corpus is — federal district courts reviewing final state-court judgments that placed the claimant in custody and that are alleged to cause constitutional injury.[208] Congress also could suspend *Rooker-Feldman* by statute for a particular case or class of cases outside of habeas, including in certain constitutional actions.[209]

§ 6.15 PRECLUSION DISTINGUISHED

Rooker-Feldman's reach expanded for a time because of its easy conflation with preclusion doctrines.[210] Lower courts frequently held that they lacked jurisdiction on *Rooker-Feldman* grounds where the federal plaintiff was trying to relitigate claims and issues previously resolved in state court proceedings, even where the case did not specifically involve a state-court loser claiming a constitutional injury caused by the state judgment itself.

The Supreme Court recently struck back, sharpening the line between *Rooker-Feldman*, a limit on district court jurisdiction, and preclusion, a common law defense to a claim. *Rooker-Feldman* does not apply to ordinary concurrent or parallel federal/state litigation in which state litigation happens to reach judgment

---

[203] *Hoblock*, 422 F.3d at 87.

[204] PJ v. Wagner, 603 F.3d 1182 (10th Cir. 2010); Marran v. Marran, 376 F.3d 143 (3d Cir. 2004).

[205] *Brown*, 668 F.3d at 443–44; Hale v. Comm. on Character & Fitness for Ill., 335 F.3d 678 (7th Cir. 2003); Stern v. Nix, 840 F.2d 208 (3d Cir. 1988).

[206] *Robins*, 631 F.3d at 925–26; *Hoblock*, 422 F.3d at 81–83; *see also Hunter*, 635 F.3d at 234 (considering but rejecting *Rooker-Feldman* in light of timing of state court judgment in election dispute).

[207] Campbell v. City of Spencer, 682 F.3d 1278 (10th Cir. 2012); Edwards v. City of Jonesboro, 645 F.3d 1014 (8th Cir. 2011); Knutson v. City of Fargo, 600 F.3d 992 (8th Cir. 2010). Supreme Court precedent has created some confusion in the takings context. In *Williamson County Reg'l Planning Comm'n v. Hamilton Bank*, 473 U.S. 172, 194–96 (1985), the Court suggested that a claim under the Takings Clause is not ripe until the claimant, having had property taken, seeks and is denied just compensation through state-court procedures. Chief Justice Rehnquist later argued that, to the extent *Williamson* makes state-court denial of just compensation an element of a federal takings claim, *Rooker-Feldman* might bar any § 1983 action seeking to challenge the constitutionality of a taking, sicne it necessarily would challenge the state court order as to compensation. San Remo Hotel, L.P. v. City & County of San Francisco, 545 U.S. 323, 351 (2005) (Rehnquist, C.J., concurring in the judgment). The Eighth Circuit has rejected this argument; the takings injury is the loss of property, not the failure of just compensation, thus a federal plaintiff asserting a takings claims challenges the executive conduct that took the property, not the state-court judgment that awarded compensation. *Edwards*, 645 F.3d at 1019 (citing *Knutson*, 600 F.3d at 995–96).

[208] 28 U.S.C. §§ 2254(b), (d); *supra* § 5.06.

[209] Act for the Relief of the Parents of Theresa Marie Schiavo, Pub. L. No. No. 109-3, § 2, 119 Stat. 15 (2005).

[210] *Supra* Ch. 5, Part C.

first.[211] It also does not incorporate principles of privity between the parties to the first and second action, but applies only where the federal plaintiff herself is a (losing) party to the first suit.[212]

Of course, that *Rooker-Feldman* does not deprive federal courts of jurisdiction does not mean the federal court will hear the case. It may have to abstain under other doctrines. More commonly, actual claim or issue preclusion may defeat the federal action.[213] The point is that the dispute is not over the district court's jurisdiction under § 1331 as interpreted in *Rooker* and *Feldman*.

§ 6.16   *ROOKER-FELDMAN* PUZZLES

Consider whether the district court can hear the following cases, in light of Rooker-Feldman, as well as general principles of issue and claim preclusion.

1. *Plaintiff is an applicant to the state bar. Under state law, the state supreme court has jurisdiction over who is admitted to practice law. Pursuant to that authority, the court has established the Board of Law Examiners ("BLE"), responsible for investigating, reporting, and certifying to the court that an applicant has the necessary "good moral character and fitness." An applicant can challenge a negative BLE admission recommendation by requesting a hearing before the BLE and then appealing the outcome of that hearing to the state supreme court. The court also has established a Judges and Lawyers Assistance Committee ("JLAC") to evaluate and assist lawyers, judges, law students, and other persons having possible mental health issues; JLAC will, on request, evaluate bar applicants and provide a report to the BLE, which the BLE then uses in its determination and recommendation to the supreme court.*

Plaintiff's bar application is referred to the BLE and then to JLAC, which conducts an evaluation and identifies some mental health problems; the BLE denies the plaintiff's bar application and the state supreme court affirms that decision and denies bar admission. Plaintiff files a § 1983 action in federal district court. The complaint names as defendants, among others, the doctors who evaluated him for JLAC and the two directors of JLAC; it alleges that the JLAC evaluations were religiously biased and that JLAC otherwise acted unconstitutionally.[214]

2. *Plaintiff owns a tract of land adjacent to a city-owned landfill; the decomposition of waste in the landfill causes methane to migrate onto the property, rendering the property unsuitable for building and causing two prospective buyers to cancel contracts to purchase the land. The plaintiff files suit in state court against the city, mayor, and members of the city council; he asserts state-law claims for inverse condemnation, trespass, nuisance, negligence and negligence per se, strict liability, and several state statutory and constitutional violations. He also makes a "reservation" of federal rights and remedies. The state court finds that*

---

[211] Exxon Mobil Corp. v. Saudi Basic Indus. Corp., 544 U.S. 280, 292 (2005).

[212] Lance v. Dennis, 546 U.S. 459, 466 (2006) (per curiam).

[213] *Exxon*, 544 U.S. at 293; Edwards v. City of Jonesboro, 645 F.3d 1014 (8th Cir. 2011).

[214] Brown v. Bowman, 668 F.3d 437 (7th Cir. 2012).

the invasion of methane onto the property constitutes a taking and awards $387,500 as the value of the property, along with a refund of more than $18,000 in property taxes paid, but no pre-judgment interest.

Plaintiff files a § 1983 action in federal court, asserting the same basic rights through the First, Fifth, and Fourteenth Amendments, as well as a claim under the Takings Clause of the Fifth and Fourteenth Amendments.[215]

PART E
ABSTENTION REVIEW

§ 6.17   ABSTENTION REVIEW PUZZLE

The chief judge of the state trial court issues a general order (applicable in all cases pending in that court) prohibiting the county sheriff from carrying out residential evictions during the Christmas holiday season or during extreme winter weather conditions.

A company that owns and manages residential rental property has a number of eviction actions pending in the court and regularly requests sheriff assistance in carrying out evictions. It files a § 1983 action against the chief judge and the sheriff, arguing that the general order violates equal protection, due process, and the Establishment Clause, and seeking an injunction ordering the state court to rescind the general order and to process evictions at its ordinary pace.[216]

Consider whether the federal court can or should hear the § 1983 action in light of all potentially applicable abstention and jurisdiction doctrines.

---

[215]   Edwards v. City of Jonesboro, 645 F.3d 1014 (8th Cir. 2011).

[216]   SKS Assocs. v. Dart, 619 F.3d 674 (7th Cir. 2010).

Chapter 7

REMEDIES

§ 7.01   INTRODUCTION TO REMEDIES

The final issue in constitutional litigation is the remedy for any plaintiff who has prevailed on the merits of her claim or has settled or otherwise resolved the dispute. All of the substantive, jurisdictional, and procedural issues previously discussed have been resolved. The plaintiff has proven (or the defendant has acknowledged) that she was deprived of a right, privilege, or immunity secured by the Constitution or laws of the United States, by a person, entity, or government acting under color of law; the plaintiff has overcome individual immunity defenses (most prominently qualified immunity); and she has overcome or avoided procedural and jurisdictional defenses, such as *Heck*, abstention, exhaustion, and preclusion. The question now is what the plaintiff can recover and what the court can award.

Section 1983 makes a defendant liable to the party injured in an "action at law, suit in equity, or other proper proceeding for redress."[1] That statutory language reflects the historic divide between law and equity. In England, Chancery Courts (or equity) developed as an alternative, supplementary, and sometimes rival adjudicative system to the existing Courts of Law (or Common Law); that divided system was carried to the United States and still existed at the state and federal levels time when the 1871 Act was enacted. The division was eliminated in federal courts with enactment of the Federal Rules of Civil Procedure in 1938, which merged law and equity into a single system in which all judicial remedies are available in a single cause of action.[2]

The phrase "action in law" now means a claim for "legal" relief — the relief historically available in courts of common law, primarily compensatory and punitive damages and other monetary relief. The phrase "suit in equity" now means a claim for equitable relief — the type of relief historically available in a court of equity, namely injunctions. The third common remedy under § 1983 is the declaratory judgment, a remedy that developed after the merger of law and equity and does not fall neatly or accurately into either category.[3]

The line between legal and equitable remedies retains its greatest modern force in dictating whether the parties are entitled to a jury trial and who serves as fact-finder. The Seventh Amendment civil jury right applies only in "Suits at common law,"[4] which has come to mean all suits in which legal rights are to be ascertained and determined, as distinct from claims seeking equitable relief.[5] There thus is a right to a jury trial in most § 1983 and *Bivens* actions seeking damages.[6]

---

[1]   42 U.S.C. § 1983.

[2]   FED. R. CIV. P. 2.

[3]   DOUGLAS LAYCOCK, MODERN AMERICAN REMEDIES: CASES AND MATERIALS 6 (4th ed. 2010).

[4]   U.S. CONST. amend. VII.

[5]   City of Monterey v. Del Monte Dunes, Ltd., 526 U.S. 687, 708–09 (1999) (quoting Parsons v. Bedford, 28 U.S. (3 Pet.) 433, 447 (1830)).

[6]   *Del Monte Dunes*, 526 U.S. at 708–10; *id.* at 723 (Scalia, J., concurring in part and concurring in the

On the other hand, because there historically was no jury in courts of equity, a claim for injunctive relief is not a "Suit at Common Law" for Seventh Amendment purposes and the court acts fact-finder.[7] Where an action seeks both damages and injunctive relief, the judge is bound by the jury's findings on any facts common to both forms of relief.[8] For declaratory judgments, where, as is typically true in § 1983 cases, the request for declaratory relief is closely tied to a claim for injunctive relief, the declaratory claim is treated as equitable, the Seventh Amendment does not apply, and the judge acts as fact-finder.[9]

Beyond the historically determined and overbroad law/equity divide, we also can distinguish between "substitutionary" and "specific" remedies. Substitutionary remedies replace what the injured plaintiff lost by substituting something in its place. Specific remedies prevent or undo harm; they involve steps either to prevent the harm from happening or to repair the harm in kind by replacing the specific thing lost or giving the plaintiff the specific thing she would have had. For purposes of constitutional litigation, compensatory and punitive damages are substitutionary remedies providing money to replace the thing that was lost. Most injunctions, declaratory relief, exclusion of evidence, and dismissal of a criminal prosecution are specific remedies, giving the plaintiff back his constitutional right to engage in protected conduct.[10]

The concept of the "private attorney general" prominent with respect to constitutional remedies. Constitutional and civil rights plaintiffs, and the lawyers who represent them, vindicate public rights by bringing private civil litigation to enforce and remedy individual violations of federal rights.[11] The term was coined by Judge Jerome Frank, who recognized that Congress might confer on non-official persons the authority to bring a suit to prevent action by an officer in violation of his powers; there is an actual controversy between that non-official person and the defendant, even if the sole or partial purpose of the action is vindication of the larger public interest.[12]

Enabling more, and more successful, civil rights litigation increases the overall level of federal constitutional rights enforcement, which inures to the public benefit. Congress thus can provide a broad range of private remedies to incentivize and enable private individuals to pursue and succeed in civil litigation. Damages for private constitutional injury compensate the injured persons for past violations of

---

judgment) (arguing that a jury is available in all § 1983 actions seeking monetary damages); Carlson v. Green, 446 U.S. 14, 22 (1980).

[7] Wilson v. Bailey, 934 F.2d 301, 305 (11th Cir. 1991).

[8] Burton v. Armontrout, 975 F.2d 543 (8th Cir. 1992).

[9] Johnson v. Randle, 2012 U.S. Dist. LEXIS 75080 (S.D. Ill. May 31, 2012); DL v. District of Columbia, 845 F. Supp. 2d 1 (D.D.C. 2011); *supra* § 5.04.

[10] DOUGLAS LAYCOCK, MODERN AMERICAN REMEDIES: CASES AND MATERIALS 5 (4th ed. 2010); John M. Greabe, *Constitutional Remedies and Public Interest Balancing*, ___ WM. & MARY BILL RTS. J. ___ (forthcoming 2013).

[11] Evans v. Jeff D., 475 U.S. 717, 745 (1986) (Brennan, J., dissenting); William B. Rubenstein, *On What a "Private Attorney General" Is — And Why It Matters*, 57 VAND. L. REV. 2129 (2004); Pamela S. Karlan, *Disarming the Private Attorney General*, 2003 U. ILL. L. REV. 183.

[12] Associated Indust. of New York State v. Ickes, 134 F.2d 694 (2d Cir. 1943).

their rights, while indirectly serving the public interest by deterring future violations and incentivizing governments and government officials to change their policies and conduct.[13] Injunctions and other prospective or specific remedies more directly benefit the public; a court order prohibiting certain unconstitutional conduct as to the plaintiff (such as future enforcement of an unconstitutional law or policy) functionally prohibits, or at least constrains, enforcement as to similarly situated members of the public. Even more obviously, a court order compelling government to affirmatively change how its public institutions operate benefits not only the plaintiff, but every member of the public who comes in contact with those institutions. Finally, by allowing prevailing plaintiffs to recover attorney's fees, Congress provides a financial incentive for quality lawyers to represent plaintiffs in constitutional cases, particularly cases involving smaller, individual, and less systemic violations worth little or no money. Attorney's fees make it easier for plaintiffs to obtain legal counsel, giving them a better opportunity to prevail and thus a better opportunity to achieve some public benefit.

PART A
"ACTION IN LAW": DAMAGES

§ 7.02 COMPENSATORY DAMAGES

The Supreme Court insists there is nothing unique about § 1983 or constitutional claims for damages purposes; whether damages are awarded and the level of damages available are determined in accordance with ordinary common law tort principles. The "basic purpose of a § 1983 damages award should be to compensate persons for injuries caused by the deprivation of constitutional rights," consistent with common law principles of damages-as-compensation prevalent in 1871. To the extent damages also deter future government and official constitutional misconduct, damages serve that value, although the deterrent should not be more formidable than what is inherent in the award of compensatory damages. The goal at common law, and thus under § 1983, is "fair compensation."[14]

A plaintiff can recover for any actual injury resulting from a constitutional violation, including out-of-pocket loss.[15] Other recoverable monetary harms include medical, hospital, and similar expenses associated with physical injuries (generally arising only in Fourth and Eighth Amendment excessive force cases and some substantive due process cases that actually produce physical injuries imposing monetary costs),[16] lost income or wages (associated with public employment discrimination[17] or lengthy incarceration[18]), the value of something taken by

---

[13] Owen v. City of Independence, 445 U.S. 622, 651 (1980); Carey v. Piphus, 435 U.S. 247, 256–57 (1978).

[14] Memphis Community Sch. Dist. v. Stachura, 477 U.S. 299 (1986); Carey v. Piphus, 435 U.S. 247, 258 (1978).

[15] *Stachura*, 477 U.S. at 306–07.

[16] Park v. Shiflett, 250 F.3d 843 (4th Cir. 2001); Bauer v. Norris, 713 F.2d 408 (8th Cir. 1983).

[17] Dossett v. First State Bank, 399 F.3d 940 (8th Cir. 2005).

government (such as property in a takings case[19]), and incidental costs incurred because of the violation (for example, having to miss work[20] or hire an attorney to defend against a wrongful prosecution[21]). The plaintiff also can recover for harm to reputation, personal humiliation, and mental and emotional distress and suffering.[22] Prisoners, however, may recover for mental or emotional injury suffered while in custody only with a showing of physical injury.[23]

The difficulty for plaintiffs is establishing causation between the constitutional violation and the monetary loss. This involves two distinct issues. First, the violation may not have caused the financial loss or, stated differently, the financial loss still may have occurred even without the constitutional violation. In *Carey v. Piphus*, plaintiffs were public school students who were suspended without an opportunity to be heard prior to their suspensions; they sought to recover for pain and suffering and mental and emotional distress. But the Court questioned whether the due process violation caused that distress and, if so, how. The plaintiff could not recover for any distress from the suspension itself; the deprivation of liberty may in fact have been proper, the plaintiffs may in fact have been properly suspended, or they may in fact have been suspended even if accorded sufficient hearings. But the plaintiffs also could not recover for the distress from the failure to accord pre-deprivation process; the Court doubted that the absence of a hearing actually caused the plaintiff pain and suffering or distress, or that she would not have incurred pain and suffering if she had a hearing before her suspension.[24]

Second, many constitutional injuries are intangible and the violation of the plaintiff's right, although causing clear constitutional harm, does not cause actual monetary loss. Physical injury is not an ordinary consequence of most constitutional violations.[25] For example, an individual denied an opportunity to participate in a public protest likely will be unable to show a monetary harm — what is the value of a lost opportunity to speak in public? Or consider *Stachura*, in which a public school teacher was suspended with pay in response to parental objections to his in-class expression, then reinstated without having to undergo an administrative evaluation of his teaching methods. Although his First Amendment rights were violated and he suffered a real constitutional injury, he suffered no lost wages or

---

[18] Connick v. Thompson, 131 S. Ct. 1350 (2011) (jury awarded $14 million against municipality for wrongful incarceration; verdict vacated because no basis for municipal liability established); Sam Kamin, *Duke Lacrosse, Prosecutorial Misconduct, and the Limits of the Civil Justice System, in* INSTITUTIONAL FAILURES: DUKE LACROSSE, UNIVERSITIES, THE NEWS MEDIA, AND THE LEGAL SYSTEM 43, 54 n.40 (Howard M. Wasserman ed., 2010).

[19] Bowlby v. City of Aberdeen, 681 F.3d 215 (5th Cir. 2012).

[20] Slicker v. Jackson, 215 F.3d 1225 (11th Cir. 2000).

[21] Michael L. Wells, *Civil Recourse, Damages-as-Redress, and Constitutional Torts*, 46 GA. L. REV. 1003 (2012).

[22] *Stachura*, 477 U.S. at 307; *Carey*, 435 U.S. at 261–62.

[23] 42 U.S.C. § 1997e(e).

[24] *Carey*, 435 U.S. at 263.

[25] Michael L. Wells, *Civil Recourse, Damages-as-Redress, and Constitutional Torts*, 46 GA. L. REV. 1019 (2012).

other monetary injury.[26] It often is impossible to place a value on, for example, the lost opportunity to speak,[27] an unlawful search and seizure of contraband that does not result in prosecution, conviction, or incarceration, or even on the use of force that does not produce physical injury.[28]

Further, while constitutional rights are absolute and a remedy must be available for any violation of those rights,[29] courts cannot monetize intangible injuries or constitutional rights themselves. In *Carey*, the plaintiff urged the Court to adopt the concept of presumed damages from common law defamation *per se*, in which injury is presumed from the harm itself and the plaintiff need not prove a compensable harm to recover substantial damages. But *Carey* rejected the analogy. Presumed damages exist in defamation because statements which are defamatory *per se* are virtually certain to cause injury to reputation, although the injury is difficult to prove. By contrast, it is not reasonable to presume that every procedural due process violation causes mental or emotional distress, given the ambiguity in causation.[30]

Moreover, mental and emotional distress is a personal injury to the plaintiff that she can easily establish in accordance with common law, even through her own testimony.[31] Thus, in *Stachura*, the Court rejected a jury instruction that allowed the jury to assign a monetary value to the constitutional right itself, in light of right's importance and significance. That, the Court insisted, was an "unwieldy tool for ensuring compliance with the Constitution," vesting juries with "unbounded discretion" to punish unpopular defendants or to award arbitrary amounts without any evidentiary basis.[32]

The answer instead is to award a nominal sum of money, recoverable even without proof of actual injury, for the right itself. Nominal damages acknowledge the absolute nature of the right, that the right has been violated, and the importance to society that rights, particularly constitutional rights, be scrupulously observed and vindicated with some remedy.[33]But they do not empower the jury to speculate about harm or causation. Nominal damages are typically[34] (although not always[35]) for $1. This means large money awards are limited exclusively to cases of severe physical injury,[36] long periods of incarceration or custody (if the plaintiff can prove the claim),[37] and perhaps lost salary from dismissal.[38]

---

[26] *Stachura*, 477 U.S. at 300–01.

[27] Lowry v. Watson Chapel Sch. Dist., 540 F.3d 752 (8th Cir. 2008); *Dossett*, 399 F.3d at 946.

[28] Frizzell v. Szabo, 647 F.3d 698 (7th Cir. 2011).

[29] *Carey*, 435 U.S. at 266.

[30] *Id.* at 263.

[31] Bogle v. McClure, 332 F.3d 1347 (11th Cir. 2003).

[32] *Stachura*, 477 U.S. at 310.

[33] *Carey*, 435 U.S. at 266.

[34] *Id.* at 266–67; Park v. Shiflett, 250 F.3d 843 (4th Cir. 2001).

[35] Williams v. Kaufman County, 352 F.3d 994 (5th Cir. 2003).

[36] Guy v. Graham, 188 F.3d 513 (9th Cir. 1999).

[37] *Connick*, 131 S. Ct. at 1355–56; Sam Kamin, *Duke Lacrosse, Prosecutorial Misconduct, and the Limits of the Civil Justice System*, *in* INSTITUTIONAL FAILURES: DUKE LACROSSE, UNIVERSITIES, THE NEWS

That many actions end up being only for nominal damages[39] has been called the "final indignity" in § 1983 litigation — the plaintiff's rights were violated and those rights were clearly established, but those rights are not worth any money.[40] The small amounts of money involved also cast doubt on the effectiveness of private damages litigation as a means of vindicating constitutional rights. Plaintiffs lose the incentive to sue given the low value of the cases, governments and public officials lose the incentive to change their conduct or to take steps to prevent similar future abuses because the cost of any judgment is low enough to be incorporated into the basic cost of doing business.

§ 7.03 ALTERNATIVE APPROACHES TO DAMAGES

Scholarly dissatisfaction with § 1983's damages regime has produced proposals for alternative approaches to damages.

[1] Statutory Liquidated Damages

Congress could establish by statute a scheme of liquidated or presumed damages for constitutional claims, assigning a presumptive value for the constitutional right that provides a minimum guaranteed recovery, even absent proof of actual harm. The liquidated amount is recoverable on top of any actual monetary losses the plaintiff might be able to prove.[41] This approach recognizes that the real value in constitutional litigation is the usually intangible worth of the right itself; even if the plaintiff suffers significant monetary losses, those losses are a consequence of the loss of that intangible constitutional right.[42] Importantly, Congress must set the level of liquidated damages high enough to be quasi-punitive, in order to impose genuine deterrence on government actors and to give plaintiffs the incentive to pursue damages claims.[43]

Of course, the Court refused to allow recovery of value-of-the-right damages in *Stachura* and *Carey*, based on its interpretation of the 1871 Act, its history, and its relation to common law. But Congress always can override common law and establish a different statutory damages regime as part of § 1983 or *Bivens*. And having Congress define the value of the constitutional right in the statute itself, addresses the *Stachura* Court's objection to vesting the jury with unbounded discretion to arbitrarily assign value to rights.

MEDIA, AND THE LEGAL SYSTEM 43, 54 n.40 (Howard M. Wasserman ed., 2010).

[38] *Dossett*, 399 F.3d at 946.

[39] Williams v. Hobbs, 662 F.3d 994 (8th Cir. 2011); *Frizzell*, 647 F.3d at 701–02.

[40] Jon O. Newman, *Suing the Lawbreakers: Proposals to Strengthen the Section 1983 Damage Remedy for Law Enforcers' Misconduct*, 87 YALE L.J. 447, 465 (1978).

[41] *Id.* at 465.

[42] Michael L. Wells, *Civil Recourse, Damages-as-Redress, and Constitutional Torts*, 46 GA. L. REV. 1003, 1009–13 (2012).

[43] Jon O. Newman, *Suing the Lawbreakers: Proposals to Strengthen the Section 1983 Damage Remedy for Law Enforcers' Misconduct*, 87 YALE L.J. 447, 465 (1978).

[2] Civil Recourse

Second, we might adopt a different model of tort recovery. Tort damages are governed by a "loss allocation" model; this model understands monetary awards as purely compensatory, designed to "make the plaintiff whole" and place her in the position she would have been in but for the defendant's harmful behavior. But an alternative model understands damages as providing "civil recourse"; the purpose of tort law is to vindicate rights against those who have violated them, independent of any monetized harm to the plaintiff. If the state did not exist, an injured person would resort to self-help to vindicate his rights. Private rights of action simply are a state-created substitute for self-help, a way for the injured person to respond to a legal wrong in lieu of taking matters into his own hands.[44] Civil litigation is the new, state-sanctioned means by which an injured person acts against those who wronged her.

Michael Wells argues that a civil recourse is a better model for constitutional damages litigation. The "rights asserted are more vital and the defendants from who redress is sought are more powerful and more dangerous," while the injuries involved are typically intangible.[45] A civil recourse model recognizes that the point of constitutional litigation is to provide the plaintiff with recourse for the violation of a protected right, regardless of whether she shows actual physical or emotional harm.

This approach also establishes necessary equivalence among constitutional rights. A plaintiff whose free speech rights were violated when police unlawfully halted a public protest stands on equal constitutional footing with a plaintiff whose Fourth Amendment rights were violated by a police beating. Such equivalence is appropriate because both cases involve violations of protected constitutional rights; under current law, however, the latter case likely results in a larger award because the plaintiff could show substantial monetary losses.[46] The free-speech plaintiff likely recovers only $1.

A civil recourse focus would compel a number of changes to current § 1983 remedies jurisprudence, including recognition of presumed damages and rejection of the *Carey/Stachura* focus on damages-as-compensation.[47]

[3] Nominal Damages, Easier Recovery

James Pfander recognizes a link between two related problems of constitutional litigation — the difficulty of recovering substantial damages for violations of many intangible rights and the high hurdle of qualified immunity. His solution is to enable and encourage plaintiffs to bring claims explicitly seeking only nominal

---

[44] Michael L. Wells, *Civil Recourse, Damages-as-Redress, and Constitutional Torts*, 46 GA. L. REV. 1003, 1010 (2012) (discussing Benjamin C. Zipursky, *Rights, Wrongs, and Recourse in the Law of Torts*, 51 VAND. L. REV. 1 (1998)).

[45] Michael L. Wells, *Civil Recourse, Damages-as-Redress, and Constitutional Torts*, 46 GA. L. REV. 1003, 1012 (2012).

[46] *Id.* at 1019.

[47] *Id.* at 1022–25.

damages of $1, while expressly waiving any claim for substantial compensatory damages, in exchange for eliminating the qualified immunity defense in such cases.[48]

Pfander argues that the main policy goals underlying qualified immunity — protecting government officials from personal liability, protecting officials from the distractions and burdens of litigation, and enabling the development and evolution of constitutional law through judicial decisions on the merits — all are furthered by allowing claims for nominal damages free of qualified immunity. Courts can clarify and vindicate constitutional norms in situations of legal uncertainty, while imposing no substantial personal liability or costs on the officers or the government that indemnifies him.[49] Nominal damages claims would function like claims for prospective relief against executive officers, which are not subject to qualified immunity[50] and which proceed without concerns for interfering with or distracting government officials from doing their jobs.

Pfander argues that such a limited, nominal-damages-only action would appeal to two classes of plaintiffs: (1) those who have suffered constitutional injuries with minimal, modest, or symbolic value, who currently must overcome a qualified immunity defense under current law; and (2) plaintiffs who have suffered substantial damages, where the unsettled state of the law means they likely will lose on qualified immunity grounds. The court and parties could focus entirely on resolving the constitutional merits and developing constitutional law without the distraction of qualified immunity or its competing policies, a change most plaintiffs should welcome.[51]

§ 7.04 PUNITIVE DAMAGES

The other monetary remedy in actions at law is punitive damages. The Supreme Court first held punitive damages are not available against municipalities,[52] then two years later held they are available against individual officers.[53] As with other areas in which it fills gaps in §1983, the Court looked to the common law in 1871, as well as the purposes of § 1983 and of punitive damages. The purposes of punitive damages — retribution and deterrence — are meaningless as to entities, independent of any retribution or deterrence of the officials themselves.[54] We achieve adequate deterrence and retribution as to a muncipality through punitive damages against the officers.[55] And the generally accepted availability of punitive damages

---

[48] James E. Pfander, *Resolving the Qualified Immunity Dilemma: Constitutional Tort Claims for Nominal Damages*, 111 Colum. L. Rev. 1601, 1610–11, 1628–29 (2011).

[49] *Id.* 1624–25, 1627–29; *see also* Camreta v. Greene, 131 S. Ct. 2020, 2044 (2011) (Kennedy, J., dissenting).

[50] Adler v. Pataki, 185 F.3d 35, 48 (2d Cir. 1999).

[51] James E. Pfander, *Resolving the Qualified Immunity Dilemma: Constitutional Tort Claims for Nominal Damages*, 111 Colum. L. Rev. 1601, 1627–28 (2011); *supra* Chapter 3, Part C.

[52] Newport v. Fact Concerts, Inc., 453 U.S. 247 (1981).

[53] Smith v. Wade, 461 U.S. 30 (1983).

[54] Newport v. Fact Concerts, Inc., 453 U.S. 247 (1981).

[55] *Smith*, 461 U.S. at 36 n.5; *Fact Concerts*, 453 U.S. at 269–70.

against individual state officers under § 1983 prompted the Court to conclude that they also are available against individual federal under *Bivens*.[56]

A plaintiff can recover punitive damages "when the defendant's conduct is shown to be motivated by evil motive or intent, or when it involves reckless or callous indifference to the federally protected rights of others." This is a subjective rather than objective standard, requiring that the defendant had "a 'subjective consciousness' of a risk of injury or illegality and a 'criminal indifference to civil obligations.' "[57]

The amount of punitive damages recoverable may be limited by the Due Process Clause, which prohibits the award of "grossly excessive" punitive damages.[58] Several considerations guide the analysis of when an award is unconstitutionally excessive: (1) the degree of reprehensibility of the misconduct (typically the most important consideration); (2) the disparity between the harm or potential harm (as indicated in the award of compensatory damages) and the punitive damages award; and (3) the difference between this remedy and the civil penalties authorized or imposed in comparable cases.[59] Extreme ratios between compensatory and punitive damages are presumptively invalid, although ratios beyond single digits may occasionally be permissible.[60]

Punitive damages arguably provide the most significant deterrence. Given the standard, punitive damages will be in play only with extreme constitutional misconduct, where the law is clearly established and qualified immunity is overcome. Many governments do not indemnify officers for the malicious or willful misconduct that will warrant punitive damages.[61] Thus, punitive damages often represent the only substantial money for which an officer will be personally on the hook.

One concern is how due process limitations on punitive damages apply when the plaintiff recovers nominal damages; after all, if ratios of 145:1 or 500:1 are invalid, that might suggest that significant punitive damages are impermissible on an award of $1 in nominal damages. But the Supreme Court's due process cases expressly recognize that strict ratios are inappropriate and higher ratios may be necessary where the plaintiff incurs only small economic damages or where the monetary value of a loss is difficult to determine.[62] Courts depart from strict ratios on constitutional claims involving extreme, particularly egregious conduct,[63] where

---

[56] Carlson v. Green, 446 U.S. 14, 22 (1980).

[57] Kolstad v. ADA, 527 U.S. 526, 536 (1999) (quoting *Smith*, 461 U.S. at 37 n.6).

[58] State Farm Mut. Auto. Ins. Co. v. Campbell, 538 U.S. 408 (2003).

[59] *Id.* at 418.

[60] *Id.* at 425; *see also* Payne v. Jones, 696 F.3d 189, 201–03 (2d Cir. 2012) (discussing different situations in which double-digit ratio may be proper and 1:1 ratio may be excessive).

[61] Martin A. Schwartz, *Should Juries Be Informed That Municipality Will Indemnify Officer's § 1983 Liability for Constitutional Wrongdoing?*, 86 Iowa L. Rev. 1209, 1220 (2001).

[62] *State Farm*, 538 U.S. at 425; BMW of N. Am. v. Gore, 517 U.S. 559, 582 (1996).

[63] Williams v. Kaufman County, 352 F.3d 994 (5th Cir. 2003); Lee v. Edwards, 101 F.3d 805 (2d Cir. 1996).

strict proportionality would entirely eliminate the ability to award or recover punitive damages.[64]

PART B
"SUIT IN EQUITY": PROSPECTIVE RELIEF

§ 7.05   INTRODUCTION TO PROSPECTIVE OR EQUITABLE RELIEF

[1]   Injunctive Relief Categorized

The primary form of prospective or relief in constitutional and civil rights litigation is the injunction, a court order prohibiting the defending parties from taking some action or compelling them to take some action. Injunctions can be categorized along several axes.

One distinguishes negative and positive injunctions. Negative injunctions order governments and officers to stop doing something — most commonly, to stop enforcing an unconstitutional law or policy. A particular law or policy violates the Constitution and is causing the plaintiff some injury, usually through the threat of enforcement, she asks the court for an injunction prohibiting executive officers from enforcing the law, leaving her free to engage in her constitutionally protected conduct. These are the cases in which abstention is likely to arise, depending on the status of state enforcement efforts and the clarity of the law to be enforced.[65] On the other hand, positive injunctions compel government and government officers to do something, to take affirmative steps or efforts to remedy a constitutional problem, defect, or violation.

A second axis distinguishes legislative and administrative injunctions. Legislative injunctions afford relief from unconstitutional legislation by prohibiting its enforcement (although not its enactment). Administrative injunctions provide relief from unconstitutional administration of programs and policies, such as public-welfare or public-benefits programs or institutions, such as schools and prisons.[66] Administrative injunctions compel government to restructure its institutions and bureaucracies, bringing their systems into constitutional compliance and preventing future violations.

Broadly speaking, legislative injunctions correspond with negative injunctions ("stop enforcing this piece of legislation"), while administrative injunctions correspond with positive injunctions ("administer state institutions and programs in a certain way to alleviate constitutional defects going forward"). The distinction also maps with how close a particular action for injunctive relief comes to the core

---

[64] *Williams*, 352 F.3d at 1016.

[65] *Supra* Chapter 6.

[66] Va. Office for Prot. & Advocacy v. Stewart, 131 S. Ct. 1632 (2011); Horne v. Flores, 557 U.S. 433 (2009); Quern v. Jordan, 440 U.S. 332 (1979); Edelman v. Jordan, 415 U.S. 651 (1974); Swann v. Charlotte-Mecklenburg Bd. of Educ., 402 U.S. 1 (1971).

of *Ex parte Young.*[67] On one view of *Young* (espoused by John Harrison and recently suggested by Justices Kennedy and Thomas in a concurring opinion), *Young* is only about true anti-suit injunctions — anticipatory or pre-emptive actions to enjoin initiation state officers from initiating judicial proceedings to enforce state law, where the claim in equity is a defense that otherwise would have been available in the enforcement proceeding.[68] In other words, the core of *Young* is a negative or legislative injunction. But *Young* has expanded to allow all prospective injunctive relief to stop or change unconstitutional behavior in all state action administering laws, policies, programs, and institutions.[69] In other words, *Young* has extended (inappropriately, Harrison suggests) to positive or administrative injunctions.

[2] Seeking Injunctive Relief

Injunctive relief consists of three distinct remedies considered at three stages of the case. First is a Temporary Restraining Order. Typically issued *ex parte*, this order lasts for a brief, defined period (in federal court, not to exceed 14 days) and is intended to preserve matters until all parties can receive notice and the court can hold a fuller adversarial hearing.[70] Second is a Preliminary Injunction. Issued following an adversarial hearing fairly early in the case, this order makes a preliminary determination on the merits and is intended to preserve the status quo until a final decision is made on the claim.[71] In constitutional cases, both a TRO and preliminary injunction, if granted, prohibit government from engaging in the allegedly unconstitutional conduct or enforcing allegedly unconstitutional policies, and allow the plaintiff to continue to engage in arguably protected conduct without fear of enforcement until the litigation is resolved.[72] Third is a Permanent Injunction; this is a final judgment on the merits, issued following a full trial on the merits of the claim.

The test for all three forms of injunctive relief consists of five conjunctive elements, with sliding levels of proof depending on the motion and the stage of proceedings.[73] First, and most importantly, a plaintiff must show a substantial likelihood of success on the merits (at the TRO and preliminary stages) or actual success on the merits of the claim (for a permanent injunction); in other words, the plaintiff must persuade the court that the challenged law or policy violates the Constitution. The showing a plaintiff must make on this prong depends on the stage of the case; the proof of unconstitutionality necessary for a permanent

---

[67] *Supra* § 4.13[3].

[68] *Stewart*, 131 S. Ct. at 1642–43 (Kennedy, J., joined by Thomas, J., concurring); John Harrison, Ex Parte Young, 60 STAN. L. REV. 989, 1009 (2008); John Harrison, *Jurisdiction, Congressional Power, and Constitutional Remedies*, 86 GEO. L.J. 2513, 2519–20 (1998).

[69] *Stewart*, 131 S. Ct. at 1638; *Quern*, 440 U.S. at 346–49.

[70] FED. R. CIV. P. 65(b)(2).

[71] Sole v. Wyner, 551 U.S. 74 (2007); Doran v. Salem Inn, Inc., 422 U.S. 922 (1975).

[72] *Doran*, 422 U.S. at 925; Steffel v. Thompson, 415 U.S. 452 (1974).

[73] Winter v. NRDC, Inc., 555 U.S. 7 (2008); Salazar v. Buono, 559 U.S. 700 (2010).

injunction is greater than the proof necessary for a TRO.[74] Again, because there historically was no jury in courts of equity and because the Seventh Amendment civil jury right applies only to "suits at Common Law," meaning claims for legal relief, the court, rather than a jury, acts as fact-finder on all claims for injunctive relief.[75]

Second, a plaintiff must show that she will suffer irreparable injury unless the injunction is issued, with irreparable injury presumed in constitutional actions.[76] Third, the plaintiff must show that she has no adequate remedy at law. This harkens to the historic divide in England between courts of law and courts of equity or chancery, a divide brought to the United States; equity was established as an alternative adjudicative system to which a party can and should turn only when resort to the common law courts (and common law remedies) would not provide sufficient relief for the injury. Fourth, the court balances whether the injury to the movant from not obtaining an injunction is greater than the injury or harm to the non-movant if the injunction is issued. Fifth, the court considers whether an injunction is in the public interest. The first and third are the primary elements in play in constitutional injunction litigation with the second element generally presumed.

A typical constitutional action for injunctive relief proceeds as follows. A federal, state, or local law, regulation, or policy is on the books and enforceable and its enforcement violates some constitutional right; the plaintiff seeks to prohibit enforcement of that law or policy (a negative/legislative injunction) or to compel affirmative changes to the way laws are administered (a positive/administrative injunction). The action names as defendants the executive officers responsible for enforcing those laws and policies, under the theory of *Ex parte Young.* These executive officers all act under color of state (or federal) law in enforcing (or threatening to enforce) the challenged laws and policies. The plaintiff is deprived of a right, privilege, or immunity secured by the Constitution from the enforcement or threatened enforcement. And the remedy sought is an injunction, making this a "suit in equity."

A plaintiff also may sue a municipal entity (although not the state or federal governments), which is a person for § 1983 purposes. In *Los Angeles County v. Humphries,* the Court clarified that the standards for municipal liability are the same for equitable relief as for damages — the plaintiff always must show that a municipal policy, custom, or failure-to-[blank] with the requisite degree of fault caused the violation sought to be enjoined.[77] As a practical matter, this requirement always will be satisfied in actions for prospective relief. Plaintiffs are challenging the constitutional validity of a particular statute, ordinance, or rule, as opposed to the past actions of an individual officer. The plaintiff can obtain prospective relief only by showing that she is suffering a current and ongoing

----

[74] *Sole,* 551 U.S. at 84.

[75] City of Monterey v. Del Monte Dunes, Ltd., 526 U.S. 687, 719 (1999); Wilson v. Bailey, 934 F.2d 301, 305 (11th Cir. 1991); *supra* § 7.01 nn.4–6; *supra* § 5.04.

[76] Obama for Am. v. Husted, 697 F.3d 423 (6th Cir. 2012).

[77] Los Angeles County v. Humphries, 131 S. Ct. 447 (2010).

injury or is threatened with a future injury, [78] she must show that a formal legal rule (such as a statute or ordinance) or semi-formal custom remains in place that, if enforced or followed, is violating or will violate her constitutional rights. Isolated or random individual misconduct, such as future use of excessive force by an unknown individual officer, is too uncertain and unpredictable to cause an ongoing or likely future injury justifying an injunction,[79] unless some policy authorizes or requires that misconduct. And if such a formal rule or policy exists, the *Monell* standard for municipal liability is satisfied.

That the policy-or-custom requirement is easily satisfied, however, does not mean it is unnecessary; it simply means the requirement will make little practical significance.[80] *Humphries* presents the rare equitable case in which liability of the defendant county officers could be disaggregated from county policy. The plaintiffs sued over delays in removing their names from an index of people accused of child abuse; they argued that the defendant county officials failed to remove their names despite repeated requests and that state law failed to establish a process for doing so.[81] Although the defendants were county-level officials, they were enforcing unconstitutional state policies. Thus, while it was proper for the court to find state law constitutionally defective and to enjoin county officers from continuing to follow and enforce those unconstitutional state policies, it was not proper to impose any remedy against the county itself, since no county (as opposed to state) policies caused the violation in the case.[82]

Along with the complaint identifying injunctive relief as the remedy sought,[83] a plaintiff files a motion for a TRO or Preliminary Injunction,[84] which, if granted, allows her to continue to engage in her arguably protected conduct without fear of enforcement of the challenged law during pendency of litigation. Prior to 1976, a claim seeking to enjoin enforcement of a state (although not local) law[85] or a federal law[86] on the ground of its unconstitutionality was heard by a three-judge district court.[87] Under current law,[88] most cases are heard by a single judge, as with any other action in the district court, except in apportionment cases or where Congress otherwise provides,[89] as by requiring in a piece of legislation that any challenges to the legislation must be heard by a three-judge court.[90]

---

[78] Los Angeles v. Lyons, 461 U.S. 95 (1983).

[79] *Cf.* Rizzo v. Goode, 423 U.S. 362 (1976).

[80] *Humphries*, 131 S. Ct. at 453.

[81] *Id.* at 449–50.

[82] *Id.* at 450.

[83] FED. R. CIV. P. 8(a)(3).

[84] FED. R. CIV. P. 65.

[85] 28 U.S.C. § 2281 (repealed).

[86] 28 U.S.C. § 2282 (repealed).

[87] *Supra* § 4.13[4].

[88] 28 U.S.C. § 2284(a); Act of Aug. 12, 1976, Pub. L. No. 94-381, 90 Stat. 1119 (1976).

[89] *See, e.g.*, 18 U.S.C. § 3626(a)(3)(B) (three-judge panel required in any request for a prisoner-release order in constitutional challenge to prison conditions).

[90] *See, e.g.*, Communications Decency Act of 1996, Pub. L. No. 104-104, § 561, 110 Stat. 133 (1996).

Current procedure for three-judge courts under § 2284 is the same as it was under the former mandatory three-judge statutes. When the lawsuit is filed, the case is assigned to a single district judge and either party can request a three-judge court. If appropriate, the assigned judge refers the case to the chief judge of the circuit, who assigns two more judges to the case, at least one of whom is a circuit judge, with the original assigned district judge as the third member of the court. The original district judge handles all preliminary matters, including discovery and any request for a temporary restraining order; the fuller hearing or trial on a preliminary or permanent injunction is before all three judges,[91] with immediate Supreme Court review.[92]

When the case is heard by a single district judge, the decision granting or denying a preliminary injunction is immediately appealable as of right to the court of appeals,[93] although the grant or denial of a TRO is not.[94] This distinction makes sense. A preliminary injunction is generally decided on a fuller record following an often-extensive adversarial hearing, sometimes with significant fact-finding that produces a meaningful record for appellate review;[95] a TRO is generally decided ex parte on less than thorough briefing and a less extensive record for review.[96]Once the decision on the preliminary injunction is appealed to the court of appeals, further review can be sought in the Supreme Court.[97] As a practical matter, many constitutional challenges to state and federal statutes reach the Supreme Court on review of the decision on the preliminary injunction.[98]

If the district court grants a preliminary injunction following a full hearing on the constitutional merits with extensive fact-finding (whether affirmed on appeal or not appealed at all), the district court may simply convert it to a permanent injunction, unless new information, evidence, or legal arguments are likely to be presented; otherwise, the court has heard and considered everything at the preliminary injunction stage and no more is necessary to make the injunction permanent.[99] The permanent injunction constitutes a final and appealable judgment.[100] Alternatively, if the district court denies a preliminary injunction and is reversed on appeal, the district court may either hold further evidentiary hearings as necessary or convert the preliminary injunction to a permanent injunction.

---

[91] 28 U.S.C. § 2284(b); Hicks v. Miranda, 422 U.S. 332, 338 (1975).

[92] 28 U.S.C. § 1253.

[93] 28 U.S.C. § 1292(a)(1).

[94] SEIU v. Nat'l Union of Healthcare Workers, 598 F.3d 1061 (9th Cir. 2010).

[95] FED. R. CIV. P. 65 (a)(2).

[96] *But see* Religious Tech. Ctr., Church of Scientology Int'l, Inc. v. Scott, 869 F.2d 1306 (9th Cir. 1989) (order denominated TRO but issued on adversarial hearing and fuller record treated as preliminary injunction and proper for immediate appeal).

[97] 28 U.S.C.§ 1254.

[98] New York State Bd. of Elections v. Lopez-Torres, 552 U.S. 196 (2008); Doran v. Salem Inn, Inc., 422 U.S. 922 (1975).

[99] Shell Co. (P.R.) v. Los Frailes Serv. Station, 605 F.3d 10 (1st Cir. 2010).

[100] 28 U.S.C. § 1291.

An injunction constitutes an ongoing court order subject to continuing judicial monitoring and enforcement. A plaintiff can move the court to enforce the injunction where the defendant is not complying with its terms and the court can issue subsequent orders to ensure compliance with its original decree.[101] With a negative injunction, this may include an order specifically precluding a renewed effort or threat to enforce a law where the court already enjoined enforcement. With a positive injunction, the court may order the parties to take whatever affirmative steps are required under the original or subsequent orders. A court also may enforce an injunction by sanctioning the parties who violate it, primarily through contempt of court.[102] Either party also may move to modify or dissolve an injunction, either because some portion no longer is appropriate or because it no longer is sufficient to remedy the constitutional violation.[103]

[3] Declaratory Relief

28 U.S.C. § 2201(a)

In a case of actual controversy within its jurisdiction, except . . . any court of the United States, upon the filing of an appropriate pleading, may declare the rights and other legal relations of any interested party seeking such declaration, whether or not further relief is or could be sought. Any such declaration shall have the force and effect of a final judgment or decree and shall be reviewable as such.

28 U.S.C. § 2202

Further necessary or proper relief based on a declaratory judgment or decree may be granted, after reasonable notice and hearing, against any adverse party whose rights have been determined by such judgment.

A second form of prospective relief is the declaratory judgment, a declaration from the court of the rights of, and legal relations between, the parties. For civil rights purposes, this means a declaration that a law is constitutionally invalid and unenforceable by the defendant against the plaintiff, and that the plaintiff is constitutionally entitled to engage in some conduct. Congress enacted the Declaratory Judgment Act in 1934, a delayed reaction to, and effort to limit, *Ex parte Young* by providing an alternative, less intrusive remedy.[104] Because the declaratory judgment was created after the law/equity merger, it is not formally classified as either legal or equitable.[105]Nevertheless, declaratory judgments are treated as equitable for Seventh Amendment purposes; the court generally acts as fact-finder,

---

[101] McDowell v. Phila. Hous. Auth., 423 F.3d 233 (3d Cir. 2005); Brennan v. Nassau County, 352 F.3d 60 (2d Cir. 2003).

[102] Ex parte Young, 209 U.S. 123, 126 (1908); Hawkins v. HHS, 665 F.3d 25 (1st Cir. 2012).

[103] Fed. R. Civ. P. 60(b); Agostini v. Felton, 521 U.S. 203 (1997); Rufo v. Inmates of Suffolk County Jail, 502 U.S. 367(1992).

[104] 28 U.S.C. §§ 2201–2202; Steffel v. Thompson, 415 U.S. 452 (1974); *supra* § 4.13[4].

[105] Douglas Laycock, Modern American Remedies: Cases and Materials 6 (4th ed. 2010).

particularly when the claim for declaratory relief is intertwined with the claim for an injunction.[106]

Declaratory judgments offer a "milder form of relief" than the "strong medicine of the injunction."[107] Federal courts can resolve constitutional issues and protect constitutional rights against infringing state laws while intruding less on federalism and state authority, since a declaratory judgment is not coercive, imposes no formal restraints on state officials, and is not enforceable through contempt. Declaratory judgments function through persuasion, convincing state officers (through the force of reason and the strength of the court's analysis) of their constitutional obligations and of the need to reconsider and change their policies or their enforcement plans.[108] The declaratory judgment may form the basis for a later injunction on a showing of the other elements for relief.[109]

As a practical matter, most plaintiffs seeking prospective relief request both remedies simultaneously.[110] But they cannot do this in actions against judges in their judicial capacity. The Supreme Court held in *Pulliam v. Allen* that judicial immunity does not protect a state court judge from a § 1983 claim for injunctive relief in federal court or prevent a federal court from enjoining a state judge.[111] *Pulliam* was limited (although not overruled) by the Federal Courts Improvement Act of 1996,[112] which added a new clause to the basic cause of action in § 1983 reading: "except that in any action brought against a judicial officer for an act or omission taken in such officer's judicial capacity, injunctive relief shall not be granted unless a declaratory decree was violated or declaratory relief was unavailable."[113] This statutory change means a plaintiff cannot immediately obtain an injunction controlling a judge acting in a judicial capacity (performing functions to which judicial immunity would otherwise attach). The plaintiff must first seek a declaration that the judge's conduct violates the Constitution; only if the declaratory judgment is obtained and ignored, or if such remedy is inadequate at the outset, will the plaintiff then be able to seek and obtain an injunction.[114]

[4] Consent Decrees

A third form of prospective relief is a consent decree, a judicial order granting injunctive relief where the details of the order have been consented to by the parties. As discussed in greater detail below, a consent decree is essentially a

---

[106] Johnson v. Randle, 2012 U.S. Dist. LEXIS 75080 (S.D. Ill. May 31, 2012); DL v. District of Columbia, 845 F. Supp. 2d 1 (D.D.C. 2011); *supra* § 5.04..

[107] *Steffel*, 415 U.S. at 466, 470–71.

[108] *Id.* at 470–71.

[109] 28 U.S.C. § 2202; Samuels v. Mackell, 401 U.S. 66 (1971).

[110] DL v. District of Columbia, 845 F. Supp. 2d 1 (D.D.C. 2011).

[111] Pulliam v. Allen, 466 U.S. 522, 543 (1984); § 3.08[3].

[112] Federal Courts Improvement Act of 1996, Pub. L. No. 104-317, 110 Stat. 3847 (1996).

[113] 42 U.S.C. § 1983 (as amended by Federal Courts Improvement Act of 1996, Pub. L. No. 104-317, 110 Stat. 3847 (1996)).

[114] Brandon E. ex rel. Listenbee v. Reynolds, 201 F.3d 194, 197–98 (3d Cir. 2000). A fuller discussion of the distinctions and connections between injunctive and declaratory relief appears, Ch. 6 and Ch. 7.

settlement on an injunction (usually a positive or administrative injunction), where the parties have negotiated and agreed to the terms of the relief provided and those terms have been incorporated into an enforceable judicial decree. A consent decree is contractual in nature, since the parties agreed to the terms, but entered with the expectation that it would be enforced like any other judicial order. A consent decree has the force and effect of a final judgment granting injunctive relief and is enforced and monitored by the court according to the same rules as all other judicial decrees.[115]

[5] Remedial Hierarchy

The historic relationship between courts of law and courts of equity, and thus between legal and equitable relief, rested on a remedial hierarchy under which legal remedies were preferred and equitable relief was available only if no adequate legal remedy were available. That hierarchy survives in the requirement that a plaintiff show she cannot obtain sufficient relief in a proceeding at law (which includes being able to assert constitutional issues as a defendant in state proceedings) in order to get an injunction.

But this hierarchy arguably has flipped in constitutional litigation, where equitable relief (injunctions and declaratory judgments) has become the preferred remedy. Significant defenses have built-up around damages claims but not equitable claims. For example, qualified immunity is grounded in an explicit concern for the negative effects of personal damages awards on government officials and their ability to perform their public functions; those concerns are absent, and qualified immunity not available,[116] when officers are defending injunctive actions that do not target or threaten their pocketbook. In fact, James Pfander's proposal to eliminate qualified immunity in nominal-damages cases rests on the idea that a claim for nominal damages is functionally the same as a claim for equitable relief because it does not impose burdensome personal liability on the defendant; since qualified immunity is not available in the latter, it is unnecessary in the former.[117]

In addition, an action for equitable relief is more consistent with the private attorney general concept. Injunctive relief more obviously and more directly inures to the public benefit and it is easier to conceptualize an action for an injunction as furthering public rather than purely private interests. If a plaintiff wins a positive injunction requiring government to take steps to alleviate unconstitutional conditions (for example, alleviating overcrowding in prison or changing discriminatory policies in public education), similarly situated prisoners or students reap the benefits of that injunction. It is less clear whether a negative injunction prohibiting state officials from enforcing a statute as to the plaintiff (for example, because his speech is constitutionally protected) necessarily prohibits

---

[115] Buckhannon Bd. & Care Home, Inc. v. W. Va. Dep't of Health & Human Res., 532 U.S. 598 (2001); Rufo v. Inmates of Suffolk County Jail, 502 U.S. 367 (1992).

[116] Adler v. Pataki, 185 F.3d 35, 48 (2d Cir. 1999).

[117] James E. Pfander, *Resolving the Qualified Immunity Dilemma: Constitutional Tort Claims for Nominal Damages*, 111 COLUM. L. REV. 1601, 1634 (2011); *supra* § 7.03[3].

officials from enforcing the statute against other, similarly situated would-be speakers who were not parties to the action. At the very least, however, a negative injunction prohibiting enforcement as to the plaintiff may function like a declaratory judgment as to enforcement against similarly situated persons, persuading the government or other courts that the law being enforced is constitutionally suspect.

§ 7.06 STANDING AND PROSPECTIVE RELIEF

A plaintiff bringing a claim in federal court must establish an "actual case or controversy" for purposes of Article III of the United States Constitution.[118] One aspect of the case-or-controversy requirement is that the plaintiff has a "personal stake in the outcome" and therefore standing to bring the action.[119] The irreducible constitutional minimum of standing is that the plaintiff suffer a personal injury that is fairly traceable to the defendant's unlawful conduct and is likely to be redressed by the requested relief.[120] The plaintiff's injury must be more than abstract; she must show that she "has sustained or is immediately in danger of sustaining some direct injury," that the injury or threat of injury is both "real and immediate," and not "conjectural" or "hypothetical,"[121] and that the threatened injury is "certainly impending."[122] Moreover, the injury must be unique to the plaintiff, not one held in common by all members of the public; a plaintiff cannot assert a "generalized" or "undifferentiated" injury on behalf of the public as a whole.[123] And no plaintiff has standing to assert a general right to be free from unconstitutional laws and policies.[124]

Showing injury-in-fact is straightforward enough in an action for retrospective relief (damages) for a past, completed constitutional injury. It is more difficult in actions for prospective relief, where the plaintiff must present facts showing that some unconstitutional rule, policy, or conduct is presently causing or immediately threatening unique, personal harm to her. Past exposure to unlawful conduct does not provide standing to seek relief against future unlawful conduct, absent present and continuing adverse effects of the past misconduct. Past wrongs at most are evidence of a real and immediate threat of future injury, but they are not sufficient by themselves without some evidence of prospective injury.[125] Standing thus may split along remedial lines, even in a single action; a plaintiff may have standing to pursue damages for past harms but not injunctive relief against future harms, even from the same policies or conduct.

---

[118] O'Shea v. Littleton, 414 U.S. 488 (1974); U.S. Const. art. III, § 2.

[119] Los Angeles v. Lyons, 461 U.S. 95 (1983).

[120] Lujan v. Defenders of Wildlife, 504 U.S. 555 (1992).

[121] *Lyons*, 461 U.S. at 102.

[122] Clapper v. Amnesty Int'l USA, 133 S. Ct. 1138, 1143 (2013).

[123] *Id.* at 111.

[124] Rizzo v. Goode, 423 U.S. 362 (1976).

[125] *Lyons*, 461 U.S. at 103, 104.

For example, a plaintiff can establish standing to challenge a municipal ordinance prohibiting nude dancing by showing that he has a present intention and desire to operate a nude-dancing establishment in the town, that he remains subject to the ordinance, and that enforcement of the ordinance prevents him from engaging in what he argues is constitutionally protected conduct.[126] A plaintiff similarly has standing to challenge threatened enforcement of a criminal trespass ordinance by showing he has a present intention and desire to distribute handbills on certain property, he is presently threatened with enforcement of the law, and the threat prevents him from engaging in this protected conduct.[127] On the other hand, a plaintiff cannot show an impending injury where he will not be subject to enforcement of the challenged regulations in the future because he will not be engaging in similar conduct in a similar context at a definite time in the future.[128]

In many anticipatory actions for prospective relief against enforcement of a constitutionally suspect law, the plaintiff is not the individual whose rights are affected, but an association or organization representing members or participants whose rights are affected. Associations or organizations generally have standing to sue on behalf of their members, and to assert their members' constitutional rights, when the members would otherwise have standing to sue in their own right, the interests the association seeks to protect are germane to its purpose, and neither the claim asserted nor the relief requested requires the participation of individual members in the lawsuit.[129] Thus, for example, a trade association can sue on behalf of all its members in challenging a restriction on all members' rights;[130] a public-advocacy group has standing to challenge a federal law infringing the freedom of speech of all of its members;[131] and a union has standing to challenge a random drug-testing policy that allegedly constitutes an unreasonable search of all of its members.[132]

Standing becomes more difficult where the constitutional challenge is not to a law regulating primary real-world conduct (such as a discriminatory employment policy or a law directly infringing protected speech), but to the policies that law enforcement agencies follow and the manner in which they investigate and enforce those laws. A plaintiff has standing when she shows that she wants to engage in particular constitutionally protected conduct (such as sponsoring nude dancing), but is prevented from doing so by a unconstitutional law or ordinance. This is especially so for pre-enforcement First Amendment claims, where courts apply "somewhat relaxed" standing rules[133] on what one court referred to a " 'hold your tongue and challenge now' approach rather than requiring litigants to speak first and take their

---

[126] Doran v. Salem Inn, Inc., 422 U.S. 922 (1975).

[127] Steffel v. Thompson, 415 U.S. 452 (1974).

[128] Marcavage v. City of New York, 689 F.3d 98 (2d Cir. 2012).

[129] Hunt v. Washington State Apple Adver. Comm'n, 432 U.S. 333, 343 (1977).

[130] *See, e.g.*, *Hunt*, 432 U.S. at 343–44; Warth v. Seldin, 422 U.S. 490 (1975) (private organization of builders and contractors).

[131] Reno v. ACLU, 521 U.S. 844 (1997) (plaintiffs were several associations of internet-based publishers and speakers).

[132] Skinner v. Railway Labor Execs. Ass'n, 489 U.S. 602 (1989).

[133] Nat'l Org. for Marriage, Inc. v. Walsh, 714 F.3d 682 (2d Cir. 2013).

chances with the consequences."[134] It is less clear where the plaintiff wants to challenge the way laws will be enforced if she should come in contact with the law enforcement or criminal justice systems. Standing here requires a presumption or speculation that the plaintiff will in the future violate some valid criminal law, bringing him into contact with constitutional violations in the underlying criminal justice process, a presumption courts are not willing to make.[135]

Two cases illustrate this point. One is *City of Los Angeles v. Lyons*. The plaintiff was stopped (properly, it appears) for a traffic violation and in the course of the stop, the police officers applied a chokehold, in accordance with municipal policy and custom, which caused him to lose consciousness and damaged his larynx. The plaintiff sought damages from the city and the officers for the injuries sustained. He also sought an injunction barring the department from teaching or authorizing the use of such chokeholds in future circumstances in which officers are not threatened with deadly force.[136]

The Court held that the plaintiff lacked standing to challenge municipal policy with respect to future use of the chokehold. He could not show a real and immediate threat that he would be stopped by police in the future or that, if stopped, he would be subject to an illegal chokehold without provocation. The plaintiff must show not only that he would have another encounter with police for a traffic violation or some other unlawful conduct; he also must show that he would be subject to a chokehold, whether because all officers always use it in all situations or because the plaintiff would resist arrest and thus warrant a chokehold. But the plaintiff could not make this showing about future events beyond speculation or conjecture.[137] The Court would not assume that Lyons would be arrested in the future. The likelihood of Lyons himself being stopped and choked was no greater than any other citizen in Los Angeles, meaning he was no more entitled to an injunction against the use of chokeholds than any other citizen.[138] His claim amounted to nothing more than an allegation that he had an undifferentiated right, in common with all other citizens, not to be subject to chokeholds in unknowable future circumstances.

The same analysis explains the Court's most recent statement on standing in constitutional actions in *Clapper v. Amnesty International USA*. A group of attorneys and human rights, media, labor, and legal organizations challenged on Fourth Amendment grounds a federal statute allowing government surveillance of communications with certain non-U.S. persons located overseas. The Court held that the plaintiffs lacked standing to challenge the surveillance law because they could not show that an injury to them was "certainly impending" as a result of the existence and possible use of the surveillance law.[139] Any future injury was

---

[134] Lopez v. Candaele, 630 F.3d 775, 785 (9th Cir. 2010).

[135] *Lyons*, 461 U.S. at 108; *Rizzo*, 423 U.S. at 372; *O'Shea*, 414 U.S. at 497; Erwin Chemerinsky, *The Story of* City of Los Angeles v. Lyons: *Closing the Federal Courthouse Doors, in* CIVIL RIGHTS STORIES 131, 148 (Myriam E. Gilles & Risa L. Goluboff eds., 2008).

[136] *Lyons*, 461 U.S. at 97–98.

[137] *Id.* at 105–06, 107–08.

[138] *Id.* at 108.

[139] Clapper v. Amnesty Intern. USA, 133 S. Ct. 1138, 1144-45, 1147 (2013).

speculative and dependent on a number of assumptions courts could not make at that point — including that the federal government would decide to intercept the communications of people with whom the plaintiffs will communicate, that those interception efforts will succeed, and that the intercepted communications will be ones to which the plaintiffs themselves are party.[140] As in *Lyons*, the plaintiffs in *Clapper* could not show with certainty if, when, or how they would come in contact with government efforts in enforcing substantive law (here by monitoring foreign telecommunications) and the Court was unwilling to speculate about or assume such contact. Plaintiffs therefore could not show a sufficient impending future injury to them caused by the wiretap law.

§ 7.07   ADMINISTRATIVE INJUNCTIONS AND STRUCTURAL REFORM LITIGATION

The line between positive and negative injunctions and between administrative and legislative injunctions can be illustrated by comparing the two Supreme Court opinions in the *Brown v. Board of Education* litigation. In *Brown I*, the Court declared that *de jure* segregation and the system of separate-but-equal in public school violated the Equal Protection Clause; the Court prohibited states from continuing to adhere to state law and operate segregated schools.[141] This was a negative or legislative injunction — a command to state and local officials to stop enforcing unconstitutional state laws requiring segregated schools. In *Brown II*, the Court, having already found that legally imposed separate-but-equal violates the Constitution, ordered recalcitrant states to act with "all deliberate speed" to integrate public schools.[142] This was a positive or administrative injunction — a command to operate and administer schools in a particular way fully integrated — and to restructure their operations and institutions bringing them into compliance with the Constitution and preventing future violations.

The experience of *Brown* demonstrates that something more than a negative, "stop enforcing unconstitutional laws" injunction is necessary to ensure that public institutions operate in a constitutional manner. Courts must impose positive obligations on government officials to change the way they administer the state education aparatus to achieve constitutional ends related to integration, financing, and the general adequacy of education.[143] Thus was born "structural reform litigation," litigation undertaken to end unconstitutional practices in public institutions through positive injunctions ordering government to fundamentally reform how it is structured and how it operates.[144] This litigation model soon expanded

---

[140] *Id.* at 1148.

[141] Brown v. Board of Educ., 347 U.S. 483 (1954) (*Brown I*).

[142] Brown v. Board of Educ., 349 U.S. 294 (1955) (*Brown II*).

[143] Charles F. Sabel & William H. Simon, *Destabilization Rights: How Public Law Litigation Succeeds*, 117 Harv. L. Rev. 1015, 1023–29 (2004).

[144] Malcolm M. Feeley & Edward L. Rubin, Judicial Policy Making and The Modern State: How The Courts Reformed America's Prisons (1998); Charles F. Sabel & William H. Simon, *Destabilization Rights: How Public Law Litigation Succeeds*, 117 Harv. L. Rev. 1015, 1016 (2004).

from schools to other public institutions: prisons and jails[145] (at one point the prison systems in 48 of 53 jurisdictions were under injunctions or consent decrees);[146] juvenile justice systems;[147] state judicial systems;[148] police departments (especially with respect to police abuse);[149] family-protection agencies;[150] state mental-health hospitals;[151] and public housing.[152]

Structural reform litigation is defined by several features. First, the judge plays a central role in litigation. She not only serves as the finder of fact (as in all equitable actions), but she plays an active role in defining the case and how it is to be resolved. As Abram Chayes, who coined the term "public law litigation,"[153] describes it, the central point is to obtain a judicial decree that adjusts affirmative future behavior through a complex, on-going regime of performance, overseen by the judge. Typically this involves the entry of a consent decree, in which the parties and the court negotiate and agree upon the precise terms and obligations imposed. The consent decree "deepens" the court's involvement in and responsibility for the litigation, with the court retaining ongoing authority to monitor compliance and enforcement of the decree, often by continuing the process of negotiation through-out the life of the order.[154] Public law litigation is arguably less adversarial and more cooperative among the parties, with government officials negotiating and consenting to terms of very broad injunctions.[155]

Second, the precise remedies ordered are not necessarily constitutionally compelled. That is, courts often impose positive obligations to remedy systemic unconstitutionality and reform institutions — even if the new obligations are not constitutionally required, even if the new obligations do not themselves prevent or undo a constitutional violation, and even if failing to do the specific things ordered is not itself unconstitutional. Structural-reform injunctions thus are best under-

---

[145] Rufo v. Inmates of Suffolk County Jail, 502 U.S. 367 (1992); Charles F. Sabel & William H. Simon, *Destabilization Rights: How Public Law Litigation Succeeds*, 117 Harv. L. Rev. 1015, 1034–43 (2004); *see generally* Malcolm M. Feeley & Edward L. Rubin, Judicial Policy Making and The Modern State: How The Courts Reformed America's Prisons (1998).

[146] Edward L. Rubin & Malcolm M. Feeley, *Judicial Policy Making and Litigation Against the Government*, 5 U. Pa. J. Const. L. 617, 657 (2003).

[147] Inmates of the R.I. Training Sch. v. Martinez, 465 F. Supp. 2d 131 (D.R.I. 2006).

[148] O'Shea v. Littleton, 414 U.S. 488 (1974).

[149] Rizzo v. Goode, 423 U.S. 362 (1976); Finch v. Peterson, 622 F.3d 725 (7th Cir. 2010); Charles F. Sabel & William H. Simon, *Destabilization Rights: How Public Law Litigation Succeeds*, 117 Harv. L. Rev. 1015, 1043–48 (2004).

[150] Nicholson v. Williams, 294 F. Supp. 2d 369 (E.D.N.Y. 2003); Nicholson v. Williams, 203 F. Supp. 2d 153 (E.D.N.Y. 2002).

[151] Pennhurst State Sch. & Hosp. v. Halderman, 451 U.S. 1 (1981); Wyatt by & through Rawlins v. Rogers, 985 F. Supp. 1356 (M.D. Ala. 1997); Charles F. Sabel & William H. Simon, *Destabilization Rights: How Public Law Litigation Succeeds*, 117 Harv. L. Rev. 1015, 1029–34 (2004).

[152] Hills v. Gautreaux, 425 U.S. 284 (1976); Charles F. Sabel & William H. Simon, *Destabilization Rights: How Public Law Litigation Succeeds*, 117 Harv. L. Rev. 1015, 1048–52 (2004).

[153] Abram Chayes, *The Role of the Judge in Public Law Litigation*, 89 Harv. L. Rev. 1281 (1976).

[154] *Id.* at 1284.

[155] *Id.*; Edward L. Rubin & Malcolm M. Feeley, *Judicial Policy Making and Litigation Against the Government*, 5 U. Pa. J. Const. L. 617, 657 (2003).

stood as substitutionary rather than specific remedies (as negative injunctions would be); they provide the plaintiff with substitute benefits going beyond what simply restores the specific constitutional liberty lost by unconstitutional misconduct.[156] Positive injunctions have altered school attendance zones and ordered busing to integrate schools,[157] ordered release of non-violent offenders to alleviate prison over-crowding,[158] ordered construction or renovation of jail facilities,[159] ordered state agencies to notify eligible citizens of their entitlement to state benefits,[160] and ordered scattered public housing outside of segregated neighborhoods.[161]

The so-called prospective compliance exception to *Ex parte Young* is particularly relevant to administrative and structural-reform injunctions.[162] Sovereign immunity does not bar prospective injunctive relief, even if it involves payment of funds from the public fisc, so long as those expenses are merely "ancillary effects" on the state treasury that are the "necessary result of compliance with decrees which by their terms were prospective in nature."[163] For example, having found that a state agency violated federal law in its administration of federal welfare funds, a court could order a state agency to provide written notice to all eligible persons of their entitlement to benefits and of the process for seeking benefits after.[164] Whatever funds the state must expend to provide that notice constitute ancillary costs, necessary for the state to comply with the injunction. And whatever additional funds the state might spend because more people apply for and obtain benefits because they know of and better understand the eligibility and application processes is a product not of the injunction itself, but of the state administering its programs in a constitutionally compliant way.[165]

While a court may compel government to take remedial action, however, it must be left to the government to decide how to pay for that action and the other details of compliance. This produces some fine distinctions. For example, where local government lacks financial resources to comply with a decree ordering school integration, a district court may order a municipality to raise additional funds and may enjoin application of state laws limiting the amount by which the local government can raise taxes, but the court itself cannot order a tax increase or

---

[156] John M. Greabe, *Constitutional Remedies and Public Interest Balancing*, ___ Wm. & Mary Bill Rts. J. ___ (forthcoming 2013).

[157] Swann v. Charlotte-Mecklenburg Board of Educ., 402 U.S. 1 (1971) (busing); Green v. County School Board, 391 U.S. 430 (1968) (rejecting freedom-of-choice model as means of desegregating schools).

[158] Brown v. Plata, 131 S. Ct. 1910 (2011).

[159] Rufo v. Inmates of Suffolk County Jail, 502 U.S. 367 (1992).

[160] Quern v. Jordan, 440 U.S. 332 (1979).

[161] Hills v. Gautreaux, 425 U.S. 284 (1976); A. Dan Tarlock, *Remedying the Irremediable: The Lessons of* Gautreaux, 64 Chi.-Kent L. Rev. 573 (1988).

[162] Milliken v. Bradley, 433 U.S. 267 (1977); Edelman v. Jordan, 415 U.S. 651 (1974); *supra* § 4.13[3].

[163] *Quern*, 440 U.S. at 337; *Edelman*, 415 U.S. at 667–68.

[164] *Quern*, 440 U.S. at 334.

[165] *Id.* at 347–49.

dictate the amount that taxes should be raised.[166]

Third, there has been a clear historical flow to judicial and political acceptance of structural reform litigation. State and local governments welcomed and even embraced early judicial efforts at institutional reform. They appreciated judicial leadership, energy, and oversight in devising and helping to implement remedial plans.[167] They also likely appreciated the political cover; hard (and sometimes expensive) choices about reforming institutions were made for them and government officials could disclaim responsibility for unpopular expenditures as having been imposed on them by the court. Because of this cooperation, federal reform litigation remedied many of the most extreme constitutional violations, notably the Plantation prison system of the South.[168]

From the late-1970s and forward, however, the bloom has been off the rose, as the unique difficulties of administrative decrees have become apparent.[169] There has been pushback against government by judicial decree[170] and against civil litigation that drags on for years.[171] There has been a reassertion of the authority of state and local political branches, rather than federal courts, to control basic administration and operation of their institutions, particularly in core areas of responsibility and particularly as it affects resource allocation decisions.[172] State and local governments also have become less willing to cooperate in creating and abiding by broad consent decrees. This perhaps results from some sense that the worst and most blatant constitutional abuses have been remedied (prisoners no longer are living on the equivalent of antebellum plantations or in cells overrun with raw sewage) and current cases (which, in common perception, focus on prisoner demands for cable television and gourmet meals) are therefore frivolous or unimportant.[173] The Supreme Court has recently rejected injunctions or consent decrees that it deemed extended too far in scope, coverage, or geographic reach beyond the precise constitutional defect found in the precise public institution.[174]

---

[166] Missouri v. Jenkins, 495 U.S. 33 (1990).

[167] MALCOLM M. FEELEY & EDWARD L. RUBIN, JUDICIAL POLICY MAKING AND THE MODERN STATE: HOW THE COURTS REFORMED AMERICA'S PRISONS 34–36 (1998); Edward L. Rubin & Malcolm M. Feeley, *Judicial Policy Making and Litigation Against the Government*, 5 U. PA. J. CONST. L. 617, 656, 657–58 (2003).

[168] Edward L. Rubin & Malcolm M. Feeley, *Judicial Policy Making and Litigation Against the Government*, 5 U. PA. J. CONST. L. 617, 656–57 (2003).

[169] MALCOLM M. FEELEY & EDWARD L. RUBIN, JUDICIAL POLICY MAKING AND THE MODERN STATE: HOW THE COURTS REFORMED AMERICA'S PRISONS 46–50 (1998).

[170] ROSS SANDLER & DAVID SCHOENBROD, DEMOCRACY BY DECREE: WHAT HAPPENS WHEN COURTS RUN GOVERNMENT (2003).

[171] Missouri v. Jenkins, 515 U.S. 70 (1995) (18-year litigation over school desegregation); Charles F. Sabel & William H. Simon, *Destabilization Rights: How Public Law Litigation Succeeds*, 117 HARV. L. REV. 1015, 1047–48 (2004) (discussing 30-plus-year history of litigation against Chicago Housing Authority).

[172] Horne v. Flores, 557 U.S. 433 (2009); Missouri v. Jenkins, 515 U.S. 70 (1995).

[173] MALCOLM M. FEELEY & EDWARD L. RUBIN, JUDICIAL POLICY MAKING AND THE MODERN STATE: HOW THE COURTS REFORMED AMERICA'S PRISONS 47 (1998); Mark Tushnet & Larry Yackle, *Symbolic Statutes and Real Laws: The Pathologies of the Antiterrorism and Effective Death Penalty Act and the Prison Litigation Reform Act*, 47 DUKE L.J. 1, 64 (1997).

[174] *Horne*, 557 U.S. at 448; Lewis v. Casey, 518 U.S. 343 (1996); *Jenkins*, 515 U.S. at 89–90; Milliken

The Court even has rejected entire structural-reform cases on "Our Federalism" grounds, insisting that federal courts must respect comity not only as to state courts, but as to all state and local institutions.[175] And even when the Supreme Court approves a broad injunctive remedy, it often does so in language suggesting such remedies should be limited, with the current case merely an extraordinary exception involving extraordinary facts and circumstances.[176]

§ 7.08   ENFORCING AND MODIFYING STRUCTURAL REFORM INJUNCTIONS

Fed. R. Civ. P. 60

* * *

(b) Grounds for Relief from a Final Judgment, Order, or Proceeding. On motion and just terms, the court may relieve a party or its legal representative from a final judgment, order, or proceeding for the following reasons:

* * *

(5) the judgment has been satisfied, released, or discharged; it is based on an earlier judgment that has been reversed or vacated; or applying it prospectively is no longer equitable; or

(6) any other reason that justifies relief.

[1]   Rule 60(b) and Structural Reform Injunctions

Structural reform litigation results in a judicial decree — whether an injunction or a consent decree — constituting a final judgment and imposing ongoing and comprehensive prospective obligations, carried out under ongoing judicial monitoring.[177] Again, this supervision may last a long time; one lawsuit to reform public housing in Chicago has been ongoing since the 1960s.[178]

The same process that produces the original judicial decree repeats itself when the parties return to the court with performance and compliance issues. A plaintiff, believing that defendant officials have not taken some required action or are acting

---

v. Bradley, 433 U.S. 267 (1977); Tomiko Brown-Nagin, Missouri v. Jenkins: *Why District Courts and Local Politics Matter, in* Civil Rights Stories 243 (Myriam E. Gilles & Risa L. Goluboff eds., 2008).

[175] Rizzo v. Goode, 423 U.S. 362 (1976); O'Shea v. Littleton, 414 U.S. 488 (1974); *see also* Nicholson v. Williams, 203 F. Supp. 2d 153, 231 (E.D.N.Y. 2002) (rejecting *Younger* defense in challenge to state administration of child protective system).

[176] Brown v. Plata, 131 S. Ct. 1910, 1924 (2011).

[177] Agostini v. Felton, 521 U.S. 203 (1997); Rufo v. Inmates of Suffolk County Jail, 502 U.S. 367 (1992).

[178] Charles F. Sabel & William H. Simon, *Destabilization Rights: How Public Law Litigation Succeeds,* 117 Harv. L. Rev. 1015, 1047–48 (2004).

in a way contrary to the decree, may file a motion to enforce the decree[179] or to hold parties or other persons in contempt for repeated failures to perform obligations imposed by the decree.[180]

From the other direction, a defendant can seek relief from an injunction or consent decree through Federal Rule of Civil Procedure 60(b); that rule allows a party to obtain relief from a final judgment or order where "applying [the decree] prospectively is no longer equitable"[181] or "for any other reason that justifies relief."[182] A district court's ability to modify an injunction or consent decree is uniquely important in structural reform litigation; because these decrees remain in place for extended periods of time, it is likely that significant legal and factual changes will occur during the life of the decree. Many long-lasting judicial decrees undergo multiple changes and modifications over the years.[183] Courts thus adopt a "flexible approach" to motions to modify, respecting the broader public interest and the special role of litigation in reforming constitutionally defective state institutions, in light of the decree's "impact on the public's right to the sound and efficient operation of its institutions"[184] and the specific desire to "return control to state and local officials as soon as a violation of federal law has been remedied."[185]

In *Rufo v. Inmates of Suffolk County*, the Court held that, in moving to modify a consent decree or injunction, the government defendant bears the burden of establishing that a "significant change in circumstances warrants revision of the decree," meaning a "significant change either in factual conditions or in law."[186] The government may show changed factual conditions by showing that new circumstances make compliance with the decree "substantially more onerous," that unforeseen obstacles have arisen, or that enforcement of the decree without modification would be detrimental to the public interest.[187] A change in legal circumstances means either a change to statutory or decisional law making the acts compelled by the judgment unlawful or, more commonly, making legal (or constitutionally permissible) the very conduct the judicial decree prohibited.[188] But changes in legal circumstances alone do not justify modifying the injunction as an "other reason" under Rule 60(b)(6).[189]

If the government makes that showing, the court decides whether the proposed modification (or dissolution) of the decree is "suitably tailored to the changed

---

[179] McDowell v. Phila. Hous. Auth., 423 F.3d 233 (3d Cir. 2005); Brennan v. Nassau County, 352 F.3d 60 (2d Cir. 2003).

[180] Hawkins v. Dep't. of Health and Human Servs., 665 F.3d 25 (1st Cir. 2012).

[181] FED. R. CIV. P. 60(b)(5).

[182] FED. R. CIV. P. 60(b)(6).

[183] *See generally Rufo*, 502 U.S. at 373–77.

[184] *Rufo*, 502 U.S. 367, 381.

[185] *Horne*, 557 U.S. at 451.

[186] *Rufo*, 502 U.S. at 383–84.

[187] *Id.* at 384.

[188] *Id.* at 388.

[189] *Agonstine*, 521 U.S. at 217.

circumstance."[190] *Rufo* identifies several considerations. The court must ensure that the modification does not "create or perpetuate" a constitutional violation or undo the constitutional remedy initially established;[191] that is, modifying or dissolving the decree should not return the parties to the conditions or circumstances that existed prior to the original decree. The court should only alter the decree as necessary to meet the problems created by changed circumstances, but no further; the original consent decree is a final judgment that should be reopened or altered only as equity requires.[192] Finally, the court owes some deference to government officials who bear " 'primary responsibility for elucidating, assessing, and solving' the problems of institutional reform, to resolve the intricacies of implementing a decree modification."[193] Ultimately, the analytical touchstone must be Rule 60(b)(5) itself, which focuses on whether continued adherence to the injunction "no longer is equitable" in light of comity and federalism considerations.[194]

The Supreme Court's increasing skepticism of institutional reform litigation has been accompanied by an increasing enthusiasm for using Rule 60(b)(5) to perform the "particularly important function" of ending or modifying injunctions or consent decrees that no longer serve their purpose of remedying unconstitutional conduct. Especially in light of the length of time in which administrative injunctions remain in force, courts should be newly vigilant in irecognizing changed facts, law, and policy that warrant reexamining the original decree and returning control from the federal courts to the political branches.[195]

One of the more unusual uses of Rule 60(b) and the motion to dissolve came in *Agostini v. Felton.*[196] In *Aguilar v. Felton* in 1985,[197] the Supreme Court held that a municipal education program (designed to implement a federal program) that sent public-school teachers into parochial schools to provide remedial education to economically disadvantaged children violated the Establishment Clause. The district court permanently enjoined the school board from sending teachers onto parochial school premises; instead, the board provided these education services (which it was federally obligated to continue providing) at public schools and at leased sites (by transporting parochial-school students to those locations) and via computer, all at significantly increased public costs.[198]

Twelve years later, the Court on a Rule 60(b) motion agreed with the school board that the injunction should be dissolved in light of changes to substantive law. Establishment Clause doctrine had significantly changed and evolved in the intervening decade, such that the analysis on which the injunction was granted and

---

[190] *Rufo*, 502 U.S. at 383.

[191] *Id.* at 391.

[192] *Id.*

[193] *Id.* at 392.

[194] FED. R. CIV. P. 60(b)(5); *Horne*, 557 U.S. at 447.

[195] *Horne*, 557 U.S. at 447–48.

[196] 521 U.S. 203, 209 (1997).

[197] 473 U.S. 402 (1985).

[198] *Agostini*, 521 U.S. at 214 (discussing *Aguilar*).

approved in *Aguilar* no longer remained good law; under Establishment Clause doctrine in 1997 (the time the Rule 60(6) motion reached the Court), the city's preferred program of sending public-school teachers into parochial schools had become constitutionally permissible and no longer unlawful. The Court thus concluded that the defendants should be relieved from the injunction; continuing to restrict the city's program, in favor of a more-expensive and more-burdensome one, was "no longer equitable" for purposes of Rule 60(b)(5) given the change in First Amendment law.[199]

Justice Ginsburg dissented for four justices on the procedural issue, describing this use of Rule 60(b) as "unprecedented."[200] *Aguilar*, and the limitation on public-school teachers going into parochial schools, remained good law right until the Court's decision in *Agostini*, which only involved the Rule 60(b) motion. A motion to modify or dissolve an injunction is not the vehicle in which the Court overrules a prior decision, rehears the legal and factual claims underlying the injunction, or establishes new law. The motion should be granted only when a decision in a different case changes the state of the law, undermining the injunction; a court cannot change the law in the course of ruling on the Rule 60(b) motion, then use the newly created law to dissolve that very injunction.[201] Ginsburg also emphasized the majority's concession that expansive use of this approach to Rule 60(b) "will not be favored," she thus "anticipate[d] that the extraordinary action taken in this case will be aberrational."[202]

[2]   Rule 60(b) and Appeals

An order modifying or dissolving an injunction, or refusing to modify or dissolve an injunction, is immediately appealable on the same terms as the original order granting or denying the injunction.[203]

But courts on occasion will consider and resolve motions not explicitly styled as modifying or dissolving, but which nevertheless affect the scope and continued vitality of administrative injunctions. Courts also may decide legal and factual issues raised in an express motion to dissolve, but without explicitly granting or denying the motion. As the D.C. Circuit explained in *Salazar v. District of Columbia*, an order may be immediately appealable under § 1292(a)(1), even if it does not by its terms "clearly" grant or deny a "specific" request to dissolve or modify an injunction, if it has the "practical effect" of granting or denying such a motion. A "practical effect" order is appealable if it " 'affect[s] predominantly all of the merits,' " or if the appellant can show: (1) that the order "might have a 'serious, perhaps irreparable consequence,' " and (2) that the order can be " 'effectually challenged' only by immediate appeal.' "[204]

---

[199]   *Id.* at 237–38.

[200]   *Id.* at 255–56 (Ginsburg, J., dissenting).

[201]   *Id.* at 256–58 (Ginsburg, J., dissenting).

[202]   *Id.* at 256 (Ginsburg, J., dissenting).

[203]   28 U.S.C. § 1292(a)(1).

[204]   Salazar v. District of Columbia, 671 F.3d 1258, 1261–62, 1264–65 (D.C. Cir. 2012) (citing Carson v. American Brands, Inc., 450 U.S. 79, 84 (1981)).

This creates a two-tier structure. Orders plainly or explicitly modifying or dissolving an injunction or refusing to do so are immediately appealable under the plain terms of § 1292(a)(1), while "practical effect" orders are appealable only if the necessary criteria are met. While this elevates form over substance, that is precisely the point of the text of § 1292(a)(i) and a doctrine distinguishing an order that " 'clearly' denies a 'specific' request" from one that only has only that practical effect.[205]

§ 7.09 PRISON LITIGATION

18 U.S.C. § 3626

(a) Requirements for relief.—

(1) Prospective relief.—

(A) Prospective relief in any civil action with respect to prison conditions shall extend no further than necessary to correct the violation of the Federal right of a particular plaintiff or plaintiffs. The court shall not grant or approve any prospective relief unless the court finds that such relief is narrowly drawn, extends no further than necessary to correct the violation of the Federal right, and is the least intrusive means necessary to correct the violation of the Federal right. The court shall give substantial weight to any adverse impact on public safety or the operation of a criminal justice system caused by the relief.

(B) The court shall not order any prospective relief that requires or permits a government official to exceed his or her authority under State or local law or otherwise violates State or local law, unless —

(i) Federal law requires such relief to be ordered in violation of State or local law;

(ii) the relief is necessary to correct the violation of a Federal right; and

(iii) no other relief will correct the violation of the Federal right.

(C) Nothing in this section shall be construed to authorize the courts, in exercising their remedial powers, to order the construction of prisons or the raising of taxes, or to repeal or detract from otherwise applicable limitations on the remedial powers of the courts.

(2) Preliminary injunctive relief.— In any civil action with

---

[205] *Salazar*, 671 F.3d at 1264.

respect to prison conditions, to the extent otherwise authorized by law, the court may enter a temporary restraining order or an order for preliminary injunctive relief. Preliminary injunctive relief must be narrowly drawn, extend no further than necessary to correct the harm the court finds requires preliminary relief, and be the least intrusive means necessary to correct that harm. The court shall give substantial weight to any adverse impact on public safety or the operation of a criminal justice system caused by the preliminary relief and shall respect the principles of comity set out in paragraph (1)(B) in tailoring any preliminary relief. Preliminary injunctive relief shall automatically expire on the date that is 90 days after its entry, unless the court makes the findings required under subsection (a)(1) for the entry of prospective relief and makes the order final before the expiration of the 90-day period.

(3) Prisoner release order.—

(A) In any civil action with respect to prison conditions, no court shall enter a prisoner release order unless—

(i) a court has previously entered an order for less intrusive relief that has failed to remedy the deprivation of the Federal right sought to be remedied through the prisoner release order; and

(ii) the defendant has had a reasonable amount of time to comply with the previous court orders.

(B) In any civil action in Federal court with respect to prison conditions, a prisoner release order shall be entered only by a three-judge court in accordance with section 2284 of title 28, if the requirements of subparagraph (E) have been met.

(C) A party seeking a prisoner release order in Federal court shall file with any request for such relief, a request for a three-judge court and materials sufficient to demonstrate that the requirements of subparagraph (A) have been met.

(D) If the requirements under subparagraph (A) have been met, a Federal judge before whom a civil action with respect to prison conditions is pending who believes that a prison release order should be considered may sua sponte request the convening of a three-judge court to determine whether a prisoner release order should be entered.

(E) The three-judge court shall enter a prisoner release order only if the court finds by clear and convincing evidence that—

(i) crowding is the primary cause of the violation of a Federal right; and

(ii) no other relief will remedy the violation of the Federal right.

(F) Any State or local official including a legislator or unit of government whose jurisdiction or function includes the appropriation of funds for the construction, operation, or maintenance of prison facilities, or the prosecution or custody of persons who may be released from, or not admitted to, a prison as a result of a prisoner release order shall have standing to oppose the imposition or continuation in effect of such relief and to seek termination of such relief, and shall have the right to intervene in any proceeding relating to such relief.

(b) Termination of relief.—

(1) Termination of prospective relief.—

(A) In any civil action with respect to prison conditions in which prospective relief is ordered, such relief shall be terminable upon the motion of any party or intervener—

(i) 2 years after the date the court granted or approved the prospective relief;

(ii) 1 year after the date the court has entered an order denying termination of prospective relief under this paragraph; or

(iii) in the case of an order issued on or before the date of enactment of the Prison Litigation Reform Act, 2 years after such date of enactment.

(B) Nothing in this section shall prevent the parties from agreeing to terminate or modify relief before the relief is terminated under subparagraph (A).

(2) Immediate termination of prospective relief.— *In any civil action with respect to prison conditions, a defendant or intervener shall be entitled to the immediate termination of any prospective relief if the relief was approved or granted in the absence of a finding by the court that the relief is narrowly drawn, extends no further than necessary to correct the violation of the Federal right, and is the least intrusive means necessary to correct the violation of the Federal right.*

(3) Limitation.— *Prospective relief shall not terminate if the court makes written findings based on the record that prospective relief remains necessary to correct a current and ongoing violation of the Federal right, extends no further than necessary to correct the violation of the Federal right, and that the prospective relief is narrowly drawn and the least intrusive means to correct the violation.*

(4) Termination or modification of relief.— *Nothing in this section shall prevent any party or intervener from seeking modification or termination before the relief is terminable under paragraph*

(1) or (2), to the extent that modification or termination would otherwise be legally permissible.

(c) Settlements.—

(1) Consent decrees.— *In any civil action with respect to prison conditions, the court shall not enter or approve a consent decree unless it complies with the limitations on relief set forth in subsection (a).*

(2) Private settlement agreements.—

(A) Nothing in this section shall preclude parties from entering into a private settlement agreement that does not comply with the limitations on relief set forth in subsection (a), if the terms of that agreement are not subject to court enforcement other than the reinstatement of the civil proceeding that the agreement settled.

(B) Nothing in this section shall preclude any party claiming that a private settlement agreement has been breached from seeking in State court any remedy available under State law.

* * *

(e) Procedure for motions affecting prospective relief.—

(1) Generally.— *The court shall promptly rule on any motion to modify or terminate prospective relief in a civil action with respect to prison conditions. Mandamus shall lie to remedy any failure to issue a prompt ruling on such a motion.*

(2) Automatic stay.— *Any motion to modify or terminate prospective relief made under subsection (b) shall operate as a stay during the period—*

(A) (i) beginning on the 30th day after such motion is filed, in the case of a motion made under paragraph (1) or (2) of subsection (b); or

(ii) beginning on the 180th day after such motion is filed, in the case of a motion made under any other law; and

(B) ending on the date the court enters a final order ruling on the motion.

(3) Postponement of automatic stay.— *The court may postpone the effective date of an automatic stay specified in subsection (e)(2)(A) for not more than 60 days for good cause. No postponement shall be permissible because of general congestion of the court's calendar.*

(4) Order blocking the automatic stay.— *Any order staying, suspending, delaying, or barring the operation of the automatic stay described in paragraph (2) (other than an order to postpone the*

> *effective date of the automatic stay under paragraph (3)) shall be treated as an order refusing to dissolve or modify an injunction and shall be appealable pursuant to section 1292(a)(1) of title 28, United States Code, regardless of how the order is styled or whether the order is termed a preliminary or a final ruling.*

Of all the areas in which legal attitudes toward structural reform litigation have changed, the most dramatic has been with respect to prisons. As one study showed, prison officials initially welcomed judicial involvement and cooperated with the court and opposing parties in working out consent decrees.[206] And at one point, 48 out of 53 corrections jurisdictions were under federal injunctions or consent decrees.[207] Structural-reform litigation ultimately succeeded in remedying the worst constitutional abuses in prison conditions, particularly in eliminating the prison plantation system that prevailed through much of the South.[208] Government willingness to continue with this cooperative approach waned, however, overcome by a heightened sense that courts were micro-managing prisons, an area demanding particular deference to the expertise of prison officials; that the worst abuses had been eliminated and new cases were focusing on frivolous concerns;[209] and that courts were imposing injunctions and consent decrees that went too far beyond the actual constitutional violation, for example, by imposing requirements as to the content of libraries in every prison in the state to remedy isolated violations of a limited right to access to courts in a few prisons.[210]

This opposition crested in 1996 in the Prison Litigation Reform Act ("PLRA"), which imposes significant limitations on civil rights litigation by prisoners relating to conditions of confinement, particularly actions for administrative injunctions. The PLRA represents an unabashed congressional effort to limit what it perceived as abusive § 1983 claims; legislative debates focused on supposedly absurd complaints from prisoners challenging the lack of premium cable television or gourmet food in the prison, in contrast with the original prison lawsuits that sought to keep cells free of raw sewage.[211]

Several features of the PLRA are noteworthy.

First, injunctive relief must be proportional to the actual constitutional violation, requiring a tighter connection between the constitutional rights infringed and the

---

[206] MALCOLM M. FEELEY & EDWARD L. RUBIN, JUDICIAL POLICY MAKING AND THE MODERN STATE: HOW THE COURTS REFORMED AMERICA'S PRISONS 34–36 (1998); Edward L. Rubin & Malcolm M. Feeley, *Judicial Policy Making and Litigation Against the Government*, 5 U. PA. J. CONST. L. 617, 658 (2003).

[207] Edward L. Rubin & Malcolm M. Feeley, *Judicial Policy Making and Litigation Against the Government*, 5 U. PA. J. CONST. L. 617, 657 (2003).

[208] *Id.* at 651–52.

[209] MALCOLM M. FEELEY & EDWARD L. RUBIN, JUDICIAL POLICY MAKING AND THE MODERN STATE: HOW THE COURTS REFORMED AMERICA'S PRISONS 46–50 (1998).

[210] Lewis v. Casey, 518 U.S. 343 (1996).

[211] Mark Tushnet & Larry Yackle, *Symbolic Statutes and Real Laws: The Pathologies of the Antiterrorism and Effective Death Penalty Act and the Prison Litigation Reform Act*, 47 DUKE L.J. 1, 64 (1997).

remedies ordered.[212] A court must find that any preliminary or permanent injunction is narrowly drawn, extends no further than necessary to correct the violation, and is the least intrusive means necessary to correct the violation.[213] Courts are specifically instructed to give "substantial weight" to considerations of public safety and the state's operation of the criminal justice system.[214] And the statute specifically disclaims any grant of power to federal courts to order tax increases or prison construction as a remedy.[215] Moreover, a court can approve and enter a consent decree only on the same terms as it may issue an injunction.[216]

Second, the PLRA imposes specific limitations on decrees ordering the release of prisoners to ease overcrowding. A prisoner release order is appropriate only if the court has previously imposed less-intrusive relief that has failed to remedy the violation and the defendant has had a "reasonable" amount of time to comply with prior orders.[217] A prisoner release order can be issued only by a three-judge district court and the three-judge court can order release only if, in addition to the findings required for all other injunctions, it finds by clear and convincing evidence that crowding is the primary cause of the constitutional violation and no relief other than release of prisoners will remedy that violation.[218] Even under this high standard, the Supreme Court did recently affirm a three-judge court's prison release order concluding that releasing prisoners was the only appropriate way to ensure proper medical and mental-health care in the prison system.[219]

Finally, a court must promptly rule on any motion to terminate or modify the injunction or consent decree.[220] The filing of that motion automatically stays the injunction, leaving the defendant free to return to its pre-decree conduct and policies until the motion is resolved.[221] The court may postpone the effective date of the automatic stay for good cause, although for not more than 60 days.[222] An order refusing or limiting the automatic stay itself constitutes an immediately appealable order under § 1292(a)(1) refusing to dissolve or modify an injunction.[223] The Supreme Court has upheld the automatic stay against a separation of powers challenge.[224]

---

[212] Lewis v. Casey, 518 U.S. 343 (1996).

[213] 18 U.S.C. §§ 3626(a)(1); *id.* § 3626(a)(2) (same standard for preliminary injunction).

[214] *Id.* § 3626(a)(1)(A).

[215] *Id.* § 3626(a)(1)(C).

[216] *Id.* § 3626(c)(1).

[217] *Id.* § 3626(a)(3)(A).

[218] *Id.* §§ 3626(a)(3)(D), (E).

[219] Brown v. Plata, 131 S. Ct. 1910 (2011).

[220] 18 U.S.C. § 3626(e)(1).

[221] *Id.* § 3626(a)(2).

[222] *Id.* § 3626(e)(3).

[223] *Id.* § 3626(e)(4).

[224] Miller v. French, 530 U.S. 327, 348 (2000).

§ 7.10 FEDERAL GOVERNMENT LITIGATION AND PROSPECTIVE CIVIL REMEDIES

42 U.S.C. § 14141

(a) Unlawful conduct

It shall be unlawful for any governmental authority, or any agent thereof, or any person acting on behalf of a governmental authority, to engage in a pattern or practice of conduct by law enforcement officers or by officials or employees of any governmental agency with responsibility for the administration of juvenile justice or the incarceration of juveniles that deprives persons of rights, privileges, or immunities secured or protected by the Constitution or laws of the United States.

(b) Civil action by Attorney General

Whenever the Attorney General has reasonable cause to believe that a violation of paragraph (1) has occurred, the Attorney General, for or in the name of the United States, may in a civil action obtain appropriate equitable and declaratory relief to eliminate the pattern or practice.

Early Reconstruction efforts at civil rights enforcement focused on government-initiated enforcement, notably through the criminal prohibition of § 242, which was enacted as § 2 of the Civil Rights Act of 1866 and reenacted as § 2 of the Civil Rights Act of 1870. And enforcement of § 242 played a significant role in the slow revival of federal civil rights enforcement in the mid-20th century[225] and during the Civil Rights Era.[226]

But underutilization of § 242 has been a subject of academic criticism in recent years.[227] Criminal prosecution imposes a number of burdens that makes obtaining convictions difficult — the higher "beyond a reasonable doubt" burden of proof applicable to all criminal cases; § 242's extraordinarily stringent specific-intent requirement;[228] and vagueness concerns associated with enforcing due process by criminal means.[229] The federal government also must strike a delicate balance to ensure that federal prosecution does not overlap or interfere with efforts of functioning state prosecutors and criminal justice systems to punish the same misconduct under state law, even where a prior state conviction results in an acquittal.[230] Section 242 thus gets relatively limited use[231] only in extraordinary

---

[225] Screws v. United States, 325 U.S. 91 (1945); United States v. Classic, 313 U.S. 299 (1941).

[226] United States v. Price, 383 U.S. 787 (1966); United States v. Guest, 383 U.S. 745 (1966).

[227] Rachel A. Harmon, *Promoting Civil Rights Through Proactive Policing Reform*, 62 Stan. L. Rev. 1, 9 (2009); John V. Jacobi, *Prosecuting Police Misconduct*, 2000 Wis. L. Rev. 789, 806, 810–11; Kami Chavis Simmons, *The Politics of Policing: Ensuring Stakeholder Collaboration in the Federal Reform of Local Law Enforcement Agencies*, 98 J. Crim. L. & Criminology 489, 501–02 (2008).

[228] United States v. Lanier, 520 U.S. 259, 265 (1997); John V. Jacobi, *Prosecuting Police Misconduct*, 2000 Wis. L. Rev. 789, 806.

[229] *Lanier*, 520 U.S. at 265; *Screws*, 325 U.S. at 106; *supra* § 2.10.

[230] United States Dep't of Justice, United States Attorneys Manual § 9-2.031 (Dual and Successive

cases — where systemic defects in the state system make state enforcement unlikely[232] or where the case is uniquely high-profile and public outrage pressures the federal government into acting in the wake of perceived state failure (either as to the original events or over the state-court result).[233]

A provision of the Violent Crime Control and Law Enforcement Act of 1993[234] empowers the Attorney General of the United States to bring civil actions on behalf of the United States, seeking equitable or prospective relief against state and local law-enforcement and juvenile justice agencies to halt systemic constitutional wrongdoing.[235] The statute expressly recognizes the need for a national response and vigorous national remedies against constitutional misconduct in local law enforcement, as well as the limited effectiveness of individual § 242 prosecutions against isolated misconduct. Section 14141 targets agencies (rather than individuals) and big-picture, systemic, policy-based violations involving a "pattern or practice" of unconstitutional conduct by law-enforcement officers and organizations.[236] Although the statute does not define pattern-or-practice, scholars suggest it incorporates the concept from employment discrimination law, and the standards from policy-or-custom municipal liability under § 1983.[237]

Enforcement of § 14141 is delegated to the Special Litigation Section of the Civil Rights Division of the Department of Justice. In response to some trigger indicating potential systemic violations — a citizen complaint, a § 1983 action, some high-profile, highly publicized incidents, or even self-referrals by the target department — the section conducts a preliminary investigation. This is followed by a comprehensive and far-reaching formal investigation. If the formal investigation reveals evidence of a pattern or practice of constitutional violations, DOJ may file a civil action in federal court seeking injunctive and declaratory relief, particularly broad structural remedies reforming how agency operates.[238]

Prosecution Policy ("Petite Policy"), *available at* http://www.justice.gov/usao/eousa/foia_reading_room/usam/title9/2mcrm.htm#9-2.031.

[231] John V. Jacobi, *Prosecuting Police Misconduct*, 2000 Wis. L. Rev. 789, 810–11.

[232] United States v. Lanier, 73 F.3d 1380, 1403 (6th Cir. 1995) (Daughtrey, J., dissenting), *rev'd*, 520 U.S. 259 (1997) (politically connected judge and former political officeholder not prosecuted for sexually assaulting litigants and underlings in his chambers and threatening them with legal or employment consequences).

[233] Koon v. United States, 518 U.S. 81, 87–88 (1996) (prosecution of police officers involved in high-profile beating of suspect, where public rioting followed state acquittals); Campbell Robertson, *5 Ex-Officers Sentenced in Post-Katrina Shootings*, The New York Times, Apr. 4, 2012 (five New Orleans police officers convicted for civil rights violations resulting from shooting in the aftermath of Hurricane Katrina and subsequent department cover-up).

[234] Violent Crime Control and Law Enforcement Act of 1993, Pub. L. No. 103-322, 108 Stat. 1786 (1993).

[235] 42 U.S.C. § 14141.

[236] Rachel A. Harmon, *Promoting Civil Rights Through Proactive Policing Reform*, 62 Stan. L. Rev. 1, 14 n.42 (2009).

[237] *Id.*; *supra* § 4.04.

[238] Rachel A. Harmon, *Promoting Civil Rights Through Proactive Policing Reform*, 62 Stan. L. Rev. 1, 14–19 (2009); Kami Chavis Simmons, *The Politics of Policing: Ensuring Stakeholder Collaboration in the Federal Reform of Local Law Enforcement Agencies*, 98 J. Crim. L. & Criminology 489, 508–11 (2008).

No civil action under § 14141 has yet gone to trial. Cases typically end either with entry of a consent decree or a Memorandum of Agreement (MOA) between the United States and the law enforcement agency. The former operates as an injunction and is enforceable as such. An MOA operates as a contract between the United States and the defendant department, enforceable through a subsequent civil action by the federal government for breach of contract and to compel performance.[239] DOJ also often takes the shorter step of sending technical assistance or investigative findings letters to the target agencies, identifying specific problems and recommending reforms that the department should undertake; such a letter could be a precursor toward a lawsuit or more formal resolution, but more often is the last public action in a case.[240] The George H.W. Bush Justice Department favored this approach, preferring cooperative investigation to adversary litigation. As a presidential candidate, Bush had spoken against DOJ dictating to state and local law enforcement how it should operate.[241] DOJ under President Bush then established a policy of working informally and collaboratively with state and local agencies to develop and implement solutions; this cooperative process was designed to achieve "buy-in" from local agencies, producing faster changes and remedies without the adversarial and hardened positioning that accompanies litigation.[242]

As of 2010, the Departments of Justice of three presidential administrations had conducted 33 full formal investigations of law-enforcement agencies. Seven resulted in federal consent decrees, seven more resulted in MOAs, 12 resulted in technical assistance or investigative findings letter, and seven did not result in any public action.[243] Moreover, one scholar notes that the government has targeted law enforcement in smaller cities (such as Pittsburgh) rather than larger cities (such as Chicago or New York).[244] Investigations also continue to take a long time, slowing the process of systemic change.[245] For example, the Obama DOJ opened an investigation into Joe Arpaio, the controversial Sheriff of Maricopa County, Arizona, in March 2009 (two months into the President's first term); the case remained active but unresolved when his second term began in January 2013.[246]

---

[239] Rachel A. Harmon, *Promoting Civil Rights Through Proactive Policing Reform*, 62 Stan. L. Rev. 1, 15–17 (2009).

[240] *Id.* at 17–19.

[241] Kami Chavis Simmons, *The Politics of Policing: Ensuring Stakeholder Collaboration in the Federal Reform of Local Law Enforcement Agencies*, 98 J. Crim. L. & Criminology 489, 518 (2008).

[242] Reauthorization of the Civil Rights Division of the United States Dep't of Justice: Hearing Before the Subcomm. On the Constitution of the House Committee on the Judiciary, 109th Cong. (2005) (prepared statement of R. Alexander Acosta, Assistant Attorney General, Civil Rights Division); Rachel A. Harmon, *Promoting Civil Rights Through Proactive Policing Reform*, 62 Stan. L. Rev. 1, 55 (2009).

[243] Rachel A. Harmon, *Promoting Civil Rights Through Proactive Policing Reform*, 62 Stan. L. Rev. 1, 15–16 (2009); Kami Chavis Simmons, *Cooperative Federalism and Police Reform: Using Congressional Spending Power to Promote Police Accountability*, 62 Ala. L. Rev. 351, 375 & nn.19–20 (2011).

[244] Kami Chavis Simmons, *Cooperative Federalism and Police Reform: Using Congressional Spending Power to Promote Police Accountability*, 62 Ala. L. Rev. 351, 375 & n.120 (2011).

[245] Kami Chavis Simmons, *The Politics of Policing: Ensuring Stakeholder Collaboration in the Federal Reform of Local Law Enforcement Agencies*, 98 J. Crim. L. & Criminology 489, 517–18 (2008).

[246] Kami Chavis Simmons, *Cooperative Federalism and Police Reform: Using Congressional*

Many scholars, initially enthusiastic about § 14141 as an alternative to an under-used § 242, have come to see it as less than an overwhelming success (if not an outright failure), given the lack of vigorous enforcement.[247] As with criminal prosecutions, DOJ remains reactive rather than proactive in its enforcement efforts. And it remains subject to the same limitations on resources[248] and political will[249] that regularly deter rigorous government.

PART C
ATTORNEY'S FEES

§ 7.11 INTRODUCTION TO ATTORNEY'S FEES

42 U.S.C. § 1988

(b) In any action or proceeding to enforce a provision of sections . . . 1983 . . . , the court, in its discretion, may allow the prevailing party, other than the United States, a reasonable attorney's fee as part of the costs, except that in any action brought against a judicial officer for an act or omission taken in such officer's judicial capacity such officer shall not be held liable for any costs, including attorney's fees, unless such action was clearly in excess of such officer's jurisdiction.

A key issue in any civil justice system is how parties finance litigation, particularly in paying for legal counsel. The United Kingdom and most Civil Law systems follow a "loser pays" system, under which the losing party pays the winning party's attorney's fees; this system arguably deters weak or frivolous lawsuits. By contrast, under the "American Rule," each party is responsible for its own costs and fees;[250] this system arguably avoids over-deterrence of risk-averse plaintiffs with potentially meritorious claims, especially in civil rights cases. Through § 1988(b), Congress has overridden the common law rule by allowing recovery of fees in actions under § 1983 and several other civil rights statutes.[251] Modern civil rights statutes generally include attorney's fees provisions.[252]

Attorney's fees lie at the core of the private attorney general. Fees provide an economic incentive to encourage capable lawyers to take civil rights and constitu-

---

Spending Power to Promote Police Accountability, 62 ALA. L. REV. 351, 374 & n.116 (2011).

[247] Rachel A. Harmon, *Promoting Civil Rights Through Proactive Policing Reform*, 62 STAN. L. REV. 1, 20–21 (2009).

[248] *Id.*

[249] Kami Chavis Simmons, *The Politics of Policing: Ensuring Stakeholder Collaboration in the Federal Reform of Local Law Enforcement Agencies*, 98 J. CRIM. L. & CRIMINOLOGY 489, 518 (2008).

[250] Buckhannon Bd. & Care Home, Inc. v. W. Va. Dep't of Health & Human Res., 532 U.S. 598, 602 (2001); Alyeska Pipeline Serv. Co. v. Wilderness Soc'y, 421 U.S. 240 (1975).

[251] 42 U.S.C. § 1988(b).

[252] 42 U.S.C. § 12205 (Americans With Disabilities Act); 42 U.S.C. § 3613(c)(2) (Fair Housing Amendments Act); 42 U.S.C. § 2000e-5(k) (Title VII of the Civil Rights Act of 1964).

tional cases.[253] Plaintiffs need competent and highly skilled counsel to bring private actions, who in turn help further the congressional goal of encouraging more and more successful private civil rights enforcement. Good lawyering also makes it more likely that the plaintiff will prevail and recover more in litigation (in legal or equitable remedies), thereby providing more compensation, more constitutional enforcement, and more deterrence of future government misconduct, all of which inure to the public interest and benefit. Attorney's fees provisions also have contributed to the creation of a civil rights bar of private attorneys and ideological organizations that subsist on fees from the cases they pursue and win. This is particularly important in actions for non-monetary prospective relief or actions that are not likely to produce large damage awards (which is to say many § 1983 and *Bivens* damages actions) — cases in which plaintiffs might otherwise have difficulty finding competent and zealous representation.

The award of attorney's fees also provides additional deterrence of government misconduct, as the officer or government ends up paying something even in low- or no-value cases. Indeed, in some cases fees may be the only cost the defendant or government pays, and therefore may constitute a significant form of liability.[254] Of course, that possibility informs a common criticism of attorney's fees — they enrich attorneys by providing a private windfall to counsel, without directly benefitting the injured plaintiff.[255] One also might argue that the public interest is not served by awarding substantial fees; that money still comes from the public fisc, thus from taxpayers, and no longer can be used for some other public purpose.[256]

Because attorney's fees are available only because of a statutory exception, the analytical touchstone is congressional intent, which controls whether fees should be available in a given case, to whom they should be available, the amount awarded, and how the award is calculated.

§ 7.12   DISCRETIONARY FEES

Section 1988(b) provides that the court "may allow" attorney's fees, vesting in the district court discretion both as to whether to award fees and as to the amount of the award.[257] But that discretion is not unbridled and must be exercised in light of the statute's purposes of enabling civil rights plaintiffs to obtain competent counsel and of incentivizing attorneys to take constitutional cases.[258] The general rule is that a court may deny fees only in limited "special circumstances" in which an award would be unjust.[259]

The statute also is written in party-neutral terms, meaning any prevailing party can recover fees from the losing party, not only a prevailing plaintiff. recovery of

---

[253] Evans v. Jeff D., 475 U.S. 717, 751–52 (1986) (Brennan, J., dissenting).

[254] *Id.* at 734.

[255] Perdue v. Kenny A., 130 S. Ct. 1662, 1676 (2010); Hensley v. Eckerhart, 461 U.S. 424, 446 (1983).

[256] *Perdue*, 130 S. Ct. at 1676–77.

[257] 42 U.S.C. § 1988(b); Sole v. Wyner, 551 U.S. 74, 77 (2007).

[258] Kay v. Ehrler, 499 U.S. 432, 438 (1991).

[259] *Hensley*, 461 U.S. at 446; Mendez v. County of San Bernardino, 540 F.3d 1109 (9th Cir. 2008).

fees by a prevailing defendant officer or government entity is the exception rather than the rule, appropriate only where the plaintiff's action is frivolous, unreasonable, or without foundation.[260] Regularly awarding fees to a prevailing defendant functionally imposes "loser pays," which risks over-deterring plaintiffs from bringing (or counsel from taking on) potentially-meritorious-but-close cases — the very cases that Congress hoped to incentivize by overriding the American Rule and providing for attorney's fees.[261] Courts thus must consider whether awarding fees in favor of a prevailing defendant and against a plaintiff is consistent with congressional purpose.[262]

§ 7.13 ATTORNEY'S FEES AND JUDGES

The final clause of § 1988(b) limits the availability of attorney's fees in actions against judges for conduct taken in their judicial capacity, "unless such action was clearly in excess of such officer's jurisdiction."[263] Congress added this clause in 1996[264] (along with the add-on clause in § 1983 requiring that judges first be subject to a declaratory judgment before any injunction can issue[265]) to overturn that part of *Pulliam v. Allen* holding that a plaintiff could recover attorney's fees from a judge (which followed from its conclusion that a federal court could enjoin a state judge).[266] The amendment to § 1988(b) statutorily establishes judicial immunity from awards of attorney's fees for all conduct for which a judge enjoys judicial immunity from damages.[267]

§ 7.14 PREVAILING PARTY

Only a "prevailing party" is entitled to recover attorney's fees under § 1988(b), so that statutory term becomes the analytical focal point. A party has prevailed when is has achieved a "material alteration of the legal relationship between the parties in a manner which Congress sought to promote in the fee statute."[268] There must be an "enduring change in the legal relationship" between the plaintiff and the defendant.[269] The party must prevail on the merits of at least some claims and must

---

[260] Christiansburg Garment Co. v. EEOC, 434 U.S. 412 (1978); Torres-Santiago v. Municipality of Adjuntas, 693 F.3d 230 (1st Cir. 2012); Sensations, Inc. v. City of Grand Rapids, 526 F.3d 291 (6th Cir. 2008).

[261] *Torres-Santiago*, 693 F.3d at 234.

[262] *See* Barnes Found. v. Township of Lower Merion, 242 F.3d 151 (3d Cir. 2001) (holding that claims were without factual support as to five defendants, warranting award of fees against plaintiffs).

[263] 42 U.S.C. § 1988(b).

[264] Federal Courts Improvement Act of 1996, Pub. L. No. 104-317, 110 Stat. 3847 (1996).

[265] 42 U.S.C. § 1983.

[266] Pulliam v. Allen, 466 U.S. 522 (1984); *supra* § 3.08[3].

[267] Brandon E. ex rel. Listenbee v. Reynolds, 201 F.3d 194 (3d Cir. 2000); Kuhn v. Thompson, 304 F. Supp. 2d 1313 (M.D. Ala. 2004).

[268] Buckhannon Bd. & Care Home, Inc. v. W. Va. Dep't of Health & Human Res., 532 U.S. 598 (2001); Farrar v. Hobby, 506 U.S. 103 (1992); Texas State Teachers Ass'n v. Garland Indep. Sch. Dist., 489 U.S. 782, 792–93 (1989).

[269] Sole v. Wyner, 551 U.S. 74 (2007).

receive some relief on the merits.[270] A party need only prevail on one claim in the action, even if she does not prevail on any others; courts do not look at who won more claims but only at whether the plaintiff prevailed on something.[271] Where such a change or material alteration in relationship has occurred, a party has prevailed; the degree of success goes not to entitlement to fees, but to the reasonableness of the fee awarded.[272]

A plaintiff is most obviously prevails when she has succeeded on the merits and received some remedy sought, such as compensatory damages, permanent injunction, or declaratory judgment.[273] A party also prevails when the court enters a consent decree; although a consent decree contains no admission of liability, it is a court order that alters the legal relationship between the parties by prohibiting or (more often) requiring the defendant to take certain steps benefitting the plaintiff and that is judicially monitored for future compliance.[274] A party also can be prevail when she recovers nominal damages; that small amount of money modifies the defendant's conduct by making him a judgment debtor obligated to pay money he otherwise would not pay and changes his legal relationship with the plaintiff, who now is a judgment creditor and can demand payment of the monetary award.[275]

On the other hand, a party has not prevailed when she obtains only preliminary or temporary injunctive relief without more, particularly where the plaintiff's constitutional arguments were specifically rejected on further consideration and permanent injunctive relief ultimately is denied.[276] Nor does a party prevail when she receives an interlocutory benefit (such as reversal of the dismissal of a claim or reversal of directed verdict), even where accompanied by favorable judicial statements.[277]

Any changes in the legal relationship must be judicially sanctioned or receive judicial imprimatur, established through an enforceable judgment, order, or consent decree. In *Buckhannon Bd. and Care Home v. West Virginia Dep't of Health and Human Services*, the Supreme Court rejected the "catalyst theory," under which a plaintiff could be a prevailing party when the defendant changes its conduct, rules, or policies in response to litigation, but without a judgment or court order compelling those changes.[278] "Prevailing party," the majority insisted, is a term of art that requires an underlying judicial decree or order; anything else is a product of a defendant's voluntary change in conduct, even if that voluntary change

---

[270] *Buckhannon*, 532 U.S. at 604; *Texas State Teachers*, 489 U.S. at 790; Hensley v. Eckerhart, 461 U.S. 424, 447–48 (1983); Gray v. Bostic, 613 F.3d 1035 (11th Cir. 2010).

[271] Diaz-Rivera v. Rivera-Rodriguez, 377 F.3d 119 (1st Cir. 2004).

[272] *Farrar*, 506 U.S. at 113–14.

[273] *Buckhannon*, 532 U.S. at 603–04.

[274] *Id.* at 604 (citing Maher v. Gagne, 448 U.S. 122 (1980)).

[275] *Farrar*, 506 U.S. at 112–13; *Gray*, 613 F.3d at 1040; Keup v. Hopkins, 596 F.3d 899 (8th Cir. 2010); St. John's Organic Farm v. Gem County Mosquito Abatement Dist., 574 F.3d 1054 (9th Cir. 2009) .

[276] *Sole*, 551 U.S. at 84–86.

[277] *Buckhannon*, 532 U.S. at 641 n.13; Hewitt v. Helms, 482 U.S. 755 (1987).

[278] *Buckhannon*, 532 U.S. at 601–02.

accomplishes precisely what the plaintiff sought to achieve by her lawsuit.[279] Although *Buckhannon* was interpreting the attorney's fee provision of the ADA rather than § 1988(b), the case made clear that other fee-shifting statutes, such as § 1988(b), were subject to the same understanding of prevailing party.[280]

In a concurring opinion, Justice Scalia defended requiring a judicial order. He argued that it is impossible to distinguish a situation in which a defendant changes his conduct or policies after the plaintiff files a lawsuit (which could make the plaintiff a prevailing party under the catalyst theory) and in which a defendant changes his conduct or policies before the plaintiff files the lawsuit but knowing that such a lawsuit might be coming (under which the plaintiff could not be a prevailing party). In either case, the defendant acts on threat of possible or potential liability, but without any legal or judicial compulsion.[281] If the latter does not provide a basis for prevailing-party status (and no one argued it should), then neither does the former.

Disagreement as to the scope of "prevailing party" is often bound-up in disagreement over the underlying policies of § 1988(b). The *Buckhannon* majority rejected the catalyst theory because fees would disincentivize defendants from settling or altering their policies through non-litigation means; the fear of attorney's fees might actually be greater than the fear or amount of actual monetary liability, prompting a defendant to continue litigating simply to avoid fees.[282] On the other hand, Justice Ginsburg insisted in dissent that the catalyst theory would prompt faster change by the defendant; if the defendant remains on the hook for potential fees, faster alteration of its conduct, whether voluntary or by decree, means lower fees.[283] Moreover, whatever judicial policy exists in favor of settlement arguably must yield to congressional policy reflected in § 1988(b) and courts should focus on that policy § 1988(b) is concerned not with whether one case settles, but with how the availability of fees in one case affects the ability of future plaintiffs to find competent counsel to vindicate their rights.[284]

Another baseline theoretical dispute is the relating power of civil rights plaintiffs and the civil rights bar and how that power affects courts' understanding and application of the fees statute. In *Buckhannon*, Justice Scalia warned that a broad conception of prevailing party rewards "extortionist" plaintiffs, who file suit and hope that the defendant caves to extra-legal pressures from the plaintiff's superior resources and "media manipulation."[285] The Court at other times has questioned the real and practical impact of superior-quality representation.[286] Justice Ginsburg responded that this has it backward. Section 1988(b) exists precisely because civil rights plaintiffs lack power and resources and need attorney's fees to attract good

---

[279] *Id.* at 603, 605.

[280] *Id.* at 602–03.

[281] *Id.* at 619 (Scalia, J., concurring).

[282] *Id.* at 608–09; *see also* Evans v. Jeff D., 475 U.S. 717, 734 (1986).

[283] *Buckhannon*, 532 U.S. at 639 (Ginsburg, J., dissenting).

[284] *Evans*, 475 U.S. at 760–61 (Brennan, J., dissenting).

[285] *Buckhannon*, 532 U.S. at 617–18 (Scalia, J., concurring).

[286] *Perdue*, 130 S. Ct. at 1674.

counsel, especially in low-value cases. As for media manipulation, civil rights plaintiffs generally lack the media clout to achieve success in the political arena; they need litigation and the counter-majoritarian judiciary to affect legal change, which they best can do with quality counsel, for which they need broadly available attorney's fees.[287] Narrowing the circumstances in which plaintiffs will be entitled to fees undermines their ability to pursue legal rights and legal change through capable counsel.[288]

§ 7.15 ATTORNEY'S FEES AND RESOLUTION OF LITIGATION

The ironic consequence of *Buckhannon* rejecting the catalyst theory is that plaintiffs now cannot simply accept when government offers to change its conduct or policies. To recover fees, plaintiffs must ensure that they obtain a consent decree or some other order reducing those agreed-to changes into an enforceable judgment with sufficient judicial imprimatur, even if it means rejecting the government voluntarily providing the very constitutional relief the plaintiffs are seeking.

This creates an odd divide between negative/legislative injunctions and positive/administrative injunctions, because a consent decree memorializing voluntary change is unneccessary as to a negative injunction. In *Buckhannon*, for example, the plaintiff assisted-living facility sought a negative injunction — to halt enforce-ment of state regulations that allegedly violated federal law. By repealing the challenged regulations, the state legislature eliminated the target of the action, leaving nothing for the court to enjoin; a court cannot order government officials not to enforce laws that no longer exist.[289] Thus, if government unilaterally amends or repeals challenged policies and moots the case just after the lawsuit is filed, it leaves nothing for the parties or court to reduce to a judgment or consent decree.[290]

Demanding some judicial decree makes more sense as to positive/administrative injunctions, whose essence is that government agrees, with court approval, to take affirmative steps to reform its institutions going forward and the court retains jurisdiction to monitor and ensure compliance with the agreed-upon changes. Even as to administrative injunctions, however, attorney's fees may become part of the process of negotiating the consent decree, often to the plaintiff's detriment. This shows that the *Buckhannon* majority was correct — defendants often really want to avoid paying attorney's fees even while agreeing to other prospective remedies.

---

[287] *Buckhannon*, 532 U.S. at 640 (Ginsburg, J., dissenting).

[288] David Luban, *Taking Out the Adversary: The Assault on Progressive Public-Interest Lawyers*, 91 CAL. L. REV. 209 (2003).

[289] *Cf.* Log Cabin Republicans v. United States, 658 F.3d 1162 (9th Cir. 2011) (repeal of federal statute rendered constitutional challenge to the statute moot).

[290] A case only becomes moot as to injunctive and declaratory relief; it remains live, and attorney's fees remain possible, if the plaintiff seeks damages for past injuries caused by enforcement of government policies or conduct. Buckhannon Bd. & Care Home, Inc. v. W. Va. Dep't of Health & Human Res., 532 U.S. 598, 608–09 (2001).

But this conflicts with the policies underlying § 1988(b) and the theory of the private attorney general.

The Court faced this issue in *Evans v. Jeff D.* In an action challenging deficiencies in educational and health care programs for children with mental and emotional handicaps, the state agreed to settle all claims in a consent decree giving the plaintiffs all the positive injunctive relief they sought — and likely more relief than the plaintiffs would have received from going to trial. But the settlement was contingent on plaintiffs waiving attorney's fees. The majority held that such a condition on the consent decree was not inconsistent with the text, history, or purpose of § 1988(b), and the district court properly accepted the consent decree with that condition. While allowing for an award of attorney's fees, § 1988(b) does not make them non-waivable or non-negotiable; the statute merely added fees to the "arsenal of remedies" available to combat civil rights violations. But it was not "invariably inconsistent" with the statute for a defendant or court to condition settlement on their waiver.[291]

In dissent, Justice Brennan rejected the conception of attorney's fees as simply one more remedy available to a private party. Instead, statutory fees serve a public function — to enable all plaintiffs to obtain legal counsel in all cases. Neither one private plaintiff, one attorney, nor the district court may waive the statutory right where it contravenes the broader public purposes behind fees, as by making it more difficult for future plaintiffs in future cases to find counsel because of the threat of similar waiver demands by future defendants.[292]

§ 7.16 CALCULATING FEES

Prevailing parties (however defined) may recover a "reasonable attorney's fee."[293] Fees are calculated using a "lodestar," the prevailing hourly rate for attorneys in the relevant legal market is multiplied by the number of hours worked on those matters on which the plaintiff prevailed, then increased or decreased by the court in "extraordinary circumstances." Courts favor the lodestar approach because it is objective, cabining the district court's discretion as to the amount of the fee it can award. It also "roughly approximates" what an attorney would have earned representing a paying client by the billable hour.[294]

The lodestar is "presumptively sufficient" to achieve § 1988(b)'s goals of attracting capable counsel to represent plaintiffs by making cases financially worthwhile, in light of prevailing conditions in the legal market. Because the lodestar presumptively includes all relevant factors that make a fee reasonable, any enhancements must be based on factors not already considered in the lodestar calculation or consideration. Any enhancements to the lodestar must be supported by specific evidence, with the fee applicant bearing the burden of persuasion as to the

---

[291] Evans v. Jeff D., 475 U.S. 717, 731–32 (1986).

[292] *Id.* at 752 (Brennan, J., dissenting); David Luban, *Taking Out the Adversary: The Assault on Progressive Public-Interest Lawyers*, 91 CAL. L. REV. 209, 242 (2003).

[293] 42 U.S.C. § 1988(b).

[294] Perdue v. Kenny A., 130 S. Ct. 1662, 1672, 1674 (2010).

reasonableness of the fee awarded. A district court must provide a "reasonably specific explanation" for the award and for any enhancements, identifying and elaborating on the factors it considered and the comparisons used to reach the award.[295] Most recently, the Supreme Court rejected superior attorney performance — that the attorneys did an exceptionally good job and achieved superior results beyond what should have been expected — as a general basis for an enhancement; while possible in some cases, such adjustments must remain "rare" and "exceptional."[296]

What constitutes a "reasonable attorney's fee" is influenced by the degree of success achieved in litigation, such that the fee award must correlate somewhat with the extent of the plaintiff's success. If a plaintiff achieves only partial or limited success (success on some claims but not others or against some parties but not others) a fee award based on the total time working on the entire case may be excessive; courts thus may have to disaggregate unrelated claims, issues, or parties where a plaintiff prevails on some and not on others.[297] In damages actions, the degree of success also considers the amount recovered in damages as compared to the amount sought.[298] And there may be circumstances in which the plaintiff recovers nothing beyond a "moral victory" that does not warrant any fee at all.[299]

A common problem is determining reasonable fee where a plaintiff recovers only nominal damages. Such a plaintiff has prevailed for § 1988(b) purposes, in that she has achieved a change in her legal relationship as to the defendant.[300] And given the "absolute" nature of constitutional rights, she has succeeded in proving a violation of a protected right.[301] But a plaintiff who recovers only nominal damages arguably has failed to prove an actual compensable injury, an essential element of a damages claim; to the extent she recovers nominal damages only because of such a failure of an element, "the only reasonable fee is usually no fee at all."[302]

In a concurring opinion in *Farrar v. Hobby*, Justice O'Connor identified three factors that courts should consider in determining whether a party who recovers nominal or minimal damages should receive a fee: (1) the difference between the amount of money sought and the nominal amount recovered; (2) the significance of the legal issues on which the plaintiff prevailed; and (3) whether the suit accomplished some "public goal."[303] The degree of success is critical.[304] For example, the plaintiff in *Farrar* recovered nominal damages from one defendant after requesting $17 million from six defendants; that dramatic difference informed the conclusion

---

[295] *Id.* at 1676.

[296] *Id.* at 1673–74.

[297] Diaz-Rivera v. Rivera-Rodriguez, 377 F.3d 119 (1st Cir. 2004).

[298] Farrar v. Hobby, 506 U.S. 103 (1992).

[299] Mercer v. Duke Univ., 401 F.3d 199, 210 (4th Cir. 2005).

[300] *Farrar*, 506 U.S. at 112–13; Keup v. Hopkins, 596 F.3d 899 (8th Cir. 2010).

[301] Carey v. Piphus, 435 U.S. 247 (1978).

[302] *Farrar*, 506 U.S. at 115 (citing City of Riverside v. Rivera, 477 U.S. 561 (1986) (Powell, J., concurring)).

[303] *Id.* at 120–22 (O'Connor, J., concurring).

[304] *Farrar*, 506 U.S. at 114; Gray v. Bostic, 613 F.3d 1035 (11th Cir. 2010).

that the plaintiff had not fully prevailed.[305] As Justice O'Connor put it, the plaintiff "asked for a bundle and got a pittance."[306] Several circuits have adopted O'Connor's approach as the controlling standard, rejecting the seemingly absolute language in *Farrar*'s majority opinion[307] and awarding at least limited attorney's fees where the plaintiff recovers nominal damages.[308] Plaintiffs can protect their ability to recover fees at the end of the action by being realistic and strategic about the strength of their case at the outset— such as recognizing when a case is likely worth only nominal damages[309] or not requesting millions of dollars in damages in a case that does not involve physical injury or long incarceration and thus is not likely to produce substantial damages.[310]

§ 7.17 ATTORNEY'S FEES PUZZLE

Steven Lefemine and the members of his church regularly engage in public demonstrations in which they display pictures of aborted fetuses as a protest against legalized abortion. In November 2005, Lefemine and other church members demonstrated, with pictures and signs, at a busy municipal intersection. Citing complaints about the graphic posters, police informed Lefemine that he would be ticketed for disturbing the peace if the signs were not discarded; the protesters disbanded. One year later, Lefemine and his group contact the police department about their intention to hold a similar public demonstration in the future and are warned that the police would undertake similar enforcement efforts.

Lefemine brings a § 1983 action, alleging violations of his First Amendment rights and seeking nominal damages, a declaratory judgment, a permanent injunction, and attorney's fees. The district court determines that Lefemine's First Amendment rights are being violated by the continued threat of future citations; the court grants a permanent injunction, prohibiting police from "engaging in content-based restrictions on [Lefemine's] display of graphic signs" under similar future circumstances. But the district court refuses to award nominal damages for interference with past demonstrations, concluding that the police defendants were entitled to qualified immunity because the illegality of their conduct was not clearly established at that time.[311]

Consider whether Lefemine now is entitled to an award of attorney's fees.

---

[305] *Id.* at 106–07.

[306] *Id.* at 120 (O'Connor, J., concurring).

[307] *Gray*, 613 F.3d at 1040; Diaz-Rivera v. Rivera-Rodriguez, 377 F.3d 119 (1st Cir. 2004); *see also* Gray v. Bostic, 625 F.3d 692, 703 (11th Cir. 2010) (Wilson, J., dissenting from denial of rehearing en banc).

[308] *Diaz-Rivera*, 377 F.3d at 126–27; *Mercer*, 401 F.3d at 208–09; *but see* Pouillon v. Little, 326 F.3d 713 (6th Cir. 2003) (denying fees).

[309] James E. Pfander, *Resolving the Qualified Immunity Dilemma: Constitutional Tort Claims for Nominal Damages*, 111 Colum. L. Rev. 1601, 1610-11 (2011).

[310] *Supra* § 7.02.

[311] Lefemine v. Wideman, 133 S. Ct. 9 (2012) (per curiam).

§ 7.18 ATTORNEY'S FEES AND PRISONER LITIGATION

42 U.S.C. § 1997e

* * *

(d) Attorney's fees

(1) In any action brought by a prisoner who is confined to any jail, prison, or other correctional facility, in which attorney's fees are authorized under section 1988 of this title, such fees shall not be awarded, except to the extent that—

(A) the fee was directly and reasonably incurred in proving an actual violation of the plaintiff's rights protected by a statute pursuant to which a fee may be awarded under section 1988 of this title; and

(B) (i) the amount of the fee is proportionately related to the court ordered relief for the violation; or

(ii) the fee was directly and reasonably incurred in enforcing the relief ordered for the violation.

(2) Whenever a monetary judgment is awarded in an action described in paragraph (1), a portion of the judgment (not to exceed 25 percent) shall be applied to satisfy the amount of attorney's fees awarded against the defendant. If the award of attorney's fees is not greater than 150 percent of the judgment, the excess shall be paid by the defendant.

(3) No award of attorney's fees in an action described in paragraph (1) shall be based on an hourly rate greater than 150 percent of the hourly rate established under section 3006A of title 18 for payment of court-appointed counsel.

In the Prison Litigation Reform Act Congress also established special rules for recovery of attorney's fees in cases brought by prisoners challenging their conditions of confinement. Fees are available only on a showing that they are "directly and reasonably incurred in providing an actual violation" of the Constitution and that the amount awarded is proportionate to the court-ordered monetary relief or is "directly and reasonably incurred" in enforcing the relief ordered for a violation.[312] Moreover, a portion of any money judgment for a prisoner must be applied to satisfy the award of attorney's fees.[313]

Recall that the PLRA reflects a blatant congressional effort to limit what it perceived as abusive § 1983 claims.[314] Congress plainly recognized that restricting attorney's fees goes a long way to restricting prisoner litigation. By limiting

---

[312] 42 U.S.C. § 1997e(d)(1).

[313] 42 U.S.C. § 1997e(d)(2).

[314] Mark Tushnet & Larry Yackle, *Symbolic Statutes and Real Laws: The Pathologies of the*

incentives for competent counsel to represent prisoners and represent them well, the act limits the ability of prisoners to litigate successfully, which may limit the incentives for the plaintiffs to even bring civil rights and constitutional cases in the first instance.

Antiterrorism and Effective Death Penalty Act and the Prison Litigation Reform Act, 47 Duke L.J. 1, 64 (1997); *supra* § 7.09.

Appendix A

THE CONSTITUTION OF THE UNITED STATES

WE THE PEOPLE of the United States, in Order to form a more perfect Union, establish Justice, insure domestic Tranquility, provide for the common defence, promote the general Welfare, and secure the Blessings of Liberty to ourselves and our Posterity, do ordain and establish this Constitution for the United States of America.

ARTICLE I

SECTION 1.

All legislative Powers herein granted shall be vested in a Congress of the United States, which shall consist of a Senate and House of Representatives.

SECTION 2.

1* The House of Representatives shall be composed of Members chosen every second Year by the People of the several States, and the Electors in each State shall have the Qualifications requisite for Electors of the most numerous Branch of the State Legislature.

2 No Person shall be a Representative who shall not have attained to the Age of twenty-five Years, and been seven Years a Citizen of the United States, and who shall not, when elected, be an Inhabitant of that State in which he shall be chosen.

3 [Representatives and direct Taxes shall be apportioned among the several States which may be included within this Union, according to their respective Numbers, which shall be determined by adding to the whole Number of free Persons, including those bound to Service for a Term of Years, and excluding Indians not taxed, three fifths of all other Persons.]** The actual Enumeration shall be made within three Years after the first Meeting of the Congress of the United States, and within every subsequent Term of ten years, in such Manner as they shall by Law direct. The Number of Representatives shall not exceed one for every thirty Thousand, but each State shall have at Least one Representative; and until such enumeration shall be made, the State of New Hampshire shall be entitled to chuse three, Massachusetts eight, Rhode-Island and Providence Plantations one, Connecticut five, New-York six, New Jersey four, Pennsylvania eight, Delaware one, Maryland six, Virginia ten, North Carolina five, South Carolina five, and Georgia three.

---

* Note: The superior number preceding the paragraphs designates the number of the clause.

** Note: The part included in brackets was changed by amendments XIII, XIV, and XV.

4 When vacancies happen in the Representation from any State, the Executive Authority thereof shall issue Writs of Election to fill such vacancies.

5 The House of Representatives shall chuse their Speaker and other Officers; and shall have the sole Power of Impeachment.

SECTION 3.

1 The Senate of the United States shall be composed of two Senators from each State, [chosen by the Legislature]* thereof, for six Years; and each Senator shall have one Vote.

2 Immediately after they shall be assembled in Consequence of the first Election, they shall be divided as equally as may be into three Classes. The Seats of the Senators of the first Class shall be vacated at the Expiration of the Second Year, of the second Class at the Expiration of the fourth Year, and the third Class at the Expiration of the sixth Year, so that one-third may be chosen every second Year; [and if Vacancies happen by Resignation, or otherwise, during the Recess of the Legislature of any State, the Executive thereof may make temporary Appointments until the next Meeting of the Legislature, which shall then fill such Vacancies].**

3 No Person shall be a Senator who shall not have attained to the Age of thirty Years, and been nine Years a Citizen of the United States, and who shall not, when elected, be an inhabitant of that State for which he shall be chosen.

4 The Vice President of the United States shall be President of the Senate, but shall have no Vote, unless they be equally divided.

5 The Senate shall chuse their other Officers, and also a President pro tempore, in the absence of the Vice President, or when he shall exercise the Office of President of the United States.

6 The Senate shall have the sole Power to try all Impeachments. When sitting for that Purpose, they shall be on Oath or Affirmation. When the President of the United States is tried, the Chief Justice shall preside: And no Person shall be convicted without the Concurrence of two-thirds of the Members present.

7 Judgment in Cases of Impeachment shall not extend further than to removal from Office, and disqualification to hold and enjoy any Office of honor, Trust, or Profit under the United States: but the Party convicted shall nevertheless be liable and subject to Indictment, Trial, Judgment, and Punishment, according to Law.

SECTION 4.

1 The Times, Places and Manner of holding Elections for Senators and Representatives, shall be prescribed in each State by the Legislature thereof; but the Congress may at any time by Law make or alter such Regulations, except as to the Places of chusing Senators.

---

* The part included in brackets was repealed by clause 1 of amendment XVII.

** The part included in brackets was changed by clause 2 of amendment XVII.

2 The Congress shall assemble at least once in every Year, and such Meeting shall [be on the first Monday in December,] unless they shall by Law appoint a different Day.*

SECTION 5.

1 Each House shall be the Judge of the Elections, Returns, and Qualifications of its own Members, and a Majority of each shall constitute a Quorum to do Business; but a smaller Number may adjourn from day to day, and may be authorized to compel the Attendance of absent Members, in such Manner, and under such Penalties as each House may provide.

2 Each House may determine the Rules of its Proceedings, punish its Members for disorderly Behavior, and, with the Concurrence of two thirds expel a Member.

3 Each House shall keep a Journal of its Proceedings, and from time to time publish the same, excepting such Parts as may in their Judgment require Secrecy; and the Yeas and Nays of the Members of either House on any question shall, at the Desire of one fifth of those Present, be entered on the Journal.

4 Neither House, during the Session of Congress, shall, without the Consent of the other, adjourn for more than three days, nor to any other Place than that in which the two Houses shall be sitting.

SECTION 6.

1 The Senators and Representatives shall receive a Compensation for their Services, to be ascertained by Law, and paid out of the Treasury of the United States. They shall in all Cases, except Treason, Felony and Breach of the Peace, be privileged from Arrest during their Attendance at the Session of their respective Houses, and in going to and returning from the same; and for any Speech or Debate in either House, they shall not be questioned in any other Place.

2 No Senator or Representative shall, during the Time for which he was elected, be appointed to any civil Office under the Authority of the United States, which shall have been created, or the Emoluments whereof shall have been encreased during such time; and no Person holding any Office under the United States, shall be a Member of either House during his Continuance in Office.

SECTION 7.

1 All Bills for raising Revenue shall originate in the House of Representatives; but the Senate may propose or concur with Amendments as on other Bills.

2 Every Bill which shall have passed the House of Representatives and the Senate, shall, before it become a Law, be presented to the President of the United States; if he approve he shall sign it, but if not he shall return it, with his Objections to that House in which it shall have originated, who shall enter the Objections at large on their Journal, and proceed to reconsider it. If after such Reconsideration two thirds of that House shall agree to pass the Bill, it shall be sent, together with

---

* The part included in brackets was changed by section 2 of amendment XX.

the Objections, to the other House, by which it shall likewise be reconsidered, and if approved by two thirds of that House, it shall become a Law. But in all such Cases the Votes of both Houses shall be determined by Yeas and Nays, and the Names of the Persons voting for and against the Bill shall be entered on the Journal of each House respectively. If any Bill shall not be returned by the President within ten Days (Sundays excepted) after it shall have been presented to him, the Same shall be a Law, in like Manner as if he had signed it, unless the Congress by their Adjournment prevent its Return, in which Case it shall not be a Law.

3 Every Order, Resolution, or Vote to which the Concurrence of the Senate and House of Representatives may be necessary (except on a question of Adjournment) shall be presented to the President of the United States; and before the Same shall take Effect, shall be approved by him, or being disapproved by him, shall be repassed by two thirds of the Senate and House of Representatives, according to the Rules and Limitations prescribed in the Case of a Bill.

SECTION 8.

1 The Congress shall have Power To lay and collect Taxes, Duties, Imposts and Excises, to pay the Debts and provide for the common Defence and general Welfare of the United States; but all Duties, Imposts and Excises shall be uniform throughout the United States;

2 To borrow money on the credit of the United States;

3 To regulate Commerce with foreign Nations, and among the several States, and with the Indian Tribes;

4 To establish an uniform Rule of Naturalization, and uniform Laws on the subject of Bankruptcies throughout the United States;

5 To coin Money, regulate the Value thereof, and of foreign Coin, and fix the Standard of Weights and Measures;

6 To provide for the Punishment of counterfeiting the Securities and current Coin of the United States;

7 To Establish Post Offices and post Roads;

8 To promote the Progress of Science and useful Arts, by securing for limited Times to Authors and Inventors the exclusive Right to their respective Writings and Discoveries;

9 To constitute Tribunals inferior to the supreme Court;

10 To define and punish Piracies and Felonies committed on the high Seas, and Offenses against the Law of Nations;

11 To declare War, grant Letters of Marque and Reprisal, and make Rules concerning Captures on Land and Water;

12 To raise and support Armies, but no Appropriation of Money to that Use shall be for a longer Term than two Years;

13 To provide and maintain a Navy;

14 To make Rules for the Government and Regulation of the land and naval Forces;

15 To provide for calling forth the Militia to execute the Laws of the Union, suppress insurrections and repel Invasions;

16 To provide for organizing, arming, and disciplining the Militia, and for governing such Part of them as may be employed in the Service of the United States, reserving to the States respectively, the Appointment of the Officers, and the Authority of training the Militia according to the discipline prescribed by Congress;

17 To exercise exclusive Legislation in all Cases whatsoever, over such District (not exceeding ten Miles square) as may, by Cession of particular States, and the acceptance of Congress, become the Seat of the Government of the United States, and to exercise like Authority over all Places purchased by the Consent of the Legislature of the State in which the Same shall be, for the Erection of Forts, Magazines, Arsenals, dock-Yards, and other needful Buildings; And

18 To make all Laws which shall be necessary and proper for carrying into Execution the foregoing Powers, and all other Powers vested by this Constitution in the Government of the United States, or in any Department or Officer thereof.

SECTION 9.

1 The Migration or Importation of Such Persons as any of the States now existing shall think proper to admit, shall not be prohibited by the Congress prior to the Year one thousand eight hundred and eight, but a tax or duty may be imposed on such Importation, not exceeding ten dollars for each Person.

2 The privilege of the Writ of Habeas Corpus shall not be suspended, unless when in Cases of Rebellion or Invasion the public Safety may require it.

3 No Bill of Attainder or ex post facto Law shall be passed.

4* No capitation, or other direct, Tax shall be laid, unless in Proportion to the Census or Enumeration herein before directed to be taken.

5 No Tax or Duty shall be laid on Articles exported from any State.

6 No preference shall be given by any Regulation of Commerce or Revenue to the Ports of one State over those of another: nor shall Vessels bound to, or from, one State be obliged to enter, clear, or pay Duties in another.

7 No money shall be drawn from the Treasury, but in Consequence of Appropriations made by Law; and a regular Statement and Account of the Receipts and Expenditures of all public Money shall be published from time to time.

8 No title of Nobility shall be granted by the United States: And no Person holding any Office of Profit or Trust under them, shall, without the Consent of the Congress, accept of any present, Emolument, Office, or Title, of any kind whatever, from any King, Prince, or foreign State.

---

* *See also* amendment XVI.

SECTION 10.

1 No State shall enter into any Treaty, Alliance, or Confederation; grant Letters of Marque and Reprisal; coin Money; emit Bills of Credit; make any Thing but gold and silver Coin a Tender in Payment of Debts; pass any Bill of Attainder, ex post facto Law, or Law impairing the Obligation of Contracts, or grant any Title of Nobility.

2 No State shall, without the Consent of the Congress, lay any Imposts or Duties on Imports or Exports, except what may be absolutely necessary for executing its inspection Laws; and the net Produce of all Duties and Imposts, laid by any State on Imports or Exports, shall be for the Use of the Treasury of the United States; and all such Laws shall be subject to the Revision and Control of the Congress.

3 No State shall, without the Consent of Congress, lay any duty of Tonnage, keep Troops, or Ships of War in time of Peace, enter into any Agreement or Compact with another State, or with a foreign Power, or engage in War, unless actually invaded, or in such imminent Danger as will not admit of delay.

ARTICLE II

SECTION 1.

1 The executive Power shall be vested in a President of the United States of America. He shall hold his Office during the Term of four Years, and, together with the Vice-President, chosen for the same Term, be elected, as follows:

2 Each State shall appoint, in such Manner as the Legislature thereof may direct, a Number of Electors, equal to the whole Number of Senators and Representatives to which the State may be entitled in the Congress: but no Senator or Representative, or Person holding an Office of Trust or Profit under the United States, shall be appointed an Elector.

[The Electors shall meet in their respective States, and vote by Ballot for two persons of whom one at least shall not be an Inhabitant of the same State with themselves. And they shall make a list of all the Persons voted for, and of the Number of Votes for each; which List they shall sign and certify, and transmit sealed to the Seat of the Government of the United States, directed to the President of the Senate. The President of the Senate shall, in the Presence of the Senate and House of Representatives, open all the Certificates, and the Votes shall then be counted. The Person having the greatest Number of Votes shall be the President, if such Number by a Majority of the whole Number of Electors appointed; and if there be more than one who have such Majority, and have an equal number of Votes, then the House of Representatives shall immediately chuse by Ballot one of them for President; and if no Person have a Majority, then from the five highest on the List the said House shall in like Manner chuse the President. But in chusing the President, the Votes shall be taken by States, the Representation from each State having one Vote; A quorum for this Purpose shall consist of a Member or Members from two-thirds of the States, and a Majority of all the States shall be necessary to a Choice. In every Case, after the Choice of the President the Person having the greatest Number of Votes of the Electors shall be the Vice President. But if there should remain two or more who have equal Votes, the Senate shall chuse from them by Ballot the Vice President.]*

3 The Congress may determine the Time of chusing the Electors and the Day on which they shall give their Votes; which Day shall be the same throughout the United States.

4 No person except a natural born Citizen, or a Citizen of the United States, at the time of the Adoption of this Constitution, shall be eligible to the Office of President; neither shall any Person be eligible to that Office who shall not have attained to the Age of thirty-five Years, and been fourteen Years a Resident within the United States.

5 In case of the removal of the President from Office, or of his Death, Resignation or Inability to discharge the Powers and Duties of the said Office, the same shall devolve on the Vice President, and the Congress may by Law provide for the Case of Removal, Death, Resignation or Inability, both of the President, and Vice President, declaring what Officer shall then act as President, and such Officer shall act accordingly, until the Disability be removed, or a President shall be elected.

6 The President shall, at stated Times, receive for his Services, a Compensation, which shall neither be encreased nor diminished during the Period for which he shall have been elected, and he shall not receive within that Period any other Emolument from the United States, or any of them.

7 Before he enter on the Execution of His Office, he shall take the following Oath or Affirmation: "I do solemnly swear (or affirm) that I will faithfully execute the Office of President of the United States, and will to the best of my Ability, preserve, protect and defend the Constitution of the United States."

SECTION 2.

1 The President shall be Commander in Chief of the Army and Navy of the United States, and of the Militia of the several States, when called into the actual Service of the United States; he may require the Opinion, in writing, of the principal Officer in each of the executive Departments, upon any subject relating to the Duties of their respective Offices, and he shall have Power to grant Reprieves and Pardons for Offences against the United States, except in Cases of Impeachment.

2 He shall have Power, by and with the Advice and Consent of the Senate, to make Treaties, provided two-thirds of the Senators present concur; and he shall nominate, and by and with the Advice and Consent of the Senate, shall appoint Ambassadors, other public Ministers and Consuls, Judges of the supreme Court, and all other Officers of the United States, whose Appointments are not herein otherwise provided for, and which shall be established by Law; but the Congress may by Law vest the Appointment of such inferior Officers, as they think proper, in the President alone, in the Courts of Law, or in the Heads of Departments.

3 The President shall have Power to fill up all Vacancies that may happen during the Recess of the Senate, by granting Commissions which shall expire at the End

---

* The part included in brackets has been superseded by section 3 of amendment XII.

of their next Session.

SECTION 3.

He shall from time to time give to the Congress Information of the State of the Union, and recommend to their Consideration such Measures as he shall judge necessary and expedient; he may, on extraordinary Occasions, convene both Houses, or either of them, and in Case of Disagreement between them, with Respect to the Time of Adjournment, he may adjourn them to such Time as he shall think proper; he shall receive Ambassadors and other public Ministers; he shall take Care that the Laws be faithfully executed, and shall Commission all the Officers of the United States.

SECTION 4.

The President, Vice President and all civil Officers of the United States, shall be removed from Office on Impeachment for, and Conviction of, Treason, Bribery, or other high Crimes and Misdemeanors.

ARTICLE III

SECTION 1.

The judicial Power of the United States, shall be vested in one supreme Court, and in such inferior Courts as the Congress may from time to time ordain and establish. The Judges, both of the supreme and inferior Courts, shall hold their Offices during good Behavior, and shall, at stated Times, receive for their Services a Compensation which shall not be diminished during their Continuance in Office.

SECTION 2.

1 The judicial Power shall extend to all Cases, in Law and Equity, arising under this Constitution, the Laws of the United States, and Treaties made, or which shall be made, under their Authority; to all Cases affecting Ambassadors, other public Ministers and Consuls; to all Cases of admiralty and maritime Jurisdiction; to Controversies to which the United States shall be a Party; to Controversies between two or more States; between a State and Citizens of another State;* between Citizens of different States; between Citizens of the same State claiming Lands under Grants of different States, and between a State, or the Citizens thereof, and foreign States, Citizens or Subjects.

2 In all Cases affecting Ambassadors, other public Ministers and Consuls, and those in which a State shall be Party, the supreme Court shall have original Jurisdiction. In all the other Cases before mentioned, the supreme Court shall have appellate Jurisidiction, both as to Law and Fact, with such Exceptions, and under such Regulations as the Congress shall make.

3 The trial of all Crimes except in Cases of Impeachment shall be by Jury; and such Trial shall be held in the State where the said Crimes shall have been

---

* This clause has been affected by amendment XI.

committed; but when not committed within any State, the Trial shall be at such Place or Places as the Congress may by Law have directed.

SECTION 3.

1 Treason against the United States shall consist only in levying War against them, or, in adhering to their Enemies, giving them Aid and Comfort. No Person shall be convicted of Treason unless on the Testimony of two Witnesses to the same overt Act, or on Confession in open Court.

2 The Congress shall have power to declare the Punishment of Treason, but no Attainder of Treason shall work Corruption of Blood, or Forfeiture except during the Life of the Person attainted.

ARTICLE IV

SECTION 1.

Full Faith and Credit shall be given in each State to the public Acts, Records, and judicial Proceedings of every other State. And the Congress may by general Laws prescribe the Manner in which such Acts, Records and Proceedings shall be proved, and the Effect thereof.

SECTION 2.

1 The Citizens of each State shall be entitled to all Privileges and Immunities of Citizens in the several States.

2 A Person charged in any State with Treason, Felony, or other Crime, who shall flee from Justice, and be found in another State, shall on demand of the executive Authority of the State from which he fled, be delivered up, to be removed to the State having Jurisdiction of the Crime.

3* [No person held to Service or Labour in one State, under the Laws thereof, escaping into another, shall, in Consequence of any Law or Regulation therein, be discharged from such Service or Labour, but shall be delivered up on Claim of the Party to whom such Service or Labour may be due.].

SECTION 3.

1 New States may be admitted by the Congress into this Union; but no new State shall be formed or erected within the Jurisdiction of any other State; nor any State be formed by the Junction of two or more States, or parts of States, without the Consent of the Legislatures of the States concerned as well as of the Congress.

2 The Congress shall have Power to dispose of and make all needful Rules and Regulations respecting the Territory or other Property belonging to the United States; and nothing in this Constitution shall be so construed as to Prejudice any Claims of the United States, or of any particular State.

---

* This clause has been affected by amendment XIII.

SECTION 4.

The United States shall guarantee to every State in this Union a Republican Form of Government, and shall protect each of them against Invasion; and on Application of the Legislature, or of the Executive (when the Legislature cannot be convened) against domestic Violence.

ARTICLE V

The Congress, whenever two-thirds of both Houses shall deem it necessary, shall propose Amendments to this Constiution, or, on the Application of the Legislatures of two-thirds of the several States, shall call a Convention for proposing Amendments, which, in either Case, shall be valid to all Intents and Purposes, as part of this Constitution when ratified by the Legislatures of three-fourths of the several States, or by Conventions in three-fourths thereof, as the one or the other Mode of Ratification may be proposed by the Congress; Provided that no Amendment which may be made prior to the Year One thousand eight hundred and eight shall in any Manner affect the first and fourth Clauses in the Ninth Section of the first Article; and that no State, without its Consent, shall be deprived of its equal Sufferage in the Senate.

ARTICLE VI

1 All Debts contracted and Engagements entered into, before the Adoption of this Constitution shall be as valid against the United States under this Constitution, as under the Confederation.

2 This Constitution, and the Laws of the United States which shall be made in Pursuance thereof; and all Treaties made, or which shall be made, under the Authority of the United States, shall be the supreme Law of the Land; and the Judges in every State shall be bound thereby, any Thing in the Constitution or Laws of any State to the Contrary notwithstanding.

3 The Senators and Representatives before mentioned, and the Members of the several State Legislatures, and all executive and judicial Officers, both of the United States and of the several States, shall be bound by Oath or Affirmation, to support this Constitution; but no religious Test shall ever be required as a Qualification to any Office or public Trust under the United States.

ARTICLE VII

The Ratification of the Conventions of nine States, shall be sufficient for the Establishment of this Constitution between the States so ratifying the Same.

Done in Convention by the Unanimous Consent of the States present the Seventeenth Day of September in the Year of our Lord one thousand seven hundred and Eighty seven and of the Independence of the United States of Americal the Twelfth. IN WITNESS wherof We have herunto subscribed our Names.

G. WASHINGTON — Presidt. and Deputy from Virginia

Attest. — WILLIAM JACKSON, Secretary.

New Hampshire. — John Langdon, Nicholas Gilman.

Massachusetts. — Nathaniel Gorham, Rufus King.

Connecticut. — Wm. Saml. Johnson, Roger Sherman.

New York. — Alexander Hamilton.

New Jersey. — Wil: Livingston, David Brearley, Wm. Paterson, Jona: Dayton.

Pennsylvania. — B. Franklin, Thomas Mifflin, Robt. Morris, Geo. Clymer, Thos. FitzSimons, Jared Ingersoll, James Wilson, Gouv Morris.

Delaware. — Geo: Read, Gunning Bedford Jun, John Dickinson, Richard Bassett, Jaco: Broom.

Maryland. — James McHenry Dan of St. Thos. Jennifer, Danl. Carroll.

Virginia. — John Blair — James Madison, Jr.

North Carolina. — Wm. Blount, Richd. Dobbs Spaight, Hu Williamson.

South Carolina. — J. Rutledge, Charles Cotesworth Pinckney, Charles Pinckney, Pierce Butler.

Georgia. — William Few, Abr. Baldwin.

AMENDMENT I

Congress shall make no law respecting an establishment of religion, or prohibiting the free exercise thereof; or abridging the freedom of speech, or of the press; or the right of the people peaceably to assemble and to petition the Government for a redress of grievances.

AMENDMENT II

A well regulated Militia, being necessary to the security of a free State, the right of the people to keep and bear Arms, shall not be infringed.

AMENDMENT III

No Soldier shall, in time of peace be quartered in any house, without the consent of the Owner, nor in time of war, but in a manner to be prescribed by law.

AMENDMENT IV

The right of the people to be secure in their persons, houses, papers, and effects, against unreasonable searches and seizures, shall not be violated, and no Warrants shall issue, but upon probable cause, supported by Oath or affirmation and particularly describing the Place to be searched, and the persons or things to be seized.

AMENDMENT V

No person shall be held to answer for a capital, or otherwise infamous crime, unless on a presentment or indictment of a Grand Jury, except in cases arising in the land or naval forces, or in the Militia, when in actual service in time of War or public danger; nor shall any person be subject for the same offence to be twice put in jeopardy of life or limb; nor shall be compelled in any criminal case to be a witness against himself, nor be deprived of life, liberty, or property, without due process of law; nor shall private property be taken for public use, without just compensation.

AMENDMENT VI

In all criminal prosecutions, the accused shall enjoy the right to a speedy and public trial, by an impartial jury of the State and district wherein the crime shall have been committed, which district shall have been previously ascertained by law, and to be informed of the nature and cause of the accusation: to be confronted with the witnesses against him; to have compulsory process for obtaining witnesses in his favor, and to have the Assistance of Counsel for his defence.

AMENDMENT VII

In suits at common law, where the value in controversy shall exceed twenty dollars, the right of trial by jury shall be preserved, and no fact tried by jury, shall be otherwise reexamined in any Court of the United States, than according to the rules of the common law.

AMENDMENT VIII

Excessive bail shall not be required, nor excessive fines imposed, nor cruel and unusual punishments inflicted.

AMENDMENT IX

The enumeration in the Constitution, of certain rights, shall not be construed to deny or disparage others retained by the people.

AMENDMENT X

The powers not delegated to the United States by the Constitution, nor prohibited by it to the States, are reserved to the States respectively, or to the people.

(Ratification of the first ten amendments was completed December 15, 1791.)

AMENDMENT XI

The Judicial power of the United States shall not be construed to extend to any suit in law or equity, commenced or prosecuted against one of the United States by Citizens of another State, or by Citizens or Subjects of any Foreign State.

(Declared ratified January 8, 1798.)

AMENDMENT XII

The electors shall meet in their respective states and vote by ballot for President and Vice-President, one of whom, at least, shall not be an inhabitant of the same state with themselves; they shall name in their ballots the person voted for as President, and in distinct ballots the person voted for as Vice-President, and they shall make distinct lists of all persons voted for as President, and of all persons voted for as Vice-President, and of the number of votes for each, which lists they shall sign and certify, and transmit sealed to the seat of the government of the United States, directed to the President of the Senate; The President of the Senate shall, in presence of the Senate and House of Representatives, open all the certificates and the votes shall then be counted; The person having the greatest number of votes for President, shall be the President, if such number be a majority of the whole number of Electors appointed; and if no person have such majority, then from the persons having the highest numbers not exceeding three on the list of those voted for as President, the House of Representatives shall choose immediately, by ballot, the President. But in choosing the President, the votes shall be taken by states, the representation from each state having one vote; a quorum for this purpose shall consist of a member or members from two-thirds of the states, and a majority of all the states shall be necessary to a choice. [And if the House of Representatives shall not choose a President whenever the right of choice shall devolve upon them, before the fourth day of March next following, then the Vice-President shall act as President, as in the case of the death or other constitutional disability of the President.]* The person having the greatest number of votes as Vice-President, shall be the Vice-President, if such number be a majority of the whole number of Electors appointed, and if no person have a majority, then from the two highest numbers on the list, the Senate shall choose the Vice-President; a quorum for the purpose shall consist of two-thirds of the whole number of Senators, and a majority of the whole number shall be necessary to a choice. But no person constitutionally ineligible to the office of President shall be eligible to that of Vice-President of the United States.

(Declared ratified September 25, 1804.)

AMENDMENT XIII

SECTION 1.

Neither slavery nor involuntary servitude, except as a punishment for crime whereof the party shall have been duly convicted, shall exist within the United States, or any place subject to their jurisdiction.

SECTION 2.

Congress shall have power to enforce this article by appropriate legislation.

(Declared ratified December 18, 1865.)

AMENDMENT XIV

SECTION 1.

All persons born or naturalized in the United States, and subject to the jurisdiction thereof, are citizens of the United States and of the State wherein they reside. No State shall make or enforce any law which shall abridge the privileges or

---

* The part included in the brackets has been superseded by section 3 of amendment XX.

immunities of citizens of the United States; nor shall any State deprive any person of life, liberty, or property, without due process of law; nor deny to any person within its jurisdiction the equal protection of the laws.

SECTION 2.

Representatives shall be apportioned among the several States according to their respective numbers, counting the whole number of persons in each State, excluding Indians not taxed. But when the right to vote at any election for the choice of electors for President and Vice-President of the United States, Representatives in Congress, the Executive and Judicial officers of a State, or the members of the Legislature thereof, is denied to any of the male inhabitants of such State, being twenty-one years of age, and citizens of the United States, or in any way abridged, except for participation in rebellion, or other crime, the basis of representation therein shall be reduced in the proportion which the number of such male citizens shall bear to the whole number of male citizens twenty-one years of age in such State.

SECTION 3.

No person shall be a Senator or Representative in Congress, or elector of President and Vice-President, or hold any office, civil or military, under the United States, or under any State, who, having previously taken an oath, as a member of Congress, or as an officer of the United States, or as a member of any State legislature, or as an executive or judicial officer of any State, to support the Constitution of the United States, shall have engaged in insurrection or rebellion against the same, or given aid or comfort to the enemies thereof. But Congress may by a vote of two-thirds of each House, remove such disability.

SECTION 4.

The validity of the public debt of the United States, authorized by law, including debts incurred for payment of pensions and bounties for services in suppressing insurrection or rebellion, shall not be questioned. But neither the United States nor any State shall assume or pay any debt or obligation incurred in aid of insurrection or rebellion against the United States, or any claim for the loss or emancipation of any slave; but all such debts, obligations and claims shall be held illegal and void.

SECTION 5.

The Congress shall have power to enforce, by appropriate legislation, the provisions of this article.

(Declared ratified July 28, 1868.)

AMENDMENT XV

SECTION 1.

The right of citizens of the United States to vote shall not be denied or abridged by the United States or by any State on account of race, color, or previous condition of servitude

SECTION 2.

The Congress shall have power to enforce this article by appropriate legislation.

(Declared ratified March 30, 1870.)

AMENDMENT XVI

The Congress shall have power to lay and collect taxes on incomes, from whatever source derived, without apportionment among the several States, and without regard to any census or enumeration.

(Declared ratified February 25, 1913.)

AMENDMENT XVII

The Senate of the United States shall be composed of two Senators from each State, elected by the people thereof, for six years; and each Senator shall have one vote. The electors in each State shall have the qualifications requisite for electors of the most numerous branch of the State legislatures.

When vacancies happen in the representation of any State in the Senate, the executive authority of such State shall issue writs of election to fill such vacancies: *Provided*, That the legislature of any State may empower the executive thereof to make temporary appointments until the people fill the vacancies by election as the legislature may direct.

This amendment shall not be so construed as to affect the election or term of any Senator chosen before it becomes valid as part of the Constitution.

(Declared ratified May 31, 1913.)

AMENDMENT XVIII

[SECTION 1.]

After one year from the ratification of this article the manufacture, sale, or transportation of intoxicating liquors within, the importation thereof into, or the exportation thereof from the United States and all territory subject to the jurisdiction thereof for beverage purposes is hereby prohibited.

[SECTION 2.]

The Congress and the several States shall have concurrent power to enforce this article by appropriate legislation.

[SECTION 3.]

This article shall be inoperative unless it shall have been ratified as an amendment to the Constitution by the legislatures of the several States, as provided in the Constitution, within seven years from the date of the submission hereof to the

States by the Congress.]*

AMENDMENT XIX

The right of citizens of the United States to vote shall not be denied or abridged by the United States or by any State on account of sex.

Congress shall have power to enforce this article by appropriate legislation.

(Declared ratified August 26, 1920.)

AMENDMENT XX

SECTION 1.

The terms of the President and Vice-President shall end at noon on the 20th day of January, and the terms of Senators and Representatives at noon on the 3d day of January, of the years in which such terms would have ended if this article had not been ratified; and the terms of their successors shall then begin.

SECTION 2.

The Congress shall assemble at least once in every year, and such meeting shall begin at noon on the 3d day of January, unless they shall by law appoint a different day.

SECTION 3.

If, at the time for the beginning of the term of the President, the President elect shall have died, the Vice-President elect shall become President. If a President shall not have been chosen before the time fixed for the beginning of his term, or if the President elect shall have failed to qualify, then the Vice-President elect shall act as President until a President shall have qualified; and the Congress may by law provide for the case wherein neither a President elect nor a Vice-President elect shall have qualified, declaring who shall then act as President, or the manner in which one who is to act shall be selected, and such person shall act accordingly until a President or Vice-President shall have qualified.

SECTION 4.

The Congress may by law provide for the case of the death of any of the persons from whom the House of Representatives may choose a President whenever the right of choice shall have devolved upon them and for the case of the death of any of the persons from whom the Senate may choose a Vice-President whenever the right of choice shall have devolved upon them.

---

* Amendment XVIII was repealed by section 1 of amendment XXI. (Declared ratified January 29, 1919.)

SECTION 5.

Sections 1 and 2 shall take effect on the 15th day of October following the ratification of this article.

SECTION 6.

This article shall be inoperative unless it shall have been ratified as an amendment to the Constitution by the legislatures of three-fourths of the several States within seven years from the date of its submission.

(Declared ratified February 6, 1933.)

AMENDMENT XXI

SECTION 1.

The eighteenth article of amendment to the Constitution of the United States is hereby repealed.

SECTION 2.

The transportation or importation into any State, Territory, or possession of the United States for delivery or use therein of intoxicating liquors, in violation of the laws thereof, is hereby prohibited.

SECTION 3.

This article shall be inoperative unless it shall have been ratified as an amendment to the Constitution by conventions in the several States, as provided in the Constitution, within seven years from the date of the submission hereof to the States by the Congress.

(Declared ratified December 5, 1933.)

AMENDMENT XXII

SECTION 1.

No person shall be elected to the office of the President more than twice, and no person who has held the office of President, or acted as President, for more than two years of a term to which some other person was elected President shall be elected to the office of the President more than once. But this article shall not apply to any person holding the office of President when this Article was proposed by the Congress, and shall not prevent any person who may be holding the office of President, or acting as President, during the term within which this Article becomes operative from holding the office of President or acting as President during the remainder of such term.

SECTION 2.

This article shall be inoperative unless it shall have been ratified as an amendment to the Constitution by the legislatures of three-fourths of the several

States within seven years from the date of its submission to the States by the Congress.

(Declared ratified March 1, 1951.)

AMENDMENT XXIII

SECTION 1.

The District constituting the seat of Government of the United States shall appoint in such manner as the Congress may direct:

A number of electors of President and Vice President equal to the whole number of Senators and Representatives in Congress to which the District would be entitled if it were a State, but in no event more than the least populous State; they shall be in addition to those appointed by the States, but they shall be considered, for the purposes of the election of President and Vice President, to be electors appointed by a State; and they shall meet in the District and perform such duties as provided by the twelfth article of amendment.

SECTION 2.

The Congress shall have power to enforce this article by appropriate legislation.

(Declared ratified April 3, 1961.)

AMENDMENT XXIV

SECTION 1.

The right of citizens of the United States to vote in any primary or other election for President or Vice President, for electors for President or Vice President, or for Senator or Representative in Congress, shall not be denied or abridged by the United States or any State by reason of failure to pay any poll tax or other tax.

SECTION 2.

The Congress shall have power to enforce this article by appropriate legislation.

(Declared ratified February 4, 1962.)

AMENDMENT XXV

SECTION 1.

In case of the removal of the President from office or of his death or resignation, the Vice President shall become President.

SECTION 2.

Whenever there is a vacancy in the office of the Vice President, the President shall nominate a Vice President who shall take office upon confirmation by a majority vote of both Houses of Congress.

SECTION 3.

Whenever the President transmits to the President pro tempore of the Senate and the Speaker of the House of Representatives his written declaration that he is unable to discharge the powers and duties of his office, and until he transmits to them a written declaration to the contrary, such powers and duties shall be discharged by the Vice President as Acting President.

SECTION 4.

Whenever the Vice President and a majority of either the principal officers of the executive departments or of such other body as Congress may by law provide, transmit to the President pro tempore of the Senate and the Speaker of the House of Representatives their written declaration that the President is unable to discharge the powers and duties of his office, the Vice President shall immediately assume the powers and the duties of the office as Acting President.

Thereafter, when the President transmits to the President pro tempore of the Senate and the Speaker of the House of Representatives his written declaration that no inability exists, he shall resume the powers and duties of this office unless the Vice President and a majority of either the principal officers of the executive department or of such other body as Congress may by law provide, transmit within four days to the President pro tempore of the Senate and the Speaker of the House of Representatives their written declaration that the President is unable to discharge the powers and duties of his office. Thereupon Congress shall decide the issue, assembling within forty-eight hours for that purpose if not in session. If the Congress, within twenty-one days after receipt of the latter written declaration, or, if Congress is not in session, within twenty-one days after Congress is required to assemble, determines by two-thirds vote of both Houses that the President is unable to discharge the powers and duties of his office, the Vice President shall continue to discharge the same as Acting President; otherwise, the President shall resume the powers and duties of his office.

(Declared ratified February 10, 1967.)

AMENDMENT XXVI

SECTION 1.

The right of citizens of the United States, who are eighteen years of age or older, to vote shall not be denied or abridged by the United States or by any State on account of age.

SECTION 2.

The Congress shall have power to enforce this article by appropriate legislation.

(Declared ratified July 1, 1971.)

AMENDMENT XXVII

No law varying the compensation for the services of the Senators and Representatives shall take effect, until an election of Representatives shall have intervened.

(Declared ratified May 7, 1992.)

Appendix B

SELECTED PROVISIONS OF THE UNITED STATES CODE AND FEDERAL RULES OF CIVIL PROCEDURE

UNITED STATES CODE
Title 18

18 U.S.C. § 241   Conspiracy against rights (§ 3 of Civil Rights Act of 1870)

If two or more persons conspire to injure, oppress, threaten, or intimidate any person in any State, Territory, Commonwealth, Possession, or District in the free exercise or enjoyment of any right or privilege secured to him by the Constitution or laws of the United States, or because of his having so exercised the same; or

If two or more persons go in disguise on the highway, or on the premises of another, with intent to prevent or hinder his free exercise or enjoyment of any right or privilege so secured—

They shall be fined under this title or imprisoned not more than ten years, or both; and if death results from the acts committed in violation of this section or if such acts include kidnapping or an attempt to kidnap, aggravated sexual abuse or an attempt to commit aggravated sexual abuse, or an attempt to kill, they shall be fined under this title or imprisoned for any term of years or for life, or both, or may be sentenced to death.

18 U.S.C. § 242   Deprivation of rights under law (§ 2 of Civil Rights Act of 1866 and Civil Rights Act of 1870)

Whoever, under color of any law, statute, ordinance, regulation, or custom, willfully subjects any person in any State, Territory, Commonwealth, Possession, or District to the deprivation of any rights, privileges, or immunities secured or protected by the Constitution or laws of the United States, or to different punishments, pains, or penalties, on account of such person being an alien, or by reason of his color, or race, than are prescribed for the punishment of citizens, shall be fined under this title or imprisoned not more than one year, or both * * *

18 U.S.C. § 3626   Appropriate remedies with respect to prision conditions (Prison Litigation Reform Act of 1996)

(a)   **Requirements for relief.—**

(1)   **Prospective relief.—**

(A) Prospective relief in any civil action with respect to prison conditions shall extend no further than necessary to correct the violation of the Federal right of a particular plaintiff or plaintiffs. The court shall not grant or approve any prospective relief unless the court finds that such relief is narrowly drawn, extends no further than necessary to correct the violation of the Federal right, and is the least intrusive means necessary to correct the violation of the Federal right. The court shall give substantial weight to any adverse impact on public safety or the operation of a criminal justice system caused by the relief.

(B) The court shall not order any prospective relief that requires or permits a government official to exceed his or her authority under State or local law or otherwise violates State or local law, unless—

(i) Federal law requires such relief to be ordered in violation of State or local law;

(ii) the relief is necessary to correct the violation of a Federal right; and

(iii) no other relief will correct the violation of the Federal right.

(C) Nothing in this section shall be construed to authorize the courts, in exercising their remedial powers, to order the construction of prisons or the raising of taxes, or to repeal or detract from otherwise applicable limitations on the remedial powers of the courts.

(2) Preliminary injunctive relief.— In any civil action with respect to prison conditions, to the extent otherwise authorized by law, the court may enter a temporary restraining order or an order for preliminary injunctive relief. Preliminary injunctive relief must be narrowly drawn, extend no further than necessary to correct the harm the court finds requires preliminary relief, and be the least intrusive means necessary to correct that harm. The court shall give substantial weight to any adverse impact on public safety or the operation of a criminal justice system caused by the preliminary relief and shall respect the principles of comity set out in paragraph (1)(B) in tailoring any preliminary relief. Preliminary injunctive relief shall automatically expire on the date that is 90 days after its entry, unless the court makes the findings required under subsection (a)(1) for the entry of prospective relief and makes the order final before the expiration of the 90-day period.

(3) Prisoner release order.—

(A) In any civil action with respect to prison conditions, no court shall enter a prisoner release order unless—

(i) a court has previously entered an order for less intrusive relief that has failed to remedy the deprivation of the Federal right sought to be remedied through the prisoner release order; and

(ii) the defendant has had a reasonable amount of time to comply with the previous court orders.

(B) In any civil action in Federal court with respect to prison conditions, a prisoner release order shall be entered only by a three-judge court in accordance with section 2284 of title 28, if the requirements of subparagraph (E) have been met.

(C) A party seeking a prisoner release order in Federal court shall file with any request for such relief, a request for a three-judge court and materials sufficient to demonstrate that the requirements of subparagraph (A) have been met.

(D) If the requirements under subparagraph (A) have been met, a Federal judge before whom a civil action with respect to prison conditions is pending who believes that a prison release order should be considered may sua sponte request the convening of a three-judge court to determine whether a prisoner release order should be entered.

(E) The three-judge court shall enter a prisoner release order only if the court finds by clear and convincing evidence that—

(i) crowding is the primary cause of the violation of a Federal right; and

(ii) no other relief will remedy the violation of the Federal right.

(F) Any State or local official including a legislator or unit of government whose jurisdiction or function includes the appropriation of funds for the construction, operation, or maintenance of prison facilities, or the prosecution or custody of persons who may be released from, or not admitted to, a prison as a result of a prisoner release order shall have standing to oppose the imposition or continuation in effect of such relief and to seek termination of such relief, and shall have the right to intervene in any proceeding relating to such relief.

(b) **Termination of relief.—**

(1) **Termination of prospective relief.—**

(A) In any civil action with respect to prison conditions in which prospective relief is ordered, such relief shall be terminable upon the motion of any party or intervener—

(i) 2 years after the date the court granted or approved the prospective relief;

(ii) 1 year after the date the court has entered an order denying termination of prospective relief under this paragraph; or

(iii) in the case of an order issued on or before the date of enactment of the Prison Litigation Reform Act, 2 years after such date of enactment.

(B) Nothing in this section shall prevent the parties from agreeing to terminate or modify relief before the relief is terminated under subparagraph (A).

(2) **Immediate termination of prospective relief.—** In any civil action with respect to prison conditions, a defendant or intervener shall be entitled to the immediate termination of any prospective relief if the relief was approved or granted in the absence of a finding by the court that the relief is narrowly drawn, extends no further than necessary to correct the violation of the Federal right, and is the least intrusive means necessary to correct the violation of the Federal right.

(3) **Limitation.—** Prospective relief shall not terminate if the court makes written findings based on the record that prospective relief remains necessary to correct a current and ongoing violation of the Federal right, extends no further than necessary to correct the violation of the Federal right, and that the prospective relief is narrowly drawn and the least intrusive means to correct the violation.

(4) **Termination or modification of relief.—** Nothing in this section shall prevent any party or intervener from seeking modification or termination before the relief is terminable under paragraph (1) or (2), to the extent that modification or termination would otherwise be legally permissible.

(c) **Settlements.—**

(1) **Consent decrees.—** In any civil action with respect to prison conditions, the court shall not enter or approve a consent decree unless it complies with the limitations on relief set forth in subsection (a).

(2) **Private settlement agreements.—**

(A) Nothing in this section shall preclude parties from entering into a private settlement agreement that does not comply with the limitations on relief set forth in subsection (a), if the terms of that agreement are not subject to court enforcement other than the reinstatement of the civil proceeding that the agreement settled.

(B) Nothing in this section shall preclude any party claiming that a private settlement agreement has been breached from seeking in State court any remedy available under State law.

* * *

(e) **Procedure for motions affecting prospective relief.—**

(1) **Generally.—** The court shall promptly rule on any motion to modify or terminate prospective relief in a civil action with respect to prison conditions. Mandamus shall lie to remedy any failure to issue a prompt ruling on such a motion.

(2) **Automatic stay.—** Any motion to modify or terminate prospective relief made under subsection (b) shall operate as a stay during the period—

(A) (i) beginning on the 30th day after such motion is filed, in the case of a motion made under paragraph (1) or (2) of subsection (b); or

(ii) beginning on the 180th day after such motion is filed, in the case of a motion made under any other law; and

(B) ending on the date the court enters a final order ruling on the motion.

(3) **Postponement of automatic stay.—** The court may postpone the effective date of an automatic stay specified in subsection (e)(2)(A) for not more than 60 days for good cause. No postponement shall be permissible because of general congestion of the court's calendar.

(4) **Order blocking the automatic stay.—**

Any order staying, suspending, delaying, or barring the operation of the automatic stay described in paragraph (2) (other than an order to postpone the effective date of the automatic stay under paragraph (3)) shall be treated as an order refusing to dissolve or modify an injunction and shall be appealable pursuant to section 1292(a)(1) of title 28, United States Code, regardless of how the order is styled or whether the order is termed a preliminary or a final ruling.

Title 26

26 U.S.C. § 7421   Prohibition of suits to restrain assessment or collection

(a) Except as provided... no suit for the purpose of restraining the assessment or collection of any tax shall be maintained in any court by any person, whether or not such person is the person against whom such tax was assessed.

* * *

Title 28

28 U.S.C. § 1253   Direct appeals from decisions of three-judge courts

Except as otherwise provided by law, any party may appeal to the Supreme Court from an order granting or denying, after notice and hearing, an interlocutory or permanent injunction in any civil action, suit or proceeding required by any Act of Congress to be heard and determined by a district court of three judges.

28 U.S.C. § 1254   Courts of appeals; certiorari; certified questions

Cases in the courts of appeals may be reviewed by the Supreme Court by the following methods:

(1) By writ of certiorari granted upon the petition of any party to any civil or criminal case, before or after rendition of judgment or decree;

(2) By certification at any time by a court of appeals of any question of law in any civil or criminal case as to which instructions are desired, and upon such certification the Supreme Court may give binding instructions or require the entire record to be sent up for decision of the entire matter in controversy.

28 U.S.C. § 1257   State courts; certiorari (prior to Supreme Court Case Selections Act, Pub. L. 100-352, 102 Stat. 662 (1988))

Final judgments or decrees rendered by the highest court of a State in which a decision could be had, may be reviewed by the Supreme Court as follows:

(1) By appeal, where is drawn in question the validity of a treaty or statute of the United States and the decision is against its validity.

(2) By appeal, where is drawn in question the validity of a statute of any state on the ground of its being repugnant to the Constitution, treaties or laws of the United States, and the decision is in favor of its validity.

(3) By writ of certiorari, where the validity of a treaty or statute of the United States is drawn in question or where the validity of a State statute is drawn in question on the ground of its being repugnant to the Constitution, treaties or laws of the United States, or where any title, right, privilege or immunity is specially set up or claimed under the Constitution, treaties or statutes of, or

commission held or authority exercised under, the United States.

For the purposes of this section, the term 'highest court of a State' includes the District of Columbia Court of Appeals."

28 U.S.C. § 1257   State courts; certiorari (as amended by Supreme Court Case Selections Act, Pub. L. 100-352, 102 Stat. 662 (1988))

(a) Final judgments or decrees rendered by the highest court of a State in which a decision could be had, may be reviewed by the Supreme Court by writ of certiorari where the validity of a treaty or statute of the United States is drawn in question or where the validity of a statute of any State is drawn in question on the ground of its being repugnant to the Constitution, treaties, or laws of the United States, or where any title, right, privilege, or immunity is specially set up or claimed under the Constitution or the treaties or statutes of, or any commission held or authority exercised under, the United States.

(b) For the purposes of this section, the term "highest court of a State" includes the District of Columbia Court of Appeals.

28 U.S.C. § 1291   Final decisions of district courts

The courts of appeals (other than the United States Court of Appeals for the Federal Circuit) shall have jurisdiction of appeals from all final decisions of the district courts of the United States...

28 U.S.C. § 1292   Interlocutory decisions

(a) Except as provided in subsections (c) and (d) of this section, the courts of appeals shall have jurisdiction of appeals from:

(1) Interlocutory orders of the district courts of the United States, the United States District Court for the District of the Canal Zone, the District Court of Guam, and the District Court of the Virgin Islands, or of the judges thereof, granting, continuing, modifying, refusing or dissolving injunctions, or refusing to dissolve or modify injunctions, except where a direct review may be had in the Supreme Court;

* * *

(b) When a district judge, in making in a civil action an order not otherwise appealable under this section, shall be of the opinion that such order involves a controlling question of law as to which there is substantial ground for difference of opinion and that an immediate appeal from the order may materially advance the ultimate termination of the litigation, he shall so state in writing in such order. The Court of Appeals which would have jurisdiction of an appeal of such action may thereupon, in its discretion, permit an appeal to be taken from such order, if application is made to it within ten days after the entry of the order: Provided, however, That application for an appeal hereunder shall not stay proceedings in the district court unless the district judge or the Court of Appeals or a judge thereof shall so order.

28 U.S.C. § 1331   Federal question

The district courts shall have original jurisdiction of all civil actions arising under the Constitution, laws, or treaties of the United States.

28 U.S.C. § 1341   Taxes by states

The district courts shall not enjoin, suspend or restrain the assessment, levy or collection of any tax under State law where a plain, speedy and efficient remedy may be had in the courts of such State.

28 U.S.C. § 1343   Civil rights and elective franchise

(a) The district courts shall have original jurisdiction of any civil action authorized by law to be commenced by any person:

* * *

(3) To redress the deprivation, under color of any State law, statute, ordinance, regulation, custom or usage, of any right, privilege or immunity secured by the Constitution of the United States or by any Act of Congress providing for equal rights of citizens or of all persons within the jurisdiction of the United States...

28 U.S.C. § 1346   United States as defendant

* * *

(b) (1) Subject to the provisions of chapter 171 of this title, the district courts, together with the United States District Court for the District of the Canal Zone and the District Court of the Virgin Islands, shall have exclusive jurisdiction of civil actions on claims against the United States, for money damages, accruing on and after January 1, 1945, for injury or loss of property, or personal injury or death caused by the negligent or wrongful act or omission of any employee of the Government while acting within the scope of his office or employment, under circumstances where the United States, if a private person, would be liable to the claimant in accordance with the law of the place where the act or omission occurred.

(2) No person convicted of a felony who is incarcerated while awaiting sentencing or while serving a sentence may bring a civil action against the United States or an agency, officer, or employee of the Government, for mental or emotional injury suffered while in custody without a prior showing of physical injury.

28 U.S.C. § 1367   Supplemental jurisdiction

(a) Except as provided * * *, in any civil action of which the district courts have original jurisdiction, the district courts shall have supplemental jurisdiction over all other claims that are so related to claims in the action within such original jurisdiction that they form part of the same case or controversy under Article III of the United States Constitution. Such supplemental jurisdiction shall include claims that involve the joinder or intervention of additional parties.

* * *

(c) The district courts may decline to exercise supplemental jurisdiction over a claim under subsection (a) if—

(1) the claim raises a novel or complex issue of State law,

(2) the claim substantially predominates over the claim or claims over which the district court has original jurisdiction,

(3) the district court has dismissed all claims over which it has original jurisdiction, or

(4) in exceptional circumstances, there are other compelling reasons for declining jurisdiction.

(d) The period of limitations for any claim asserted under subsection (a), and for any other claim in the same action that is voluntarily dismissed at the same time as or after the dismissal of the claim under subsection (a), shall be tolled while the claim is pending and for a period of 30 days after it is dismissed unless State law provides for a longer tolling period.

28 U.S.C. § 1738   State and territorial statutes and judicial proceedings; full faith and credit (Full Faith and Credit Act)

* * *

Such Acts, records and judicial proceedings or copies thereof, so authenticated, shall have the same full faith and credit in every court within the United States and its Territories and Possessions as they have by law or usage in the courts of such State, Territory or Possession from which they are taken.

28 U.S.C. § 2201   Creation of remedy (Declaratory Judgment Act)

(a) In a case of actual controversy within its jurisdiction, except with respect to Federal taxes other than actions brought under section 7428 of the Internal Revenue Code of 1986, a proceeding under section 505 or 1146 of Title 11 or in any civil action involving an antidumping or countervailing duty proceeding regarding a class or kind of merchandise of a free trade area country (as defined in section 516A(f)(10) of the Tariff Act of 1930), as determined by the administering authority, any court of the United States, upon the filing of an appropriate pleading, may declare the rights and other legal relations of any interested party seeking such declaration, whether or not further relief is or could be sought. Any such declaration shall have the force and effect of a final judgment or decree and shall be reviewable as such.

28 U.S.C. § 2202   Further relief (Declaratory Judgment Act)

Further necessary or proper relief based on a declaratory judgment or decree may be granted, after reasonable notice and hearing, against any adverse party whose rights have been determined by such judgment.

28 U.S.C. § 2241   Power to grant writ

(a) Writs of habeas corpus may be granted by the Supreme Court, any justice thereof, the district courts and any circuit judge within their respective jurisdictions. The order of a circuit judge shall be entered in the records of the district court of the district wherein the restraint complained of is had.

(b) The Supreme Court, any justice thereof, and any circuit judge may decline to entertain an application for a writ of habeas corpus and may transfer the application for hearing and determination to the district court having jurisdiction to entertain it.

(c) The writ of habeas corpus shall not extend to a prisoner unless—

(1) He is in custody under or by color of the authority of the United States or is committed for trial before some court thereof; or

(2) He is in custody for an act done or omitted in pursuance of an Act of Congress, or an order, process, judgment or decree of a court or judge of the United States; or

(3) He is in custody in violation of the Constitution or laws or treaties of the United States; or

(4) He, being a citizen of a foreign state and domiciled therein is in custody for an act done or omitted under any alleged right, title, authority, privilege, protection, or exemption claimed under the commission, order or sanction of any foreign state, or under color thereof, the validity and effect of which depend upon the law of nations; or

(5) It is necessary to bring him into court to testify or for trial.

28 U.S.C. § 2253   Appeal

* * *

(c) (1) Unless a circuit justice or judge issues a certificate of appealability, an appeal may not be taken to the court of appeals from—

(A) the final order in a habeas corpus proceeding in which the detention complained of arises out of process issued by a State court; or

(B) the final order in a proceeding under section 2255

(2) A certificate of appealability may issue under paragraph (1) only if the applicant has made a substantial showing of the denial of a constitutional right.

(3) The certificate of appealability under paragraph (1) shall indicate which specific issue or issues satisfy the showing required by paragraph (2).

28 U.S.C. § 2254   State custody; remedies in Federal courts

(a) The Supreme Court, a Justice thereof, a circuit judge, or a district court shall entertain an application for a writ of habeas corpus in behalf of a person in custody pursuant to the judgment of a State court only on the ground that he is in custody in violation of the Constitution or laws or treaties of the United States.

(b) (1) An application for a writ of habeas corpus on behalf of a person in custody pursuant to the judgment of a State court shall not be granted unless it appears that—

(A) the applicant has exhausted the remedies available in the courts of the State; or

(B) (i) there is an absence of available State corrective process; or

(ii) circumstances exist that render such process ineffective to protect the rights of the applicant.

(2) An application for a writ of habeas corpus may be denied on the merits, notwithstanding the failure of the applicant to exhaust the remedies available in the courts of the State.

(3) A State shall not be deemed to have waived the exhaustion requirement or be estopped from reliance upon the requirement unless the State, through counsel, expressly waives the requirement.

(c) An applicant shall not be deemed to have exhausted the remedies available in the courts of the State, within the meaning of this section, if he has the right under the law of the State to raise, by any available procedure, the question presented.

(d) An application for a writ of habeas corpus on behalf of a person in custody pursuant to the judgment of a State court shall not be granted with respect to any claim that was adjudicated on the merits in State court proceedings unless the adjudication of the claim—

(1) resulted in a decision that was contrary to, or involved an unreasonable application of, clearly established Federal law, as determined by the Supreme Court of the United States; or

(2) resulted in a decision that was based on an unreasonable determination of the facts in light of the evidence presented in the State court proceeding.

(e) (1) In a proceeding instituted by an application for a writ of habeas corpus by a person in custody pursuant to the judgment of a State court, a determination of a factual issue made by a State court shall be presumed to be correct. The applicant shall have the burden of rebutting the presumption of correctness by clear and convincing evidence.

(2) If the applicant has failed to develop the factual basis of a claim in State court proceedings, the court shall not hold an evidentiary hearing on the claim unless the applicant shows that—

(A) the claim relies on—

(i) a new rule of constitutional law, made retroactive to cases on collateral review by the Supreme Court, that was previously unavailable; or

(ii) a factual predicate that could not have been previously discovered through the exercise of due diligence; and

(B) the facts underlying the claim would be sufficient to establish by clear and convincing evidence that but for constitutional error, no reasonable factfinder would have found the applicant guilty of the underlying offense.

(f) If the applicant challenges the sufficiency of the evidence adduced in such State court proceeding to support the State court's determination of a factual issue made therein, the applicant, if able, shall produce that part of the record pertinent to a determination of the sufficiency of the evidence to support such determination. If the applicant, because of indigency or other reason is unable to produce such part of the record, then the State shall produce such part of the record and the Federal court shall direct the State to do so by order directed to an appropriate State official. If the State cannot provide such pertinent part of the record, then the court shall determine under the existing facts and circumstances what weight shall be given to the State court's factual determination.

(g) A copy of the official records of the State court, duly certified by the clerk of such court to be a true and correct copy of a finding, judicial opinion, or other reliable written indicia showing such a factual determination by the State court shall be admissible in the Federal court proceeding.

(h) Except as provided in section 408 of the Controlled Substances Act, in all proceedings brought under this section, and any subsequent proceedings on review, the court may appoint counsel for an applicant who is or becomes financially unable to afford counsel, except as provided by a rule promulgated by the Supreme Court pursuant to statutory authority. Appointment of counsel under this section shall be governed by section 3006A of title 18

(i) The ineffectiveness or incompetence of counsel during Federal or State collateral post-conviction proceedings shall not be a ground for relief in a proceeding arising under section 2254.

28 U.S.C. § 2281   (repealed by Act of Aug. 12, 1976, Pub. L. 94-381, 90 Stat. 1119 (1976))

An interlocutory or permanent injunction restraining the enforcement, operation or execution of a State statute on grounds of unconstitutionality should not be granted unless the application has been heard and determined by a three-judge district court.

28 U.S.C. § 2282   (repealed by Act of Aug. 12, 1976, Pub. L. 94-381, 90 Stat. 1119 (1976))

An interlocutory or permanent injunction restraining the enforcement, operation or execution of any Act of Congress on grounds of unconstitutionality should not be granted unless the application therefor has been heard and determined by a three-judge district court.

28 U.S.C. § 2283   Stay of state court proceedings (Anti-Injunction Act):

A court of the United States may not grant an injunction to stay proceedings in a State court except as expressly authorized by Act of Congress, or where necessary in aid of its jurisdiction, or to protect or effectuate its judgments.

28 U.S.C. § 2284   Three-judge court; when required; composition; procedure (as amended by Act of Aug. 12, 1976, Pub. L. 94-381, 90 Stat. 1119 (1976))

(a) A district court of three judges shall be convened when otherwise required by Act of Congress, or when an action is filed challenging the constitutionality of the apportionment of congressional districts or the apportionment of any statewide legislative body.

(b) In any action required to be heard and determined by a district court of three judges under subsection (a) of this section, the composition and procedure of the court shall be as follows:

(1) Upon the filing of a request for three judges, the judge to whom the request is presented shall, unless he determines that three judges are not required, immediately notify the chief judge of the circuit, who shall designate two other judges, at least one of whom shall be a circuit judge. The judges so designated, and the judge to whom the request was presented, shall serve as members of the court to hear and determine the action or proceeding.

(2) If the action is against a State, or officer or agency thereof, at least five days' notice of hearing of the action shall be given by registered or certified mail to the Governor and attorney general of the State.

(3) A single judge may conduct all proceedings except the trial, and enter all orders permitted by the rules of civil procedure except as provided in this subsection. He may grant a temporary restraining order on a specific finding, based on evidence submitted, that specified irreparable damage will result if the order is not granted, which order, unless previously revoked by the district judge, shall remain in force only until the hearing and determination by the district court of three judges of an application for a preliminary injunction. A single judge shall not appoint a master, or order a reference, or hear and determine any application for a preliminary or permanent injunction or motion to vacate such an injunction, or enter judgment on the merits. Any action of a single judge may be reviewed by the full court at any time before final judgment.

28 U.S.C. § 2679   Exclusiveness of remedy (Westfall Act)

* * *

(b) (1) The remedy against the United States provided by sections 1346 (b) and 2672 of this title for injury or loss of property, or personal injury or death arising or resulting from the negligent or wrongful act or omission of any employee of the Government while acting within the scope of his office or employment is exclusive of any other civil action or proceeding for money damages by reason of the same subject matter against the employee whose act or omission gave rise to the claim or against the estate of such employee. Any other civil action or proceeding for money damages arising out of or relating to the same subject matter against the employee or the employee's estate is precluded without regard to when the act or omission occurred.

(2) Paragraph (1) does not extend or apply to a civil action against an employee

of the Government—

> (A) which is brought for a violation of the Constitution of the United States, or

> (B) which is brought for a violation of a statute of the United States under which such action against an individual is otherwise authorized.

(c) The Attorney General shall defend any civil action or proceeding brought in any court against any employee of the Government or his estate for any such damage or injury. The employee against whom such civil action or proceeding is brought shall deliver within such time after date of service or knowledge of service as determined by the Attorney General, all process served upon him or an attested true copy thereof to his immediate superior or to whomever was designated by the head of his department to receive such papers and such person shall promptly furnish copies of the pleadings and process therein to the United States attorney for the district embracing the place wherein the proceeding is brought, to the Attorney General, and to the head of his employing Federal agency.

28 U.S.C. § 14141   Cause of action

(a)   Unlawful conduct

It shall be unlawful for any governmental authority, or any agent thereof, or any person acting on behalf of a governmental authority, to engage in a pattern or practice of conduct by law enforcement officers or by officials or employees of any governmental agency with responsibility for the administration of juvenile justice or the incarceration of juveniles that deprives persons of rights, privileges, or immunities secured or protected by the Constitution or laws of the United States.

(b)   Civil action by Attorney General

Whenever the Attorney General has reasonable cause to believe that a violation of paragraph (1) has occurred, the Attorney General, for or in the name of the United States, may in a civil action obtain appropriate equitable and declaratory relief to eliminate the pattern or practice.

Title 42

42 U.S.C. § 1981   Equal right under the law (§ 1 of Civil Rights Act of 1866 and Civil Rights Act of 1870)

(a)   Statement of equal rights

All persons within the jurisdiction of the United States shall have the same right in every State and Territory to make and enforce contracts, to sue, be parties, give evidence, and to the full and equal benefit of all laws and proceedings for the security of persons and property as is enjoyed by white citizens, and shall be subject to like punishment, pains, penalties, taxes, licenses, and exactions of every kind, and to no other.

(b)   "Make and enforce contracts" defined

For purposes of this section, the term "make and enforce contracts" includes the making, performance, modification, and termination of contracts, and the enjoyment of all benefits, privileges, terms, and conditions of the contractual relationship.

(c)   Protection against impairment

The rights protected by this section are protected against impairment by nongovernmental discrimination and impairment under color of State law.

42 U.S.C. § 1982   Property rights of citizens (§ 1 of Civil Rights Act of 1866 and Civil Rights Act of 1870)

All citizens of the United States shall have the same right, in every State and Territory, as is enjoyed by white citizens thereof to inherit, purchase, lease, sell, hold, and convey real and personal property.

42 U.S.C. § 1983   Civil action for deprivation of rights (§ 1 of Ku Klux Klan Act of 1871)

Every person who, under color of any statute, ordinance, regulation, custom, or usage, of any State or Territory or the District of Columbia, subjects, or causes to be subjected, any citizen of the United States or other person within the jurisdiction thereof to the deprivation of any rights, privileges, or immunities secured by the Constitution and laws, shall be liable to the party injured in an action at law, suit in equity, or other proper proceeding for redress, except that in any action brought against a judicial officer for an act or omission taken in such officer's judicial capacity, injunctive relief shall not be granted unless a declaratory decree was violated or declaratory relief was unavailable. For the purposes of this section, any Act of Congress applicable exclusively to the District of Columbia shall be considered to be a statute of the District of Columbia.

42 U.S.C. § 1988   Proceedings in violation of civil rights

(a)   Applicability of statutory and common law

The jurisdiction in civil and criminal matters conferred on the district courts by the provisions of titles 13, 24, and 70 of the Revised Statutes for the protection of all persons in the United States in their civil rights, and for their vindication, shall be exercised and enforced in conformity with the laws of the United States, so far as such laws are suitable to carry the same into effect; but in all cases where they are not adapted to the object, or are deficient in the provisions necessary to furnish suitable remedies and punish offenses against law, the common law, as modified and changed by the constitution and statutes of the State wherein the court having jurisdiction of such civil or criminal cause is held, so far as the same is not inconsistent with the Constitution and laws of the United States, shall be extended to and govern the said courts in the trial and disposition of the cause, and, if it is of a criminal nature, in the infliction of punishment on the party found guilty.

(b) In any action or proceeding to enforce a provision of sections . . . 1983 . . . , the court, in its discretion, may allow the prevailing party, other than the United States, a reasonable attorney's fee as part of the costs, except that in any action brought against a judicial officer for an act or omission taken in such officer's judicial capacity such officer shall not be held liable for any costs, including attorney's fees, unless such action was clearly in excess of such officer's jurisdiction.

42 U.S.C. § 1997e   Suits by prisoners

* * *

(d) Attorney's fees

(1) In any action brought by a prisoner who is confined to any jail, prison, or other correctional facility, in which attorney's fees are authorized under section 1988[1] of this title, such fees shall not be awarded, except to the extent that—

(A) the fee was directly and reasonably incurred in proving an actual violation of the plaintiff's rights protected by a statute pursuant to which a fee may be awarded under section 1988[1] of this title; and

(B) (i) the amount of the fee is proportionately related to the court ordered relief for the violation; or

(ii) the fee was directly and reasonably incurred in enforcing the relief ordered for the violation.

(2) Whenever a monetary judgment is awarded in an action described in paragraph (1), a portion of the judgment (not to exceed 25 percent) shall be applied to satisfy the amount of attorney's fees awarded against the defendant. If the award of attorney's fees is not greater than 150 percent of the judgment, the excess shall be paid by the defendant.

(3) No award of attorney's fees in an action described in paragraph (1) shall be based on an hourly rate greater than 150 percent of the hourly rate established under section 3006A of title 18 for payment of court-appointed counsel.

(4) Nothing in this subsection shall prohibit a prisoner from entering into an agreement to pay an attorney's fee in an amount greater than the amount authorized under this subsection, if the fee is paid by the individual rather than by the defendant pursuant to section 1988[1] of this title.

(e)   Limitation on recovery

No Federal civil action may be brought by a prisoner confined in a jail, prison, or other correctional facility, for mental or emotional injury suffered while in custody without a prior showing of physical injury.

FEDERAL RULES OF CIVIL PROCEDURE

Fed. R. Civ. P. 60 Relief from a judgment or order

* * *

(b) Grounds for Relief from a Final Judgment, Order, or Proceeding. On motion and just terms, the court may relieve a party or its legal representative from a final judgment, order, or proceeding for the following reasons:

(1) mistake, inadvertence, surprise, or excusable neglect;

(2) newly discovered evidence that, with reasonable diligence, could not have been discovered in time to move for a new trial under Rule 59(b);

(3) fraud (whether previously called intrinsic or extrinsic), misrepresentation, or misconduct by an opposing party;

(4) the judgment is void;

(5) the judgment has been satisfied, released, or discharged; it is based on an earlier judgment that has been reversed or vacated; or applying it prospectively is no longer equitable; or

(6) any other reason that justifies relief.

* * *

Fed. R. Civ. P. 65 Injunctions and restraining orders

(a) Preliminary Injunction.

(1) *Notice.* The court may issue a preliminary injunction only on notice to the adverse party.

(2) *Consolidating the Hearing with the Trial on the Merits.* Before or after beginning the hearing on a motion for a preliminary injunction, the court may advance the trial on the merits and consolidate it with the hearing. Even when consolidation is not ordered, evidence that is received on the motion and that would be admissible at trial becomes part of the trial record and need not be repeated at trial. But the court must preserve any party's right to a jury trial.

(b) Temporary Restraining Order.

(1) *Issuing Without Notice.* The court may issue a temporary restraining order without written or oral notice to the adverse party or its attorney only if:

(A) specific facts in an affidavit or a verified complaint clearly show that immediate and irreparable injury, loss, or damage will result to the movant before the adverse party can be heard in opposition; and

(B) the movant's attorney certifies in writing any efforts made to give notice and the reasons why it should not be required.

(2) *Contents; Expiration.* Every temporary restraining order issued without notice must state the date and hour it was issued; describe the injury and state why it is irreparable; state why the order was issued without notice; and be promptly filed in the clerk's office and entered in the record. The order expires at the time after entry — not to exceed 14 days — that the court sets, unless before that time the court, for good cause, extends it for a like period or the adverse party consents to a longer extension. The reasons for an extension must be entered in the record.

(3) *Expediting the Preliminary-Injunction Hearing.* If the order is issued without notice, the motion for a preliminary injunction must be set for hearing at the earliest possible time, taking precedence over all other matters except hearings on older matters of the same character. At the hearing, the party who obtained the order must proceed with the motion; if the party does not, the court must dissolve the order.

(4) *Motion to Dissolve.* On 2 days' notice to the party who obtained the order without notice— or on shorter notice set by the court— the adverse party may appear and move to dissolve or modify the order. The court must then hear and

decide the motion as promptly as justice requires.

(c) Security. The court may issue a preliminary injunction or a temporary restraining order only if the movant gives security in an amount that the court considers proper to pay the costs and damages sustained by any party found to have been wrongfully enjoined or restrained. The United States, its officers, and its agencies are not required to give security.

(d) Contents and Scope of Every Injunction and Restraining Order.

(1) *Contents.* Every order granting an injunction and every restraining order must:

(A) state the reasons why it issued;

(B) state its terms specifically; and

(C) describe in reasonable detail — and not by referring to the complaint or other document — the act or acts restrained or required.

(2) *Persons Bound.* The order binds only the following who receive actual notice of it by personal service or otherwise:

(A) the parties;

(B) the parties' officers, agents, servants, employees, and attorneys; and

(C) other persons who are in active concert or participation with anyone described in Rule 65(d)(2)(A) or (B).

(e) Other Laws Not Modified. These rules do not modify the following:

* * *

(3) 28 U.S.C. § 2284, which relates to actions that must be heard and decided by a three-judge district court.

(f) Copyright Impoundment. This rule applies to copyright-impoundment proceedings.

TABLE OF CASES

[References are to pages]

[References are to pages]

[References are to pages]

E

F

G

[References are to pages]

[References are to pages]

[References are to pages]

[References are to pages]

[References are to pages]

[References are to pages]

[References are to pages]

TABLE OF STATUTES

[References are to pages]

[References are to pages]

INDEX

[References are to sections.]

[References are to sections.]

[References are to sections.]

[References are to sections.]

[References are to sections.]

[References are to sections.]